# Favorite Throws & Table Toppers to Crochet™

Annie's Attic®

# Favorite Throws & Table Toppers to Crochet



**EDITORS** Carol Alexander, Brenda Stratton
**ASSOCIATE EDITORS** Lisa M. Fosnaugh, Kristine Frye
**COPY SUPERVISOR** Michelle Beck
**COPY EDITORS** Mary O'Donnell, Beverly Richardson, Judy Weatherford

**PHOTOGRAPHY** Tammy Christian, Don Clark, Matthew Owen, Jackie Schaffel
**PHOTO STYLISTS** Tammy Nussbaum, Tammy M. Smith

**ART DIRECTOR** Brad Snow
**PRODUCTION MANAGER** Brenda Gallmeyer
**GRAPHIC ARTS SUPERVISOR** Ronda Bechinski
**GRAPHIC ARTIST** Pam Gregory
**PRODUCTION ASSISTANT** Cheryl Kempf, Marj Morgan, Judy Neuenschwander
**TECHNICAL ARTIST** Nicole Gage

**PUBLISHING DIRECTOR** David J. McKee
**EDITORIAL DIRECTOR** Gary Richardson
**MARKETING DIRECTOR** Dan Fink

Printed in China
First Printing: 2006

Hardcover:
ISBN-10: 1-59635-111-X
ISBN-13: 978-1-59635-111-0

Softcover:
ISBN-10: 1-59635-128-4
ISBN-13: 978-1-59635-128-8

Library of Congress Control Number: 2006929809

Every effort has been made to ensure the accuracy and completeness of the instructions in this book. However, we cannot be responsible for human error or for the results when using materials other than those specified in the instructions, or for variations in individual work.

1 2 3 4 5 6 7 8 9

# Cozy throws and delicate table toppers have always ranked high on the list of favorite projects among crocheters. Whether made for oneself or as treasured gifts for family and friends, each of the beautiful projects contained in this book are an expression of love.

Crocheters who are hooked on creating warm, comfortable throws enjoy the entire process of crocheting these large, snuggly projects. They get excited about starting each new design and eagerly browse through their library of patterns to select the perfect throw for the occasion, whether it's a special housewarming or wedding gift, birthday or anniversary present, or a charitable donation to help comfort the homeless and disaster victims.

The exquisite doilies and table toppers included here are reminiscent of the beautiful heirloom pieces your grandmother may have crocheted long ago as she turned simple thread into delicate and intricate masterpieces to be preserved as family treasures. From grandmothers to mothers to daughters, timeless thread creations have long been part of many family traditions.

It is our hope that this delightful collection of favorite throws and table toppers will inspire you with many wonderful choices to crochet a variety of treasured gifts that can reach across and connect the generations.

# Contents

## Fabulous Florals

## Pretty Pineapples

## Fancy Filet

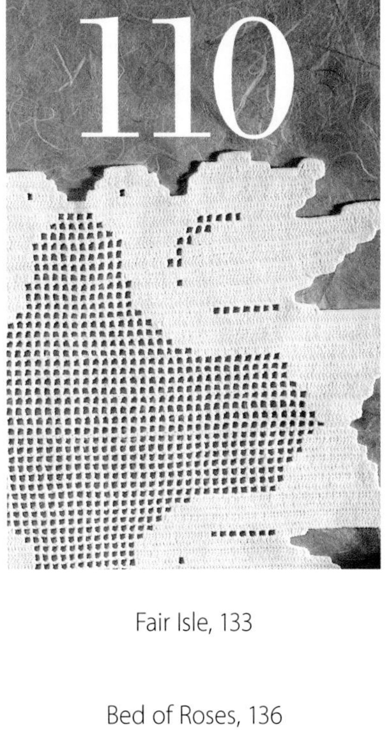

## Tempting Textures

## Happy Holidays

206

Bits & Pieces

254

280

# Posies on Parade

DESIGN BY DOT DRAKE

Dainty motifs of colorful posies dance around the center and outer edge of this divine doily masterpiece that always makes a statement of gracious beauty and style wherever it's displayed.

EXPERIENCED

**FINISHED SIZE**
20 inches in diameter

**MATERIALS**
Size 10 crochet cotton:
325 yds white
150 yds each rose, jade and pink
Size 7/1.65mm steel crochet hook or size needed to obtain gauge
Starch

**GAUGE**
Rnds 1–3 = 2¼ inches in diameter

**SPECIAL STITCHES**
**Picot:** Ch 3, sl st in first ch of ch-3.

**Cluster (cl):** Holding last lp of each st on hook, work number and sts as stated in indicated place, yo, pull through all lps on hook.

## INSTRUCTIONS

**ROSE MOTIF**
**Rnd 1 (RS):** With pink, ch 7, sl st in first ch to form ring, ch 1, 15 sc in ring, join with sl st in beg sc. *(15 sc)*

**Rnd 2:** Ch 1, sc in first sc, ch 4, sk next 2 sc, [sc in next sc, ch 4, sk next 2 sc] around, join with sl st in beg sc. *(5 ch-4 sps)*

**Rnd 3:** Ch 1, (sc, ch 3, 3 dc, ch 3, 3 dc, ch 3, sc) in each ch-4 sp around, join with sl st in beg sc.

**Rnd 4:** Inserting hook around only 1 strand of cotton at back of sc of rnd 2, ch 1, sc over same strand of cotton, ch 6, [inserting hook around only 1 strand of cotton at back of sc st of rnd 2, sc over strand of cotton, ch 6] around, join with sl st in beg sc. Fasten off.

**Rnd 5:** Join rose with sl st in any ch-6 sp, ch 1, (sc, ch 3, 3 dc, ch 3, 3 dc, ch 3, sc) in same ch sp and in each ch-6 sp around, join with sl st in beg sc. Fasten off.

**Rnd 6:** Join jade with sl st in center ch-3 sp of any petal of rnd 5, ch 3 *(counts as first st)*, dc in same ch sp *(beg cl)*, ch 5, 2-dc **cl** *(see Special Stitches)* in same ch-3 sp, ch 8, (2-dc cl, ch 5, 2-dc cl) in next center ch-3 sp of next petal, ch 8] around, join with sl st in top of beg cl. Fasten off.

**REMAINING ROSE MOTIFS**
Make 9.

**Rnds 1–5:** Rep rnds 1–5 of Rose Motif.

**Rnd 6:** Joining Motifs to form a circle, rep rnd 6 with the exception of 1 side edge, instead of working ch 5 between cls, ch 2, sc in ch-5 sp of previous Motif between cls, ch 2, instead of working ch 8, ch 4, sc in ch-8 sp of previous motif, ch 4, on 10th *(last)* Rose Motif join 2 sides to close circle, joining to 9th Rose Motif and first Rose Motif.

**CENTER FLOWER**
**Rnd 1 (RS):** With pink, ch 5, sl st in first ch to form ring, ch 1, 10 sc in ring, join with sl st in beg sc. *(10 sc)*

**Rnd 2:** Ch 4, 2-tr cl in first sc, ch 4, [3-tr cl in next sc, ch 4] around, join with sl st in top of beg cl. Fasten off.

**Rnd 3:** Join jade with sl st in any ch-4 sp, ch 1, (4 sc, ch 4, sl st in first ch of ch-4, 4 sc) in same ch-4 sp and in each ch-4 sp around, join with sl st in beg sc. Fasten off.

**JOINING**
**Rnd 1 (RS):** This rnd joins the Rose Motif ring to the Center Flower; holding Rose Motif ring, join white with sl st in any ch-8 sp at center of ring, ch 1, 10 sc in ch-8 sp on inside of circle, ch 10, pull up lp, remove hook, insert hook in first sc of 10-sc group, pick up dropped lp, pull through st on hook, (5 sc, **picot**—*see Special Stitches*, 4 sc) in ch-10 sp, 2 dtr cl in each of next 2 ch-4 sps of rnd 3 of Center Flower, (4 sc, picot, 5 sc) in same ch-10 sp, sl st in 10th sc that was worked in ch-8 sp, 2 sc in next ch-5 sp of rnd 6 of Rose Motif, ch 3, sc in side of last sc, 2 sc in next ch-5 sp of rnd 6 of next

Rose Motif, *10 sc in next ch-8 sp on inside of circle, ch 10, pull up lp, remove hook, insert hook in first sc of 10-sc group, pick up dropped lp and pull through lp on hook, (5 sc, picot, 4 sc) in ch-10 sp, dtr cl in each of next 2 ch-4 sps of rnd 3 of Center Flower, working first dtr of cl in same ch-4 sp as last dtr and next dtr of cl in next ch-4 sp, (4 sc, picot, 5 sc) in same ch-10 sp, sl st in 10th sc that was worked in ch-8 sp, 2 sc in ch-5 sp of rnd 6 of Rose Motif, ch 3, sc in side of last sc, 2 sc in next ch-5 sp of rnd 6 of next Rose Motif, rep from * around, working first half of last dtr cl in same ch-4 sp as previous dtr and last half of dtr cl in same ch-4 sp as first half of first dtr cl, join with sl st in beg sc. Fasten off.

**OUTER FLOWER RING**

***Note:*** *Make 15 each rose and pink Flowers on rnds 1 and 2, alternating colors around as Flowers are joined; rnd 3 will be worked with jade.*

**Rnds 1–3:** Rep rnds 1–3 of Center Flower on first Flower ring.

Rep rnds 1 and 2 on next Outer Flower.

**Rnd 3 (joining):** Join jade in any ch-4 sp, ch 1, [4 sc, ch 1, sc in ch-4 sp of previous flower, ch 1, sl st in last sc on working Flower, 4 sc in same ch-4 sp] twice, [4 sc, ch 4, sl st in first ch of ch-4, 4 sc in same ch-4 sp] 8 times, join with sl st in beg sc. Fasten off.

Continue to rep rnds 1 and 2, and rnd 3 of joining, leaving 2 ch-4 sps unworked on each Motif on inside of circle between joining and 4 unworked ch-4 sps on each Motif on outer edge of circle between joining. Last Flower is joined to previous Flower and first Flower to close ring. Set aside.

**OUTER ROSE MOTIF BORDER**

**Rnd 1 (RS):** Join white in first ch-8 sp to the left of joining of 2 Rose Motifs, ch 1, [15 sc in ch-8 sp, 7 sc in next ch-5 sp between dc cl sts, 15 sc in next ch-8 sp, 3 sc in next ch-5 sp at Motif joining, sc in sp between Motifs joining, 3 sc in next ch-5 sp at Motif joining] around entire outer edge, join with sl st in beg sc. *(440 sc)*

**Rnd 2:** Sl st across to 5th sc of 15-sc group, ch 8 *(counts as first dc and ch-5)*, dc in same st as beg ch-8, sk next 5 sc, (dc, ch 5, dc) in next sc, (dc, ch 5, dc) in sp between last sc of 15-sc group and first sc of 7-sc group, (dc, ch 5, dc) in sp between last sc of 7-sc group and next sc of 15-sc group, sk next 4 sc, (dc, ch 5, dc) in next sc, sk next 5 sc, (dc, ch 5, dc) in next sc, [(dc, ch 5, dc) in 5th sc of next 15-sc group, sk next 5 sc, (dc, ch 5, dc) in next sc, (dc, ch 5, dc) in sp between last sc of 15-sc group and first sc of 7-sc group, (dc, ch 5, dc) in sp between last sc of 7-sc group and next sc of 15-sc group, sk next 4 sc, (dc, ch 5, dc) in next sc, sk next 5 sc, (dc, ch 5, dc) in next sc] around, join with sl st in 3rd ch of beg ch-8. *(60 ch-5 sps)*

**Rnd 3:** Sl st to center of ch-5 sp, ch 1, sc in same ch-5 sp, picot, [ch 7, sc in next ch-5 sp, picot] around, ending with ch 3, tr in beg sc to position hook in center of last ch-7 sp to beg following rnd.

**Rnd 4:** Ch 1, sc in first ch sp, picot, [ch 7, sc in next ch-7 sp, picot] around, ending with ch 3, tr in beg sc.

**Rnds 5–7:** Rep rnd 4.

**Rnd 8:** Ch 1, sc in first ch sp, ch 5, [sc in next ch-7 sp, ch 5] around, join with sl st in beg sc.

**Rnd 9:** Ch 1, sc in first st, 8 sc in ch-5 sp, [sc in next sc, 8 sc in next ch-5 sp] around, join with sl st in beg sc.

**Rnd 10:** Ch 5 *(counts as first dc and ch-2)*, sk next 2 sc, [dc in next sc, ch 2, sk next 2 sc] around, join with sl st in 3rd ch of beg ch-5.

***Note:*** *Next rnd will join the 2 inner ch-4 sps of each Flower of Outer Flower Ring to Doily.*

**Rnd 11 (RS):** Ch 1, beg in first st, *sc in next dc of rnd 10, [2 sc in next ch-2 sp, sc in next dc] twice, 2 sc in next ch-2 sp, ch 10, pull up lp, remove hook, insert hook in 8th sc to the right *(2nd sc of the 9 sc sts worked)*, pick up dropped lp, (5 sc, picot, 4 sc) in ch-10 sp, working in 2 ch-4 sps of Flower on Outer Flower Ring, yo, insert hook in first unworked ch-4 sp, yo, pull up lp, yo, pull through 2 lps on hook, yo, insert hook in 2nd ch-4 sp of same Flower, yo, pull up lp, yo, pull through 2 lps on hook, yo, pull through all lps on hook, (4 sc, picot, 5 sc) in same ch-10 sp, sc in next dc of rnd 10, [2 sc in next ch-2 sp, sc in next dc] twice, 2 sc in next ch-2 sp, ch 10, pull up lp, remove hook, insert hook in 8th sc to the right *(2nd sc of the 9 sc sts worked)*, pick up dropped lp, (5 sc, picot, 4 sc, picot, 4 sc, picot, 5 sc) in ch-10 sp, rep from * around, join with sl st in beg sc. Fasten off.

**OUTER BORDER**

**Rnd 1 (RS):** Working on outer edge of Outer Flower Ring in the 4 ch-4 sps of each Flower, join white with sl st in first unworked ch-4 sp of any Flower, ch 1, sc in same ch-4 sp, [ch 7, sc in next ch-4 sp] 3 times, ch 4, *sc in first ch-4 sp of next Flower, [ch 7, sc in next ch-4 sp] 3 times, ch 4, rep from * around, join with sl st in beg sc.

**Rnd 2:** Ch 1, *(4 sc, picot, {sc, picot} twice, 4 sc) in each of next 3 ch-7 sps, 2 sc in next ch-4 sp, rep from * around, join with sl st in beg sc. Fasten off.

With WS facing, starch lightly and press. ■

# Rose Splendor

DESIGN BY BRENDA STRATTON

With an ornate beauty that belies its simplicity, this stunning thread throw evokes the feel of formal elegance, yet can perfectly accent any room with easy-living style for a look that's extraordinary.

INTERMEDIATE

### FINISHED SIZE

58 x 70 inches, excluding Tassels

### MATERIALS

South Maid size 10 crochet cotton (400 yds per ball):
- 18 balls #1 white

South Maid size 10 crochet cotton (350 yds per ball):
- 14 balls #493 French rose
- 5 balls #449 forest green

Size G/6/4mm crochet hook or size needed to obtain gauge
Tapestry needle
Sewing needle
Sewing thread to match French rose
59 pearl 6mm beads

### GAUGE

Motif across center from point to point = 10 inches; 6 dc = 1 inch; 2 dc rnds = 1 inch

### PATTERN NOTE

Hold 2 strands of same-color crochet cotton together throughout.

### SPECIAL STITCHES

**Puff stitch (puff st):** [Insert hook in st, yo, pull up lp in indicated st, yo] 4 times, yo, pull through all lps on hook.

**Shell:** 5 dc in indicated st.

**Corner shell:** 7 dc in indicated st.

**Beginning corner shell (beg corner shell):** Ch 3 *(counts as first dc)*, 6 dc in indicated st.

## INSTRUCTIONS

### MOTIF

Make 59.

### ROSE FRONT

**Rnd 1 (RS):** Beg at center front with 2 strands of French rose held tog, ch 4, sl st in first ch to form ring, ch 1, [sc in ring, ch 3] 6 times, join with sl st in beg sc. *(6 sc, 6 ch-3 sps)*

**Rnd 2:** [(Hdc, 3 dc, hdc) in next ch-3 sp, sl st in next sc] 6 times. *(6 petals)*

**Rnd 3:** Holding petals forward, ch 1, sc in first st, ch 3, [sc in next sl st, ch 3] 5 times, join with sl st in beg sc. *(6 sc, 6 ch-3 sps)*

**Rnd 4:** [(Hdc, 5 dc, hdc) in next ch-3 sp, sl st in next sc] 6 times. *(6 petals)*

**Rnd 5:** Holding petals forward, ch 1, sc in first st, ch 4, [sc in next sl st, ch 4] 5 times, join with sl st in beg sc. *(6 sc, 6 ch-4 sps)*

**Rnd 6:** [(Hdc, 7 dc, hdc) in next ch-4 sp, sl st in next sc] 6 times. *(6 petals)*

**Rnd 7:** Holding petals forward, ch 1, sc in first st, ch 5, [sc in next sl st, ch 5] 5 times, join with sl st in beg sc. Fasten off. *(6 sc, 6 ch-5 sps)*

### LEAF

Make 6.

Join 2 strands of forest green with sl st in any sc of rnd 7, ch 6, 3 sc in 2nd ch from hook, hdc in next ch, dc in each of next 3 chs, sl st in next ch-5 sp, ch 2, sl st in sc at base of beg ch-6, ch 2, sl st in next ch-5 sp on opposite side, working in opposite side of foundation ch of ch-6, dc in each of next 3 chs, hdc in next ch, join with sl st in beg sc. Fasten off.

### ROSE BACK

**Rnd 1:** With WS of Rose Front facing, join 2 strands of French rose with sl st around **front** of **post** *(see Stitch Guide)* of any sc of rnd 1 of Rose Front, ch 1, sc around base of same sc, ch 3, [sc around base of next sc of rnd 1, ch 3] 5 times, join with sl st in beg sc. *(6 sc, 6 ch-3 sps)*

**Rnd 2:** Sl st in next ch-3 sp, holding Leaves to back of work, ch 3, 4 dc in same st, sl st in next ch-5 sp of rnd 7 of Rose Front, [5 dc in next ch-3 sp, sl st in next ch-5 sp of rnd 7 of Rose Front] 5 times, join with sl st in 3rd ch of beg ch-3. Fasten off.

### BACKGROUND

**Rnd 8:** With RS of Rose Front facing,

join 2 strands of white with sl st through both Rose Front and Rose Back in sp between any 2 Leaves to beg first corner, holding Leaves forward, (ch 3, tr, ch 2, tr, dc) in same sp, ch 3, sc in center dc of next 5-dc group of rnd 2 of Rose Back, ch 3, [(dc, tr, ch 2, tr, dc) in next sp, ch 3, sc in center dc of next 5-dc group on rnd 2 of Rose Back, ch 3] 5 times, join with sl st in 3rd ch of beg ch-3.

**Rnd 9:** Sl st in next ch-2 sp, ch 3, (dc, ch 2, 2 dc) in same ch sp, [ch 3, sc in next ch-3 sp] twice, ch 3, *(2 dc, ch 2, 2 dc) in next ch-2 sp, [ch 3, sc in next ch-3 sp] twice, ch 3, rep from * around, join with sl st in 3rd ch of beg ch-3. *(24 dc, 18 ch-3 sps)*

**Rnd 10:** Sl st in corner ch-2 sp, ch 3, (dc, ch 2, 2 dc] in same ch sp, dc in each of next 2 dc, 2 dc in next ch sp, catching **back lp** *(see Stitch Guide)* of center sc at point of Leaf to secure, tr in next sp, 2 dc in next sp, dc in each of next 2 dc, [(2 dc, ch 2, 2 dc) in next corner ch-2 sp, dc in each of next 2 dc, 2 dc in next sp, catching back lp of center sc at point of Leaf to secure, tr in next sp, 2 dc in next sp, dc in each of next 2 dc] around, join with sl st in 3rd ch of beg ch-3. *(78 sts)*

**Rnd 11:** Sl st in corner ch-2 sp, ch 3, (dc, ch 2, 2 dc) in same ch sp, dc in each of next 13 sts, [(2 dc, ch 2, 2 dc) in next corner ch-2 sp, dc in each of next 13 sts] 5 times, join with sl st in 3rd ch of beg ch-3. *(102 dc)*

**Rnd 12:** Sl st in corner ch-2 sp, ch 3, (dc, ch 2, 2 dc) in same ch sp, dc in each of next 17 sts, [(2 dc, ch 2, 2 dc) in next corner ch-2 sp, dc in each of next 17 sts] 5 times, join with sl st in 3rd ch of beg ch-3, pull up lp, remove hook, **do not fasten off.** *(126 dc)*

**Rnd 13:** Join 2 strands of French rose with sl st in any corner ch-2 sp, ch 1, (sc, ch 5, sc) in same corner ch-2 sp, ch 7, **puff st** *(see Special Stitches)* around post of first dc following ch-2 sp at corner on rnd 10, ch 6, sc around post of 8th dc after ch-2 sp on corner of rnd 12, ch 6, puff st around post of tr in rnd 10, ch 6, sc around post of 14th dc after ch-2 sp on corner of rnd 12, ch 6, puff st around post of last dc before corner on rnd 10, ch 7, [(sc, ch 5, sc) in next corner ch-2 sp on rnd 12, ch 7, puff st around post of first dc following ch-2 sp at corner on rnd 10, ch 6, sc around post of 8th dc after ch-2 sp on corner of rnd 12, ch 6, puff st around post of tr in rnd 10, ch 6, sc around post of 14th dc after ch-2 sp on corner of rnd 12, ch 6, puff st around post of last dc before corner on rnd 10, ch 7] 5 times, join with sl st in beg sc. Fasten off.

**Rnd 14:** Pick up dropped lp of white, sl st in next sc and ch-2 sp, ch 3, (dc, ch 1, sl st) in back lp of 3rd ch of ch-5 sp of rnd 13, ch 1, sk next sc, next ch 5 and sc of rnd 13, 2 dc in same sp of rnd 12, dc in each of next 7 dc, **dc dec** *(see Stitch Guide)* in next sc of rnd 13 and next dc of rnd 12, dc in each of next 5 dc, dc dec in next sc of rnd 13 and next dc of rnd 12, dc in each of next 7 dc, *in next corner ch-2 sp work (2 dc, ch 1, sl st) in back lp of 3rd ch of ch-5 sp of rnd 13, ch 1, sk next sc, next ch 5 and sc of rnd 13, 2 dc in same sp of rnd 12, dc in each of next 7 dc, dc dec in next sc on rnd 13 and next dc of rnd 12, dc in each of next 5 dc, dc dec in next sc of rnd 13 and next dc of rnd 12, dc in each of next 7 dc, rep from * around, join with sl st in 3rd ch of beg ch-3. Fasten off. *(150 dc)*

**FILL-IN MOTIF**

Make 8.

**Row 1:** Beg at inner edge and working outward, with 2 strands of white, ch 26, dc in 4th ch from hook, dc in each ch across, turn. *(24 dc)*

**Rows 2–10:** Ch 3, dc in same st, dc in each dc across to last dc, 2 dc in

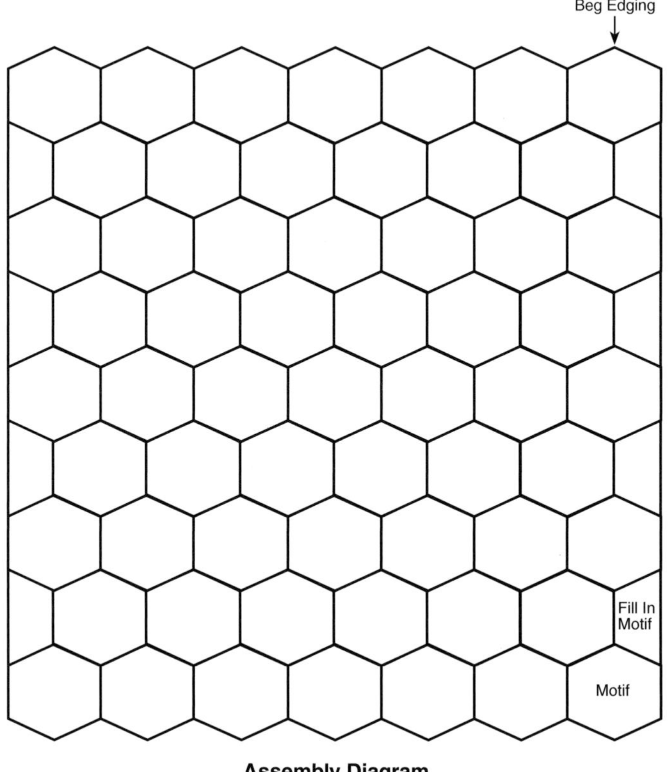

**Assembly Diagram**

last dc, turn. At the end of row 10, fasten off. *(43 dc at end of last row)*

### ASSEMBLY

Sew Motifs tog with 2 strands white cotton according to assembly diagram.

With sewing needle and rose-colored thread, sew 1 pearl bead to the center of each Motif.

### EDGING

**Rnd 1 (RS):** Join 2 strands of white with sc at first point at top of throw as indicated on diagram, sc in each st around, inc and dec at inner and outer point as necessary to maintain shape, join with sl st in beg sc. Fasten off.

***Note:*** *On rnd 2, adjust the placement of sts to allow for the corner shells to fall at outer points and for sc dec sts to fall at inner points on short ends of throw.*

**Rnd 2:** Join 2 strands French rose with sl st at same point as rnd 1, **beg corner shell** *(see Special Stitches)* in same st, sk 2 sc, sl st in next sc, sk next 2 sc, [**shell** *(see Special Stitches)* in next sc, sk next 2 sc, sl st in next sc, sk next 2 sc] 4 times, **sc dec** *(see Stitch Guide)* at inner point, [shell in next sc, sk next 2 sc, sl st in next sc, sk next 2 sc] 4 times, sk next 2 sc, ***corner shell** *(see Special Stitches)* in next st, sk next 2 sc, sl st in next sc, sk next 2 sc, [shell in next sc, sk next 2 sc, sl st in next sc, sk next 2 sc] 4 times, sc dec at inner point, [shell in next sc, sk next 2 sc, sl st in next sc, sk next 2 sc] 4 times, sk next 2 sc*, rep between * across top edge of throw, corner shell in last point, sk next 2 sc, sl st in next sc, sk next 2 sc, **shell in next sc, sk next 2 sc, sl st in next sc, sk next 2 sc**, rep between ** across straight edge of throw, rep between * across bottom of throw, rep between ** across last straight edge of throw, join with sl st in 3rd ch of beg ch-3. Fasten off.

### TASSEL

Make 14.

With French rose, cut 48 strands of crochet cotton each 10 inches in length. Holding all strands tog, tie a separate length of crochet cotton tightly around strands at center. Fold strands in half at tied point and tie a 10-inch length tightly around folded strands 1¼ inches below top. Blend ends of tying strand in with Tassel strands.

Using tying length at top of each Tassel.

Attach Tassel to center dc of shell at point.

Attach a Tassel to each point on each short end of coverlet. Trim ends even. ■

# Tapestry Floral

DESIGN BY GLENDA WINKLEMAN

Delicate cross-stitch bouquets on a Tunisian crochet background create the look of fine embroidery in this elegant, old-fashioned throw. Dainty shells add a pretty petaled edging.

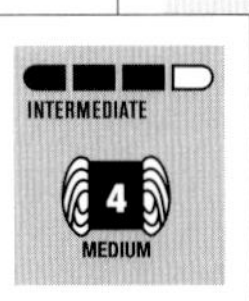


**FINISHED SIZE**
45 x 61 inches

**MATERIALS**
TLC Essentials medium (worsted) weight yarn (6 oz/312 yds/170g per skein):
8 skeins #2316 winter white
2 skeins #2772 light country rose
1 skein #2531 light plum
1 oz/50 yds/28g each #2220 butter, #2222 baby yellow, #2673 medium thyme
Size J/10/6mm afghan crochet hook or size needed to obtain gauge
Size J/10/6mm crochet hook
Tapestry needle

**GAUGE**
**With size J afghan hook:** 12 afghan sts = 3 inches; 10 rows = 3 inches

## INSTRUCTIONS

**BLOCK**
Make 12.

**Row 1:** With size J afghan crochet hook and winter white, ch 40, insert hook in 2nd ch from hook, yo, pull up lp, [insert hook in next ch, yo, pull up lp] across leaving all lps on hook *(40 lps on hook)*, yo, pull through first lp on hook, [yo, pull through 2 lps on hook] across until 1 lp rem on hook. Last lp on hook, counts as first st on next row.

**Row 2:** [With yarn to front of work on right-hand side of next vertical bar, insert hook in next vertical bar, yarn underneath and to back of hook, yo, pull through st, with yarn to back of work, insert hook in next vertical bar, yo, pull yarn through] across to last st, yarn to back of work, insert hook in last st, yo, pull yarn through st *(40 lps on hook)*, yo, pull through first lp on hook, [yo, pull through 2 lps on hook] across until 1 lp rem on hook.

**Row 3:** First lp counts as first st, [with yarn to back of work, insert hook in next vertical bar, yo, pull up lp, with yarn to front of work right-hand side of next vertical bar, insert hook in next vertical bar, yarn underneath and to back of hook, yo, pull yarn through st] across to last st, with yarn to back of work, insert hook in last st, yo, pull yarn through st *(40 lps on hook)*, yo, pull through first lp on hook, [yo pull through 2 lps on hook] across until 1 lp rem on hook.

**Rows 4 & 5:** Rep rows 2 and 3.

**Row 6:** *With yarn to front of work on right-hand side of next vertical bar, insert hook in next vertical bar, yarn underneath and to back of hook, yo, pull yarn through st, with yarn to back of work, insert hook in next vertical bar, yo, pull yarn through bar *, rep between * twice, [with yarn to back, insert hook in next vertical bar, yo, pull up a lp] 28 times, rep between * twice, yarn to back of work, insert hook in last st, yo, pull yarn through *(40 lps on hook)*, yo, pull through first lp on hook, [yo, pull through 2 lps on hook] across until 1 lp rem on hook.

**Row 7:** *With yarn to back of work, insert hook in next vertical bar, yo, pull up lp, with yarn to front of work on right-hand side of vertical bar, insert hook in next vertical bar, yarn underneath and to back of hook, yo, pull yarn through *, rep between *, [with yarn to back, insert hook in next vertical bar, yo, pull up lp] 28 times, rep between * 3 times, with yarn to back of work, insert hook in last st, yo, pull yarn through st *(40 lps on hook)*, yo, pull through first lp on hook, [yo, pull through 2 lps on hook] across until 1 lp rem on hook.

**Rows 8–33:** Rep rows 6 and 7 alternately 13 times.

**Row 34:** Rep row 2.

**Row 35:** Rep row 3.

**Row 36:** Rep row 2.

**Row 37:** [With yarn to back, sl st in next vertical bar, with yarn to front,

sl st in next vertical bar] across. Fasten off.

**BLOCK BORDER**

**Rnd 1 (RS):** With size J crochet hook, join light country rose with sc in top right corner st of Block, [ch 1, sk next st, sc in next st] across to next corner, ch 2, working in ends of rows, sc in end of row, [ch 1, sk next row, sc in next row] across to last row from corner, sc in next row, ch 2, working in starting ch on opposite side of row 1, sc in first ch, [ch 1, sk next ch, sc in next ch] across to next corner, ch 2, working across ends of rows, sc in end of row, [ch 1, sk next row, sc in next row] across, ending with ch 2, join with sl st in beg sc. Fasten off.

**Rnd 2:** Join winter white with sl st in first st, ch 3 *(counts as first dc),* dc in each ch-1 sp and each sc around, working (dc, ch 2, dc) in each corner ch-2 sp, join with sl st in 3rd ch of beg ch-3.

**Rnd 3:** Ch 1, sc in each of first 7 dc, sk next dc, *sc in each of next 7 dc, sk next dc*, rep between * across to last 8 dc before next corner, sc in each of next 8 dc, (sc, ch 2, sc) in corner ch-2 sp, sc in each dc down to next corner ch-2 sp, (sc, ch 2, sc) in corner ch-2 sp, sc in each of next 8 dc, rep between * across to last 8 dc before next corner, sc in each of next 8 dc, (sc, ch 2, sc) in corner ch-2 sp, sc in each dc across to next corner, (sc, ch 2, sc) in corner ch-2 sp, sc in next dc, join with sl st in beg sc. Fasten off.

**EMBROIDERY**

With **cross-stitch,** work floral design *(see Chart)* on center front of each Block according to Chart.

**ASSEMBLY**

With size J crochet hook and winter white, working in **back lps** *(see Stitch Guide)* only, sl st Blocks tog in 4 rows of 3 Blocks. When joining Blocks tog, make sure that each corner of 4 Blocks and all other corners are evenly sp so that design will not be distorted.

**AFGHAN BORDER**

**Rnd 1 (RS):** With size J crochet

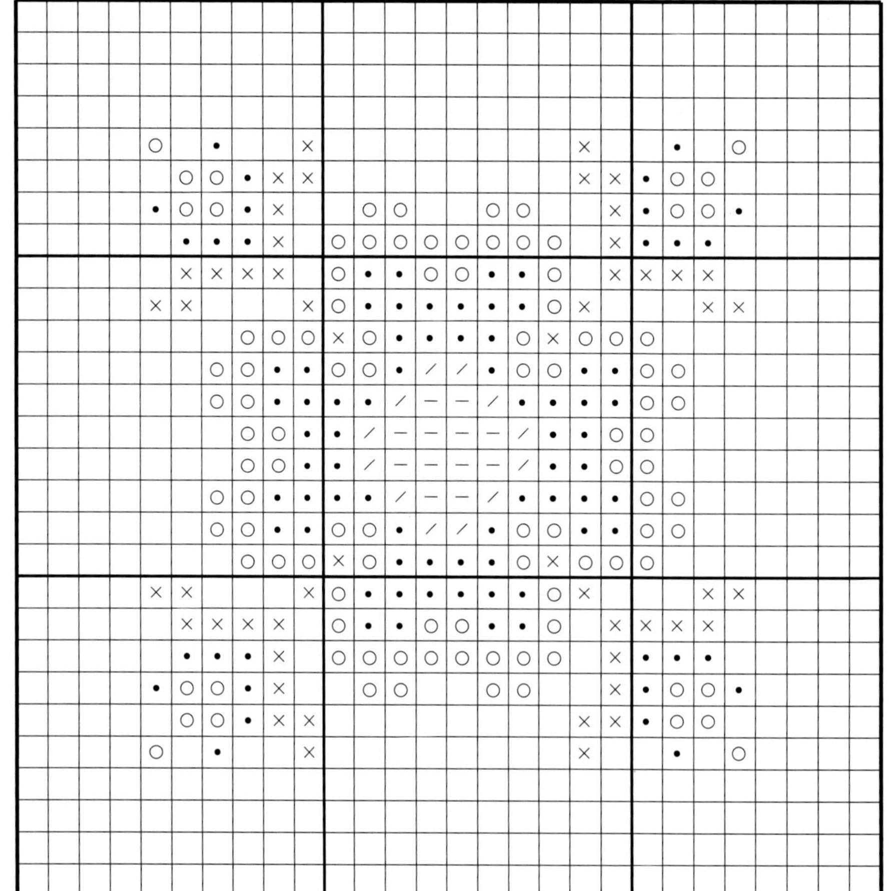


**Tapestry Floral Chart**

**COLOR KEY**
- ○ Light country rose
- • Light plum
- × Medium thyme
- ⁄ Baby blue
- – Butter

hook, join winter white with sc in top right corner sc, sc in each sc and each ch sp on each side of each joining seam around, working (sc, ch 2, sc) in each corner ch-2 sp, join with sl st in beg sc.

**Rnd 2:** Ch 3 *(counts as first dc)*, dc in sc to right of beg ch-3, *[sk next sc, dc in next sc, dc in sk sc] across to last sc before corner, dc in next sc, (2 dc, ch 2, 2 dc) in corner ch-2 sp, working down length, [sk next sc, dc in next sc, dc in sk sc] across to next corner, (2 dc, ch 2, 2 dc) in corner ch-2 sp, rep from * around, join with sl st in 3rd ch of beg ch-3.

**Rnd 3:** Ch 1, sc in each dc around, with (sc, ch 2, sc) in each corner ch-2 sp, join with sl st in beg sc.

**Rnd 4:** Ch 3, dc in sc to right of beg ch-3, *[sk next sc, dc in next sc, dc in sk sc] across to last sc before corner, dc in next sc, (dc, ch 2, dc) in corner ch-2 sp, working down length, [sk next sc, dc in next sc, dc in sk sc] across to corner, (dc, ch 2, dc) in corner ch-2 sp, rep from * around, ending with sk next sc, dc in next sc, dc in sk sc, join with sl st in 3rd ch of beg ch-3. Fasten off.

**Rnd 5:** Join light country rose in right-hand corner dc, ch 1, sc in each dc around, with 4 sc in each corner ch-2 sp, join with sl st in beg sc. Fasten off.

**Rnd 6:** Join light plum with sl st in joining sc, ch 1, (hdc, dc, ch 1, tr, ch 1, dc, hdc) in same st, [sk next sc, sc in next sc, sk next sc, (hdc, dc, ch 1, tr, ch 1, dc, hdc) in next sc] around to last 9 sc, sk next 2 sc, sc in next sc, sk next sc, (hdc, dc, ch 1, tr, ch 1, dc, hdc) in next sc, sk next 2 sc, sc in next sc, sk next sc, join with sl st in top of beg hdc. Fasten off. ■

# Jardin Des Fleurs

DESIGN BY DOT DRAKE

Timeless style and exquisite detail are beautifully rendered in this breathtaking, heirloom-quality tablecloth that brings to mind the gracious living and hospitality of Grandmother's house.

INTERMEDIATE

**FINISHED SIZE**
62 inches across

**MATERIALS**
Size 10 crochet cotton:
4,000 yds white
Size 8/1.50mm steel crochet hooks or size needed to obtain gauge
Beading needle
Pink sewing thread
456 tiny pink seed beads

**GAUGE**
Rnds 1–5 = 2½ inches across

**PATTERN NOTE**
Using instructions, work First Motif and Next Motif according to assembly diagram.

**SPECIAL STITCHES**
**Chain-3 picot (ch-3 picot):** Ch 3, sl st in top of last st made.

**Chain-6 picot (ch-6 picot):** Ch 6, sl st in 3rd st from hook.

**Corner joining:** 4 sc in next ch sp, ch 2, sc in corresponding corner ch sp of adjacent Motif, ch 2, 4 sc in same ch sp on this Motif.

**Side joining:** Sc in each of next 4 sts, [ch 1, sc in corresponding ch-3 picot on adjacent Motif, ch 1, sl st in top of last st made on this Motif, sc in each of next 3 sts] 21 times.

## INSTRUCTIONS

**TABLECLOTH**

**FIRST MOTIF**
**Rnd 1:** Ch 6, sl st in first ch to form ring, ch 1, 12 sc in ring, join with sl st in beg sc. *(12 sc)*

**Rnd 2:** Ch 1, sc in first st, ch 4, sk next st, [sc in next st, ch 4, sk next st] around, join with sl st in beg sc. *(6 ch sps)*

**Rnd 3:** Sl st in first ch sp, ch 3 *(counts as first dc)*, 4 dc in same ch sp, ch 3, [5 dc in next ch sp, ch 3] around, join with sl st in 3rd ch of beg ch-3. *(30 dc, 6 ch sps)*

**Rnd 4:** Ch 3, dc in next st, 2 dc in next st, dc in each of next 2 sts, ch 5, sk next ch sp, [dc in each of next 2 sts, 2 dc in next st, dc in each of next 2 sts, ch 5, sk next ch sp] around, join with sl st in 3rd ch of beg ch-3. *(36 dc, 6 ch sps)*

**Rnd 5:** Ch 4 *(counts as first tr)*, **tr dec** *(see Stitch Guide)* in next 2 sts, tr dec in next 3 sts, ch 5, sc in next ch sp, **ch-3 picot** *(see Special Stitches)*, *ch 3, [tr dec in next 3 sts] twice, ch 3, sc in next ch sp, ch-3 picot, rep from * around, ch 2, join with hdc in top of first tr dec forming last ch sp.

**Rnd 6:** Ch 12 *(counts as first dc and ch-9)*, [dc in next ch sp, ch 5, dc in next ch sp, ch 9] 5 times, dc in last ch sp, ch 3, join with hdc in 3rd ch of beg ch-12. *(12 ch sps)*

**Rnd 7:** Ch 6 *(counts as first dc and ch-3)*, *11 dc in next ch-9 sp, ch 3, (dc, ch 3, dc) in center ch of next ch-5 sp, ch 3, rep from * 4 times, 11 dc in last ch-9 sp, ch 3, dc in same ch sp as ch-6, ch 3, join with sl st in 3rd ch of beg ch-6.

**Rnd 8:** Ch 6, sk next ch sp, *dc in each of next 11 sts, ch 3, sk next ch sp**, [dc in next st, ch 3, sk next ch sp] twice, rep from * around, ending last rep at **, dc in last st, ch 3, join with sl st in 3rd ch of beg ch-6.

**Rnd 9:** Ch 6, sk next ch sp, *dc in each of next 4 sts, ch 6, sk next st, sc in next st, ch 6, sk next st, dc in each of next 4 sts, ch 3, sk next ch sp, dc in next st, ch 5, sk next ch sp**, dc in next st, ch 3, rep from * around, ending last rep at **, join with sl st in 3rd ch of beg ch-6.

**Rnd 10:** Ch 6, sk next ch sp, *dc in each of next 3 sts, ch 6, sk next st, [sc in next ch sp, ch 6] twice, sk next st, dc in each of next 3 sts, ch 3, sk next ch sp, dc in next st, **ch-6 picot** *(see Special Stitches)*, ch 3, sk next ch sp**, dc in next st, ch 3, sk next ch

sp, rep from * around, ending last rep at **, join with sl st in 3rd ch of beg ch-6.

**Rnd 11:** Ch 6, sk next ch sp, *dc in each of next 3 sts, 2 dc in next ch sp, ch 6, sc in next ch sp, ch 6, 2 dc in next ch sp, dc in each of next 3 sts, ch 3, sk next ch sp, dc in next st, ch 7, sk next ch-6 picot and next ch-3 sp**, dc in next st, ch 3, sk next ch sp, rep from * around, ending last rep at **, join with sl st in 3rd ch of beg ch-6.

**Rnd 12:** Ch 3, dc in same st, ch 3, sk next ch sp and next st, *dc in each of next 4 sts, 2 dc in next ch sp, ch 6, 2 dc in next ch sp, dc in each of next 4 sts, ch 4, sk next st and next ch sp, 2 dc in next st, ch 3, (dc, ch 3, dc) in center ch of next ch-7 sp, ch 3**, 2 dc in next st, ch 4, sk next ch sp and next st, rep from * around, ending last rep at **, join with sl st in 3rd ch of beg ch-3.

**Rnd 13:** Ch 3, dc in next st, ch 4, sk next ch sp and next st, *dc in each of next 5 sts, 5 dc in next ch sp, dc in each of next 5 sts, ch 4, sk next st and next ch sp, dc in each of next 2 sts, ch 3, dc in next st, 7 dc in next ch sp, dc in next st, ch 3, sk next ch sp**, dc in each of next 2 sts, ch 4, sk next ch and next st, rep from * around, ending last rep at **, join with sl st in 3rd ch of beg ch-3.

**Rnd 14:** Ch 3, dc in next st, ch 4, sk next ch sp and next st, *dc in each of next 13 sts, ch 4, sk next st and next ch sp, dc in each of next 2 sts, ch 3, sk next ch sp, 2 dc in next st, dc in each of next 3 sts, 3 dc in next st, dc in each of next 3 sts, 2 dc in next st, ch 3, sk next ch sp**, dc in each of next 2 sts, ch 4, sk next ch sp and next st, rep from * around, ending last rep at **, join with sl st in 3rd ch of beg ch-3.

**Rnd 15:** Ch 3, dc in next st, ch 4, sk next ch sp and next st, *dc in each of next 11 sts, ch 4, sk next st and next ch sp, dc in each of next 2 sts, ch 3, sk next ch sp, dc in next st, [sk next st, (dc, ch 2, dc) in next st] 5 times, sk next st, dc in next st, ch 3, sk next ch sp**, dc in each of next 2 sts, ch 3, sk next ch sp and next st, rep from * around, ending last rep at **, join with sl st in 3rd ch of beg ch-3.

**Rnd 16:** Ch 3, dc in next st, ch 4, sk next ch sp and next st, *dc in each of next 9 sts, ch 4, sk next st and next ch sp, dc in each of next 2 sts, ch 3, dc in each of next 2 sts, [2 dc in next ch sp, dc in each of next 2 sts] 4 times, 2 dc in next ch sp, dc in next st, 2 dc in next st, ch 3, sk next ch sp**, dc in each of next 2 sts, ch 4, sk next ch sp and next st, rep from * around, ending last rep at **, join with sl st in 3rd ch of beg ch-3.

**Rnd 17:** Ch 3, dc in next st, ch 4, sk next ch sp and next st, *dc each of in next 7 sts, ch 4, sk next st and next ch sp, dc in each of next 2 sts, ch 3, sk next ch sp, dc in next st, [sk next st, (dc, ch 2, dc) in next st] 10 times, sk next st, dc in next st, ch 3, sk next ch sp**, dc in each of next 2 sts, ch 4, sk next ch sp and next st, rep from * around, ending last rep at **, join with sl st in 3rd ch of beg ch-3.

**Rnd 18:** Ch 3, dc in next st, ch 4, sk next ch sp and next st, *dc in each of next 5 sts, ch 4, sk next st and next ch sp, dc in each of next 2 sts, ch 3, sk next ch sp, dc in each of next 2 sts, [2 dc in next ch sp, dc in each of next 2 sts] 9 times, 2 dc in next ch sp, dc in next st, 2 dc in next st, ch 3, sk next ch sp**, dc in each of next 2 sts, ch 4, sk next ch sp and next st, rep from * around, ending last rep at **, join with sl st in 3rd ch of beg ch-3.

**Rnd 19:** Ch 3, dc in next st, ch 4, sk next ch sp and next st, *dc in each of next 3 sts, ch 4, sk next st and next ch sp, dc in each of next 2 sts, ch 3, sk next ch sp, dc in next st, [ch 1, sk next st, dc in next st] 21 times, ch 3, sk next ch sp**, dc in each of next 2 sts, ch 4, sk next ch sp and next st, rep from * around, ending last rep at **, join with sl st in 3rd ch of beg ch-3.

**Rnd 20:** Ch 3, dc in next st, ch 4, sk next ch sp and next st, *dc in next st, ch 4, sk next st and next ch sp, dc in each of next 2 sts, ch 3, sk next ch sp, dc in next st, [ch 2, sk next ch sp, dc in next st] 21 times, ch 3, sk next ch sp**, dc in each of next 2 sts, ch 4, sk next ch sp and next st, rep from * around, ending last rep at **, join with sl st in 3rd ch of beg ch-3.

**Rnd 21:** Ch 3, dc in next st, *ch 3, sk next ch sp, sc in next st, ch 3, sk next ch sp, dc in each of next 2 sts, [ch 3, sk next ch sp, dc in next st] 22 times, ch 3, sk next ch sp**, dc in each of next 2 sts, rep from * around, ending last rep at **, join with sl st in 3rd ch of beg ch-3.

**Rnd 22:** Ch 3, dc in next st, sk next 2 ch sps, dc in each of next 2 sts, *ch 3, sk next ch sp, [sc in next ch sp, ch 3] 21 times, sk next ch sp**, dc in each of next 2 sts, sk next 2 ch sps, dc in each of next 2 sts, rep from * around, ending last rep at **, join with sl st in 3rd ch of beg ch-3.

**Rnd 23:** Sl st in next st, ch 1, sc in next sp between sts, sk next 2 sts, [3 sc in each of next 22 ch sps, sc in sp between next 2-dc groups] 5 times, 3 sc in each of last 22 ch sps, join with sl st in beg sc. *(402 sc)*

**Rnd 24:** Ch 3, [dc in each of next 34 sts, ch 7, dc in each of next 33 sts] 5 times, dc in each of next 34 sts, ch 7, dc in each of last 32 sts, join with sl st in 3rd ch of beg ch-3. *(402 dc)*

**Rnd 25:** Ch 1, sc in each of first 2 sts, [ch-3 picot, sc in each of next 3 sts] 11 times, (4 sc, ch 4, 4 sc) in next ch sp *(corner made)*, *sc in each of next 4 sts, [ch-3 picot, sc in each of next 3 sts] 21 times, (4 sc, ch 4, 4 sc) in next ch sp *(corner made)*, rep from * 4 times, sc in each of next 4 sts, [ch-3 picot, sc in each of next 3 sts] 9 times, ch-3 picot, sc in last st, join with sl st in beg sc. Fasten off.

**NEXT MOTIF**

**Rnds 1–24:** Rep rnds 1–24 of First Motif.

**Rnd 25:** Ch 1, sc in each of first 2 sts, [ch-3 picot, sc in each of next 3 sts] 11 times, work **corner joining** *(see Special Stitches)*, [**side joining** *(see Special Stitches)*, corner joining] number of times needed to join Motif tog, to complete the rnd, *sc in each of next 4 sts, [ch-3 picot, sc in each of next 3 sts] 21 times, (4 sc, ch 4, 4 sc) in next ch sp *(corner made)*, rep from * around to last 32 sts, sc in each of next 4 sts, [ch-3 picot, sc in each of next 3 sts] 9 times, ch-3 picot, sc in last st, join with sl st in beg sc. Fasten off.

Work rem Motifs *(see Pattern Note)* according to Assembly Diagram.

**FINISHING**

For **circles**, join with sl st in any corner ch-4 sp, ch 12, sl st in same ch sp, ch 1, ({5 sc, ch-3 picot} 3 times, 5 sc) in ch-12 sp, working on side of last circle made *(first circle made)*, sl st in same worked ch-4 sp, ch 25, drop lp from hook, insert hook in same worked ch-4 sp at opposite side of first circle, pick up lp, (2 sc, 2 hdc, 5 dc, ch-3 picot, {5 dc, ch-3 picot} 5 times, 5 dc, 2 hdc, sc) in ch-25 sp, sl st in ch-4 sp *(2nd circle made)*. Fasten off.

Rep circles in each corner ch-4 sp around.

Using beading needle and sewing thread, sew 24 seed beads to center of each Motif. ■

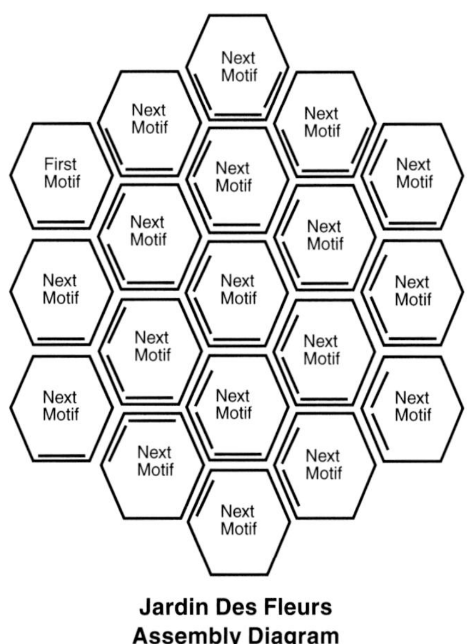


**Jardin Des Fleurs Assembly Diagram**

# Crystal Treasure

DESIGN BY JENNIFER McCLAIN

Rows of beautiful flowers captured in delicate, lace-edged panels create the gracious, old-time charm and elegance of this easy strip design that's as pretty as an English country garden.

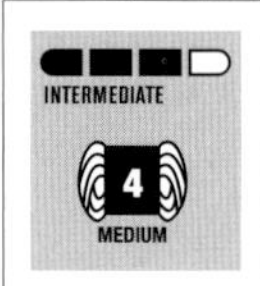


**FINISHED SIZE**
52 x 61 inches, excluding Fringe

**MATERIALS**
Medium (worsted) weight yarn:
50 oz/2,500 yds/1,418g white
11 oz/550 yds/312g pink
7 oz/350 yds/198g green
3 oz/150 yds/85g dark pink
Sizes G/6/4mm and H/8/5mm crochet hooks or sizes needed to obtain gauge
Tapestry needle

**GAUGE**
**Size G hook:** 2 sc and 2 V-sts = 2¼ inches; 3 sc rows and 2 V-st rows in pattern = 2¼ inches

**Size H hook:** Block is 6 inches square

**PATTERN NOTE**
Use size H hook for Blocks and size G hook for Border.

**SPECIAL STITCHES**
**Beginning cluster (beg cl):** Ch 2, [yo, insert hook in same sp, yo, pull lp through, yo, pull through 2 lps on hook] 3 times, yo, pull through all lps on hook.

**Cluster (cl):** Yo, insert hook in next ch sp, yo, pull lp through, yo, pull through 2 lps on hook, [yo, insert hook in same sp, yo, pull lp through, yo, pull through 2 lps on hook] 3 times, yo, pull through all lps on hook.

**Puff stitch (puff st):** Yo, insert hook in ch sp, yo, pull up ⅝-inch-long lp, [yo, insert hook in same sp, yo, pull up ⅝-inch-long lp] twice, yo, pull through all lps on hook.

**Beginning V-stitch (beg V-st):** Ch 4, dc in same st.

**V-stitch (V-st):** (Dc, ch 1, dc) in indicated st or ch sp.

**Long single crochet (lsc):** Working over next ch sp, sc in next, sk next st or ch on row before last.

**INSTRUCTIONS**

**STRIP**
Make 4.

**BLOCK**
Make 10.

**Rnd 1:** With dark pink and size H hook *(see Pattern Note)*, ch 2, 8 sc in 2nd ch from hook, join with sl st in beg sc. *(8 sc)*

**Rnd 2:** Ch 1, sc in first st, ch 2, [sc in next st, ch 2] around, join with sl st in beg sc. Fasten off. *(8 ch-2 sps)*

**Rnd 3:** Join pink with sl st in any ch sp, **beg cl** *(see Special Stitches)*, ch 3, [**cl** *(see Special Stitches)* in next ch sp, ch 3] around, join with sl st in beg cl. Fasten off. *(8 cls, 8 ch-3 sps)*

**Rnd 4:** Join green with sl st in any ch sp, ch 1, (**puff st**—*see Special Stitches*, ch 2, puff st) in same ch sp, ch 3, *(puff st, ch 2, puff st) in next ch sp, ch 3, rep from * around, join with sl st in beg puff st. Fasten off. *(16 puff sts, 8 ch-3 sps, 8 ch-2 sps)*

**Rnd 5:** Join white with sc in any ch-2 sp, *ch 1, working over next ch-3 sp, 3 dc in next cl on rnd before last, ch 1, sc in next ch-2 sp on last rnd, ch 1, working over next ch-3 sp, (3 tr, ch 2, 3 tr) in next cl on rnd before last, ch 1**, sc in next ch-2 sp on last rnd, rep from * around, ending last rep at **, join with sl st in beg sc. *(24 tr, 16 ch-1 sps, 12 dc, 8 sc, 4 ch-2 sps)*

**Rnd 6:** Sl st in first ch-1 sp, ch 1, sc in same ch sp, ch 1, *sk next st, sc in next st, ch 1, [sc in next ch-1 sp, ch 1] twice, sk next st, sc in next st, ch 1, sk next st, (sc, ch 2, sc) in next corner ch-2 sp, ch 1, sk next st, sc in next st, ch 1, sk next st**, [sc in next ch-1 sp, ch 1] twice, rep from * around, ending last rep at **, sc in last ch-1 sp, ch 1, join with sl st in beg sc. *(32 ch-1 sps, 4 ch-2 sps)*

**Rnd 7:** Sl st in first ch-1 sp, ch 1, 2 sc in same ch sp, 2 sc in each ch-1 sp and 3 sc in each corner ch-2 sp around, join with sl st in beg sc. Fasten off. *(76 sc)*

Placing Blocks tog side to side to form Strip, with white, sew tog across 20 sts *(from center st of 1 corner to center st of other corner).*

**BORDER**

**Row 1:** Working across 1 long edge of Strip, join white with sc in first center corner st, [sc in each st across to next joined corner st before seam, hdc in joined corner st, dc in seam, hdc in next joined corner st after seam] across to last Block, sc in each st across ending in center corner st, turn. *(209 sts)*

**Row 2:** Working this row in **back lps** *(see Stitch Guide)* only, ch 1, sl st in each st across, turn.

**Row 3:** Working in rem lps of row 1, ch 1, sc in first st, [sk next st, **V-st** *(see Special Stitches)* in next st, sk next st, sc in next st] across, turn. *(53 sc, 52 V-sts)*

**Row 4:** Working this row in **front lps** *(see Stitch Guide)* only, **beg V-st** *(see Special Stitches)*, [sc in ch sp of next V-st, V-st in next sc] across, turn. *(53 V-sts, 52 sc)*

**Row 5:** Working this row in back lps only, sl st in first st, sl st in next ch sp, ch 1, sc in same ch sp, [V-st in next sc, sc in next V-st] across, turn.

**Rows 6 & 7:** Rep rows 4 and 5.

**Row 8:** Working this row in back lps only, ch 1, sl st in each st and in each ch across, turn. Fasten off.

**Row 9:** Working in rem lps of row 7, join pink with sc in first st, [ch 1, sk next st or ch, sc in next st or ch] across, **do not turn.** Fasten off. *(105 sc, 104 ch-1 sps)*

**Row 10:** Join white with sc in first st, **lsc** *(see Special Stitches)*, [ch 1, sk next st, lsc] across to last st, sc in last st, **do not turn**. Fasten off. *(104 lsc, 103 ch-1 sps, 2 sc)*

**Row 11:** Join pink with sc in first st, ch 1, sk next st, [lsc, ch 1, sk next st] across to last st, sc in last st, **do not turn.** Fasten off. *(104 ch-1 sps, 103 lsc, 2 sc)*

**Row 12:** Join white with sc in first st, 2 lsc in each lsc on row before last across to last lsc, lsc in last lsc, sc same lsc and last st on last row tog. Fasten off. *(209 sc)*

Rep on opposite edge.

With H hook and white, hold 2 Strips RS tog, matching sts of last row on Border, sc Strips tog. Rep with rem Strips.

**EDGING**

Working in sts and in ends of rows across 1 short end, with H hook and white, join with sc in first row, sc evenly across to opposite corner, fasten off.

Rep on opposite end.

**FRINGE**

For each Fringe, cut 1 strand white 16 inches long. Fold in half, insert hook in st, pull fold through, pull all loose ends through fold, tighten. Trim ends even.

Attach Fringe in each st across short ends of Afghan. ■

# Purple Mums

DESIGN BY BRENDA STRATTON

The floral beauty of New England in autumn is captured in the colorful mums that are the focal point of this enchanting afghan that perfectly blends the contrast of rich texture and lacy stitch work.

**FINISHED SIZE**
52½ x 73½ inches

**MATERIALS**
Medium (worsted) weight yarn:
- 49 oz/2,450 yds/1,389g white
- 23 oz/1,150 yds/652g lavender
- 14 oz/700 yds/397g dark sage
- 11 oz/550 yds/312g lilac
- 2 oz/100 yds/57g bright yellow

Sizes G/6/4mm and H/8/5mm crochet hook or sizes needed to obtain gauge
Tapestry needle

**GAUGE**
Mum Motifs: 8 inches square

Fill-in Motifs: 4 inches square

**PATTERN NOTES**
Using assembly diagram as guide, join Motifs together as work progresses.

Use size G hook for flowers and leaves only. Remainder of Motifs are crocheted with size H hook.

**INSTRUCTIONS**

**FIRST MUM MOTIF**
**Rnd 1:** With size G hook *(see Pattern Notes)* and bright yellow, ch 4, sl st in first ch to form ring, ch 1, 8 sc in ring, join with sl st in beg sc. Fasten off. *(8 sc)*

**Rnd 2:** For **front petals**, working in **front lps** *(see Stitch Guide)* for this rnd only, join lavender with sl st in any sc, [ch 7, sl st in 2nd ch from hook, sc in next ch, hdc in each of next 4 chs, sl st in next sc of rnd 1] around, join with sl st in beg sl st. *(8 petals)*

**Rnd 3:** For **back petals,** sl st in first **back lp** *(see Stitch Guide)* of rnd 1, holding petals of rnd 2 forward and working in back lps only, rep rnd 2, ending with sl st to bottom of first petal of this rnd. Fasten off. *(8 petals)*

**Rnd 4:** For **leaf base,** join dark sage with sl st in sl st between any 2 petals of rnd 3, [ch 4, sl st between next 2 petals, sl st in sp between next 2 petals] around, ending with sl st in first sl st. *(4 ch-4 sps)*

**Rnd 5:** For **leaves**, *sl st in next ch-4 sp, ch 1, 3 sc in same ch-4 sp, ch 1, turn, [sc in each of next 3 sc, ch 1, turn] 3 times, **sc dec** *(see Stitch Guide)* in next 2 sc, sc in next sc, ch 1, turn, sc dec in next 2 sc, fasten off, join dark sage with sl st in same ch-4 sp, ch 1, 3 sc in same ch-4 sp, ch 1, turn, [sc in each of next 3 sc, ch 1, turn] 3 times, sc dec in next 2 sc, sc in next sc, ch 1, turn, sc dec in next 2 sc, fasten off, rep from * in each of next 3 ch-4 sps. *(8 leaves)*

**Rnd 6:** For **center**, with size G hook and bright yellow, ch 3, 7 hdc in 3rd ch from hook, join with sl st in 3rd ch of beg ch-3. Leaving long end, fasten off.

Thread tapestry needle with long end and sew RS of center over rnd 1 of center of flower.

**Rnd 7:** With size H hook, join white with sc in ch-4 sp of rnd 4 between any 2 leaves, holding all petals and leaves forward, ch 1, sc in same ch sp, ch 3, [sc in ch-4 sp between next 2 petals, ch 3] around, join with sl st in beg sc. *(8 ch-3 sps)*

**Rnd 8:** Sl st in next ch sp, ch 3, (2 dc, ch 2, 3 dc) in same ch sp, 3 dc in next ch sp, [(3 dc, ch 2, 3 dc) in next ch-3 sp, 3 dc in next ch-3 sp] around, join with sl st in 3rd ch of beg ch-3. *(36 dc)*

**Rnd 9:** For **anchor**, sl st in ch-2 sp, holding petals forward and picking up st in back of leaves as necessary to anchor them to rnd being worked, ch 3, (dc, ch 2, 2 dc) in same ch sp, dc in each dc across, [(2 dc, ch 2, 2 dc) in next ch-2 sp, dc in each dc across] around, join with sl st in 3rd ch of beg ch-3. *(52 dc)*

**Rnd 10:** Sl st in corner ch-2 sp, ch 3, (dc, ch 2, 2 dc) in same ch sp, dc in each dc across, [(2 dc, ch 2, 2 dc) in next ch-2 sp, dc in each dc across]

around, join with sl st in 3rd ch of beg ch-3. Fasten off. *(68 dc)*

**Rnd 11:** Join lilac with sl st in any corner ch-2 sp, ch 1, (sc, {ch 3, sc} 3 times) in same ch sp, sk next 2 dc, [(sc, ch 3, sc) in next dc, sk next 2 dc] 5 times, *(sc, {ch 3, sc} 3 times) in next ch sp, sk next 2 dc, [(sc, ch 3, sc) in next dc, sk next 2 dc] 5 times, rep from * around, join with sl st in beg sc. Fasten off. *(32 ch-3 sps)*

**Rnd 12:** Join lavender with sl st in center ch-3 sp at any corner, ch 1, (sc, ch 3, sc) in same ch sp, [(sc, ch 3, sc) in next ch sp] around, join with sl st in beg sc. Fasten off.

**Rnd 13:** Join white with sl st in ch-3 sp at any corner, ch 1, (sc, {ch 3, sc} 3 times) in same ch sp, [(sc, ch 3, sc) in next ch sp] 7 times, *[(sc, {ch 3, sc} 3 times) in next corner ch sp, [(sc, ch 3, sc) in next ch sp] 7 times, rep from * around, join with sl st in beg sc. Fasten off. *(40 ch-3 sps)*

**Rnd 14:** Join white with sl st in center corner ch-3 sp, ch 1, (sc, ch 5, sc) in same ch-3 sp, *[(sc, ch 3, sc) in next ch-3 sp] 9 times**, (sc, ch 5, sc) in next center corner ch-3 sp, rep from * around, ending last rep at **, join with sl st in beg sc. Fasten off.

**REMAINING MUM MOTIFS**
Make 59.

**Rnds 1–13:** Rep rnds 1–13 of First Mum Motif.

**Rnd 14:** Rep rnd 14 of First Mum Motif, working at each center corner, (sc, ch 2, sl st in adjacent ch-5 sp, ch 2, sc) in same ch-3 sp and replacing the (sc, ch 3, sc) in each ch-3 sp with [sc in ch-3 sp, ch 1, sl st in corresponding lp on previously worked Motif, ch 1, sc in same ch-3 sp] rep across side to be joined to previous Motif, join with sl st in beg sc. Fasten off.

**FILL-IN MOTIF**
Make 20.

**Rnd 1:** With size H hook and white, ch 4, sl st in first ch to form ring, ch 2, 2 hdc in ring, ch 2, [3 hdc in ring, ch 2] 3 times, join with sl st in 2nd ch of beg ch-2. Fasten off. *(12 hdc)*

**Rnd 2:** Join lilac with sl st in any ch-2 sp, ch 1, (sc, {ch 3, sc} 3 times) in same ch sp, sk next hdc, (sc, ch 3, sc) in next hdc, sk next hdc, *(sc, {ch 3, sc} 3 times) in next ch-2 sp, sk next hdc, (sc, ch 3, sc) in next hdc, sk next hdc, rep from * around, join with sl st in beg sc. Fasten off. *(16 ch-3 sps)*

**Rnd 3:** Join lavender with sl st in center ch-3 sp of any corner, ch 1, (sc, ch 3, sc) in same ch-3 sp, *(sc, ch 3, sc) in next ch-3 sp, rep from * around, join with sl st in beg sc. Fasten off.

**Rnd 4:** Join white with sl st in corner ch-3 sp, ch 1, (sc, {ch 3, sc} 3 times) in same ch-3 sp, *[(sc, ch 3, sc) in next ch-3 sp] 3 times**, (sc, {ch 3, sc} 3 times) in next corner ch-3 sp, rep from * around, ending last rep at **, join with sl st in beg sc. Fasten off. *(24 ch-3 sps)*

**Rnd 5:** Join white with sl st in center corner ch-3 sp, rep rnd 3, replacing (sc, ch 3, sc) in next lp with (sc, ch 1, sl st in corresponding ch sp on previously worked Motif, ch 1, sc) in next ch-3 sp on sides to be joined.

**Purple Mums Assembly Diagram**

**TASSEL**
Make 18.

Cut 30 strands of white yarn each 12 inches long. Holding all strands tog at center, tie a separate length of yarn around strands at center. Fold strands in half at tied point and tie 12-inch length of yarn around folded strands 1¼ inches below top. Blend tying ends in with strands of Tassel, trim ends.

Sew Tassel to each of the 9 bottom points on each end of Afghan. Trim ends even. ■

# Rickrack Daisies

DESIGN BY BRENDA STRATTON

It's said that daisies don't tell, but the creative use of rickrack braid in this unusual, eye-catching table topper reveals a secret crochet technique that's based on the past, but just as appealing today.

INTERMEDIATE

**FINISHED SIZE**
14 inches square

**MATERIALS**
Size 10 crochet cotton:
400 yds white
Size 9/1.25mm steel crochet hook or size needed to obtain gauge
Sewing needle
Beading needle
Sewing thread: blue, white
Package blue medium rickrack
360 yellow seed beads
Liquid seam sealer

**GAUGE**
Motif = 4¼ inches across

**PATTERN NOTES**
Cut 9 pieces rickrack according to Fig. 1 with 14 points across top edge and 13 points across bottom edge.

Apply seam sealer to raw edges.

Fold into circle, overlapping section A over section B according to Fig. 1, sew to secure. There will be 12 points on outside edge and 12 points on inside edge.

When working through point of rickrack, if it is hard to get head of hook through point, use a sharp darning needle to make a hole in rickrack before inserting hook.

**SPECIAL STITCHES**
**V-stitch (V-st):** (Dc, ch 2, dc) in next ch sp or st.

**Shell:** (2 dc, ch 3, 2 dc) in next ch sp.

**Joined shell:** 2 dc in next ch sp, ch 1, sl st in ch sp of next shell on other Motif, ch 1, 2 dc in same ch sp on this Motif.

**Cluster (cl):** Holding back last lp of each st on hook, 2 dc in next ch sp, yo, pull through all lps on hook.

**Cluster shell (cl shell):** ({**Cl** *(see Special Stitches)*, ch 2} twice, cl) in next ch sp.

**INSTRUCTIONS**

**FIRST ROW**

**FIRST MOTIF**
**Rnd 1:** Ch 4, sl st in first ch to form ring, ch 2 *(does not count as first hdc)*, 12 hdc in ring, join with sl st in top of beg hdc. *(12 hdc)*

**Rnd 2:** Ch 5, sl st in any point of 1 rickrack circle on inside edge of circle, hdc in next ch of ch-5, dc in each of next 4 chs, sl st in top of first hdc on rnd 1, *sl st in top of next hdc on rnd 1, (ch 5, sl st) in next point on inside edge of rickrack, hdc in next ch of ch-5 just made, dc in each of next 4 chs, sl st in top of same hdc on rnd 1, rep from * around, join with sl st in beg sl st. Fasten off.

**Rnd 3:** Join with sl st in any point on outside edge of same rickrack circle, ch 5 *(counts as dc and ch-2 sp)*, dc in same sp, ch 5, ***V-st** *(see Special Stitches)* in next point, ch 5, rep from * around, join with sl st in 3rd ch of beg ch-5.

**Rnd 4:** Sl st in next ch sp, ch 7 *(counts as first tr and ch-3 sp)*, (tr, ch 5, tr, ch 3, tr) in same ch sp, [2 dc in next ch-5 sp, V-st in ch sp of next V-st] twice, 2 dc in next ch sp, *(tr, ch 3, tr, ch 5, tr, ch 3, tr) in next corner ch sp, [2 dc in next ch-5 sp, V-st in

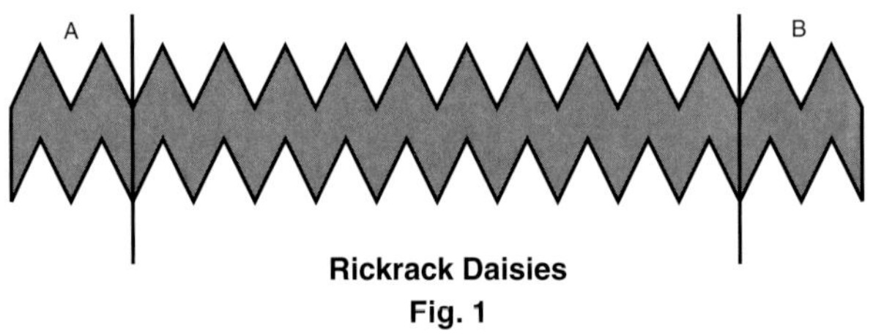


Rickrack Daisies
Fig. 1

ch sp of next V-st] twice, 2 dc in next ch sp, rep from * around, join with sl st in 4th ch of beg ch-7.

**Rnd 5:** Sl st in next ch sp, ch 6, dc in same sp, (tr, ch 3, tr, ch 5, tr, ch 3, tr) in next ch-5 sp, (dc, ch 3, dc) in next ch sp, [dc in each of next 2 dc, V-st in next V-st] twice, 2 dc in next 2 dc, *(dc, ch 3, dc) in next ch sp, (tr, ch 3, tr, ch 5, tr, ch 3, tr) in next ch-5 sp, (dc, ch 3, dc) in next ch sp, [dc in each of next 2 dc, V-st in next V-st] twice, 2 dc in next 2 dc, rep from * around, join with sl st in 3rd ch of ch-6.

**Rnd 6:** (Sl st, ch 3, dc, ch 3, 2 dc) in next ch sp *(counts as first shell)*, *sl st in next ch sp, (**shell**—*see Special Stitches*, ch 5, shell) in next corner ch sp, sl st in next ch sp, shell in next ch sp, [sl st in sp between next 2 dc, shell in next V-st] twice, sl st in sp between next 2 dc**, shell in next ch sp, rep from * around, ending last rep at **, join with sl st in 3rd ch of beg ch-3. Fasten off.

**2ND MOTIF**

**Rnds 1–5:** Work rnds 1–5 of First Motif.

**Rnd 6:** (Sl st, ch 3, dc, ch 3, 2 dc) in next ch sp, sl st in next ch sp, shell in next corner ch-5 sp, ch 2, sl st in corresponding corner ch sp on last Motif, ch 2, 2 dc in same ch sp on this Motif, ch 1, sl st in next ch sp on other Motif, ch 1, 2 dc in same ch sp on this Motif, sl st in next ch sp, **joined shell** *(see Special Stitches)* in next ch sp, [sl st in sp between next 2 dc, joined shell in next V-st] twice, sl st in sp between next 2 dc, joined shell in next ch sp, sl st in next ch sp, joined shell in next ch sp, ch 2, sl st in next corner ch sp on other Motif, ch 2, shell in same ch sp on this Motif, sl st in next ch sp, shell in next ch sp, [sl st in sp between next 2 dc, shell in next V-st] twice, sl st in sp between next 2 dc, shell in next ch sp, *sl st in next ch sp, (shell, ch 5, shell) in next corner ch-5 sp, sl st in next ch sp, shell in next ch sp, [sl st in sp between next 2 dc, shell in next V-st] twice, sl st in sp between next 2 dc*, shell in next ch sp, rep between *, join with sl st in 3rd ch of beg ch-3. Fasten off.

Work 2nd Motif once more for total of 3 Motifs on this row.

**2ND ROW**

**FIRST MOTIF**

Working on bottom of First Motif of last row, work same as First Row, 2nd Motif.

**2ND MOTIF**

**Rnds 1–5:** Work rnds 1–5 of First Motif.

**Rnd 6:** (Sl st, ch 3, dc, ch 3, 2 dc) in next ch sp, sl st in next ch sp, shell in next corner ch sp, working on bottom of next Motif on last row, ch 2, sl st in corresponding corner ch sp on other Motif, ch 2, 2 dc in same ch sp on this Motif, ch 1, sl st in next ch sp on other Motif, ch 1, 2 dc in same ch sp on this Motif, *sl st in next ch sp, joined shell in next ch sp, [sl st in sp between next 2 dc, joined shell in next V-st] twice, sl st in sp between next 2 dc, joined shell in next ch sp, sl st in next ch sp, 2 dc in next corner ch sp, ch 1, sl st in next ch sp on other Motif, ch 1, 2 dc in same ch sp on this Motif, ch 2, sl st in next corner ch sp on other Motif, ch 2, 2 dc in same ch sp on this Motif*, joining to side of last Motif on this row, ch 1, sl st in corresponding sp on other Motif, ch 1, 2 dc in same ch sp on this Motif, rep between *, ch 3, 2 dc in same ch sp, sl st in next ch sp, shell in next ch sp, [sl st in sp between next 2 dc, shell in next V-st] twice, sl st in sp between next 2 dc, shell in next ch sp, sl st in next ch sp, (shell, ch 5, shell) in next corner ch-5 sp, sl st in next ch sp, shell in next ch sp, [sl st in sp between next 2 dc, shell in next V-st] twice, sl st in sp between next 2 dc, join with sl st in 3rd ch of beg ch-3. Fasten off.

Work 2nd Motif once more for total of 3 Motifs on this row.

Work 2nd Row once more for total of 3 rows.

**EDGING**

**Rnd 1:** Join with sc in sl st before 1 corner, ch 1, *(**cl shell**—see *Special Stitches*, ch 2) in each of next 2 ch sps, [cl shell in next ch sp, ch 1, sc in next sl st or joining sl st, ch 1] 17 times, rep from * twice, (cl shell, ch 2) in each of next 2 ch sps, [cl shell in next ch sp, ch 1, sc in next sl st or joining sl st, ch 1] 16 times, cl shell in last ch sp, join with sl st in beg sc.

**Rnd 2:** Sl st in next ch, sl st in next cl, sl st in each of next 2 chs, sl st in next cl, ch 1, (sc, ch 3, sc) in same cl, ◊*ch 7, (sc, ch 3, sc) in center cl of next shell*, rep between *, [ch 5, (sc, ch 3, sc) in center cl of next shell] 17 times, rep from ◊ twice, rep between * twice, rep between [ ] 16 times, ch 5, join with sl st in beg sc.

**Rnd 3:** Sl st in next ch sp, ch 1, (sc, ch 3, sc) in same ch sp, [◊ch 3, sl st in next ch-7 sp, ch 3, (sc, ch 3, sc, ch 5, sc, ch 3, sc) in next ch-3 sp, ch 3, sl st in next ch-7 sp, ch 3◊, *(sc, ch 3, sc) in next ch-3 sp, ch 2, sl st in next ch-5 sp, ch 2*, rep between * 16 times, (sc, ch 3, sc) in next ch-3 sp] twice, rep between ◊, rep between * 17 times, join with sl st in beg sc. Fasten off.

**FINISHING**

Thread beading needle with white sewing thread, insert needle from back to front through rnd 1 of any Motif, sew 40 beads to rnd 1 covering hdc sts completely, secure.

Rep on each Motif. ■

# Rose Lattice

DESIGN BY VALMAY FLINT

With the Victorian charm and classic beauty of vintage doilies that might have graced your grandmother's table, this unique design features roses joined with an interesting lattice technique.

INTERMEDIATE

**FINISHED SIZE**
16 x 18 inches

**MATERIALS**
Size 20 crochet cotton:
- 150 yds white
- 150 yds pink

Size 9/1.25mm steel crochet hook or size needed to obtain gauge

**GAUGE**
Rose = 1¼ inches across; 7 joined roses = 4 inches

**SPECIAL STITCHES**
**Beginning shell (beg shell):** Ch 3 *(counts as first dc)*, (2 dc, ch 2, 3 dc) in same sp.

**Shell:** (3 dc, ch 2, 3 dc) in next ch sp.

**Picot:** Ch 3, sc in 3rd ch from hook.

**Joining chain space (joining ch sp):** Ch 2, drop lp from hook, insert hook through center of specified ch sp on other Rose, pull dropped lp through.

## INSTRUCTIONS

**FIRST MOTIF**

**CENTER ROSE**
**Rnd 1:** With pink, ch 5, sl st in first ch to form ring, ch 1, [sc in ring, ch 4] 6 times, join with sl st in beg sc. *(6 sc, 6 ch sps)*

**Rnd 2:** Sl st in first ch sp, ch 1, (sc, 3 dc, sc) in same ch sp and in each ch sp around, join with sl st in beg sc.

**Rnd 3:** Working behind last rnd, ch 1, sc around front of **post** *(see Stitch Guide)* of sc of sc below on rnd before last, ch 6, [sc around post of next sc on rnd before last, ch 6] around, join with sl st in beg sc.

**Rnd 4:** Sl st in first ch sp, ch 1, (sc, 3 dc, ch 2, 3 dc, sc) in same ch sp and in each ch sp around, join with sl st in beg sc. Fasten off.

**2ND ROSE**
**Rnds 1–3:** Rep rnds 1–3 of Center Rose.

**Rnd 4:** Sl st in first ch sp, ch 1, (sc, 3 dc) in same ch sp, joining to Center Rose *(see assembly diagram)*, work **joining ch sp** *(see Special Stitches)* in any ch sp on Center Rose, (3 dc, sc) in same ch sp on this Rose, (sc, 3 dc, ch 2, 3 dc, sc) in each ch sp around, join with sl st in beg sc. Fasten off.

**3RD ROSE**
**Rnds 1–3:** Rep rnds 1–3 of Center Rose.

**Rnd 4:** Sl st in first ch sp, ch 1, (sc, 3 dc) in same ch sp, joining to Center Rose, work joining ch sp in next unjoined ch sp on Center Rose *(see Assembly Diagram)*, (3 dc, sc) in

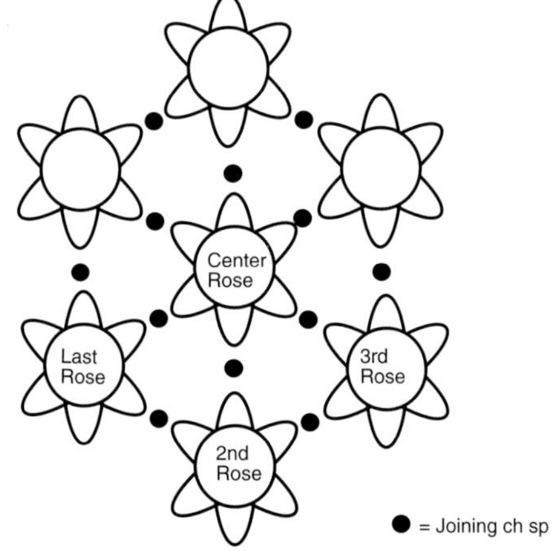

**Rose Lattice Assembly Diagram**

same ch sp on this Rose, (sc, 3 dc) in next ch sp, joining to last Rose, work joining ch sp in corresponding ch sp on other Rose *(see Assembly Diagram)*, (3 dc, sc) in same ch sp on this Rose, (sc, 3 dc, ch 2, 3 dc, sc) in each ch sp around, join with sl st in beg sc. Fasten off.

**4TH–6TH ROSES**
Rep 3rd Rose 3 times.

**LAST ROSE**
**Rnds 1–3:** Rep same rnds of Center Rose.

**Rnd 4:** Sl st in first ch sp, ch 1, (sc, 3 dc) in same ch sp, joining to Center Rose, work joining ch sp in last unjoined ch sp on Center Rose, (3 dc, sc) in same ch sp on this Rose, (sc, 3 dc) in next ch sp, joining to last Rose, work joining ch sp in corresponding ch sp on other Rose, (3 dc, sc) in same ch sp on this Rose, (sc, 3 dc, ch 2, 3 dc, sc) in each of next 3 ch sps, (sc, 3 dc) in last ch sp, joining to 2nd Rose *(see Assembly Diagram)*, work joining ch sp in corresponding ch sp on other Rose, (3 dc, sc) in same sp on this Rose, join with sl st in beg sc. Fasten off.

**EDGING**
**Rnd 1:** Working around outer edge of Roses, join white with sc in first unjoined ch sp after joining on any Rose, ch 9, [sc in next ch sp, ch 9] around, join with sl st in beg sc. *(18 ch sps)*

**Rnd 2:** Sl st in first ch sp, ch 3, 11 dc in same ch sp, 12 dc in each ch sp around, join with sl st in 3rd ch of beg ch-3. *(216 dc)*

**Rnd 3:** Ch 5 *(counts as first dc and ch-2 sp)*, sk next 2 sts, [dc in next st, ch 2, sk next 2 sts] around, join with sl st in 3rd ch of beg ch-5. *(72 dc, 72 ch sps)*

**Rnd 4:** Sl st in first ch sp, **beg shell** *(see Special Stitches)*, ch 4, sk next 2 ch sps, [**shell** *(see Special Stitches)* in next ch sp, ch 4, sk next 2 ch sps] around,

join with sl st in 3rd ch of beg ch-3. Fasten off. *(24 shells, 24 ch sps)*

**Rnd 5:** Join pink with sl st in ch sp of first shell, beg shell, ch 2, (sc, ch 3, sc) in next ch sp, ch 2, *shell in ch sp of next shell, ch 2, (sc, ch 3, sc) in next ch sp, ch 2, rep from * around, join with sl st in 3rd ch of beg ch-3. Fasten off.

**Rnd 6:** Join white with sl st in first shell, beg shell, ch 6, sk next 3 ch sps, [shell in next shell, ch 6, sk next 3 ch sps] around, join with sl st in 3rd ch of beg ch-3. Fasten off.

**Rnd 7:** Join pink with sl st in first shell, beg shell, ch 3, (sc, ch 3, sc) in next ch sp, ch 3, *shell in next shell, ch 3, (sc, ch 3, sc) in next ch sp, ch 3*, rep between *, [3 dc in next ch sp, ch 49, dc in 4th ch from hook, dc in each ch across, 3 dc in same shell in last rnd, ch 3, (sc, ch 3, sc) in next ch sp, ch 3] 4 times, rep between * twice, rep between [ ] 4 times, rep between * around, join with sl st in 3rd ch of beg ch-3. Fasten off.

**2ND MOTIF**

**CENTER ROSE, 2ND ROSE, 3RD–6TH ROSE & LAST ROSE**
Work same as First Motif, Center Rose, 2nd Rose, 3rd–6th Rose and Last Rose.

**EDGING**
**Rnds 1–6:** Rep same rnds of First Motif's Edging.

**Rnd 7:** Join pink with sl st in first shell, beg shell, ch 3, (sc, ch 3, sc) in next ch sp, ch 3, *shell in next shell, ch 3, (sc, ch 3, sc) in next ch sp, ch 3*, rep between *, [3 dc in next ch sp, ch 49, dc in 4th ch from hook, dc in each ch across, 3 dc in same shell on last rnd, ch 3, (sc, ch 3, sc) in next ch sp, ch 3] 4 times, 3 dc in next shell, joining to 2 shells between strips on First Motif, ch 1, sc in ch sp of corresponding shell on First Motif, ch 1, 3 dc in same shell on this Motif, ch 3, (sc, ch 3, sc) in next ch sp, ch 3, 3 dc in next shell, ch 1, sc in ch sp of next shell on First Motif, ch 1, 3 dc in same shell on this Motif, ch 3, (sc, ch 3, sc) in next ch sp, ch 3, rep between [ ] 4 times, rep between * around, join with sl st in 3rd ch of beg ch-3. Fasten off.

**BORDER**

**Rnd 1:** Working around entire outer edge of both Motifs, join white with sl st in first shell on last rnd of either Motif, beg shell, ch 6, sk next 3 ch sps, [shell in next shell, ch 6, sk next 3 ch sps] twice, *[shell in end of next strip on other Motif, ch 6] 4 times being careful not to twist strips, [pick up next strip on this Motif, weave over and under strips of other Motif, shell in end of woven strip, ch 6, pick up next strip on this Motif, weave under and over strips of other Motif, shell in end of woven strip, ch 6] twice being careful not to twist strips*, [shell in next shell, ch 6, sk next 3 ch sps] 14 times, rep between *, [shell in next shell, ch 6, sk next 3 ch sps] 11 times, join with sl st in 3rd ch of beg ch-3. Fasten off.

**Rnd 2:** Join pink with sl st in first shell, beg shell, ch 3, (sc, ch 3, sc) in next ch sp, ch 3, *shell in next shell, ch 3, (sc, ch 3, sc) in next ch sp, ch 3, rep from * around, join with sl st in 3rd ch of beg ch-3. Fasten off.

**Rnd 3:** Join white with sl st in first shell, beg shell, ch 7, sk next 3 ch sps, [shell in next shell, ch 7, sk next 3 ch sps] around, join with sl st in 3rd ch of beg ch-3. Fasten off.

**Rnd 4:** Join pink with sl st in first shell, ch 3, 2 dc in same sp, **picot** *(see Special Stitches)*, 3 dc in same ch sp, ch 3, (sc, ch 3, sc) in next ch sp, ch 3, *(3 dc, picot, 3 dc) in next shell, ch 3, (sc, ch 3, sc) in next ch sp, ch 3, rep from * around, join with sl st in 3rd ch of beg ch-3. Fasten off. ■

# Midnight Pansies

DESIGN BY CAROL ALEXANDER

Pretty pansies in rich, bright colors float in lacy white squares on a dramatic black background. Filigree crochet accents suggest the look of fancy wrought iron for an elegant, ornate effect.

**FINISHED SIZE**
54 x 72 inches

**MATERIALS**
Medium (worsted) weight yarn:
38½ oz/1,925 yds/1,091g each black and white
14 oz/700 yds/397g green
3½ oz/175 yds/99g each lemon, red, blue, lilac and hot orange
Size G/6/4mm crochet hook or size needed to obtain gaug
Tapestry needle

**GAUGE**
Pansy Motif = 2½ inches in diameter
Center Motif = 3¾ inches
Center Motif Extensions: 4 sc = 1 inch; 4 sc rows = 1 inch
Corner Motif = 5¾ inches
Completed square = 18 inches

**SPECIAL STITCHES**
**Beginning corner shell (beg corner shell):** Ch 3 *(counts as first dc)* (2 dc, ch 3, 3 dc) in corner ch sp.

**Corner shell:** (3 dc, ch 3, 3 dc) in corner ch sp.

**Shell:** (2 dc, ch 1, 2 dc) in st indicated.

**Picot:** Ch 4, sl st in 4th ch from hook.

## INSTRUCTIONS

### FIRST LARGE SQUARE

#### PANSY MOTIF
For each Large Square, make 5 Pansy Motifs, 1 each with flower petals *(rnd 2)* worked in lilac, red, lemon, blue and hot orange. Arrange pansy colors for Corner and Center Pansy Squares as desired when assembling for each Large Square.

**Rnd 1:** Beg at center with black, ch 4, sl st in first ch to form ring, working over beg yarn tail, [ch 2, 2 dc in ring, ch 2, sl st in ring] 3 times. Fasten off. *(3 center petals)* Pull beg yarn tail firmly to pull center opening nearly closed, weave in and secure on back side.

**Rnd 2:** Join petal color with sl st in sl st between any 2 center petals of rnd 1, [(ch 4, 3 dtr, ch 4, sl st) in same st] twice *(2 large bottom petals made)*, [ch 3, 3 dc in each of 2 dc of next center petal, ch 3, sl st in next sl st between center petals] 3 times, now working in **back lps** *(see Stitch Guide)* only around outside edge of next 2 large bottom petals, *ch 1, sl st in next st*, rep between * to end of 2nd petal. Fasten off.

Flatten and arrange petals of rnd 2 as shown, with side petals in front of and overlapping top and bottom petals, and bottom right petal overlapping bottom left petal. Tack all overlaps securely in place to hold. With yellow, embroider 3 straight sts on center of pansy as shown, with the center st slightly longer than the 1 on each side.

#### CENTER PANSY SQUARE
**Rnd 1:** With back of Pansy facing and bottom petals on top, join white to back of flower at base of overlap of bottom petals, working on back of flower, ch 6, sl st in center bar on back of center st of next side petal, ch 6, sl st in center bar on back of center st of top petal, ch 6, sl st in center bar on back of center st of other side petal, ch 6, sl st in base of first ch-6, turn. *(4 ch-6 sps)*

**Rnd 2:** With RS of Pansy now facing, sl st in next ch-6 sp, ch 3 *(counts as first dc)*, *2 dc in same ch sp, tr in

same ch sp catching lp on center of bottom Pansy petal approximately ¼ inch from edge, ch 1, (tr, 3 dc) in same ch sp*, (3 dc, tr, ch 1, tr, 3 dc) in each of next 2 ch-6 sps, dc in next ch-6 sp, rep between * once, join with sl st in **front lp** *(see Stitch Guide)* of 3rd ch of beg ch-3.

**Rnd 3:** Working in front lps only this rnd, *4 hdc in next st, work dec in next 2 sts as follows: insert hook in next st, yo, pull lp through, insert hook in next st, yo, pull through st and 2 lps on hook *(dec made)*, 5 dc in next st *(corner ch-1)*, dec as before, 4 hdc in next st, dec as before, rep from * 3 times, join with sl st in beg sl st. Fasten off. *(12 scallops)*

**Rnd 4:** Join black in the unworked back lp of any corner ch-1 of rnd 2, working in the unworked back lps of rnd 2, ch 2, hdc in same st catching lp on top center back of corner scallop of rnd 3, ch 2, 2 hdc in same st, *[hdc in each of next 2 sts, hdc in next st catching lp on top center back *(just below back lps)* of next scallop of rnd 3] twice, hdc in each of next 2 sts**, 2 hdc in corner ch-1 catching lp on top center back *(just below back lps)* of corner scallop with 2nd of these hdc, ch 2, 2 hdc in corner st, rep from * 3 times, ending last rep at **, join with sl st in 2nd ch of beg ch-2, sl st in next hdc, sl st in corner ch-2 sp. **Do not fasten off.**

#### FIRST EXTENSION

**Row 1:** Ch 1, sc in corner sp, sc in each of next 12 hdc, sc in next corner ch-2 sp, turn. *(14 sc)*

**Rows 2–22:** Ch 1, sc in each sc across, turn. Fasten off at end of row 22.

#### 2ND, 3RD & 4TH EXTENSIONS

With RS facing, join black with sl st in same corner ch-2 sp where last sc of row 1 of previous Extension is worked, rep rows 1-22 of First Extension.

#### CORNER PANSY SQUARE

Make 4.

**Rnd 1:** With green, rep rnd 1 of Center Pansy Square. *(4 ch-6 sps)*

**Rnd 2:** With RS of Pansy facing, *in next ch-6 sp work (sl st, ch 1, hdc, 3 dc, hdc, ch 1), sl st in same sp catching lp on center back of bottom Pansy petal approximately ⅜ inch from edge, (ch 1, hdc, 3 dc, hdc, ch 1) in same ch-6 sp*, in each of next 2 ch-6 sps work (sl st, ch 1, hdc, 3 dc, hdc, ch 1) twice, rep between * once, join with sl st in beg sl st. Fasten off. *(8 scallops)*

**Rnd 3:** With Pansy facing, join white with sl st in center bar on back of center dc of right scallop of the 2 scallops centered behind top Pansy petal, ch 4, [sl st to lp on top back of center st of next scallop, ch 4] 7 times, join with sl st in base of beg ch-4. *(8 ch-4 sps)*

**Rnd 4:** Sl st in first ch-4 sp, ch 3, 5 dc in same ch sp, [(3 tr, ch 3, 3 tr) in next ch-4 sp, 6 dc in next ch-4 sp] 3 times, (3 tr, ch 3, 3 tr) in last ch-4 sp, join with sl st in 3rd ch of beg ch-3.

**Rnd 5:** Ch 3, dc in each of next 8 sts, *(2 tr, ch 1, 2 tr) in corner ch-3 sp, dc in each of next 12 sts, rep from * twice, (2 tr, ch 1, 2 tr) in next corner ch-3 sp, dc in each of last 3 sts, join with sl st in front lp of 3rd ch of beg ch-3.

**Rnd 6:** Working in front lps only this

rnd, ch 2, 3 hdc in same st, *[dec in next 2 sts as on rnd 3 of Center Pansy Square, 4 hdc in next st] 3 times, sl st in next st, 5 dc in corner ch-1 sp**, rep between [ ] twice, rep from * 3 times, ending last rep at **, dec in next 2 sts, 4 hdc in next st, dec in next 2 sts, join with sl st in 2nd ch of beg ch-2. Fasten off.

**Rnd 7:** Join black with sl st to bottom back of center dc of any 5-dc corner scallop, ch 2, hdc in same place catching lp on top center back of same scallop, ch 2, 2 hdc in same place, *working in back lps of rnd 5, [hdc in each of next 2 sts, hdc in next st catching lp on top center back of next scallop of rnd 6] 5 times, hdc in next st**, 2 hdc in bottom back of center dc of next 5-dc corner scallop catching lp on top center back of same scallop with 2nd of these hdc, ch 2,2 hdc in same place, rep from * 3 times, ending last rep at **, join with sl st in 2nd ch of beg ch-2. Fasten off.

#### ASSEMBLY OF PANSY SQUARES

With black, sew 4 Corner Pansy Squares in place to insets of Center Pansy Square Extensions as shown in photo, sewing underneath both lps of sts on edge of Motifs.

#### FILIGREES

Make 4.

**Row 1:** With white, ch 29, sl st in 2nd ch from hook and in each of next 6 chs, **picot** *(see Special Stitches)*, sl st in each of next 7 chs, picot 3 times, sl st in each of next 7 chs, picot, sl st in each of last 7 chs, join with sl st in beg sl st of row. Fasten off.

Arrange each Filigree on Large Square in a diamond shape as shown in photo, with bottom end behind scalloped edges of Center Pansy Square.

Pin in place to hold and sew to square, making sure to keep all Filigrees uniform in arrangement.

#### LARGE SQUARE EDGING

**Rnd 1:** Join black with sl st in any corner ch-2 sp, ch 3, (dc, ch 2, 2 dc) in same ch sp, * evenly sp 55 dc across to next corner**, (2 dc, ch 2, 2 dc) in corner ch-2 sp, rep from * 3 times, ending last rep at **, join with sl st in 3rd ch of beg ch-3. Fasten off.

**Rnd 2:** Join white with sl st in any corner ch-2 sp, ch 3, (dc, ch 2, 2 dc) in same ch sp, *dc in each dc across to next corner**, (2 dc, ch 2, 2 dc) in corner ch-2 sp, rep from * 3 times, ending last rep at **, join with sl st in 3rd ch of beg ch-3. Fasten off.

**Rnd 3:** Join green in any corner ch-2 sp, **beg corner shell** *(see Special Stitches)* in same ch sp, *ch 1, sk next st, sl st in next st, [ch 1, sk next 2 sts, **shell** *(see Special Stitches)* in next st, ch 1, sk next 2 sts, sl st in next st] 10 times, ch 1, sk last st before corner sp**, **corner shell** *(see Special Stitches)* in corner sp, rep from * 3 times, ending last rep at **, join with sl st in 3rd ch of beg ch-3. Fasten off.

#### 2ND LARGE SQUARE

Rep instructions for First Large Square through rnd 2 of Edging.

**Rnd 3 (joining rnd):** Work same as rnd 3 of Edging for First Large Square to first corner of joining side; on joining side, work the ch-3 of each corner shell as (ch 1, sl st in ch-3 sp of corresponding corner shell on First Large Square, ch 1), and the ch-1 of each shell as sl st in ch-1 sp of corresponding shell on First Large Square. Complete rem of rnd same as for First Large Square.

Make and join 10 more Large Squares same as 2nd Large Square in a pattern of 3 squares across and 4 down. ■

# Gardenias in Bloom

DESIGN BY JOSIE RABIER

With delicate stitch patterns that emulate the look of fine crochet lace, this light, airy doily accented with dainty gardenias adds a touch of old-world charm to even the most contemporary setting.

INTERMEDIATE

**FINISHED SIZE**
26 inches in diameter

**MATERIALS**
Size 10 crochet cotton:
650 yds white
Size 7/1.65mm steel crochet hook or size needed to obtain gauge
Starch

**GAUGE**
Rnds 1–3 = 2 inches in diameter,
2 shell rnds = 1 inch

**SPECIAL STITCHES**
**Shell:** (3 dc, ch 3, 3 dc) in indicated st or ch sp.

**Beginning shell (beg shell):** Sl st in indicated st or ch sp, ch 3 *(counts as first dc)*, (2 dc, ch 3, 3 dc) in same st or ch sp.

## INSTRUCTIONS

**DOILY**
**Rnd 1 (RS):** Ch 5, sl st in first ch to form ring, ch 3 *(counts as first dc)*, 23 dc in ring, join with sl st in 3rd ch of beg ch-3. *(24 dc)*

**Rnd 2:** Ch 3 *(counts as first dc)*, dc in next dc, ch 2, [dc in each of next 2 dc, ch 2] around, join with sl st in 3rd ch of beg ch-3.

**Rnd 3:** Ch 3, dc in next dc, ch 3, [dc in each of next 2 dc, ch 3] around, join with sl st in 3rd ch of beg ch-3.

**Rnd 4:** Ch 3, dc in same st as beg ch-3, 2 dc in next dc, *sk next ch-3 sp, 2 dc in each of next 2 dc, ch 5, sk next ch-3 sp**, 2 dc in each of next 2 dc, rep from * around, ending last rep at **, join with sl st in 3rd ch of beg ch-3. *(48 dc, 6 ch-5 sps)*

**Rnd 5:** Ch 3, dc in each of next 2 dc, *sk next 2 dc, dc in each of next 3 dc, ch 5, sl st in next ch-5 sp, ch 5**, dc in each of next 3 dc, rep from * around, ending last rep at **, join with sl st in 3rd ch of beg ch-3. *(36 dc, 12 ch-5 sps)*

**Rnd 6:** Ch 3, dc in next dc, *sk next 2 dc, dc in each of next 2 dc, [ch 5, sl st in next ch-5 sp] twice, ch 5**, dc in each of next 2 dc, rep from * around, ending last rep at **, join with sl st in 3rd ch of beg ch-3. *(24 dc, 18 ch-5 sps)*

**Rnd 7:** Ch 3, *sk next 2 dc, dc in next dc, [ch 5, sl st in next ch-5 sp] 3 times, ch 5**, dc in next dc, rep from * around, ending last rep at **, join with sl st in 3rd ch of beg ch-3, sl st in 3rd ch of next ch-5 sp. *(12 dc, 24 ch-5 sps)*

**Rnd 8:** Ch 8 *(counts as first dc, ch-5)*, dc in same sp as beg ch-8, *[(dc, ch 5, dc) in 3rd ch of next ch-5 sp] 3 times, ch 3, sk next 2 dc**, (dc, ch 5, dc) in 3rd ch of next ch-5 sp, rep from * around, ending last rep at **, join with sl st in 3rd ch of beg ch-8, sl st in next ch-5 sp.

**Rnd 9:** Ch 3, 4 dc in same ch sp, *5 dc in each of next 3 ch-5 sps, 5 dc in next ch-3 sp**, 5 dc in next ch-5 sp, rep from * around, ending last rep at **, join with sl st in 3rd ch of beg ch-3. *(150 dc)*

**Rnd 10:** Ch 3, dc in next dc, *(dc, ch 5, dc) in next dc**, dc in each of next 4 dc, rep from * around, ending last rep at **, dc in each of last 2 dc,

join with sl st in 3rd ch of beg ch-3, sl st in next ch-5 sp.

**Rnd 11: Beg shell** *(see Special Stitches)* in same ch-5 sp, **shell** *(see Special Stitches)* in each ch-5 sp around, join with sl st in 3rd ch of beg ch-3, sl st in ch-3 sp. *(30 shells)*

**Rnd 12:** Beg shell in same ch-3 sp, shell in each ch-3 sp around, join with sl st in 3rd ch of beg ch-3. Fasten off.

**FIRST FLOWER**

**Rnd 1:** Ch 4, 15 dc in 4th ch from hook *(first 3 chs count as first dc)*, join with sl st in 4th ch of beg ch-4. *(16 dc)*

**Rnd 2:** [Ch 3, 6 dc in same dc as beg ch-3, sk next dc, sl st in next dc] 8 times. *(8 petals)*

**Rnd 3:** Holding petals forward and working in sk dc of previous rnd, sl st in next sk dc, [ch 5, sl st in next sk dc of previous rnd] around, ending with sl st in same dc as beg ch-5, sl st in next ch-5 sp. *(8 ch-5 sps)*

**Rnd 4:** Beg shell in same ch-5 sp, 3 dc in next ch-5 sp, ch 1, sl st in ch-3 sp of any shell on rnd 12 of Doily, ch 1, 3 dc in same ch-5 sp of Flower, 3 dc in next ch-5 sp, ch 1, sl st in next ch-3 sp of shell on rnd 12 of Doily, ch 1, 3 dc in same ch-5 sp of Flower, shell in each of next 5 rem ch-5 lps of Flower, join with sl st in 3rd ch of beg ch-3. Fasten off.

**2ND FLOWER**

**Rnds 1–3:** Rep rnds 1–3 of First Flower.

**Rnd 4:** Working counterclockwise, beg shell in same ch-5 sp, 3 dc in next ch-5 sp, ch 1, sk 4 shells on previous Flower, sl st in next ch-3 sp of next shell, ch 1, 3 dc in same ch-5 sp on working Flower, 3 dc in next ch-5 sp, ch 1, sl st in next ch-3 sp of previous Flower, ch 1, 3 dc in same ch-5 sp on working flower *(working flower joined to 2 shells of previous flower)*, [3 dc in next ch-5 sp, ch 1, sl st in next unworked ch-3 sp on rnd 12 of Doily, ch 1, 3 dc in same ch-5 sp] twice, shell in each of rem 4 ch-5 sps on working Flower, join with sl st in 3rd ch of beg ch-3. Fasten off.

**3RD–14TH FLOWERS**

**Rnds 1–3:** Rep rnds 1–3 of First Flower.

**Rnd 4:** Work the same as for 2nd Flower with the exception of sk 2 shells of previous Flower instead of 4 shells.

**15TH FLOWER**

**Rnds 1–3:** Rep rnds 1–3 of First Flower.

**Rnd 4:** Rep the same as for previous Flowers, except after joining 2 shells to rnd 12 of Doily, join next 2 shells to next 2 shells of First Flower, shell in next 2 shells of working Flower, join with sl st in 3rd ch of beg ch-3. **Do not fasten off.**

**DOILY CONTINUED**

**Rnd 13:** Sl st in ch-3 sp of first shell, beg shell in same ch sp, shell in next ch-3 sp of shell, *ch 5, sk next 3 dc, tr in next dc, sk next 4 dc, tr in next dc, ch 5**, [shell in ch-3 sp of next shell] twice, rep from * around, ending last rep at **, join with sl st in 3rd ch of beg ch-3.

**Rnd 14:** Sl st in ch-3 sp, beg shell in same ch sp, *ch 7, shell in next shell, ch 3, sk next 2 dc, tr in next dc, sk ch-5 sps, tr in next dc, ch 3**, shell in next shell, rep from * around, ending last rep at **, join with sl st in 3rd ch of beg ch-3.

**Rnd 15:** Sl st in ch-3 sp, beg shell in same ch sp, *16 tr in next ch-7 sp, shell in next shell, ch 3, sk next ch-3 sp, sl st in each of next 2 tr, ch 3**, shell in next shell, rep from * around, ending last rep at **, join with sl st in 3rd ch of beg ch-3. *(15 pineapple bases)*

**Rnd 16:** Sl st in ch-3 sp, beg shell in shell, *dc in each of next 2 tr, [ch 1, dc in each of next 2 tr] 7 times, shell in next shell, sk ch-3 sps**, shell in next shell, rep from * around, ending last rep at **, join with sl st in 3rd ch of beg ch-3.

**Rnd 17:** Sl st in ch-3 sp, beg shell in shell, *ch 3, sl st in next ch-1 sp, [ch 5, sl st in next ch-1 sp] 6 times, ch 3**, [shell in next shell] twice, rep from * around, ending last rep at **, shell in next shell, join with sl st in 3rd ch of beg ch-3.

**Rnd 18:** Sl st in ch-3 sp, beg shell in shell, *ch 3, sl st in next ch-5 sp, [ch 5, sl st in next ch-5 sp] 5 times, ch 3**, [shell in next shell] twice, rep from * around, ending last rep at **, shell in next shell, join with sl st in 3rd ch of beg ch-3.

**Rnd 19:** Sl st in ch-3 sp, beg shell in shell, *ch 3, sl st in next ch-5 sp, [ch 5, sl st in next ch-5 sp] 4 times, ch 3, shell in next shell, ch 5**, shell in next shell, rep from * around, ending last rep at **, join with sl st in 3rd ch of beg ch-3.

**Rnd 20:** Sl st in ch-3 sp, beg shell in shell, *ch 3, sl st in next ch-5 sp, [ch 5, sl st in next ch-5 sp] 3 times, ch 3, shell in next shell, ch 5, sl st in next ch-5 sp, ch 5**, shell in next shell, rep from * around, ending last rep at **, join with sl st in 3rd ch of beg ch-3.

**Rnd 21:** Sl st in ch-3 sp, beg shell in shell, *ch 3, sl st in next ch-5 sp, [ch 5, sl st in next ch-5 sp] twice, ch 3, shell in next shell, [ch 5, sl st in next ch-5 sp] twice, ch 5**, shell in next shell, rep from * around, ending last rep at **, join with sl st in 3rd ch of beg ch-3.

**Rnd 22:** Sl st in ch-3 sp, beg shell in shell, *ch 3, sl st in next ch-5 sp, ch 5, sl st in next ch-5 sp, ch 3, shell in next shell, ch 5, sl st in next ch-5 sp, 8 tr in next ch-5 sp, sl st in next ch-5 sp, ch 5**, shell in next shell, rep from * around, ending last rep at **, join with sl st in 3rd ch of beg ch-3.

**Rnd 23:** Sl st in ch-3 sp, beg shell in shell, *ch 3, sl st in rem ch-5 sp, ch 3, shell in next shell, ch 5, sl st in next ch-5 sp, 2 tr in each of next 2 tr, [ch 3, 2 tr in each of next 2 tr] 3 times, sl st in next ch-5 sp, ch 5**, shell in next shell, rep from * around, ending last rep at **, join with sl st in 3rd ch of beg ch-3.

**Rnd 24:** Sl st in ch-3 sp, beg shell in shell, *sk next 2 ch-3 sps, shell in next shell, sk next ch-5 sp, holding back last lp of each st on hook, 2 dtr in next tr *(3 lps on hook)*, dtr in each of next 2 tr *(5 lps on hook)*, 2 dtr in next tr *(7 lps on hook)*, yo, pull through all lps on hook, ch 1 to lock *(6-dtr cl)*, [ch 7, sl st in next ch-3 sp, ch 7, 6-dtr cl in next 4 tr] 3 times, sk next ch-5 sp**, shell in next shell, rep from * around, ending last rep at **, join with sl st in 3rd ch of beg ch-3. Fasten off.

Starch lightly and press. ■

# Beaded Roses

DESIGN BY CAROL ALEXANDER

Lush, pink roses cascading in a waterfall of creamy white crochet lace give vintage style and classic elegance to this one-of-a-kind throw that's the perfect accent for a soft, feminine room.

**FINISHED SIZE**
54 x 72 inches

**MATERIALS**
Medium (worsted) weight yarn:
40 oz/2,000 yds/1,134g soft white
16 oz/800 yds/454g each pink and green
Size H/8/5mm crochet hook or size needed to obtain gauge
Sewing needle
Sewing thread
86 white pearl 6mm beads

**GAUGE**
Rose Motif = 6½ inches across
Fill-in Motif = 4 inches across

**PATTERN NOTE**
Using instructions, work First Motif and Next Motif according to assembly diagram.

**SPECIAL STITCHES**

**Single crochet picot (sc picot):** Ch 1, sc in top of last st made.

**Cluster (cl):** Ch 4, holding last lps of each st on hook, 3 dtr in same st as last st made, yo, pull through all lps on hook.

**V-stitch (V-st):** (Dc, ch 1, dc) in next picot.

**Joining V-stitch (joining V-st):** Ch 7, sl st in 4th ch from hook *(picot made)*, ch 6, sl st in 4th ch from hook *(picot made)*, ch 2, dc in picot at top of next petal on rnd 7 of this Motif, sl st in ch sp of corresponding V-st on adjacent Motif, dc in same picot as last dc made on this Motif, [ch 6, sl st in 3rd ch from hook] twice, ch 3, dc in next ch-5 sp on rnd 7, sl st in back 2 strands at top of 2nd tr on next leaf of rnd 6.

## INSTRUCTIONS

**FIRST MOTIF**

**Rnd 1:** With pink, ch 5, sl st in first ch to form ring, ch 5 *(counts as dc and ch-2 sp)*, [dc in ring, ch 2] 5 times, join with sl st in 3rd ch of beg ch-5. *(6 dc, 6 ch sps)*

**Rnd 2:** For **bottom petals,** (sl st, ch 2, 2 dc, **sc picot**–*see Special Stitches*, dc, ch 2, sl st) in each ch sp around, join with sl st in **front lp** *(see Stitch Guide)* of beg sl st. *(6 petals)*

**Rnd 3:** For **top petals**, working in front of last petals made, (sl st, ch 2, 2 dc, ch 2, sl st) around **front** of **post** *(see Stitch Guide)* of each dc on rnd 1 around, join with sl st in beg sl st.

**Rnd 4:** For **center**, working in front of last petals made, ch 3, [sl st around post at bottom of next worked dc on rnd 1, ch 3] around, join with sl st in joining sl st of last rnd. Fasten off.

**Rnd 5:** Working behind bottom petals, join green with sl st in **back lp** *(see Stitch Guide)* of first sl st on any petal, ch 4, [sl st in back lp of first sl st on next petal, ch 4] around, join with sl st in first ch of beg ch-4. *(6 ch sps)*

**Rnd 6:** For **leaves,** (sl st, ch 1, dc, tr) in first ch sp, tr in back 2 strands of 2nd dc on corresponding bottom petal, ch 3, sl st in top of last st made *(picot made)*, (tr, dc, ch 1, sl st) in same ch sp, *(sl st, ch 1, dc) in next ch sp, tr in back 2 strands of 2nd dc on corresponding bottom petal, ch 3, sl st in top of last st made *(picot)*, (tr, dc, ch 1, sl st) in same ch sp, rep from * around, join with sl st in beg sl st. Fasten off.

**Rnd 7:** For **petals**, working behind leaves, join white with sl st in back lp of any sl st on rnd 5, **cl** *(see Special Stitches)*, ch 3, sl st in top of last st made *(picot)*, ch 7, sl st in same st as last cl, *ch 5, *(sl st, cl, ch 3, sl st in top of last st made, ch 7, sl st) in back lp of next sl st on rnd 5, rep from * around, ch 2, join with dc in first ch at base of beg ch-4. *(6 petals)*

**Rnd 8:** Ch 3, sl st in back 2 strands at top of 2nd tr on leaf of rnd 6, *ch 7, sl st in 4th ch from hook *(picot)*, ch 6, sl st in 3rd ch from hook *(picot)*, ch 2, **V-st** *(see Special Stitches)* in picot

at top of next petal on rnd 7, [ch 6, sl st in 3rd ch from hook] twice, ch 3**, dc in next ch-5 sp on rnd 7, sl st in back 2 strands at top of 2nd tr on next leaf of rnd 6, rep from * around, ending last rep at **, join with sl st in 3rd ch of beg ch-3. Fasten off.

**NEXT MOTIF**

**Rnds 1–7:** Rep rnds 1–7 of First Motif.

**Rnd 8:** Ch 3, sl st in back 2 strands at top of 2nd tr on leaf of rnd 6, work **joining V-st** *(see Special Stitches)* number of times needed to join Motif or Motifs tog *(see Assembly Diagram)*; to complete the rnd, *ch 7, sl st in 4th ch from hook *(picot)*, ch 6, sl st in 3rd ch from hook *(picot)*, ch 2, V-st in picot at top of next petal on rnd 7, [ch 6, sl st in 3rd ch from hook] twice, ch 3**, dc in next ch-5 sp on rnd 7, sl st in back 2 strands at top of 2nd tr on next leaf of rnd 6, rep from * around, ending last rep at **, join with sl st in 3rd ch of beg ch-3. Fasten off.

Sew 1 bead to center of each Motif.

**FILL-IN MOTIF**

**Rnd 1:** With white, ch 4, sl st in first ch to form ring, ch 4 *(counts as hdc and ch-2 sp)*, [hdc in ring, ch 2] 5 times, join with sl st in 2nd ch of beg ch-4. *(6 hdc, 6 ch sps)*

**Rnd 2:** Ch 2, sl st in first corresponding picot of any 2-picot group on Motif, hdc in next ch sp, sl st in corresponding picot of same picot group on Motif, [hdc in next st, sl st in first corresponding picot of next 2-picot group on Motif, hdc in next ch sp on this Motif, sl st in 2nd picot of same group] 5 times, join with sl st in 2nd ch of beg ch-2. Fasten off.

Rep Fill-In Motif in sp between Motifs. ■

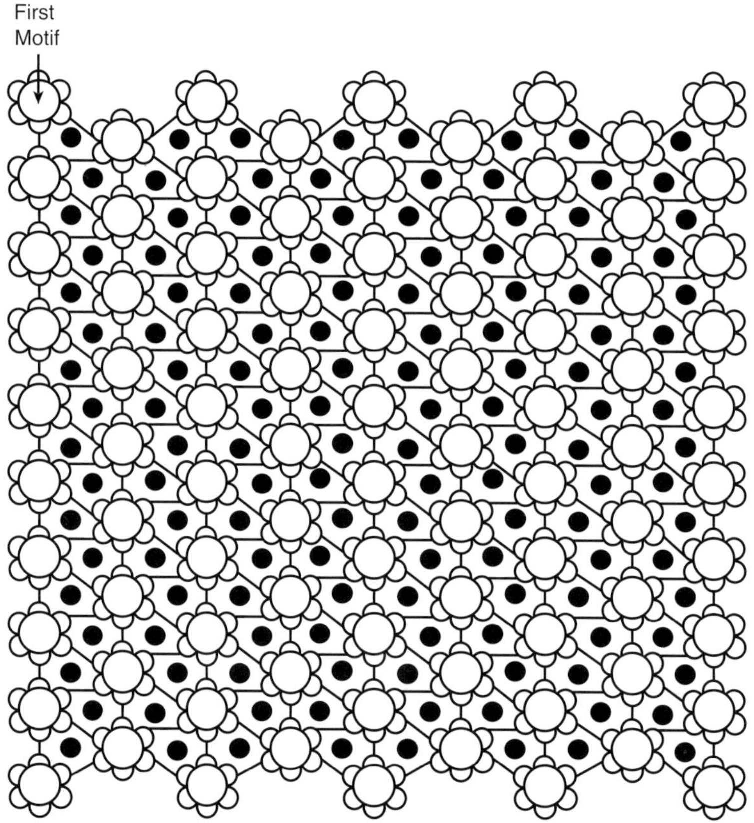


**Beaded Roses
Assembly Diagram**

# Lily Pond

DESIGN BY JOSIE RABIER

The perfect blend of soothing green colors, large flowers and generous leaves captured in this striking, oval-shaped doily bring to mind the quiet tranquility of a peaceful country pond.

RMEDIATE

**FINISHED SIZE**
14¾ x 22 inches

**MATERIALS**
Size 10 crochet cotton:
450 yds shaded greens
Size 7/1.65mm steel crochet hook or size needed to obtain gauge

**GAUGE**
7 dc = 1 inch; 7 dc rows = 2 inches

**PATTERN NOTE**
As Motifs are completed they are joined together in a strip of 3.

**SPECIAL STITCH**
**Cluster (cl):** Holding last lp of each st on hook, 5 tr in next ch sp, yo, pull through all lps on hook.

## INSTRUCTIONS

**FIRST MOTIF**
**Rnd 1 (RS):** Ch 8, sl st in first ch to form ring, ch 3 *(counts as first dc)*, 23 dc in ring, join. *(24 dc)*

**Rnd 2:** Ch 3, dc in next dc, ch 3, [dc in each of next 2 dc, ch 3] around, join with sl st in 3rd ch of beg ch-3.

**Rnd 3:** Sl st in ch-3 sp, ch 3, 4 dc in same ch-3 sp, [5 dc in next ch-3 sp] around, join with sl st in 3rd ch of beg ch-3.

**Rnd 4:** Ch 2 *(does not count as dc)*, **tr dec** *(see Stitch Guide)* in next 5 dc, *ch 7, tr dec in next 5 dc, ch 5, sl st in same dc as last tr of dec, sl st in next dc, ch 5, beg in same dc as last sl st, tr dec in next 5 dc, rep from * around, join with sl st in top of beg tr dec. Fasten off. *(12 tr dec, 6 ch-7 sps)*

**2ND MOTIF**
**Rnds 1–3:** Rep rnds 1–3 of First Motif.

**Rnd 4:** Ch 2, tr dec in next 5 dc, ch 3, sl st in 4th ch of ch-7 on previous Motif, ch 3, tr dec in next 5 dc, ch 5, sl st in same dc as last tr of dec, sl st in next dc, ch 5, beg in same dc as last sl st, tr dec in next 5 dc, ch 3, sl st in 4th ch of next ch-7 sp of previous Motif, ch 3, tr dec in next 5 dc, [ch 5, sl st in same dc as last tr of dec, sl st in next dc, ch 5, beg in same dc as last sl st, tr dec in next 5 dc, ch 7, tr dec in next 5 dc] 4 times, ch 5, sl st in same dc as last tr of dec, sl st in next dc. Fasten off.

**3RD MOTIF**
**Rnds 1–3:** Rep rnds 1–3 of First Motif.

**Rnd 4:** Rep rnd 4 of 2nd Motif, joining 3rd Motif to opposite end of First Motif leaving 1 ch-7 sp on each side of First Motif unworked.

**FILL-IN CLUSTERS**
*With RS facing, working over ch-3 sps of joining sps between Motifs, join with sl st in first ch-3 sp, ch 5, **cl** *(see Special Stitch)* in same ch-3 sp, ch 7, cl in next ch-3 sp, ch 5, sl st in same ch-3 sp. Fasten off.

Rep from * 3 times.

**DOILY**
**Rnd 1 (RS):** Join with sl st in unworked ch-7 sp of First Motif *(center Motif)*, ch 1, *9 sc in ch-7 sp, ch 5, [dc in 3rd ch of next ch-5 sp at side edge of dec on rnd 4 of Motif] twice, ch 5, rep from * around, join with sl st in beg sc. *(14 groups of 9 sc)*

**Rnd 2:** Ch 3, dc in same st, 2 dc in each of next 8 sc, sk next 2 chs, dc in 3rd ch of next ch-5 sp, ch 5, sk next 2 chs, dc in 3rd ch of next ch-5 sp, [2 dc in each of next 9 sc, sk next 2 chs, dc in 3rd ch of ch-5 sp, ch 5, sk next 2 chs, dc in 3rd ch of next ch-5 sp] around, join with sl st in 3rd ch of beg ch-3.

**Rnd 3:** Ch 3, dc in each of next 18 dc, sl st in next ch-5 sp, [dc in each of next 20 dc, sl st in next ch-5 sp] around, ending with dc in last dc, join with sl st in 3rd ch of beg ch-3.

**Rnd 4:** Ch 3, dc in each of next 17 dc, sk next 2 dc, [dc in each of next 18 dc, sk next 2 dc] around, join with sl st in 3rd ch of beg ch-3.

**Rnd 5:** Ch 3, sk next dc, dc in each of next 14 dc, sk next dc, dc in next dc, ch 5, [dc in next dc, sk next dc, dc in each of next 14 dc, sk next dc, dc in next dc, ch 5] around, join with sl st in 3rd ch of beg ch-3.

**Rnd 6:** Ch 3, sk next dc, dc in each of next 12 dc, sk next dc, dc in next dc, ch 5, sl st in next ch-5 sp, ch 5, [dc in next dc, sk next dc, dc in each of next 12 dc, sk next dc, dc in next dc, ch 5, sl st in next ch-5 sp, ch 5] around, join with sl st in 3rd ch of beg ch-3.

**Rnd 7:** Ch 3, sk next dc, dc in each of next 10 dc, sk next dc, dc in next dc, [ch 5, sl st in next ch-5 sp] twice, ch 5, *dc in next dc, sk next dc, dc in each of next 10 dc, sk next dc, dc in next dc, [ch 5, sl st in next ch-5 sp] twice, ch 5, rep from * around, join with sl st in 3rd ch of beg ch-3.

**Rnd 8:** Ch 3, sk next dc, dc in each of next 8 dc, sk next dc, dc in next dc, ch 3, [(dc, ch 3, dc) in 3rd ch of next ch-5 sp, ch 3] 3 times, *dc in next dc, sk next dc, dc in each of next 8 dc, sk next dc, dc in next dc, ch 3, [(dc, ch 3, dc) in 3rd ch of ch-5 sp, ch 3] 3 times, rep from * around, join with sl st in 3rd ch of beg ch-3.

**Rnd 9:** Ch 3, sk next dc, dc in each of next 6 dc, sk next dc, dc in next dc, ch 3, sk next ch-3 sp, 4 dc in each of next 5 ch-3 sps, ch 3, sk next ch-3 sp, *dc in next dc, sk next dc, dc in each of next 6 dc, sk next dc, dc in next dc, ch 3, sk next ch-3 sp, 4 dc in each of next 5 ch-3 sps, ch 3, sk next ch-3 sp, rep from * around, join with sl st in 3rd ch of beg ch-3.

**Rnd 10:** Ch 3, sk next dc, dc in each of next 4 dc, sk next dc, dc in next dc, ch 3, dc in each of next 20 dc, ch 3, *dc in next dc, sk next dc, dc in each of next 4 dc, sk next dc, dc in next dc, ch 3, dc in each of next 20 dc, ch 3, rep from * around, join with sl st in 3rd ch of beg ch-3.

**Rnd 11:** Ch 3, sk next dc, dc in each of next 2 dc, sk next dc, dc in next dc, ch 3, dc in each of next 20 dc, ch 3, *dc in next dc, sk next dc, dc in each of next 2 dc, sk next dc, dc in next dc, ch 3, dc in each of next 20 dc, ch 3, rep from * around, join with sl st in 3rd ch of beg ch-3.

**Rnd 12:** Ch 3, sk next 2 dc, dc in next dc, ch 3, dc in each of next 4 dc, sk next 2 dc, dc in each of next 4 dc, ch 5, dc in each of next 4 dc, sk next 2 dc, dc in each of next 4 dc, ch 3, [dc in next dc, sk next 2 dc, dc in next dc, ch 3, dc in each of next 4 dc, sk next 2 dc, dc in each of next 4 dc, ch 5, dc in each of next 4 dc, sk next 2 dc, dc in each of next 4 dc, ch 3] around, join with sl st in 3rd ch of beg ch-3.

**Rnd 13:** Sl st across next dc, ch-3 sp and in first dc of 4-dc group, ch 3, dc in each of next 2 dc, sk next 2 dc, dc in each of next 3 dc, ch 5, sl st in ch-5 sp, ch 5, dc in each of next 3 dc, sk next 2 dc, dc in each of next 3 dc, ch 5, sk next ch-3 sp, sl st in sp between next 2 dc, ch 5, [dc in each of next 3 dc, sk next 2 dc, dc in each of next 3 dc, ch 5, sl st in next ch-5 sp, ch 5, dc in each of next 3 dc, sk next 2 dc, dc in each of next 3 dc, ch 5, sk next ch-3 sp, sl st in sp between next 2 dc, ch 5] around, join with sl st in 3rd ch of beg ch-3.

**Rnd 14:** Ch 3, dc in next dc, sk next 2 dc, dc in each of next 2 dc, [ch 5, sl st in next ch-5 sp] twice, ch 5, dc in each of next 2 dc, sk next 2 dc, dc in each of next 2 dc, [ch 5, sl st in next ch-5 sp] twice, ch 5, *dc in each of next 2 dc, sk next 2 dc, dc in each of next 2 dc, [ch 5, sl st in next ch-5 sp] twice, ch 5, dc in each of next 2 dc, sk next 2 dc, dc in each of next 2 dc, [ch 5, sl st in next ch-5 sp] twice, ch 5, rep from * around, join with sl st in 3rd ch of beg ch-3.

**Rnd 15:** Ch 3, sk next 2 dc, dc in next dc, ch 5, sl st in next ch-5 sp, 10 dc in next ch-5 sp, sl st in next ch-5 sp, ch 5, dc in next dc, sk next 2 dc, dc in next dc, ch 5, sl st in next ch-5 sp, 10 dc in next ch-5 sp, sl st in next ch-5 sp, ch 5, [dc in next dc, sk next 2 dc, dc in next dc, ch 5, sl st in next ch-5 sp, 10 dc in next ch-5 sp, sl st in next ch-5 sp, ch 5, dc in next dc, sk next 2 dc, dc in next dc, ch 5, sl st in next ch-5 sp, 10 dc in next ch-5 sp, ch 5] around, join with sl st in 3rd ch of beg ch-3.

**Rnd 16:** Sl st in 3rd ch of next ch-5 sp, ch 2, tr dec in next 5 dc, ch 5, sl st in same dc as last tr of dec, sl st in next dc, ch 5, beg in same dc as ch-5, tr dec in next 5 dc, sl st in next ch-5 sp, ch 5, sl st in next ch-5 sp, [tr dec in next 5 dc, ch 5, sl st in same dc as last tr of dec, sl st in next dc, ch 5, beg in same dc as ch-5, tr dec in next 5 dc, sl st in next ch-5 sp, ch 5, sl st in next ch-5 sp] around, join with sl st in beg dec. Fasten off.

Starch and press Doily as desired. ■

# Gingham Garden

DESIGN BY CAROL ALEXANDER

Strips of plush pink flowers alternating with pretty gingham panels come together in perfect harmony in this enchanting floral throw that's a perfect accent for your spring or summer decor.

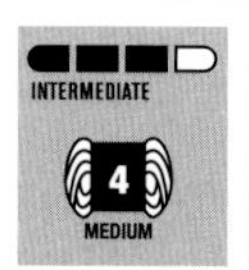


**FINISHED SIZE**
51 x 69 inches

**MATERIALS**
Medium (worsted) weight yarn:
32 oz/1,600 yds/907g white
21 oz/1,050 yds/595g light rose
14 oz/700 yds/397g rose
7 oz/350 yds/198g sage green
Size H/8/5mm crochet hook or size needed to obtain gauge
Tapestry needle

**GAUGE**
Panel A Motif = 5½ inches
Panel B = 4 sc = 1 inch; 4 sc rows = 1 inch; panel = 3½ inches wide

**PATTERN NOTE**
**Change color** *(see Stitch Guide)* in last stitch made. Carry dropped color along top of stitches and work over it with new color.

## INSTRUCTIONS

**MOTIF**
Make 60.

**Rnd 1:** With rose, ch 4, sl st in first ch to form ring, ch 3 *(counts as first dc)*, 11 dc in ring, join with sl st in 3rd ch of beg ch-3. Fasten off. *(12 dc)*

**Rnd 2:** Join white with sl st in first st, ch 3, dc in same st, 2 dc in each dc around, join with sl st in 3rd ch of beg ch-3. *(24 dc)*

**Rnd 3:** Ch 2 *(counts as first hdc)*, hdc in each of next 4 dc, 2 hdc in next dc, [hdc in each of next 5 dc, 2 hdc in next dc] 3 times, join with sl st in 2nd ch of beg ch-2. Fasten off. *(28 hdc)*

**FLOWER PETALS**
With RS facing, join light rose with sl st around **front** of **post** *(see Stitch Guide)* of any dc on rnd 1 of Motif, *ch 1, (sc, ch 1, hdc, ch 1) around post of same dc, sl st in lp on front of post of dc on rnd 2 directly behind to tack petal, ch 1, sc around post of last hdc made, hdc around post of same dc on rnd 1, sl st around post of next dc on rnd 1, rep from * 11 times, tacking petals to every other dc of rnd 2, join with sl st in beg sc. Fasten off.

**MOTIF CONTINUED**
**Rnd 4:** Join sage green with sl st in any hdc of rnd 3, ch 3, (3 dc, ch 2, 4 dc) in same sc, *ch 1, sk next 2 sts, sc in next st, ch 2, sc in next st, ch 1, sk next 2 sts**, (4 dc, ch 2, 4 dc) in next st, rep from * around, ending last rep at **, join with sl st in 3rd ch of beg ch-3. Fasten off.

**Rnd 5:** Join white with sl st in any corner ch-2 sp, ch 1, *3 sc in corner ch-2 sp, ch 5, (dc, ch 3, dc) in next ch-2 sp, ch 5, rep from * around, join

with sl st in beg sc.

**Rnd 6:** Ch 1, *sc in each of next 3 sc, (hdc, 3 dc) in next ch-5 sp, (3 tr, ch 2, 3 tr) in next ch-3 sp *(corner group)*, (3 dc, hdc) in next ch-5 sp, rep from * around, join with sl st in beg sc. Fasten off.

**PANEL A**
Make 5.

With tapestry needle and matching yarn, whipstitch Motifs with RS tog to form strip 12 Motifs long.

**EDGING**
With RS facing, join white with sl st in corner ch-2 sp at right end of long edge of strip, ch 1, 2 sc in same corner sp, [sc in each of next 17 sts across to next Motif joining, 2 sc in each of 2 corner sps at joining] 11 times, sc in each of next 17 sts across to last corner sp, 2 sc in last corner sp. Fasten off. *(252 sc)*

Rep on opposite long edge of strip.

**OUTSIDE PANEL B**
Make 2.

**Row 1 (RS):** With white, ch 252, with rose, ch 1 more, dropping white, beg in 2nd ch from hook [sc in each of next 4 chs, **change colors** *(see Pattern Note)* to light rose, sc in each of next 4 chs, change to rose] 31 times, sc in each of last 4 chs, turn. *(252 sc)*

**Rows 2–4:** Ch 1, sc in each sc across, following established color sequence, turn. At end of row 4, change to light rose on last sc. Fasten off rose.

**Row 5:** Ch 1, [sc in each of next 4 sc, change to white, sc in each of next 4 sc, change to light rose] 31 times, sc in each of last 4 sc, turn.

**Rows 6–8:** Ch 1, sc in each sc across, following established color sequence, turn. At end of row 8, change to rose on last sc. Fasten off white.

**Rows 9–12:** Ch 1, sc in each sc across, following color sequence established in rows 1–4. At end of row 12, fasten off.

**INSIDE PANEL B**
Make 4.

**Rows 1–12:** Rep rows 1–12 of Outside Panel B.

**Row 13:** With WS facing, join white with sl st in first st at right end of row 12, **turn,** sl st in each sc across. Fasten off.

**ASSEMBLY**
With RS tog, whipstitch Panels A and Inside Panels B tog alternately, beg with Panel A. Whipstitch foundation ch of Outside Panels B on each outside edge of Panels A.

**BORDER**
**Rnd 1:** With RS facing, join white with sl st in any corner, ch 3 *(counts as first dc)*, (dc, ch 2, 2 dc) in corner, evenly sp dc around, working (2 dc, ch 2, 2 dc) at each corner, join with sl st in 3rd ch of beg ch-3.

**Rnd 2:** Sl st in next dc and next ch-2 sp, ch 3, (dc, ch 2, 2 dc) in same ch sp, *dc in each dc across to next corner ch-2 sp**, (2 dc, ch 2, 2 dc) in corner sp, rep from * around, ending last rep at **, join with sl st in 3rd ch of beg ch-3. Fasten off.

***Note:*** *On following rnd, adjust spacing of sts as needed when working between ** to accommodate st sequence, keeping number of scallops on opposite sides equal.*

**Rnd 3:** Join sage green with sl st in any corner ch-2 sp, ch 1, *(sc, 3 dc, sc) in corner ch-2 sp, sk next st, **(sc, dc) in next st, (2 dc, sc) in next st, sk next 2 sts, rep from ** across, ending 3 sts from next corner ch-2 sp, (sc, dc) in next st, (2 dc, sc) in next st, sk last st before corner sp, rep from * 3 times, join with sl st in beg sc. Fasten off. ■

# Calla Lilly

DESIGN BY ROSANNE KROPP

As graceful and lovely as its natural counterpart, the delicate, cup-shaped bloom of the calla lily is charmingly replicated in the lavish ruffles of this breath-taking, picture-perfect doily.

INTERMEDIATE

**FINISHED SIZE**
15 inches in diameter

**MATERIALS**
Size 10 crochet cotton:
350 yds cream
Size 7/1.65mm steel crochet hook or size needed to obtain gauge
Fabric stiffener

**GAUGE**
9 tr = 1 inch; 2 tr rnds = 1 inch

**SPECIAL STITCHES**
**Beginning cluster (beg cl):** Ch 2 *(does not count as dc)*, holding back last lp of each st on hook, work number of dc as indicated in place, yo, pull through all lps on hook.

**Cluster (cl):** Holding back last lp of each st on hook, work number of dc as indicated, yo, pull through all lps on hook.

**INSTRUCTIONS**

**DOILY**
**Rnd 1 (RS):** Ch 10, sl st in first ch to form ring, ch 3 *(counts as first dc)*, 23 dc in ring, join with sl st in 3rd ch of beg ch-3. *(24 dc)*

**Rnd 2:** Ch 2, **dc dec** *(see Stitch Guide)* in next 2 dc, ch 4, [dc dec in last st worked and in next 2 dc, ch 4] around, join with sl st in top of beg cl. *(12 dc dec, 12 ch-4 sps)*

**Rnd 3:** Sl st in ch-4 sp, **beg 2-dc cl** *(see Special Stitches)* in same ch sp, ch 6, [**3-dc cl** *(see Special Stitches)* in next ch-4 sp, ch 6] around, join with sl st in top of beg cl. *(12 cls, 12 ch-6 sps)*

**Rnd 4:** [7 sc in next ch-6 sp, sl st in top of next cl] around. *(84 sc, 12 sl sts)*

**Rnd 5:** [Ch 8, sk next 7 sc, sl st in **back lp** *(see Stitch Guide)* only of next sl st] around.

**Rnd 6:** Sl st in next ch, *ch 2, [dc in next ch, ch 1] 5 times, dc in next ch, ch 2, sl st in next ch, working over top of next sl st, sl st in back lp only of sl st of rnd 4, sl st in first ch on next ch-8 sp, rep from * around, ending with sl st between last and first scallops. *(12 scallops)*

**Rnd 7:** Holding scallops forward, [ch 9, sk next scallop, sl st in back lp only of sl st between scallops] around. *(12 ch-9 sps)*

**Rnd 8:** Sl st in next ch, *ch 2, [dc in next ch, ch 1] 6 times, dc in next ch, ch 2, sl st in next ch, working over top of next sl st, sl st in back lp only of sl st on rnd before last, sl st in first ch of next ch-9 sp, rep from * around, ending with sl st in back lp only of sl st between last and first scallops.

**Rnds 9 & 10:** Rep rnds 7 and 8.

**Rnd 11:** Sl st in next sl st, sl st in each of next 2 chs, sl st in next dc, sl st in next ch, sl st in next dc, ch 1, sc in same st, ch 7, *sk next 3 dc, sc in next dc, ch 7, sc in 2nd dc worked on next scallop, ch 7, rep from * around, join with sl st in beg sc. *(24 ch-7 sps)*

**Rnd 12:** Sl st in each of next 2 chs, sl st in next ch sp, *ch 1, (tr, ch 1) 7 times in next ch sp, sl st in next ch sp, rep from * around, join with sl st in beg st.

**Rnd 13:** [Sl st in next ch, sl st in next

tr] twice, ch 1, sc in same st, *ch 8, sk next 3 tr, sc in next tr, ch 8**, sc in 2nd tr worked on next scallop, rep from * around, ending last rep at **, join with sl st in beg sc. *(24 ch-8 sps)*

**Rnd 14:** Ch 1, 9 sc in each ch-8 sp around, join with sl st in beg sc. *(216 sc)*

**Rnd 15:** Sl st in next sc *(2nd sc of 9-sc group)*, ch 1, sc in same st, *[ch 5, sc in next sc] 6 times, sk last sc of sc group, ch 4, sk next 4 sc, sc in next sc, ch 4, sk next 5 sc**, sc in 2nd sc of next sc group, rep from * around, ending last rep at **, join with sl st in beg sc.

**Rnd 16:** Sl st in next ch-5 sp, ch 1, sc in same ch sp, *[ch 5, sc in next ch-5 sp] 5 times, ch 4, sk next ch-4 sp, sc in next sc, ch 4, sk next ch-4 sp**, sc in next ch-5 sp, rep from * around, ending last rep at **, join with sl st in beg sc.

**Rnd 17:** Sl st in next ch-5 sp, ch 1, sc in same ch sp, *[ch 5, sc in next ch-5 sp] 4 times, ch 3, sk next ch-4 sp, 3 tr in next sc, ch 3, sk next ch-4 sp**, sc in next ch-5 sp, rep from * around, ending last rep at **, join with sl st in beg sc.

**Rnd 18:** Sl st in next ch-5 sp, ch 1, sc in same ch sp, *[ch 5, sc in next ch-5 sp] 3 times, ch 2, 2 tr in next tr, (tr, ch 1, tr) in next tr, 2 tr in next tr, ch 2, sk next ch-3 sp**, sc in next ch-5 sp, rep from * around, ending last rep at **, join with sl st in beg sc.

**Rnd 19:** Sl st in next ch-5 sp, ch 1, sc in same ch sp, *[ch 5, sc in next ch-5 sp] twice, ch 1, 2 tr in next tr, tr in next tr, 2 tr in next tr, ch 2, sk next ch-1 sp, 2 tr in next tr, tr in next tr, 2 tr in next tr, ch 1**, sc in next ch-5 sp, rep from * around, ending last rep at **, join with sl st in beg sc.

**Rnd 20:** Sl st in next ch-5 sp, ch 1, sc in same ch sp, *ch 5, sc in next ch-5 sp, 2 tr in next tr, tr in each of next 3 tr, 2 tr in next tr, ch 5, sk next ch-2 sp, 2 tr in next tr, tr in each of next 3 tr, 2 tr in next tr**, sc in next ch-5 sp, rep from * around, ending last rep at **, join with sl st in beg sc.

**Rnd 21:** Sl st in next ch-5 sp, ch 1, sc in same ch sp, *2 tr in next tr, tr in each of next 6 tr, ch 5, sc in next ch-5 sp, ch 5, tr in each of next 6 tr, 2 tr in next tr**, sc in next ch-5 sp, rep from * around, ending last rep at **, join with sl st in beg sc.

**Rnd 22:** Sl st in each of next 3 tr, ch 4 *(counts as first tr)*, tr in each of next 5 tr, *[ch 5, sc in next sp] twice, ch 5, tr in each of next 6 tr, sk next 2 tr, sk next sc, sk next 2 tr**, tr in each of next 6 tr, rep from * around, ending last rep at **, join with sl st in 4th ch of beg ch-4.

**Rnd 23:** Ch 5 *(counts as first tr and ch-1)*, *sk next 3 tr, sc in next tr, ch 5, sc in next ch sp, 10 dc in next ch sp, sc in next ch sp, ch 5, sk next tr, sc in next tr, ch 1, sk next 3 tr, tr in next tr, ch 5**, tr in next tr, ch 1, rep from * around, ending last rep at **, join with sl st in 4th ch of beg ch-5.

**Rnd 24:** Sl st in next ch, sl st in next sc, sl st in each of next 2 chs, sl st in next ch sp, * 2-dc cl in next dc, ch 4, [3-dc cl in each of next 2 dc, ch 4] 4 times, 2-dc cl in next dc, sl st in next sp, ch 7, sk next ch-1 sp, sc in next ch-5 sp, ch 7, sk next ch-1 sp, sl st in next ch-5 sp, rep from * around, join with sl st in top of beg 2-dc cl.

**Rnd 25:** Sl st in next ch, sl st in next sp, ch 1, sc in same ch sp, *[ch 5, sc in next ch sp] 5 times, ch 7, sc in next ch sp, ch 5**, sc in next ch sp, rep from * around, ending last rep at **, join with sl st in beg sc.

**Rnd 26:** Sl st in each of next 2 chs, sl st in next sp, ch 1, sc in same ch sp, [ch 5, sc in next ch sp] 4 times, *ch 3, (tr, ch 5, tr) in next ch-7 sp, ch 3, [sc in next ch sp, ch 5] 5 times**, sc in next ch sp, rep from * around, ending last rep at **, join with sl st in beg sc. Fasten off.

**Rnd 27:** Sk first ch-5 sp worked on rnd 26, join with sl st in next ch-5 sp, ch 5 *(counts as first tr, ch-1)*, ({tr, ch 1} 12 times, tr) in same ch sp, *[ch 5, sc in next ch-5 sp] twice, ch 5, sc in next ch-3 sp, ch 5, ({tr, ch 1} 13 times, tr) in next ch-5 sp, ch 5, sc in next ch-3 sp, [ch 5, sc in next ch-5 sp] twice, ch 5, ({tr, ch 1} 13 times, tr) in next ch-5 sp, rep from * around, join with sl st in 4th ch of beg ch-5.

**Rnd 28:** Ch 6 *(counts as first tr, ch-2)*, [tr in next tr, ch 2] 12 times, tr in next tr, *[ch 5, sc in next ch sp] 4 times, ch 5, [tr in next tr, ch 2] 13 times, tr in next tr, rep from * around, join with sl st in 4th ch of beg ch-6.

**Rnd 29:** Ch 7 *(counts as first tr, ch-3)*, [tr in next tr, ch 3] 12 times, tr in next tr, *[ch 5, sc in next ch sp] 5 times, ch 5, [tr in next tr, ch 3] 13 times, tr in next tr, rep from * around, join with sl st in 4th ch of beg ch-7. Fasten off.

**Rnd 30:** Join with sl st in last ch-5 worked on previous rnd, ch 1, sc in same ch sp, *[ch 4, tr in last sc worked, ch 3, sl st in top of tr *(picot)*, sc in next tr] 14 times, ch 4, tr in last sc worked, sc in next ch-5 sp, drop lp from hook, insert hook in first sc worked on same ruffle *(which is sc in which first picot was worked)*, pick up dropped lp, pull through st on hook, [ch 5, sc in next unworked ch-5 sp] 5 times, rep from * around, join with sl st in beg sc. Fasten off.

Stiffen Doily according to manufacturer's directions.

Shape and allow to dry completely. ■

# Diamond Floral

DESIGN BY BRENDA STRATTON

Flawlessly beautiful in design and rich with dimension, texture and color, this gorgeous doily is a treat for the eyes, and its variety of interesting stitch patterns will showcase your crocheting skills.

INTERMEDIATE

**FINISHED SIZE**
14½ inches in diameter

**MATERIALS**
Size 10 crochet cotton:
150 yds each white, rose and spruce
Size 7/1.65mm steel crochet hook or size needed to obtain gauge
Tapestry needle
Sewing needle
Sewing thread

**GAUGE**
Rnds 1–4 = 2¼ inches

**SPECIAL STITCHES**
**Popcorn (pc):** 5 dc in st indicated, drop lp from hook, insert hook from front to back in first dc, pick up lp and pull through.

**Split cluster (split cl):** Holding back last lp of each st on hook, [2 dtr in next ch-4 sp] twice, yo, pull through all lps on hook.

## INSTRUCTIONS

**DOILY**

**Rnd 1:** With white, ch 8, sl st in first ch to form ring, ch 3 *(counts as first dc)*, 23 dc in ring, join with sl st in 3rd ch of beg ch-3. *(24 dc)*

**Rnd 2:** Ch 3, dc in each of next 2 dc, ch 2, [dc in each of next 3 dc, ch 2] around, join with sl st in 3rd ch of beg ch-3.

**Rnd 3:** Ch 3, dc in same st, dc in next dc, 2 dc in next dc, ch 2, sk next ch-2 sp, [2 dc in next dc, dc in next dc, 2 dc in next dc, ch 2, sk next ch-2 sp] around, join with sl st in 3rd ch of beg ch-3.

**Rnd 4:** Ch 3, dc in each of next 4 dc, ch 2, dc in next ch-2 sp, ch 2, [dc in each of next 5 dc, ch 2, dc in next ch-2 sp, ch 2] around, join with sl st in 3rd ch of beg ch-3. *(48 dc)*

**Rnd 5:** Ch 3, dc in each of next 4 dc, ch 2, [dc in next ch-2 sp, ch 2] twice, *dc in each of next 5 dc, ch 2, [dc in next ch-2 sp, ch 2] twice, rep from * around, join with sl st in 3rd ch of beg ch-3. *(56 dc)*

**Rnd 6:** Ch 3, dc in each of next 4 dc, ch 2, dc in next ch-2 sp, ch 2, **pc** *(see Special Stitches)* in next ch-2 sp, ch 2, dc in next ch-2 sp, ch 2, [dc in each of next 5 dc, ch 2, dc in next ch-2 sp, ch 2, pc in next ch-2 sp, ch 2, dc in next ch-2 sp, ch 2] around, join with sl st in 3rd ch of beg ch-3. *(56 dc, 8 pc)*

**Rnd 7:** Ch 3, dc in each of next 4 dc, ch 2, dc in next ch-2 sp, ch 2, [pc in next ch-2 sp, ch 2] twice, dc in next ch-2 sp, ch 2, *dc in each of next 5 dc, ch 2, dc in next ch-2 sp, ch 2, [pc in next ch-2 sp, ch 2] twice, dc in next ch-2 sp, ch 2, rep from * around, join with sl st in 3rd ch of beg ch-3. *(56 dc, 16 pc)*

**Rnd 8:** Ch 3, dc in each of next 4 dc, ch 2, dc in next ch-2 sp, ch 2, [pc in next ch-2 sp, ch 2] 3 times, dc in next ch-2 sp, ch 2, *dc in each of next 5 dc, ch 2, dc in next ch-2 sp, ch 2, [pc in next ch-2 sp, ch 2] 3 times, dc in next ch-2 sp, ch 2, rep from * around, join with sl st in 3rd ch of beg ch-3. *(56 dc, 24 pc)*

**Rnd 9:** Ch 3, dc in each of next 4 dc, ch 2, dc in next ch-2 sp, ch 2, [pc in next ch-2 sp, ch 2] 4 times, dc in next ch-2 sp, ch 2, *dc in each of next 5 dc, ch 2, dc in next ch-2 sp, ch 2, [pc in next ch-2 sp, ch 2] 4 times, dc in next ch-2 sp, ch 2, rep from * around, join with sl st in 3rd ch of beg ch-3. *(56 dc, 32 pc)*

**Rnd 10:** Sl st in each of next 2 dc, ch 3, *dc in each of next 2 dc, 2 dc in next ch-2 sp, ch 2, dc in next ch-2 sp, ch 2, [pc in next ch-2 sp, ch 2] 3 times, dc in next ch-2 sp, ch 2, 2 dc in next ch-2 sp, dc in each of next 2 dc**, (dc, ch 2, dc) in next dc, rep from * around, ending last rep at **, (dc, ch 2) in same st as beg ch-3, join with sl st in 3rd ch of beg ch-3. *(96 dc, 24 pc)*

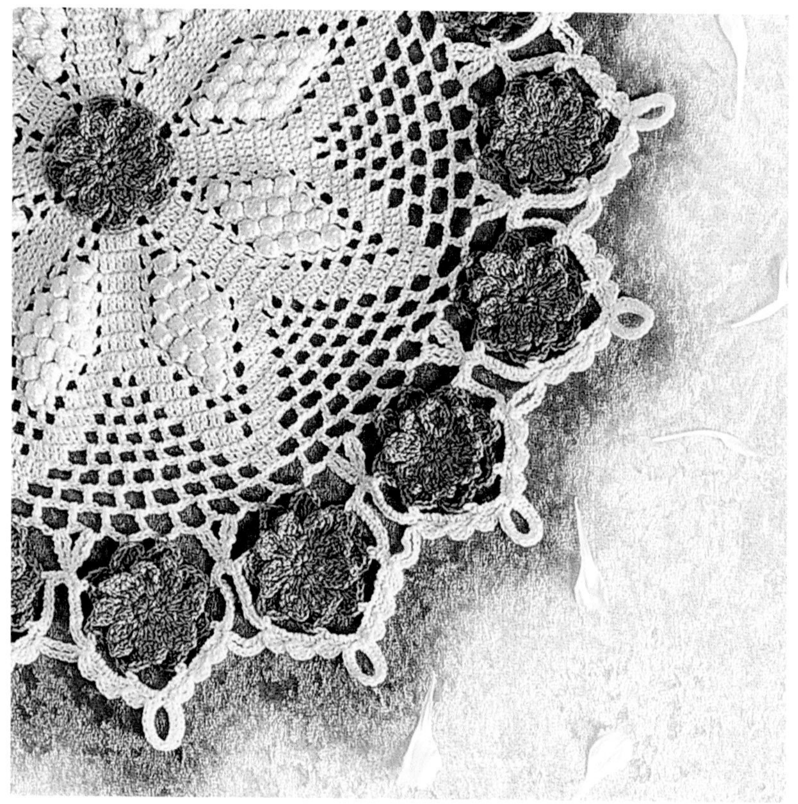

**Rnd 11:** Sl st in each of next 2 dc, ch 3, dc in each of next 2 dc, 2 dc in next ch-2 sp, ch 2, dc in next ch-2 sp, ch 2, [pc in next ch-2 sp, ch 2] twice, dc in next ch-2 sp, ch 2, 2 dc in ch-2 sp, dc in each of next 3 dc, ch 2, dc in next ch-2 sp, ch 2, sk next 2 dc, *dc in each of next 3 dc, 2 dc in next ch-2 sp, ch 2, dc in next ch-2 sp, ch 2, [pc in next ch-2 sp, ch 2] twice, dc in next ch-2 sp, ch 2, 2 dc in next ch-2 sp, dc in each of next 3 dc, ch 2, dc in next ch-2 sp, ch 2, sk next 2 dc, rep from * around, join with sl st in 3rd ch of beg ch-3. *(104 dc, 16 pc)*

**Rnd 12:** Sl st in each of next 2 dc, ch 3, dc in each of next 2 dc, 2 dc in next ch-2 sp, ch 2, dc in next ch-2 sp, ch 2, pc in next ch-2 sp, ch 2, dc in next ch-2 sp, ch 2, 2 dc in next ch-2 sp, dc in each of next 3 dc, ch 2, [dc in next ch-2 sp, ch 2] twice, sk next 2 dc, *dc in each of next 3 dc, 2 dc in next ch-2 sp, ch 2, dc in next ch-2 sp, ch 2, pc in next ch-2 sp, ch 2, dc in next ch-2 sp, ch 2, 2 dc in next ch-2 sp, dc in each of next 3 dc, ch 2, [dc in next ch-2 sp, ch 2] twice, sk next 2 dc, rep from * around, join with sl st in 3rd ch of beg ch-3. *(112 dc, 8 pc)*

**Rnd 13:** Sl st in each of next 2 dc, ch 3, dc in each of next 2 dc, 2 dc in next ch-2 sp, ch 2, [dc in next ch-2 sp, ch 2] twice, 2 dc in next ch-2 sp, dc in each of next 3 dc, sk next 2 dc, ch 2, [dc in next ch-2 sp, ch 2] 3 times, sk next 2 dc, *dc in each of next 3 dc, 2 dc in next ch-2 sp, ch 2, [dc in next ch-2 sp, ch 2] twice, 2 dc in next ch-2 sp, dc in each of next 3 dc, sk next 2 dc, ch 2, [dc in next ch-2 sp, ch 2] 3 times, sk next 2 dc, rep from * around, join with sl st in 3rd ch of beg ch-3. *(120 dc)*

**Rnd 14:** Sl st in each of next 2 dc, ch 3, dc in each of next 2 dc, 2 dc in next ch-2 sp, ch 2, dc in next ch-2 sp, ch 2, 2 dc in next ch-2 sp, dc in each of next 3 dc, sk next 2 dc, ch 2, [dc in next ch-2 sp, ch 2] 4 times, sk next 2 dc, *dc in each of next 3 dc, 2 dc in next ch-2 sp, ch 2, dc in next ch-2 sp, ch 2, 2 dc in next ch-2 sp, dc in each of next 3 dc, sk next 2 dc, ch 2, [dc in next ch-2 sp, ch 2] 4 times, sk next 2 dc, rep from * around, join with sl st in 3rd ch of beg ch-3.

**Rnd 15:** Sl st in each of next 2 dc, ch 3, dc in each of next 2 dc, 2 dc in next ch-2 sp, ch 2, 2 dc in next ch-2 sp, dc in each of next 3 dc, sk next 2 dc, ch 3, [dc in next ch-2 sp, ch 3] 5 times, sk next 2 dc, *dc in each of next 3 dc, 2 dc in next ch-2 sp, ch 2, 2 dc in next ch-2 sp, dc in each of next 3 dc, sk next 2 dc, ch 3, [dc in next ch-2 sp, ch 3] 5 times, sk next 2 dc, rep from * around, join with sl st in 3rd ch of beg ch-3.

**Rnd 16:** Sl st in each of next 2 dc, ch 3, dc in each of next 2 dc, dc in next ch-2 sp, dc in each of next 3 dc, sk next 2 dc, ch 3, [dc in next ch-3 sp, ch 3] 6 times, sk next 2 dc, *dc in each of next 3 dc, dc in next ch-2 sp, dc in each of next 3 dc, sk next 2 dc, ch 3, [dc in next ch-3 sp, ch 3] 6 times, sk next 2 dc, rep from * around, join with sl st in 3rd ch of beg ch-3.

**Rnd 17:** Sl st in each of next 2 dc, ch 3, dc in each of next 2 dc, ch 3, [dc in next ch-3 sp, ch 3] 7 times, sk next 2 dc, *dc in each of next 3 dc, ch 3, [dc in next ch-3 sp, ch 3] 7 times, sk next 2 dc, rep from * around, join with sl st in 3rd ch of beg ch-3.

**Rnd 18:** Sl st in each of next 2 dc, sl st in next ch-3 sp, ch 7, [dc in next ch-3 sp, ch 4] around, join with sl st in 3rd ch of ch-7. Fasten off.

**FIRST FLOWER**

**Rnd 1:** With rose, ch 4, sl st in first ch to form ring, ch 2 *(counts as hdc)*, 7 hdc in ring, join with sl st in 2nd ch of beg ch-2. *(8 hdc)*

**First Petal**

**Row 1:** Ch 3, 3 dc in same st, turn.

**Row 2:** Ch 3, pull up lp in same st as turning ch-3 and in next st, [yo, pull through 2 lps] twice, pull up lp in next st and in top of beg ch-3 of row 1, [yo, pull through 2 lps] twice, turn.

**Row 3:** Ch 1, pull up lp in each of next 2 sts and in top of turning ch, yo, pull through all lps on hook, ch 1, sl st in top of last st worked, 4 sl sts down side edge of Petal, sl st in next st of rnd 1.

**Remaining Petals**

**Rows 1–3:** Rep rows 1–3 of First Petal. Fasten off.

**Leaves**

**Rnd 1:** With WS facing, join spruce with sl st to center back of any Petal, ch 3, [sl st to center back of next Petal, ch 3] 7 times, join with sl st in base of beg ch-3, turn. *(8 ch-3 sps)*

**Rnd 2:** [(Hdc, dc, tr, ch 1, tr, dc, hdc) in next ch-3 sp, sl st in next sl st] 8 times. Fasten off.

**REMAINING FLOWERS**

Make 16.

Rep First Flower through rnd 1 of Leaves.

**Rnd 2 (joining):** [(Hdc, dc, tr, ch 1, tr, dc, hdc) in next ch-3 sp, sl st in next sl st] 6 times, [(hdc, dc, tr) in next ch-3 sp, sl st in ch-4 sp on Doily, (tr, dc, hdc) in same ch-3 sp, sl st in next sl st] twice. Fasten off. Sk 2 ch-4 sps on Doily between Flowers.

With sewing needle and white thread, sew First Flower to center of Doily, positioning 1 Leaf in center of each of 8 radiating spokes at center of Doily.

**EDGING**

**Rnd 1:** Join white with sc in **back lp** *(see Stitch Guide)* of ch-1 sp of first unworked Leaf on lower right of any Flower, *[ch 7, sc in back lp of ch-1 sp of next leaf] 5 times, ch 2, **split cl** *(see Special Stitches)* in sk ch-4 sps on rnd 18 on Doily, ch 2**, sc in back lp of ch-1 sp of first unworked Leaf on next Flower, rep from * around, ending last rep at **, join with sl st in beg sc.

**Rnd 2:** Sl st in next ch-7 sp, ch 1, 7 sc in same ch sp, *7 sc in next ch-7 sp, (4 sc, ch 10, sc in last sc made, 3 sc) in next ch-7 sp, 7 sc in each of next 2 ch-7 sps, 2 sc in next ch-2 sp, sc in next split cl, 2 sc in next ch-2 sp**, 7 sc in next ch-7 sp, rep from * around, ending last rep at **, join with sl st in beg sc.

**Rnd 3:** Sl st in each of next 8 sc, *[ch 3, dc in same sc, sk next 2 sc, sl st in next sc] 3 times, 15 sc in next ch-10 sp, [ch 3, dc in same sc, sk next 2 sc, sl st in next sc] 3 times, ch 7, trtr in same sc, sk next 19 sc, sl st in next sc, rep from * around, join with sl st in base of beg ch-3. Fasten off. ■

# Double Delight

DESIGN BY BABETTE COURTNEY

This blue-ribbon design features two winning versions that are equally wonderful. Choose the pattern using the popcorn stitch, or the alternate version that's made using cluster stitches.

EXPERIENCED

**FINISHED SIZE**
19 inches in diameter

**MATERIALS**
Size 10 crochet cotton:
500 yds white
Size 7/1.65mm steel crochet hook or size needed to obtain gauge
Tapestry needle

**GAUGE**
Rnds 1–4 = 2½ inches; 4 shell rnds = 1½ inches

**SPECIAL STITCHES**
**Popcorn Stitch Version**

**Popcorn (pc):** 7 dc in indicated ch sp, pull up lp, remove hook, insert hook in first dc of 7-dc group, pick up dropped lp, pull through st on hook.

**Beginning popcorn (beg pc):** Ch 3 *(counts as first dc)*, 6 dc in indicated ch sp, pull up lp, remove hook, insert hook in top of beg ch-3, pick up dropped lp, pull through st on hook.

**Cluster Stitch Version**

**Cluster (cl):** Holding last lp of each st on hook, 5 dc in indicated ch sp, yo, pull through all lps.

**Beginning cluster (beg cl):** Ch 2, holding last lp of each st on hook, 4 dc in indicated ch sp, yo, pull through all lps on hook.

**Both Versions**

**Shell:** (3 dc, ch 3, 3 dc) in indicated ch sp or st.

**Beginning shell (beg shell):** Sl st in indicated st, ch 3 *(counts as first dc)*, (2 dc, ch 3, 3 dc) in same st or sp.

**INSTRUCTIONS**

**DOILY**
**Rnd 1:** Ch 6, sl st in first ch to form ring, ch 1, 13 sc in ring, join with sl st in beg sc. *(13 sc)*

**Rnd 2:** Ch 3 *(counts as first dc)*, dc in each st around, join with sl st in 3rd ch of beg ch-3. *(13 dc)*

**Rnd 3:** Ch 1, 2 sc in each st around, join with sl st in beg sc. *(26 sc)*

**Rnd 4:** Ch 1, sc in first st, ch 3, [sc in next st, ch 3] around, join with sl st in beg sc. *(26 ch-3 lps)*

**Rnd 5:** Sl st in next ch-3 sp, ch 1, sc in same ch-3 sp, [ch 4, sc in next ch-3 sp] around, ending with ch 2, dc in beg sc to position hook in center of last ch sp.

**Rnd 6:** Ch 1, sc in last ch sp made, [ch 5, sc in next ch sp] around, ending with ch 3, dc in beg sc.

**Rnds 7–9:** Ch 1, sc in last sp made, [ch 6, sc in next ch sp] around, ending with ch 3, tr in beg sc.

**Rnd 10:** Ch 1, sc in last ch sp made, *ch 4, sc in next ch sp, ch 8**, sc in next ch sp, rep from * around, ending last rep at **, join with sl st in beg sc. *(13 ch-4 sps, 13 ch-8 sps)*

**Rnd 11:** Sl st in ch-4 sp, ch 3, 6 dc in same ch sp, ch 3, sc in next ch-8 sp, ch 3, [7 dc in next ch-4 sp, ch 3, sc in next ch-8 sp, ch 3] around, join with sl st in 3rd ch of beg ch-3. *(13 small pineapple bases)*

**Rnd 12:** Sl st in sp between ch-3 and next dc, ch 1, sc in same ch sp, *[ch 2, sc in next sp between dc sts] 5 times, [ch 3, sc in next ch-3 sp] twice, ch 3**, sc in next sp between dc, rep from * around, ending last rep at **, join with sl st in beg sc. *(104 ch sps)*

**Rnd 13:** Sl st in next ch-2 sp, ch 1, sc in same ch-2 sp, *[ch 2, sc in next ch-2 sp] 4 times, [ch 3, sc in next ch-3 sp] 3 times, ch 3**, sc in next ch-2 sp, rep from * around, ending last rep at **, join with sl st in beg sc.

**Rnd 14:** Sl st in next ch-2 sp, ch 1, sc in same ch-2 sp, *[ch 2, sc in next

ch-2 sp] 3 times, [ch 3, sc in next ch-3 sp] 4 times, ch 3**, sc in next ch-2 sp, rep from * around, ending last rep at **, join with sl st in beg sc.

**Rnd 15:** Sl st in next ch-2 sp, ch 1, sc in same ch-2 sp, *[ch 2, sc in next ch-2 sp] twice, [ch 3, sc in next ch-3 sp] 5 times, ch 3**, sc in next ch-2 sp, rep from * around, ending last rep at **, join with sl st in beg sc.

**Rnd 16:** Sl st in next ch-2 sp, ch 1, sc in same ch-2 sp, *ch 2, sc in next ch-2 sp, [ch 3, sc in next ch-3 sp] 6 times, ch 3**, sc in next ch-2 sp, rep from * around, ending last rep at **, join with sl st in beg sc.

**Rnd 17:** Sl st in next ch sp, ch 1, sc in same ch sp, [ch 3, sc in next ch sp] around, ending with ch 1, dc in beg sc. *(104 ch sps)*

**Rnd 18:** Ch 1, sc in last ch sp made, ch 3, [sc in next ch sp, ch 3] around, join with sl st in beg sc.

***Notes:*** *Before beg rnd 19, decide if you want to work pcs or cls for rnds 19–25. The pcs will create a raised surface and the cls will maintain the flat surface.*
*The pattern will indicate to work a pc. However, if you choose to make the cl st version, replace the pc st directions with those for the cl st.*

**Rnd 19:** Sl st in next ch-3 sp *(this ch-3 sp will be centered directly above the last ch-2 sp of a small pineapple)*, **beg pc** *(see Special Stitches)* in same ch sp, *[ch 3, sc in next ch sp] 3 times**, ch 3, **pc** *(see Special Stitches)* in next ch-3 sp, rep from * around, ending last rep at **, ch 1, dc in top of beg pc. *(26 pc)*

**Rnd 20:** Beg pc in last ch sp made, ch 3, pc in next ch-3 sp, *[ch 3, sc in next ch sp] twice**, [ch 3, pc in next ch sp] twice, rep from * around, ending last rep at **, ch 1, dc in top of beg pc. *(52 pc)*

**Rnd 21:** Beg pc in last ch sp made, [ch 3, pc in next ch sp] twice, *ch 4, sc in next ch-3 sp, ch 4, pc in ch sp between pc, ch 4, sk next ch-3 sp, sc in next ch-3 sp, ch 4, [pc in next ch-3 sp, ch 3] twice, pc in next ch-3 sp, rep from * around, ending with ch 1, dc in top of beg pc. *(52 pc)*

**Rnd 22:** Beg pc in same sp, *[ch 3, pc in next ch-3 sp] 3 times, [ch 5, sc in next ch-4 sp] twice, ch 5**, pc in next ch-3 sp, rep from * around, ending last rep at **, join with sl st in top of beg pc.

**Rnd 23:** Sl st in next ch-3 sp, beg pc in same sp, *[ch 3, pc in next ch-3 sp] twice, [ch 5, sc in next ch sp] 3 times, ch 5**, pc in next ch-3 sp, rep from * around, ending last rep at **, join with sl st in top of beg pc. *(39 pc)*

**Rnd 24:** Sl st in next ch-3 sp, beg pc in same ch sp, *ch 3, pc in next ch-3 sp, [ch 5, sc in next ch sp] 4 times, ch 5**, pc in next ch-3 sp, rep from * around, ending last rep at **, join with sl st in top of beg pc. *(26 pc)*

**Rnd 25:** Sl st in next ch-3 sp, beg pc in same ch-3 sp, *[ch 5, sc in next ch sp] 5 times**, ch 5, pc in next ch-3 sp, rep from * around, ending last rep at **, ch 2, dc in top of beg pc. *(13 pc)*

**Rnd 26:** Ch 1, sc in same ch sp, [ch 5, sc in next ch sp] around, ending with ch 2, dc in beg sc.

***Note:*** *13-dc groups of rnd 27 will be directly above each pc of rnd 25.*

**Rnd 27:** Ch 1, sc in same ch sp as beg ch-1, *13 dc in next ch sp, sc in next ch sp**, [ch 5, sc in next ch sp] 4 times, rep from * around, ending last rep at **, [ch 5, sc in next ch sp] 3 times, ch 2, dc in beg sc. *(13 pineapple bases)*

**Rnd 28: Beg shell** *(see Special Stitches)* in same ch sp, *ch 3, sc in first dc of 13-dc group, [ch 3, sc in next dc] 12 times, ch 3, **shell** *(see Special Stitches)* in next ch-5 sp, sc in next ch-5 sp, ch 5, sc in next ch-5 sp**, shell in next ch-5 sp, rep from * around, ending last rep at **, join with sl st in 3rd ch of beg ch-3.

**Rnd 29:** Sl st in ch-3 sp of shell, beg shell in ch-3 sp of shell, *ch 3, sk next ch-3 sp, sc in next ch-3 sp, [ch 3, sc in next ch-3 sp] 11 times, ch 3, sk next ch-3 sp, shell in next ch-3 sp of next shell, ch 3, sc in next ch-5 sp, ch 3**, shell in ch-3 sp of next shell, rep from * around, ending last rep at **, join with sl st in 3rd ch of beg ch-3.

**Rnd 30:** Ch 3, dc in each of next 2 dc, *ch 3, 3 dc in ch-3 sp of shell, ch 3, sk next ch-3 sp, sc in next ch-3 sp, [ch 3, sc in next ch-3 sp] 10 times, ch 3, sk next ch-3 sp, 3 dc in next ch-3 sp of next shell, ch 3, dc in each of next 3 dc of same shell **, dc in each of next 3 dc of next shell, rep from * around, ending last rep at**, join with sl st in 3rd ch of beg ch-3.

**Rnd 31:** Ch 3, dc in each of next 2 dc, *ch 3, 3 dc in ch-3 sp of shell, ch 3, sk next ch-3 sp, sc in next ch-3 sp, [ch 3, sc in next ch-3 sp] 9 times, ch 3, sk next ch-3 sp, 3 dc in ch-3 sp of next shell, ch 3, dc in each of next 3 dc of same shell**, dc in each of next 3 dc of next shell, rep from * around, ending last rep at **, join with sl st in 3rd ch of beg ch-3.

**Rnd 32:** Sl st in ch-3 sp of shell, (ch 3, 2 dc, {ch 3, 3 dc} twice) in same ch-3 sp of shell *(double shell)*, *ch 3, sk next ch-3 sp, sc in next ch-3 sp, [ch 3, sc in next ch-3 sp] 8 times, ch 3, sk next ch-3 sp, (3 dc, {ch 3, 3 dc} twice) in ch-3 sp of next shell, ch 3, sc in sp between 3rd and 4th dc of 6-dc group, ch 3**, (3 dc, {ch 3, 3 dc} twice) in next ch-3 sp of shell *(double shell)*, rep from * around, ending last rep at **, join with sl st in 3rd ch of beg ch-3, sl st across next 2 dc, next ch-3 sp, next 3 dc and in next ch-3 sp.

**PINEAPPLE FINISHING**

**Row 33:** Beg shell in ch-3 sp of shell, ch 3, sk next ch-3 sp, sc in next ch-3 sp, [ch 3, sc in next ch-3 sp] 7 times, ch 3, sk next ch-3 sp, shell in next ch-3 sp of shell, ch 5, sl st in 3rd ch from hook, turn.

**Row 34:** Ch 2, shell in ch-3 sp of shell, ch 3, sk next ch-3 sp, sc in next ch-3 sp, [ch 3, sc in next ch-3 sp] 6 times, ch 3, sk next ch-3 sp, shell in next shell, ch 5, sl st in 3rd ch from hook, turn.

**Row 35:** Ch 2, shell in ch-3 sp of shell, ch 3, sk next ch-3 sp, sc in next ch-3 sp, [ch 3, sc in next ch-3 sp] 5 times, ch 3, sk next ch-3 sp, shell in next shell, ch 5, sl st in 3rd ch from hook, turn.

**Row 36:** Ch 2, shell in ch-3 sp of shell, ch 3, sk next ch-3 sp, sc in next ch-3 sp, [ch 3, sc in next ch-3 sp] 4 times, ch 3, sk next ch-3 sp, shell in next shell, ch 5, sl st in 3rd ch from hook, turn.

**Row 37:** Ch 2, shell in ch-3 sp of shell, ch 3, sk next ch-3 sp, sc in next ch-3 sp, [ch 3, sc in next ch-3 sp] 3 times, ch 3, sk next ch-3 sp, shell in next shell, ch 5, sl st in 3rd ch from hook, turn.

**Row 38:** Ch 2, shell in ch-3 sp of shell, ch 3, sk next ch-3 sp, sc in next ch-3 sp, [ch 3, sc in next ch-3 sp] twice, ch 3, sk next ch-3 sp, shell in next shell, ch 5, sl st in 3rd ch from hook, turn.

**Row 39:** Ch 2, shell in ch-3 sp of shell, ch 3, sk next ch-3 sp, [sc in next ch-3 sp, ch 3] twice, sk next ch-3 sp, shell in next shell, ch 5, sl st in 3rd ch from hook, turn.

**Row 40:** Ch 2, shell in ch-3 sp of shell, ch 3, sk next ch-3 sp, sc in next ch-3 sp, ch 3, sk next ch-3 sp, shell in next shell, ch 5, sl st in 3rd ch from hook, turn.

**Row 41:** Ch 2, [3 dc in next ch-3 sp of shell] twice, ch 5, sl st in 3rd ch from hook, turn.

**Row 42:** Ch 2, dc in each of next 6 dc, pull up lp, remove hook, insert hook in first dc of 6-dc group, pick up dropped lp and pull through st on hook, ch 1 to lock. Fasten off.

With finished Pineapple to the right, join crochet cotton in 2nd ch-3 sp of next unworked double shell to left of finished Pineapple, rep rows 33–42.

Rep until all 13 Pineapples are completed. ■

# Regency Square

DESIGN BY MAGGIE WELDON

Elaborate blocks of gorgeous pineapples produce an afghan that's both cozy and attractive. No matter if your room is laid-back and casual or prim and proper, this throw will accent your living space with style.

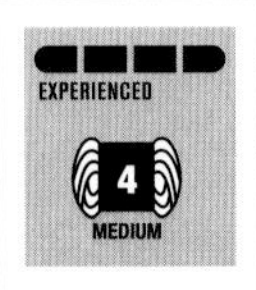


**FINISHED SIZE**
50 x 73 inches

**MATERIALS**
Medium (worsted) weight yarn:
46 oz/2,300 yds/1,304g green
Size I/9/5.5mm crochet hook or size needed to obtain gauge
Tapestry needle

**GAUGE**
Rnds 1 and 2 = 3 inches; Block = 23 inches square

**PATTERN NOTE**
This afghan may ruffle until blocked.

**SPECIAL STITCHES**

**Beginning shell (beg shell):** Ch 3 *(counts as first dc)*, (2 dc, ch 2, 3 dc) in same ch sp.

**Shell:** (3 dc, ch 2, 3 dc) in next ch sp.

**Beginning double shell (beg double shell):** Ch 3, (2 dc, {ch 2, 3 dc} twice) in same sp.

**Double shell:** ({3 dc, ch 2} twice, 3 dc) in next ch sp.

**V-stitch (V-st):** (Dc, ch 2, dc) in next st.

## INSTRUCTIONS

**BLOCK**
Make 6.

**Rnd 1:** Ch 4, sl st in first ch to form ring, ch 4, [dc in ring, ch 1] 7 times, join with sl st in 3rd ch of beg ch-4. *(8 dc, 8 ch sps)*

**Rnd 2:** Sl st in first ch sp, ch 3, 2 dc in same ch sp, ch 2, [3 dc in next ch sp, ch 2] around, join with sl st in 3rd ch of beg ch-3.

**Rnd 3:** Sl st in each of next 2 sts, sl st in next ch sp, **beg shell** *(see Special Stitches)*, ch 1, sc in next ch sp, ch 1, [**shell** *(see Special Stitches)* in next ch sp, ch 1, sc in next ch sp, ch 1] around, join with sl st in 3rd ch of beg ch-3. *(4 shells, 4 sc)*

**Rnd 4:** Sl st in each of next 2 sts, sl st in next ch sp, beg shell, ch 1, (dc, ch 3, dc) in next sc, ch 1, *shell in ch sp of next shell, ch 1, (dc, ch 3, dc) in next sc, ch 1, rep from * around, join with sl st in 3rd ch of beg ch-3.

**Rnd 5:** Sl st in each of next 2 sts, sl st in next ch sp, beg shell, *ch 2, sk next ch-1 sp, 10 dc in next ch-3 sp, ch 2, sk next ch-1 sp**, shell in next shell, rep from * around, ending last rep at **, join with sl st in 3rd ch of beg ch-3.

**Rnd 6:** Sl st in each of next 2 sts, sl st in next ch sp, beg shell, *ch 2, sk next ch-2 sp, dc in next dc, [ch 1, dc in next dc] 9 times, ch 2, sk next ch-2 sp**, shell in next shell, rep from * around, ending last rep at **, join with sl st in 3rd ch of beg ch-3.

**Rnd 7:** Sl st in each of next 2 sts, sl st in next ch sp, **beg double shell** *(see Special Stitches)*, *ch 2, sk next ch-2 sp, sc in next ch-1 sp, [ch 3, sc in next ch-1 sp] 8 times, ch 2, sk next ch-2 sp**, **double shell** *(see Special Stitches)* in next shell, rep from * around, ending last rep at **, join with sl st in 3rd ch of beg ch-3.

**Rnd 8:** Sl st in each of next 2 sts, sl st in next ch sp, beg shell, *ch 3, shell in next ch-2 sp, ch 2, sk next ch-2 sp, sc in next ch-3 sp, [ch 3, sc in next ch-3 sp] 7 times, ch 2, sk next ch-2 sp**, shell in first ch sp of next double shell, rep from * around, ending last rep at **, join with sl st in 3rd ch of beg ch-3.

**Rnd 9:** Sl st in each of next 2 sts, sl st in next ch sp, beg shell, *ch 2, tr in 2nd ch of next ch-3 sp, [ch 1, tr in same ch] 4 times, ch 2, shell in next shell, ch 2, sk next ch-2 sp, sc in next ch-3 sp, [ch 3, sc in next ch-3 sp] 6 times, ch 2, sk next ch-2 sp**, shell in next shell, rep from * around, ending last rep at **, join with sl st in 3rd ch of beg ch-3.

**Rnd 10:** Sl st in each of next 2 sts, sl st in next ch sp, beg shell, *ch 2, sk next ch-2 sp, sc in next ch-1 sp, [ch 3, sc in next ch-1 sp] 3 times, ch 2, sk next ch-2 sp, shell in next shell, ch 2, sk next ch-2 sp, sc in next ch-3 sp, [ch 3, sc in next ch-3 sp] 5 times, ch 2, sk next ch-2 sp**, shell in next shell, rep from * around, ending last rep at **, join with sl st in 3rd ch of beg ch-3.

**Rnd 11:** Sl st in each of next 2 sts, sl st in next ch sp, beg double shell, *ch 5, sk next ch-2 sp, sc in next ch-3 sp, [ch 3, sc in next ch-3 sp] twice, ch 5, sk next ch-2 sp, double shell in next shell, ch 2, sk next ch-2 sp, sc in next ch-3 sp, [ch 3, sc in next ch-3 sp] 4 times, ch 2, sk next ch-2 sp**, double shell in next shell, rep from * around, ending last rep at **, join with sl st in 3rd ch of beg ch-3.

**Rnd 12:** Sl st in each of next 2 sts, sl st in next ch sp, beg shell, *ch 3, shell in next ch-2 sp, ch 5, sk next ch-5 sp, sc in next ch-3 sp, ch 5, sc in next ch-3 sp, ch 5, sk next ch-5 sp, shell in next ch-2 sp, ch 3, shell in next ch-2 sp, ch 2, sk next ch-2 sp, sc in next ch-3 sp, [ch 3, sc in next ch-3 sp] 3 times, ch 2, sk next ch-2 sp**, shell in first ch sp of next double shell, rep from * around, ending with last rep at **, join with sl st in 3rd ch of beg ch-3.

**Rnd 13:** Sl st in each of next 2 sts, sl st in next ch sp, beg shell, *◊ch 3, (dc, ch 3, dc) in 2nd ch of next ch-3 sp, ch 3, shell in next shell◊, ch 5, sk next ch-5 sp, (sc, ch 5, sc) in next ch-5 sp, ch 5, sk next ch-5 sp, shell in next shell, rep between ◊, ch 2, sk next ch-2 sp, sc in next ch-3 sp, [ch 3, sc in next ch-3 sp] twice, ch 2, sk next ch-2 sp**, shell in next shell, rep from * around, ending last rep at **, join with sl st in 3rd ch of beg ch-3.

**Rnd 14:** Sl st in each of next 2 sts, sl st in next ch sp, beg shell, *◊ch 3, sk next ch-3 sp, shell in next ch-3 sp, ch 3, sk next ch-3 sp, shell in next shell◊, ch 5, sk next ch-5 sp, (tr, ch 7, tr) in next ch-5 sp, ch 5, sk next ch-5 sp, shell in next shell, rep between ◊, ch 2, sk next ch-2 sp, sc in next ch-3 sp, ch 3, sc in next ch-3 sp, ch 2, sk next ch-2 sp**, shell in next shell, rep from * around, ending last rep at **, join with sl st in 3rd ch of beg ch-3.

**Rnd 15:** Sl st in each of next 2 sts, sl st in next ch sp, beg shell, *[ch 3, sk next ch-3 sp, shell in next shell] twice, ch 3, sk next ch-5 sp, double shell in next ch-7 sp, ch 3, sk next ch-5 sp, shell in next shell, [ch 3, sk next ch-3 sp, shell in next shell] twice, ch 3, sk next ch-2 sp, sc in next ch-3 sp, ch 3, sk next ch-2 sp**, shell in next shell, rep from * around, ending last rep at **, join with sl st in 3rd ch of beg ch-3.

**Rnd 16:** Sl st in each of next 2 sts, sl st in next ch sp, beg shell, ch 3, sk next ch-3 sp, [shell in next shell, ch 3, sk next ch-3 sp] twice, *(3 dc, ch 5, 3 dc) in first ch sp of next double shell, ch 7, (3 dc, ch 5, 3 dc) in 2nd ch sp of same shell, [ch 3, sk next ch-3 sp, shell in next shell] 3 times, ch 3, sk next 2 ch-3 sps**, [shell in next shell, ch 3, sk next ch-3 sp] 3 times, rep from * around, ending last rep at **, join with sl st in 3rd ch of beg ch-3.

**Rnd 17:** Sl st in each of next 2 sts, sl st in next ch sp, beg shell, ch 3, [shell in next shell, ch 3] twice, *sk next ch-3 sp, shell in next ch-5 sp, ch 3, (3 tr, ch 5, 3 tr) in next ch-7 sp, ch 3, shell in next ch-5 sp, ch 3**, [shell in next shell, ch 3] 6 times, rep from * around, ending last rep at **, [shell in next shell, ch 3] 3 times, join with sl st in 3rd ch of beg ch-3.

**Rnd 18:** Sl st in each of next 2 sts, sl st in next ch sp, ch 3, 2 dc in same ch sp, 4 tr in next ch-3 sp, [3 dc in next shell, 4 tr in next ch-3 sp] 3 times, (4 tr, ch 3, 4 tr) in next ch-5 sp, *4 tr in next ch-3 sp, [3 dc in next shell, 4 tr in next ch-3 sp] 8 times, (4 tr, ch 3, 4 tr) in next ch-5 sp, rep from * twice, 4 tr in next ch-3 sp, [3 dc in next shell, 4 tr in next ch-3 sp] 4 times, join with sl st in 3rd ch of beg ch-3. Fasten off. *(68 sts across each side between corner ch-3 sps)*

Holding Blocks WS tog, matching sts, sew tog through **back lps** *(see Stitch Guide)* in 2 rows of 3 Blocks each.

**BORDER**

**Rnd 1:** Working around entire outer edge of afghan, with RS facing, join with sl st in corner ch sp before 1 short end, ch 3, (dc, ch 2, 2 dc) in same ch sp, dc in each st and each ch sp on each side of seams around with (2 dc, ch 2, 2 dc) in each corner ch sp, join with sl st in 3rd ch of beg ch-3. *(142 dc across each short end between corner ch sps, 212 dc across each long edge between corner ch sps)*

**Rnd 2:** Sl st in next st, sl st in next ch sp, ch 7, dc in same ch sp, *sk next st, [**V-st** *(see Special Stitches)* in next st, sk next 2 sts] across to next corner ch sp, (dc, ch 4, dc) in next ch sp, sk next 2 sts, [V-st in next st, sk next 2 sts] across to next corner ch sp*, (dc, ch 4, dc) in next ch sp, rep between * once, join with sl st in 3rd ch of beg ch-7.

**Rnd 3:** Sl st in first corner ch sp, ch 3, 6 dc in same ch sp, *sl st in sp between next 2 dc, [5 dc in next ch sp, sl st in sp between next 2 dc] across to next corner ch sp**, 7 dc in next ch sp, rep from * around, ending last rep at **, join with sl st in 3rd ch of beg ch-3. Fasten off. ■

# Reflections

DESIGN BY JOSIE RABIER

A splash of buttery yellow and mint green make this doily a must for any cheery room. The ribbon-like band woven around its center draws the eye to blooming yellow daises, the perfect complement to spring.

RMEDIATE

**FINISHED SIZE**
15 x 20 inches

**MATERIALS**
Size 10 crochet cotton:
400 yds white
50 yds each maize and mint green
Size 9/1.25mm steel crochet hook or size needed to obtain gauge
Sewing needle
Sewing thread

**GAUGE**
8 dc = 1 inch

## INSTRUCTIONS

**DOILY CENTER**

**Row 1:** With white, ch 4, 8 dc in 4th ch from hook, turn. *(9 dc)*

**Rows 2–22:** Ch 3 *(counts as first dc)*, dc in each dc across, turn. *(9 dc)*

**Row 23:** Ch 3, [yo, insert hook in next dc, yo, pull through 2 lps on hook] 8 times, yo, pull through all lps on hook, ch 1 to lock, **do not turn.**

**DOILY**

**Rnd 1 (RS):** Working around outer edge of Doily Center, ch 7, sl st in same st, 2 sc in end of row 23, [(sl st, ch 7, sl st) in end of next row, 2 sc in end of next row] 11 times, (sl st, ch 7, sl st) in opposite side of starting ch, 2 sc end of row 1, [(sl st, ch 7, sl st) in end of next row, 2 sc in end of next row] 11 times. *(48 sc, 24 ch-7 sps)*

**Rnd 2:** Sl st in next ch-7 sp, ch 4 *(counts as first tr)*, 16 tr in same sp, [sl st in next ch-7 sp, 11 tr in next ch-7 sp] 5 times, sl st in next ch-7 sp, 17 tr in next ch-7 sp, [sl st in next ch-7 sp, 11 tr in next ch-7 sp] 5 times, sl st in next ch-7 sp, join with sl st in 4th ch of beg ch-4.

**Rnd 3:** Sl st in 3rd tr, *[ch 7, sk next 2 tr, sl st in next tr] 4 times, **ch 7, sk next 4 tr, sl st in next tr, [ch 7, sk next 2 tr, sl st in next tr] twice**, rep between ** 4 times, ch 7, sk next 4 tr, sl st in next tr, rep from * around, join with sl st in same st as beg ch-7. *(40 ch-7 sps)*

**Rnd 4:** Sl st in 4th ch of next ch-7 sp, [ch 7, sl st in next ch-7 sp] 9 times, *ch 7, sk next ch-7 sp, sl st in next ch-7 sp, ch 7, sl st in next ch-7 sp *, rep between * once, [ch 7, sl st in next ch-7 sp] 14 times, rep between * twice, [ch 7, sl st in next ch-7 sp] 4 times, ch 7, join with sl st in same st as beg ch-7. *(36 ch-7 sps)*

**Rnd 5:** Sl st in 4th ch of ch-7 sp, *14 tr in next ch-7 sp, sl st in next ch-7 sp, ch 9, sl st in 4th ch of next ch-7 sp, rep from * around.

**Rnd 6:** Sl st in first tr, ch 4, tr in same st, *2 tr in each of next 13 tr, [sl st in next ch-9 sp, tr in each of next 14 tr] 5 times, sl st in next ch-9 sp*, 2 tr in next tr, rep between *, join with sl st in 4th ch of beg ch-4.

**Rnd 7:** Ch 3, dc in next tr, *[ch 1, dc in each of next 2 tr] 13 times, **dc in each of next 2 tr, [ch 1, dc in each of next 2 tr] 6 times**, rep between ** 4 times***, dc in each of next 2 tr, rep from * to ***, join with sl st in 3rd ch of beg ch-3.

**Rnd 8:** Sl st in next ch-1 sp, ch 3, dc in same ch sp, *[ch 1, 2 dc in next ch-1 sp] 5 times, ch 3, (sl st, ch 9, sl st) in next ch-1 sp, **ch 3, 2 dc in next ch-1 sp, [ch 1, 2 dc in next ch-1 sp] 5 times, ch 3, sk next 2 dc, (sl st, ch 9, sl st) in sp between dc**, rep between ** 5 times, ch 3*** 2 dc in next ch-1 sp, rep from * around, ending last rep at ***, join.

**Rnd 9:** Sl st in next ch-1 sp, ch 3, dc in same ch sp, [ch 1, 2 dc in next ch-1 sp] 4 times, *ch 3, 9 dc in ch-9 sp, ch 3**, 2 dc in next ch-1 sp, [ch 1, 2 dc in next ch-1 sp] 4 times, rep from * around, ending last rep at **, join.

**Rnd 10:** Sl st in next ch-1 sp, ch 3, dc in same ch sp, [ch 1, 2 dc in next ch-1 sp] 3 times, *ch 3, sk next ch-3 sp, dc in each of next 4 dc, (dc, ch 5, dc) in next dc, dc in each of next 4 dc, ch 3, sk next ch-3 sp**, 2 dc in next ch-1 sp, [ch 1, 2 dc in next ch-1 sp] 3 times, rep from * around, ending last rep at **, join with sl st in 3rd ch of beg ch-3.

**Rnd 11:** Sl st in next ch-1 sp, ch 3, dc in same ch sp, *[ch 1, 2 dc in next ch-1 sp] twice, ch 3, sk next ch-3 sp, dc in each of next 5 dc, ch 5, sl st in next ch-5 sp, ch 5, dc in each of next 5 dc, ch 3, sk next ch-3 sp**, 2 dc in next ch-1 sp, rep from * around, ending last rep at **, join with sl st in 3rd ch of beg ch-3.

**Rnd 12:** Sl st in next ch-1 sp, ch 3, dc in same ch sp, *ch 1, 2 dc in next ch-1 sp, ch 3, dc in each of next 5 dc, ch 5, sl st in next ch-5 sp, 5 dc in next sl st, sl st in next ch-5 sp, ch 5, dc in each of next 5 dc, ch 3**, 2 dc in next ch-1 sp, rep from * around, ending last rep at **, join with sl st in 3rd ch of beg ch-3. Fasten off.

**POINT FINISHING**

**Row 13 (RS):** Join white with sl st in 3rd dc of 5-dc worked in sl st of previous rnd, ch 3, dc in each of next 2 dc, sl st in next ch-5 sp, ch 5, dc in each of next 5 dc, ch 3, 2 dc in next ch-1 sp, ch 3, sk ch-3 sp, dc in each of next 5 dc, ch 5, sl st in next ch-5 sp, dc in each of next 3 dc, turn.

**Row 14:** Ch 3, dc in each of next 2 dc, sl st in next ch-5 sp, ch 5, dc in each of next 5 dc, sk next ch-3 sp, 2 dc and next ch-3 sp, dc in each of next 5 dc, ch 5, sl st in next ch-5 sp, dc in each of next 3 dc, turn.

**Row 15:** Ch 3, dc in each of next 2 dc, sl st in next ch-5 sp, ch 5, dc in each of next 10 dc, ch 5, sl st in next ch-5 sp, dc in each of next 3 dc, turn.

**Row 16:** Ch 3, dc in each of next 2 dc, sl st in next ch-5 sp, ch 5, dc in next dc, sk next 2 dc, dc in each of next 4 dc, sk next 2 dc, dc in next dc, ch 5, sl st in next ch-5 sp, dc in each of next 3 dc, turn.

**Row 17:** Ch 3, dc in each of next 2 dc, sl st in next ch-5 sp, ch 5, [yo, insert hook in next dc, yo, pull up lp, yo, pull through 2 lps on hook] 6 times, yo, pull through all lps on hook, ch 5, sl st in next ch-5 sp, dc in each of next 3 dc, turn.

**Row 18:** Ch 3, dc in each of next 2 dc, sl st in next ch-5 sp, ch 5, sl st in next ch-5 sp, dc in each of next 3 dc, turn.

**Row 19:** Ch 3, dc in each of next 2 dc, sl st in next ch-5 sp, dc in each of next 3 dc, turn.

**Row 20:** Ch 5, beg in same st as beg ch-5, *yo twice, insert hook in next st, yo, pull up lp, [yo, pull through 2 lps on hook] twice, rep from * 5 times, yo, pull through all lps on hook. Fasten off.

**Rows 21–188:** Rep rows 13–20 consecutively 11 times.

**MINT GREEN BAND**

**Row 1:** With mint green, ch 9, dc in 4th ch from hook, dc in each of last 5 chs, turn. *(7 dc)*

**Rows 2–70:** Ch 3, dc in each of next 6 dc, turn. At the end of row 70, leave length of crochet cotton. Fasten off.

Beg at rounded end of Doily below double pineapple, [pass band under 2 ch sps of rnd 3 that connect to base of pineapple, over next 2 ch sps of rnd 4] around, sew ends of Band tog.

**FLOWER**

Make 2.

**Rnd 1 (RS):** With mint green, ch 6, sl st in first ch to form a ring, ch 3 *(counts as first dc)*, 23 dc in ring, join with sl st in 3rd ch of beg ch-3. *(24 dc)*

**Rnd 2:** [Ch 7, sk next 2 dc, sl st in next dc] around, ending with sl st in same st as beg ch-7. *(8 ch-7 sps)*

**Rnd 3:** Sl st in ch-7 sp, [ch 4, 7 tr, ch 4, sl st in same ch sp, sl st in next ch-7 sp] around. Fasten off. *(8 petals)*

**Rnd 4 (RS):** Working in sk dc of rnd 1 and in front of mint green petals, join maize with [sl st in first sk st of 2 sk sts of rnd 1, 11 tr in first sk dc of rnd 1 of next 2 sk sts] 4 times. *(4 petals)*

**Rnd 5:** *[Ch 3, sk next tr, sl st in next tr] 5 times, sl st in next tr, sl st in sl st, sl st in next dc, rep from * around. Fasten off.

Sew 1 Flower over each end 17-tr group of rnd 2 of Doily Center.

Starch lightly and press. ■

# Pineapple Rose Garden

DESIGN BY CAROL ALEXANDER

Delicately shaded roses accented with pearl beads seem to float on this lovely doily. Its dimension, beautiful stitching and enduring charm will make it a beloved favorite for years to come.

EXPERIENCED

**FINISHED SIZE**
18 inches in diameter

**MATERIALS**
Size 10 crochet cotton:
- 270 yds white
- 20 yds shaded pinks
- 40 yds each rose and celery

Size 6/1.80mm steel crochet hook or size needed to obtain gauge
Tapestry needle
Sewing needle
Sewing thread
9 white 6mm pearl beads
Starch

**GAUGE**
Completed center rose and leaves = 2⅞ inches in diameter; 3 tr cl shells = 1¼ inches

**SPECIAL STITCHES**
**Beginning double crochet cluster (beg 3-dc cl)**: Holding back last lp of each dc on hook, dc in each of next 2 dc, yo, pull through all lps on hook.

**3-double crochet cluster (3-dc cl):** Holding back last lp of each dc on hook, dc in each of next 3 dc, yo, pull through all lps on hook .

**Single crochet picot (sc picot):** Ch 2, sc around top of post of last st made.

**Picot:** Ch 3, sl st in top of last st made.

**Treble crochet cluster (tr cl):** Holding last lp of each st on hook, 3 tr in indicated st, yo, pull through all lps on hook.

**Beginning treble crochet cluster (beg tr cl):** Ch 3, holding last lp of each st on hook, 2 tr in same st as beg ch, yo, pull through all lps on hook.

**Split treble crochet cluster (split tr cl):** Holding back last lp of each st on hook, 4 tr in each of next 2 ch sps, yo, pull through all lps on hook.

**Treble crochet cluster shell (tr-cl shell):** (Tr cl, ch 3, tr cl) in indicated st.

**Beginning treble crochet cluster shell (beg tr-cl shell):** (Beg tr cl, ch 3, tr cl) in indicated st.

**INSTRUCTIONS**

**CENTER ROSE**
**Rnd 1 (RS):** With rose, ch 5, sl st in first ch to form ring, ch 5 *(counts as first dc and ch-2)*, [dc in ring, ch 2] 7 times, join with sl st in 3rd ch of beg ch-5. *(8 ch-2 sps)*

**Rnd 2:** (Sl st, ch 3, 3 tr, ch 3, sl st) in each ch-2 sp around, join with sl st in same sp as beg sl st.

**Rnd 3:** [Ch 4, working behind petal, sl st between next 2 petals] 8 times, join with sl st at base of beg ch-4, pull up lp of shaded pinks, drop rose.

**Rnd 4:** (Sl st, ch 3, 4 tr, ch 3, sl st) in each ch-3 sp around, join with sl st in same st as beg sl st. *(8 petals)*

**Rnd 5:** [Ch 5, working behind petal, sl st between next 2 petals] 8 times, join with sl st at base of beg ch-5, pull up lp of rose, drop shaded pinks. *(8 ch-4 sps)*

**Rnd 6:** (Sc, dc, 5 tr, dc, sc) in each ch-5 sp around, join with sl st in beg sc. Fasten off.

**ROSE CENTER**

Join shaded pinks with sl st around post of any dc of rnd 1, ch 1, (sc, dc, 2 tr, dc, sc) around front of **post** *(see Stitch Guide)* of same dc and around post of each dc of rnd 1, join with sl st in beg sc. Fasten off.

Flatten and smooth all petal layers.

**LEAVES**

**Rnd 7:** Join celery with sl st to back of any petal of rnd 6 at bottom center, ch 4, [sl st in back of next petal at bottom center, ch 4] 7 times, join with sl st at base of beg ch-4. *(8 ch-4 sps)*

**Rnd 8:** (Sl st, ch 3, 3 dtr, **sc picot**—*see Special Stitches*, 2 dtr, ch 4, sl st) in each ch-4 sp around. Fasten off. *(8 leaves)*

**DOILY**

**Rnd 9:** Join white with sl st in sc picot of any Leaf, ch 4, (tr, ch 6, 2 tr) in same st, ch 6, *(2 tr, ch 6, 2 tr) in sc picot of next Leaf, ch 5, rep from * 6 times, join with sl st in 4th ch of beg ch-4.

**Rnd 10:** Sl st in next tr, sl st in each of next 2 chs, ch 3, (2 dc, ch 3, 3 dc) in same ch-6 sp, *ch 3, (sc, ch 3, sc) in next ch-6 sp, ch 3**, (3 dc, ch 3, 3 dc) in next ch-6 sp, rep from * around, ending last rep at **, join with sl st in 3rd ch of beg ch-3.

**Rnd 11:** Ch 3, **beg 3-dc cl** *(see Special Stitches)*, *ch 1, ({dc, ch 1} 4 times, dc) in next ch-3 sp, **3-dc cl** *(see Special Stitches)*, ch 4, sk next ch-3 sp, sc in next ch-3 sp, ch 4, sk next ch-3 sp**, 3-dc cl in next 3 dc, rep from * around, ending last rep at **, join with sl st in top of beg cl.

**Rnd 12:** [Sl st in next ch-1, sl st in next dc] twice, *sc in next ch-1 sp, ch 9, **split tr cl** *(see Special Stitches)*, ch 9, sk next cl, next ch-1 sp, next dc, next ch-1 sp, and next dc, rep from * 7 times, join with sl st in beg sc.

**Rnd 13:** Sl st to center of next ch-9 sp, ch 1, sc in same ch sp, *ch 4, (3 tr, ch 3, 3 tr) in top of next split cl, ch 4, sc in next ch-9 sp, ch 9**, sc in next ch-9 sp, rep from * around, ending last rep at **, join with sl st in beg sc.

**Rnd 14:** Sl st in each of next 4 chs, sl st in next tr, **beg tr cl** *(see Special Stitches)* in same st, *ch 7, sk next 2 tr, (**tr cl**—*see Special Stitches*, ch 7, tr cl) in next ch-3 sp, ch 7, sk next 2 tr, tr cl in next tr, **picot** *(see Special Stitches)*, (tr cl, ch 7, tr cl) in next ch-9 sp, picot**, tr cl in next tr, rep from * around, ending last rep at **, join with sl st in top of beg cl.

**Rnd 15:** Sl st to center of first ch-7 sp, ch 7 *(counts as first tr and ch-3)*, tr in same ch sp, *[ch 5, (tr, ch 3, tr) in next ch-7 sp] twice, ch 5, tr cl in next ch-7 sp, picot, ch 5**, (tr, ch 3, tr) in next ch-7 sp, rep from * around, ending last rep at **, join with sl st in 4th ch of beg ch-7.

**Rnd 16:** Sl st to center of next ch-3 sp, **beg tr-cl shell** *(see Special Stitches)* in same ch sp, *ch 3, sk next ch-5 sp, 9 tr in next ch-3 sp, ch 3, sk next ch-5 sp, **tr-cl shell** *(see Special Stitches)* in next ch-3 sp, [ch 3, sc in next ch-5 sp] twice, ch 3**, tr-cl shell in next ch-3 sp, rep from * around, ending last rep at **, join with sl st in top of beg tr cl.

**Rnd 17:** Sl st in ch-3 sp of beg tr-cl shell, beg tr-cl shell in same sp, *ch 3, sk next ch-3 sp, sc in next tr, [ch 3, sc in next tr] 8 times, ch 3, sk next ch-3 sp, tr-cl shell in ch-3 sp of next tr-cl shell, ch 5, sk next ch-3 sp, sc in next ch-3 sp, ch 5, sk next ch-3 sp**, tr-cl shell in ch-3 sp of next tr-cl shell, rep from * around, ending last rep at **, join with sl st in top of beg tr cl.

**Rnd 18:** Sl st in ch-3 sp of beg tr-cl shell, beg tr-cl shell in same ch sp, *ch 3, sk next ch-3 sp, sc in next ch-3 sp, [ch 3, sc in next ch-3 sp] 7 times, ch 3, sk next ch-3 sp, tr-cl shell in ch-3 sp of next tr-cl shell, ch 3, sc in next ch-5 sp, ch 5, sc in next ch-5 sp, ch 3**, tr-cl shell in ch-3 sp of next

**Rnd 20:** Sl st into ch-3 sp of shell, beg tr-cl shell in same ch sp, *ch 3, sk next ch-3 sp, sc in next ch-3 sp, [ch 3, sc in next ch-3 sp] 5 times, ch 3, sk next ch-3 sp, tr-cl shell in next ch-3 sp of shell, ch 3, sc in next ch-3 sp, ch 5, sc in next ch-5 sp, ch 3**, tr-cl shell in next ch-3 sp of shell, rep from * around, ending last rep at **, join with sl st in top of beg cl.

**Rnd 21:** Sl st into ch-3 sp of shell, beg tr-cl shell in same sp, *ch 3, sk next ch-3 sp, sc in next ch-3 sp, [ch 3, sc in next ch-3 sp] 4 times, ch 3, sk next ch-3 sp, tr-cl shell in next ch-3 sp of shell, ch 7, sk next ch-3 sp, sc in next ch-5 sp, ch 7, sk next ch-3 sp**, tr-cl shell in ch-3 sp of shell, rep from * around, ending last rep at **, join with sl st in top of beg cl.

**Rnd 22:** Sl st into ch-3 sp of shell, beg tr-cl shell in same sp, *ch 3, sk next ch-3 sp, sc in next ch-3 sp, [ch 3, sc in next ch-3 sp] 3 times, ch 3, sk next ch-3 sp, tr-cl shell in next ch-3 sp of shell, ch 3, sc in next ch-7 sp, ch 11, sc in next ch-7 sp, ch 3**, tr-cl shell in next ch-3 sp of shell, rep from * around, ending last rep at **, join with sl st in top of beg cl.

**Rnd 23:** Sl st into ch-3 sp of shell, beg tr-cl shell in same sp, *ch 3, sk next ch-3 sp, sc in next ch-3 sp, [ch 3, sc in next ch-3 sp] twice, ch 3, sk next ch-3 sp, tr-cl shell in ch-3 sp of next shell, ch 9, sk next ch-3 sp, (3 tr, ch 3, 3 tr) in next ch-11 sp, ch 9, sk next ch-3 sp**, tr-cl shell in next ch-3 sp of shell, rep from * around, ending last rep at **, join with sl st in top of beg tr cl.

**Rnd 24:** Sl st into ch-3 sp of shell, beg tr-cl shell in same sp, *ch 3, sk next ch-3 sp, sc in next ch-3 sp, ch 3, sc in next ch-3 sp, ch 3, sk next ch-3 sp, tr-cl shell in next ch-3 sp of next shell, ch 5, sc in next ch-9 sp, ch 5, **dc dec** *(see Stitch Guide)* in next 3 tr, ch 3, (dc, ch 3) 4 times in next ch-3 sp, dc dec in next 3 tr, ch 5, sc in next ch-9 sp, ch 5**, tr-cl shell in next ch-3 sp of shell, rep from * around, ending last rep at **, join with sl st in top of beg cl.

**Rnd 25:** Sl st into ch-3 sp of shell, beg tr-cl shell in same sp, *ch 3, sk next ch-3 sp, sc in next ch-3 sp, ch 3, sk next ch-3 sp, tr-cl shell in next ch-3 sp of shell, [ch 7, sc in next ch-5 sp] twice, ch 7, sk next ch-3 sp, [sc in next ch-3 sp, ch 7, sk next ch-3 sp] twice, [sc in next ch-5 sp, ch 7] twice**, tr-cl shell in ch-3 sp of next shell, rep from * around, ending last rep at **, join with sl st in top of beg cl.

**Rnd 26:** Sl st in ch-3 sp of shell, beg tr-cl shell in same sp, *sk next 2 ch-3 sps, tr-cl shell in next ch-3 sp of shell, ch 3, sc in next ch-7 sp, ch 3, (3 dc, ch 3, 3 dc) in next ch-7 sp, ch 3, sc in next ch-7 sp, ch 5, (3 dc, ch 3, 3 dc) in next ch-7 sp, ch 5, sc in next ch-7 sp, ch 3, (3 dc, ch 3, 3 dc) in next ch-7 sp, ch 3, sc in next ch-7 sp, ch 3 **, tr-cl shell in next ch-3 sp of shell, rep from * around, ending last rep at **, join with sl st in top of beg cl.

**Rnd 27:** Sl st in next ch-3 sp, ch 3, 2 dc in same sp, *picot, 3 dc in next ch-3 sp, [ch 3, (sc, picot) in next sc, ch 3, dc dec in next 3 dc, picot, ch 3, (dc, picot, ch 2) twice in next ch-3 sp, (dc, picot, ch 3) in same ch sp, dc dec in next 3 dc, picot] 3 times, ch 3, (sc, picot) in next sc, ch 3**, 3 dc in next ch-3 sp, rep from * around, ending last rep at **, join with sl st in 3rd ch of beg ch-3. Fasten off.

#### SMALL ROSE

Make 8.

**Rnd 1:** With rose, ch 5, sl st in first ch to form ring, ch 5 *(counts as first dc and ch-2)*, [dc in ring, ch 2] 7 times, join with sl st in 3rd ch of beg ch-5.

**Rnd 2:** (Sc, dc, 3 tr, dc, sc) in each ch-2 sp around, join with sl st in beg sc. Fasten off.

#### SMALL ROSE CENTER

Join shaded pinks with sl st around post of any dc of rnd 1, ch 1, (sc, 3 dc, sc) around post of same dc and around post of each dc around, join with sl st in beg sc. Fasten off.

Flatten and smooth petals.

#### SMALL ROSE LEAVES

Make 2.

With WS of Small Rose facing, join celery with sl st to back of any petal at bottom center, [ch 4, sl st to bottom center back of next petal] twice, **turn,** (sl st, ch 3, 3 tr, sc picot, 2 tr, ch 3, sl st) in each of next 2 ch-4 sps. Fasten off.

#### FINISHING

Starch Doily and block to size.

Using photo as guide for positioning, sew Roses between pineapples. Sew 1 pearl bead to center of each Small Rose and to center of Center Rose. ■

# Octagon Lace

DESIGN BY MAGGIE WELDON

Winter white, rose pink and sage green form a color palette as classic as this afghan's vintage design. Lacy octagon blocks and delicate roses make it a lovely accent for any feminine room.

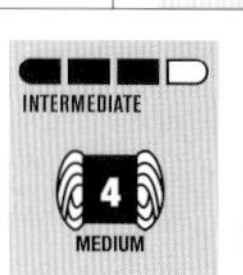


**FINISHED SIZE**
49 x 73 inches

**MATERIALS**
Medium (worsted) weight yarn:
42 oz/2,100 yds/1,191g winter white
3½ oz/175 yds/99g each pink and green
Size I/9/5.5mm crochet hook or size needed to obtain gauge
Tapestry needle
Stitch marker

**GAUGE**
Rnds 1–4 = 6¾ inches
Octagon = 12 inches across
Filler Square = 4½ inches square

**SPECIAL STITCHES**
**Beginning cluster (beg cl):** Ch 3, holding last lp of each st on hook, 2 dc in same ch sp, yo, pull through all lps on hook.

**Cluster (cl):** Holding last lp of each st on hook, 3 dc in ch sp, yo, pull through all lps on hook.

## INSTRUCTIONS

**OCTAGON**
Make 24.

**Rnd 1:** With winter white, ch 4, sl st in first ch to form ring, ch 5, [dc in ring, ch 2] 5 times, join with sl st in 3rd ch of beg ch-5. *(6 dc, 6 ch sps)*

**Rnd 2:** Ch 3, 3 dc in next ch sp, [dc in next st, 3 dc in next ch sp] around, join with sl st in 3rd ch of beg ch-3. *(24 dc)*

**Rnd 3:** Ch 4, [dc in next st, ch 1] around, join with sl st in 3rd ch of beg ch-4. *(24 dc, 24 ch sps)*

**Rnd 4:** Sl st in next ch sp, **beg cl** *(see Special Stitches)*, ch 2, [**cl** *(see Special Stitches)* in next ch sp, ch 2] around, join with sl st in top of beg cl.

**Rnd 5:** Sl st in first ch sp, beg cl, [ch 2, cl in next ch sp] twice, ch 5, *cl in next ch sp, [ch 2, cl in next ch sp] twice, ch 5, rep from * around, join with sl st in beg cl.

**Rnd 6:** Sl st in first ch-2 sp, beg cl, ch 2, cl in next ch-2 sp, ch 5, sc in next ch-5 sp, ch 5, *cl in next ch-2 sp, ch 2, cl in next ch-2 sp, ch 5, sc in next ch-5 sp, ch 5, rep from * around, join with sl st in top of beg cl.

**Rnd 7:** Sl st in first ch-2 sp, beg cl, ch 5, [sc in next ch-5 sp, ch 5] twice, *cl in next ch-2 sp, ch 5, [sc in next ch-5 sp, ch 5] twice, rep from * around, join with sl st in top of beg cl. *(24 ch sps)*

**Rnd 8:** Ch 5, dc in same st, 3 dc in next ch sp, 5 dc in next ch sp, 3 dc in next ch sp, *(dc, ch 2, dc) in next cl, 3 dc in next ch sp, 5 dc in next ch sp, 3 dc in next ch sp, rep from * around, join with sl st in 3rd ch of beg ch-5. Fasten off. *(13 dc across each side between ch sps)*

**LEAVES**
With green, ch 15, sl st in 2nd ch from hook, *sc in next ch, hdc in next ch, dc in each of next 2 chs, hdc in next ch, sl st in each of next 2 chs, hdc in next ch, dc in each of next 2 chs, hdc in next ch, sc in next ch*, (sl st, ch 1, sl st) in last ch, working on opposite side of ch, rep between *, sl st in last ch, ch 1, join with sl st in beg sl st. Fasten off.

Sew Leaves to center of Octagon.

## ROSE

With pink, ch 11, (4 sc, sl st) in 2nd ch from hook, (4 sc, sl st) in each of next 2 chs, (4 hdc, sl st) in each of next 2 chs *(mark last st made)*, (4 dc, sl st) in each of last 5 chs, roll in a rose shape, sl st in marked st. Fasten off. Remove st marker.

Sew Rose to center of Octagon over Leaves.

## FILLER SQUARE

Make 15.

**Rnd 1:** With winter white, ch 4, sl st in first ch to form ring, beg cl, ch 3, [cl in ring, ch 3] 7 times, join with sl st in top of beg cl. *(8 cls, 8 ch sps)*

**Rnd 2:** Sl st in first ch sp, ch 1, (sc, ch 5, sc) in same ch sp, ch 4, sc in next ch sp, ch 4, *(sc, ch 5, sc) in next ch sp, ch 4, sc in next ch sp, ch 4, rep from * around, join with sl st in beg sc.

**Rnd 3:** Sl st in first ch-5 sp, ch 3, (2 dc, ch 2, 3 dc) in same ch sp, 3 dc in next ch-4 sp, dc in next sc, 3 dc in next ch-4 sp, *(3 dc, ch 2, 3 dc) in next ch-5 sp, 3 dc in next ch-4 sp, dc in next sc, 3 dc in next ch-4 sp, rep from * around, join with sl st in 3rd ch of beg ch-3. Fasten off. *(13 dc across each side between corner ch sps)*

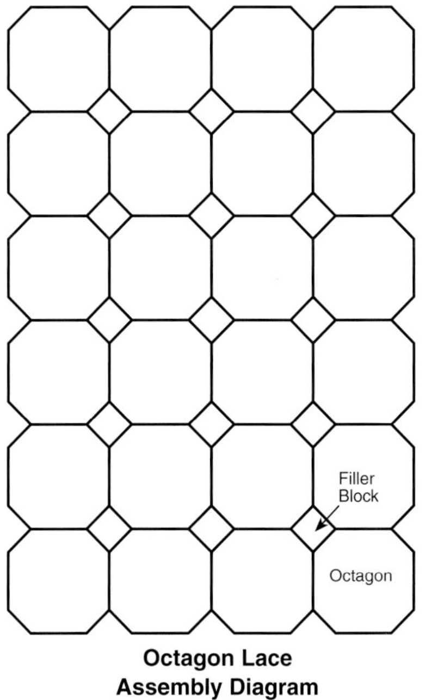

**Octagon Lace Assembly Diagram**

Matching sts and ch sps, sew Octagons and Filler Squares tog through **back lps** *(see Stitch Guide)* according to Assembly Diagram.

## EDGING

Working around entire outer edge, join winter white with sc in any corner ch sp, (tr, sc) in same ch sp, tr in next st, [sc in next st, tr in next st] around to next corner ch sp, *(sc, tr, sc) in next corner ch sp, tr in next st, [sc in next st, tr in next st] around to next corner ch sp, rep from * around, join with sl st in beg sc. Fasten off. ■

# Queen's Treasure

DESIGN BY JOSIE RABIER

Classic beauty and elegance define this intricate doily that is fit for a queen's dressing table or accenting any surface in your castle. Equally perfect for a formal parlor or a lady's boudoir, it is sure to impress!

INTERMEDIATE

**FINISHED SIZE**
27 inches in diameter

**MATERIALS**
Caron Grandma's Best size 10 crochet cotton (650 yds per ball): 2 balls #21 white
Size 7/1.65mm steel crochet hook or size needed to obtain gauge
Starch

**GAUGE**
8 dc = 1 inch; 4 shell rnds = 2½ inches

**SPECIAL STITCHES**
**Shell:** (3 dc, ch 3, 3 dc) in indicated st.

**Beginning double shell (beg double shell):** Beg shell in next ch-3 sp of shell, ch 3, 3 dc in same ch-3 sp.

**Double shell (Shell, ch 3, 3 dc):** in ch-3 sp of shell.

**Beginning shell (beg shell):** Ch 3 *(counts as first dc)*, (2 dc, ch 3, 3 dc) in indicated st.

**Beginning split cluster (beg split cl):** Ch 2, holding last lp of each dc on hook, dc in next dc, sk next 2 dc, dc in each of next 2 dc, yo, pull through all lps on hook.

**Split cluster (split cl):** Holding last lp of each dc on hook, dc in each of next 2 dc, sk next 2 dc, dc in each of next 2 dc, yo, pull through all lps on hook.

**Popcorn (pc):** 3 dc in each of next 2 tr, pull up lp, remove hook, insert hook in first dc of 6-dc group, pick up dropped lp, pull through st on hook, ch 1 to lock.

## INSTRUCTIONS

### DOILY

**Rnd 1:** Ch 6, sl st in first ch to form ring, ch 3 *(counts as first dc)*, 23 dc in ring, join with sl st in 3rd ch of beg ch-3. *(24 dc)*

**Rnd 2:** Ch 3, dc in each of next 2 dc, ch 5, [dc in each of next 3 dc, ch 5] around, join with sl st in 3rd ch of beg ch-3.

**Rnd 3:** Ch 3, *5 dc in center dc, dc in next dc, sl st in next ch-5 sp**, dc in next dc, rep from * around, ending last rep at **, join with sl st in 3rd ch of beg ch-3.

**Rnd 4:** Ch 3, dc in each of next 2 dc, (dc, ch 3, dc) in next dc, *dc in each of next 6 dc, (dc, ch 3, dc) in next dc, rep from * around, ending with dc in each of last 3 dc, join with sl st in 3rd ch of beg ch-3.

**Rnd 5:** Sl st in each of next 2 dc, sl st across ch-3 sp and into next dc, ch 3, dc in each of next 2 dc, *sk next 2 dc, dc in each of next 3 dc, ch 5, sk next ch-3 sp**, dc in each of next 3 dc, rep from * around, ending last rep at **, join with sl st in 3rd ch of beg ch-3.

**Rnd 6:** **Beg split cl** *(see Special Stitches)* in next 6 dc, ch 5, **shell** *(see Special Stitches)* in 3rd ch of next ch-5 sp, ch 5 [**split cl** *(see Special Stitches)* in next 6 dc, ch 5, shell in 3rd ch of next ch-5 sp, ch 5] around, join with sl st in top of beg split cl.

**Rnd 7:** **Beg shell** *(see Special Stitches)* in ch-3 sp of shell, *ch 5, sl st in next ch-5 sp, ch 7, sl st in next ch-5 sp, ch 5**, shell in next ch-3 sp of shell, rep from * around, ending last rep at **, join with sl st in 3rd ch of beg ch-3.

**Rnd 8:** Beg shell in next ch-3 sp of shell, *ch 3, sl st in ch-5 sp, 12 tr in ch-7 sp, sl st in next ch-5 sp, ch 3**, shell in ch-3 sp of next shell, rep from * around, ending last rep at **, join with sl st in 3rd ch of beg ch-3. *(8 pineapple bases)*

**Rnd 9:** Beg shell in next ch-3 sp of shell, *ch 3, **pc** *(see Special Stitches)*, [ch 5, pc] 5 times, ch 3**, shell in ch-3 sp of next shell, rep from * around, ending last rep at **, join with sl st in 3rd ch of beg ch-3.

**Rnd 10:** Beg shell in next ch-3 sp of

shell, *sk next ch-3 sp, 6 dc in each of next 5 ch-5 sps**, shell in ch-3 sp of next shell, rep from * around, ending last rep at **, join with sl st in 3rd ch of beg ch-3.

**Rnd 11: Beg double shell** *(see Special Stitches)*, *sk next 3 dc of shell, dc in each of next 4 dc, sk next 2 dc, dc in each of next 18 dc, sk next 2 dc, dc in each of next 4 dc**, **double shell** *(see Special Stitches)*, rep from * around, ending last rep at **, join with sl st in 3rd ch of beg ch-3.

**Rnd 12:** Beg shell in next ch-3 sp of shell, *shell in next ch-3 sp of shell, sk next 3 dc of shell, dc in each of next 4 dc, sk next 2 dc, dc in each of next 14 dc, sk next 2 dc, dc in each of next 4 dc**, shell in next ch-3 sp of shell, rep from * around, ending last rep at **, join with sl st in 3rd ch of beg ch-3.

**Rnd 13:** Beg shell in next ch-3 sp of

shell, *ch 5, sk 2 dc of shell, sl st in each of next 2 dc, ch 5, shell in next ch-3 sp of shell, sk next 3 dc of shell, dc in each of next 4 dc, sk next 2 dc, dc in each of next 10 dc, sk next 2 dc, dc in each of next 4 dc**, shell in next ch-3 sp of shell, rep from * around, ending last rep at **, join with sl st in 3rd ch of beg ch-3.

**Rnd 14:** Beg shell in next ch-3 sp of shell, *ch 5, sl st in next ch-5 sp, ch 7, sl st in next ch-5 sp, ch 5, shell in next ch-3 sp of shell, sk next 3 dc of shell, dc in each of next 4 dc, sk next 2 dc, dc in each of next 6 dc, sk next 2 dc, dc in each of next 4 dc**, shell in next ch-3 sp of shell, rep from * around, ending last rep at **, join with sl st in 3rd ch of beg ch-3.

**Rnd 15:** Beg shell in next ch-3 sp of shell, *ch 5, sl st in next ch-5 sp, ch 5, sl st in next ch-7 sp, ch 5, sl st in next ch-5 sp, ch 5, shell in next ch-3 sp of shell, sk next 3 dc of shell, dc in each of next 4 dc, sk next 2 dc, dc in each of next 2 dc, sk next 2 dc, dc in each of next 4 dc**, shell in next ch-3 sp of shell, rep from * around, ending last rep at **, join with sl st in 3rd ch of beg ch-3.

**Rnd 16:** Beg shell in next ch-3 sp of shell, *[ch 5, sl st in next ch-5 sp] 4 times, ch 5, shell in next ch-3 sp of shell, sk next 3 dc of shell, dc in each of next 4 dc, sk next 2 dc, dc in each of next 4 dc**, shell in next ch-3 sp of shell, rep from * around, ending last rep at **, join with sl st in 3rd ch of beg ch-3.

**Rnd 17:** Beg shell in next ch-3 sp of shell, *[ch 5, sl st in next ch-5 sp] 5 times, ch 5, shell in ch-3 sp of next shell, sk next 3 dc of shell, dc in each of next 3 dc, sk next 2 dc, dc in each of next 3 dc**, shell in next ch-3 sp of shell, rep from * around, ending last rep at **, join with sl st in 3rd ch of beg ch-3.

**Rnd 18:** Beg shell in next ch-3 sp of shell, *[ch 5, sl st in next ch-5 sp] 6 times, ch 5, shell in next ch-3 sp of shell, sk next 3 dc of shell, dc in each of next 2 dc, sk next 2 dc, dc in each of next 2 dc**, shell in ch-3 sp of next shell, rep from * around, ending last rep at **, join with sl st in 3rd ch of beg ch-3.

**Rnd 19:** Beg shell in next ch-3 sp of shell, *[ch 5, sl st in next ch-5 sp] 7 times, ch 5, shell in ch-3 sp of next shell, sk next 3 dc of shell, dc in next dc, sk next 2 dc, dc in next dc**, shell in ch-3 sp of next shell, rep from * around, ending last rep at **, join with sl st in 3rd ch of beg ch-3, sl st into 2nd ch of ch-3 sp of shell.

**Rnd 20:** *[Ch 5, 2 dc in 3rd ch of next ch-5 sp] 8 times, ch 5, sl st in next ch-3 sp of shell, ch 5**, sl st in next ch-3 sp of shell, rep from * around, ending last rep at **, join with sl st in same st as beg sl st.

**Rnd 21:** Ch 3, dc in same sp as beg ch-3, *[ch 5, sk next ch-5 sp, 2 dc in each of next 2 dc] 8 times, ch 5**, 2 dc in each of next 2 sl sts, rep from * around, ending last rep at **, join with sl st in 3rd ch of beg ch-3.

**Rnd 22:** Ch 3, dc in each of next 3 dc, ch 5, [dc in each of next 4 dc, ch 5] around, join with sl st in 3rd ch of beg ch-3.

**Rnds 23–27:** Rep rnd 22.

**Rnd 28:** Ch 5, dc in each of next 3 dc, *ch 5, **dc dec** *(see Stitch Guide)* in next 4 dc**, [ch 5, dc in each of next 4 dc] twice, rep from * around, ending last rep at **, ch 5, dc in each of next 4 dc, ch 5, join with sl st in 3rd ch of beg ch-3.

### POINT FINISHING

**Row 29 (RS):** Ch 3, dc in each of next 3 dc, sl st in ch-5 sp, ch 5, sl st in next ch-5 sp, dc in each of next 4 dc, turn.

**Row 30:** Ch 3, dc in each of next 3 dc, sl st in next ch-5 sp, dc in each of next 4 dc, turn.

**Rows 31 & 32:** Ch 3, dc in each of next 7 dc, turn.

**Row 33 (RS):** Ch 2, holding last lp of each dc on hook, dc in each of next 2 dc, sk next 2 dc, dc in each of next 3 dc, yo, pull through all lps on hook, ch 1 to lock. Fasten off.

With RS facing and Finished Point to the right, join with sl st in first dc of next 4-dc group, rep rows 29–33. Rep around; at the end of last rep, **do not fasten off.**

### TRIM

**Rnd 34 (RS):** *Ch 7, (dtr, sl st) in top of cl, ch 7, dtr in top of same cl, sk side edge of cl, 3 sc in next row, ch 7, dtr in same row, sk next row, [3 sc in end next row] twice, 5 sc over ch-5 sp, [3 sc in end next row] twice, [ch 7, dtr in end of same row, sk next row**, 3 sc in next row] twice, rep from * around, ending last rep at **, join with sl st in top of beg cl. Fasten off.

### INNER RUFFLE

**Rnd 1 (RS):** Join white with sl st in any ch-5 sp of rnd 20, ch 1, 7 hdc in same ch sp, ch 5, sl st in next ch-5 sp, ch 5, [7 hdc in next ch-5 sp, ch 5, sl st in next ch-5 sp, ch 5] around, join with sl st in top of beg hdc.

**Rnd 2:** Ch 3, dc in same st, *ch 3, 2 dc in next hdc, [ch 3, 2 tr in next hdc] 3 times, [ch 2, 2 dc in next hdc] twice, sl st in next ch-5 sp, ch 7, sl st in next ch-5 sp**, 2 dc in next hdc, rep from * around, ending last rep at **, join with sl st in 3rd ch of beg ch-3, sl st in next ch-3 sp.

**Rnd 3:** *[Ch 7, dtr in same ch-3 sp, sl st in next ch-3 sp] 5 times, sl st in ch-7 sp, sl st in next ch-3 sp, rep from * around, ending with last sl st in first ch-3 sp. Fasten off.

Starch lightly and press. ■

# Exotic Beauty

DESIGN BY LUCILLE LAFLAMME

The beauty of floral motifs and the ageless charm of the pineapple stitch come together in a timeless pattern that showcases a tradition of gracious hospitality in its cheerful and inviting design.

RMEDIATE

**FINISHED SIZE**
14 x 18 inches

**MATERIALS**
Size 10 crochet cotton:
180 yds white
115 yds peach
40 yds green
Size 7/1.65mm steel crochet hook or size needed to obtain gauge

**GAUGE**
Motif = 2 inches across

**SPECIAL STITCHES**
**Beginning popcorn (beg pc):** Ch 3 *(counts as first dc)*, 4 dc in ring, drop lp from hook, insert hook in top of ch-3, pull dropped lp through.

**Popcorn (pc):** 5 dc in ring, drop lp from hook, insert hook in first dc of group, pull dropped lp through st.

**Joining:** Ch 2, sl st in corresponding picot of adjacent Motif, ch 2, sl st in top of last st made on this Motif.

**Picot:** Ch 4, sl st in top of last st made.

**Shell:** (2 dc, ch 3, 2 dc) in center ch of next ch sp.

**Cluster (cl):** Holding last lp of each st on hook, 3 tr in next ch sp, yo, pull through all lps on hook.

## INSTRUCTIONS

**CENTER**
For **first row,** work First Motif, work Next Motif 4 times for total of 5 Motifs in first row.

For **2nd row,** work Next Motif onto top of First Motif and Next Motif made on first row, work Next Motif 3 times for total of 4 Motifs in 2nd row.

For **3rd row**, work Next Motif onto bottom of First Motif and Next Motif made on first row, work Next Motif 3 times for total of 4 Motifs in 3rd row.

**FIRST MOTIF**
**Rnd 1:** With peach, ch 6, sl st in first ch to form ring, **beg pc** *(see Special Stitches)*, ch 4, ****pc** *(see Special Stitches)*, ch 4, rep from * twice, join with sl st in top of beg pc. *(4 pc, 4 ch sps)*

**Rnd 2:** Ch 1, sc in first st, ch 4, sc in next ch sp, ch 4, [sc in next st, ch 4, sc in next ch sp, ch 4] around, join with sl st in beg sc. *(8 ch sps)*

**Rnd 3:** (Sl st, ch 3, 3 dc) in first ch sp, **picot** *(see Special Stitches)*, 4 dc in same ch sp, (4 dc, picot, 4 dc) in each ch sp around, join with sl st in 3rd ch of beg ch-3. Fasten off.

**NEXT MOTIF**
**Rnd 1:** With peach, ch 6, sl st in first ch to form ring, beg pc, ch 4, [pc in ring, ch 4] 3 times, join with sl st in top of beg pc. *(4 pc, 4 ch sps)*

**Rnd 2:** Ch 1, sc in first st, ch 4, sc in next ch sp, ch 4, [sc in next st, ch 4, sc in next ch sp, ch 4] around, join with sl st in beg sc. *(8 ch sps)*

**Rnd 3:** (Sl st, ch 3, 3 dc) in first ch sp, work **joining** *(see Special Stitches, see black lines on Assembly Diagram)*, 4 dc in same ch sp on this Motif, [4 dc, work joining, 4 dc] number of times needed to join Motif or Motifs tog, to complete the rnd, (4 dc, picot, 4 dc) in each ch sp around, join with sl st in 3rd ch of beg ch-3. Fasten off.

**BORDER**
**Rnd 1:** Working around outer edge, join white with sl st in picot on last Motif made on first row *(see Assembly Diagram)*, ch 13 *(counts as tr and ch-9)*, *tr in next picot, [ch 7, sc in next picot] 3 times, [ch 9, sc in next picot, ch 7, sc in next picot] 3 times, ch 7, sc in next picot, ch 7, tr in next picot, ch 9, tr in next picot, [ch 7, sc in next picot] twice, ch 7*, tr in next picot, ch 9, rep between *, join with sl st in 4th ch of beg ch-13. *(32 ch sps)*

**Rnd 2:** Ch 3, dc in each st and in each ch around, join with sl st in 3rd ch of beg ch-3. Fasten off. *(276 dc)*

**Rnd 3:** Join green with sc in first st, ch 7, sk next 5 sts, [sc in next st, ch 7, sk next 5 sts] around, join with sl st in beg sc. *(46 ch sps)*

**Rnd 4:** Sl st in each of first 4 chs of first ch sp, (ch 3, dc, ch 3, 2 dc) in same ch, [ch 3, **shell** *(see Special Stitches)* in center ch of next ch sp] 4 times, shell in center ch of each of next 10 ch sps, [ch 3, shell in center ch of next ch sp] 13 times, shell in center ch of each of next 10 ch sps, [ch 3, shell in center ch of next ch sp] 8 times, ch 3, join with sl st in 3rd ch of beg ch-3. Fasten off. *(46 shells, 26 ch-3 sps)*

**Rnd 5:** Working in ch sps of shells and in ch-3 sps, join white with sc in ch sp of 4th shell, ch 5, [sc in next ch

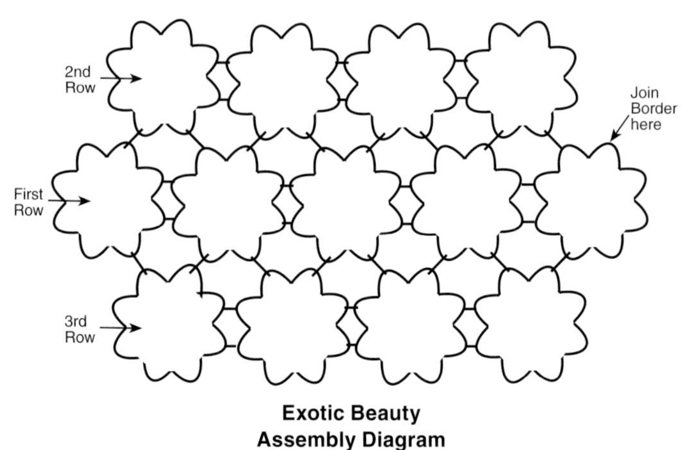


**Exotic Beauty Assembly Diagram**

sp, ch 5] around, join with sl st in beg sc. *(72 ch sps)*

**Rnd 6:** Sl st in each of first 3 chs of first ch sp, ch 1, sc in same ch sp, ch 5, [sc in next ch sp, ch 5] around, join with sl st in beg sc.

**Rnd 7:** Sl st in each of first 3 chs of first ch sp, ch 3, 8 dc in same ch sp, [ch 2, sc in next ch sp, ch 5, sc in next ch sp, ch 2, 9 dc in next ch sp] 4 times, *ch 2, sc in next ch sp, [ch 5, sc in next ch sp] twice, ch 2, 9 dc in next ch sp*, rep between * 5 times, (ch 2, sc in next ch sp, ch 5, sc in next ch sp, ch 2, 9 dc in next ch sp] 4 times, rep between * 5 times, ch 2, sc in next ch sp, [ch 5, sc in next ch sp] twice, ch 2, join with sl st in 3rd ch of beg ch-3. *(180 dc, 72 ch sps)*

**Rnd 8:** Ch 4 *(counts as dc and ch-1)*, dc in next dc, [ch 1, dc in next dc] 7 times, *ch 2, sk next ch sp, sc in next ch sp, ch 2, sk next ch sp, dc in first dc of next dc group, [ch 1, dc in next dc] 8 times*, rep between * 3 times, **ch 2, sk next ch sp, sc in next ch sp, ch 5, sc in next ch sp, ch 2, sk next ch sp, dc in first dc of next dc group, [ch 1, dc in next dc] 8 times**, rep between ** 5 times, rep between * 4 times, rep between ** 5 times, ch 2, sk next ch sp, sc in next ch sp, ch 5, sc in next ch sp, ch 2, sk last ch sp, join with sl st in 3rd ch of beg ch-4.

**Rnd 9:** Ch 1, sc in first ch sp, [ch 5, sc in next ch sp] 7 times, *ch 3, sk next 2 ch sps, sc in next ch sp, [ch 5, sc in next ch sp] 7 times*, rep between * 3 times, **ch 3, sk next ch sp, sc in next ch sp, ch 3, sk next ch sp, sc in next ch sp, [ch 5, sc in next ch sp] 7 times**, rep between ** 5 times, rep between * 4 times, rep between ** 5 times, ch 3, sk next ch sp, sc in next ch sp, ch 3, sk last ch sp, join with sl st in beg sc.

**Rnd 10:** Ch 1, sc in first ch sp, [ch 5, sc in next ch sp] 6 times, *ch 3, sk next ch sp, sc in next ch sp, [ch 5, sc in next ch sp] 6 times*, rep between * 3 times, **ch 5, sk next 2 ch sps, sc in next ch sp, [ch 5, sc in next ch sp] 6 times**, rep between ** 5 times, rep between * 4 times, rep between ** 5 times, ch 5, sk last 2 ch sps, join with sl st in beg sc.

**Rnd 11:** Ch 1, sc in first ch sp, [ch 5, sc in next ch sp] 5 times, *ch 3, sk next ch sp, sc in next ch sp, [ch 5, sc in next ch sp] 5 times*, rep between * 3 times, **ch 5, sk next ch sp, sc in next ch sp, [ch 5, sc in next ch sp] 5 times**, rep between ** 5 times, rep between * 4 times, rep between ** 5 times, ch 5, sk last ch sp, join with sl st in beg sc.

**Rnd 12:** Ch 1, sc in first ch sp, [ch 5, sc in next ch sp] 4 times, *ch 4, sk next ch sp, sc in next ch sp, [ch 5, sc in next ch sp] 4 times*, rep between * 3 times, **ch 7, sk next ch sp, sc in next ch sp, [ch 5, sc in next ch sp] 4 times**, rep between ** 5 times, rep between * 4 times, rep between ** 5 times, ch 7, sk last ch sp, join with sl st in beg sc.

**Rnd 13:** Ch 1, sc in first ch sp, [ch 5, sc in next ch sp] 3 times, *ch 6, sk next ch sp, sc in next ch sp, [ch 5, sc in next ch sp] 3 times*, rep between * 3 times, **ch 9, sk next ch sp, sc in next ch sp, [ch 5, sc in next ch sp] 3 times**, rep between ** 5 times, rep between * 4 times, rep between ** 5 times, ch 9, sk last ch sp, join with sl st in beg sc.

**Rnd 14:** Ch 1, sc in first ch sp, [ch 5, sc in next ch sp] twice, *ch 9, sk next ch sp, sc in next ch sp, [ch 5, sc in next ch sp] twice*, rep between * 3 times, **ch 14, sk next ch sp, sc in next ch sp, [ch 5, sc in next ch sp] twice**, rep between ** 5 times, rep between * 4 times, rep between ** 5 times, ch 14, sk last ch sp, join with sl st in beg sc.

**Rnd 15:** Ch 1, sc in first ch sp, [ch 9, sc in next ch sp, ch 12, sk next ch sp, sc in next ch sp] 4 times, [ch 9, sc in next ch sp, ch 17, sk next ch sp, sc in next ch sp] 6 times, [ch 9, sc in next ch sp, ch 12, sk next ch sp, sc in next ch sp] 4 times, [ch 9, sc in next ch sp, ch 17, sk next ch sp, sc in next ch sp] 5 times, ch 9, sc in next ch sp, ch 17, sk last ch sp, join with sl st in beg sc. Fasten off.

**Rnd 16:** Join green with sl st in 6th ch of beg ch-12 sp, ch 3, dc in same ch, ch 4, 2 dc in next ch, [ch 8, sc in next ch sp, ch 8, 2 dc in 6th ch of next ch-12 sp, ch 4, 2 dc in next ch of same ch sp] 3 times, ch 8, sc in next ch sp, *ch 6, (2 dc, ch 4, 2 dc) in 6th ch of next ch-17 sp, ch 3, sk next 5 chs, (2 dc, ch 4, 2 dc) in next ch, ch 6, sc in next ch sp*, rep between * 5 times, [ch 8, 2 dc in 6th ch of next ch-12 sp, ch 4, 2 dc in next ch, ch 8, sc in next ch sp] 4 times, rep between * 6 times, ch 8, join with sl st in 3rd ch of beg ch-3. Fasten off.

**Rnd 17:** Join peach with sl st in first ch-4 sp, ch 4, *yo twice, insert hook in same ch sp, yo, pull through, [yo, pull through 2 lps on hook] twice, rep from *, yo, pull through all lps on hook *(beg cl)*, (ch 3, **cl**—*see Special Stitches*—in same ch sp) twice, **ch 7, sk next ch sp, sc in next sc, ch 7, sk next ch sp, ({cl, ch 3} twice, cl) in next ch sp**, rep between ** twice, ch 7, sk next ch sp, sc in next sc, ◊ch 5, sk next ch sp, ({cl, ch 3} twice, cl) in next ch sp, ch 4, sc in next ch sp, ch 4, ({cl, ch 3} twice, cl) in next ch sp, ch 5, sk next ch sp, sc in next sc◊, rep between ◊ 5 times, ch 5, sk next ch sp, ({cl, ch 3} twice, cl) in next ch sp, rep between ** 3 times, ch 7, sk next ch sp, sc in next sc, rep between ◊ 6 times, ch 5, sk last ch sp, join with sl st in top of beg cl. Fasten off.

**Rnd 18:** Join white with sc in first cl, picot, 3 sc in each ch-3 sp, 7 sc in each ch-7 sp, 4 sc in each ch-4 sp, 5 sc in each ch-5 sp and (sc, picot) in each cl around, join with sl st in beg sc. Fasten off. ■

# Blue Velvet

DESIGN BY JOSIE RABIER

This classy doily speaks of cordial warmth and generous living. Worked in true blue or a striking variation, this time-honored pineapple design melds tradition with a bold look that's all new.

INTERMEDIATE

**FINISHED SIZE**
34 inches in diameter

**MATERIALS**
South Maid size 10 crochet cotton (350 yds per ball):
3 balls #482 true blue
Size 7/1.65mm steel crochet hook or size needed to obtain gauge

**GAUGE**
Rnds 1–4 = 3⅛ inches in diameter

**SPECIAL STITCHES**
**Double shell:** ({3 dc, ch 3} twice, 3 dc) in indicated ch sp.

**Shell:** (3 dc, ch 3, 3 dc) in indicated ch sp.

## INSTRUCTIONS

**DOILY**

**Rnd 1:** Ch 10, sl st in first ch to form ring, ch 3 *(counts as first dc)*, 31 dc in ring, join with sl st in 3rd ch of beg ch-3. *(32 dc)*

**Rnd 2:** Ch 3, dc in each dc around, join with sl st in 3rd ch of beg ch-3. *(32 dc)*

**Rnd 3:** Ch 3, dc in same st, 2 dc in each dc around, join with sl st in 3rd ch of beg ch-3. *(64 dc)*

**Rnd 4:** Rep rnd 2.

**Rnd 5:** Ch 3, dc in next dc, ch 5, *sk next 2 dc, dc in each of next 2 dc, ch 5, rep from * around, join with sl st in 3rd ch of beg ch-3. *(16 ch-5 sps)*

**Rnd 6:** Ch 3, dc in same st, *ch 5, 2 dc in next dc, sl st in next ch-5 sp**, 2 dc in next dc, rep from * around, ending last rep at **, join with sl st in 3rd ch of beg ch-3.

**Rnd 7:** Sl st in next dc and in ch-5 sp, ch 4 *(counts as first tr)*, 8 tr in same sp, sl st in next sl st, *9 tr in next ch-5 sp, sl st in next sl st, rep from * around, join with sl st in 4th ch of beg ch-4. *(16 groups of 9 tr each)*

**Rnd 8:** Sl st across to 5th tr of 9-tr group, *ch 7, sk next 2 tr, dc in next tr, dc in 2nd tr of next tr group, ch 7, sk next 2 tr**, sl st in next tr, rep from * around, ending last rep at **, join with sl st at base of beg ch-7.

**Rnd 9:** Sl st to 4th ch of ch-7 sp, ch 7, *sl st in 4th ch of next ch-7 sp, ch 7, rep from * around, join with sl st at base of beg ch-7. *(32 ch-7 sps)*

**Rnd 10:** Sl st in ch-7 sp, ch 4, 15 tr in same sp, *sl st in 4th ch of next ch-7 sp, [ch 7, sl st in 4th ch of next ch-7 sp] twice**, 16 tr in next ch-7 sp, rep from * around, ending last rep at **, join with sl st in 4th ch of beg ch-4.

**Rnd 11:** Ch 4, tr in same st, 2 tr in each of next 15 tr, *sl st in 4th ch of next ch-7 sp, ch 7, sl st in 4th ch of next ch-7 sp**, 2 tr in each of next 16 tr, rep from * around, ending last rep at **, join with sl st in 4th ch of beg ch-4.

**Rnd 12:** Ch 3, dc in next tr, *[ch 1, dc in each of next 2 tr] 15 times, sl st in 4th ch of next ch-7 sp**, dc in each of next 2 tr, rep from * around, ending last rep at **, join with sl st in 3rd ch of beg ch-3. *(8 groups of 32 dc)*

**Rnd 13:** Sl st in next dc and in next ch-1 sp, ch 3, dc in same ch sp, *[ch 1, 2 dc in next ch-1 sp] 14 times**, 2 dc in first ch-1 sp of next 32-dc group, rep from * around, ending last rep at **, join with sl st in 3rd ch of beg ch-3. *(8 groups of 30 dc)*

**Rnd 14:** Sl st in next dc and in next ch-1 sp, ch 3, dc in same ch sp, *[ch 1, 2 dc in next ch-1 sp] 13 times**, 2 dc in first ch-1 sp of next 30-dc group, rep from * around, ending last rep at **, join with sl st in 3rd ch of beg ch-3. *(8 groups of 28 dc)*

**Rnd 15:** Sl st in next dc and in next ch-1 sp, ch 3, dc in same ch sp, *[ch 1, 2 dc in next ch-1 sp] 12 times**, 2 dc in first ch-1 sp of next 28-dc group, rep from * around, ending last rep at **, join with sl st in 3rd ch of beg-ch 3. *(8 groups of 26 dc)*

**Rnd 16:** Sl st in next dc and next ch-1 sp, ch 3, dc in same ch sp, *[ch 1, 2 dc in next ch-1 sp] 11 times, ch 5**, 2 dc in first ch 1 sp of next 26-dc group, rep from * around, ending last rep at **, join with sl st in 3rd ch of beg ch-3. *(8 groups of 24 dc)*

**Rnd 17:** Sl st in next dc and in next ch-1 sp, ch 3, dc in same ch sp, *[ch 1, 2 dc in next ch-1 sp] 10 times, ch 5, sl st in 3rd ch of next ch-5 sp, ch 5**, 2 dc in first ch-1 sp of next 24-dc group, rep from * around, ending last rep at **, join with sl st in 3rd ch of beg ch-3. *(8 groups of 22 dc)*

**Rnd 18:** Sl st in next dc and next ch-1 sp, ch 3, dc in same ch sp, *[ch 1, 2 dc in next ch-1 sp] 9 times, [ch 5, sl st in 3rd ch of next ch-5 sp] twice, ch 5**, 2 dc in first ch-1 sp of next 22-dc group, rep from * around, ending last rep at **, join with sl st in 3rd ch of beg ch-3. *(8 groups of 20 dc)*

**Rnd 19:** Sl st in next dc and in next ch-1 sp, ch 3, dc in same ch sp, *[ch 1, 2 dc in next ch-1 sp] 8 times, ch 3, sl st in 3rd ch of next ch-5 sp, **double shell** *(see Special Stitches)* in next ch-5 sp, sl st in 3rd ch of next ch-5 sp, ch 3**, 2 dc in first ch-1 sp of next 20-dc group, rep from * around, ending last rep at **, join with sl st in 3rd ch of beg ch-3. *(8 groups of 18 dc)*

**Rnd 20:** Sl st in next dc and in next ch-1 sp, ch 3, dc in same ch sp, *[ch 1, 2 dc in next ch-1 sp] 7 times, ch 5, sk next ch-3 sp, **shell** *(see Special Stitches)* in next ch-3 sp, ch 5, shell in next ch-3 sp, ch 5**, 2 dc in first ch-1 sp of next 18-dc group, rep from * around, ending last rep at **, join with sl st in 3rd ch of beg ch-3. *(8 groups of 16 dc)*

**Rnd 21:** Sl st in next dc and in next ch-1 sp, ch 3, dc in same ch sp, *[ch 1, 2 dc in next ch-1 sp] 6 times, ch 5, shell in ch sp of next shell, ch 5, sl st in 3rd ch of next ch-5 sp, ch 5, shell in ch sp of next shell, ch 5**, 2 dc in first ch-1 sp of next 16-dc group, rep from * around, ending last rep at **, join with sl st in 3rd ch of beg ch-3. *(8 groups of 14 dc)*

**Rnd 22:** Sl st in next dc and in next ch-1 sp, ch 3, dc in same sp, *[ch 1, 2 dc in next ch-1 sp] 5 times, ch 5, shell in next shell, [ch 5, sl st in 3rd ch of next ch-5 sp] twice, ch 5, shell in next shell, ch 5**, 2 dc in first ch-1 sp of next 14-dc group, rep from * around, ending last rep at **, join with sl st in 3rd ch of beg ch-3. *(8 groups of 12 dc)*

**Rnd 23:** Sl st in next dc and in next ch-1 sp, ch 3, dc in same ch sp, *[ch 1, 2 dc in next ch-1 sp] 4 times, ch 5, shell in next shell, ch 3, sl st in 3rd ch of next ch-5 sp, double shell in next ch-5 sp, sl st in 3rd ch of next ch-5 sp, ch 3, shell in next shell, ch 5**, 2 dc in first ch-1 sp of next 12-dc group, rep from * around, ending last rep at **, join with sl st in 3rd ch of beg ch-3. *(8 groups of 10 dc)*

**Rnd 24:** Sl st in next dc and in next ch-1 sp, ch 3, dc in same ch sp, *[ch 1, 2 dc in next ch-1 sp] 3 times, ch 5, shell in next shell, ch 5, sk next ch-3 sp, shell in next ch-3 sp, ch 5, shell in next ch-3 sp, ch 5, shell in next shell, ch 5**, 2 dc in first ch-1 sp of next 10-dc group, rep from * around, ending last rep at **, join with sl st in 3rd ch of beg ch-3. *(8 groups of 8 dc)*

**Rnd 25:** Sl st in next dc and in next ch-1 sp, ch 3, dc in same ch sp, *[ch 1, 2 dc in next ch-1 sp] twice, ch 5, shell in next shell, [ch 5, sl st in 3rd ch of next ch-5 sp, ch 5, shell in next shell] 3 times, ch 5 **, 2 dc in first ch-1 sp of next 8-dc group, rep from * around, ending last rep at **, join with sl st in 3rd ch of beg ch-3. *(8 groups of 6 dc)*

**Rnd 26:** Sl st in next dc and in next ch-1 sp, ch 3, dc in same ch sp, *ch 1, 2 dc in next ch-1 sp, ch 5, shell in next shell, [ch 5, sl st in 3rd ch of next ch-5 sp, ch 7, sl st in 3rd ch of next ch-5 sp, ch 5, shell in next shell] 3 times, ch 5**, 2 dc in first

# Angel Whispers

DESIGN BY JOSIE RABIER

Delicate stitching as intricate as an angel's wing in a soft and unassuming cream make for an heirloom-quality piece sure to grace the homes of future generations.

ERIENCED

**FINISHED SIZE**
18½ inches in diameter

**MATERIALS**
South Maid size 10 crochet cotton (350 yds per ball):
1 ball #430 cream
Size 7/1.65mm steel crochet hook or size needed to obtain gauge

**GAUGE**
Rnds 1–3 = 2 inches in diameter

**SPECIAL STITCHES**
**Beginning shell (beg shell):** Ch 3 *(counts as first dc)*, (2 dc, ch 3, 3 dc) in same st or ch sp.

**Shell:** (3 dc, ch 3, 3 dc) in indicated st or ch sp.

**Beginning double shell (beg double shell):** Ch 3 *(counts as first dc)*, (2 dc, {ch 3, 3 dc} twice) in same st or ch sp.

**Double shell:** ({3 dc, ch 3} twice, 3 dc) in indicated st or ch sp.

## INSTRUCTIONS

**DOILY**

**Rnd 1 (RS):** Ch 6, sl st in first ch to form ring, ch 1, 16 hdc in ring, join with sl st in beg hdc. *(16 hdc)*

**Rnd 2:** Ch 3 *(counts as first dc)*, dc in same st, 2 dc in each hdc around, join with sl st in 3rd ch of beg ch-3. *(32 dc)*

**Rnd 3:** Ch 3, [2 dc in next dc, dc in next dc] around, join with sl st in 3rd ch of beg ch-3. *(48 dc)*

**Rnd 4:** Ch 3, dc in each dc around, join with sl st in 3rd ch of beg ch-3.

**Rnd 5:** [Ch 11, sl st in same st, ch 7, 3 dtr in same st, sk next 3 dc, sl st in next dc] around, join with sl st in base of beg ch-11.

**Rnd 6:** Sl st to 5th ch of ch-11, ch 4 *(counts as first tr)*, 10 tr in same sp, 11 tr in each ch-11 sp around, join with sl st in 4th ch of beg ch-4. *(12 groups of 11 tr)*

**Rnd 7:** *Ch 7, 3 dtr in same st, sk next 4 tr, (sl st, ch 11, sl st) in next tr, ch 7, 3 dtr in same tr, sk next 4 tr, sl st in next tr, ch 13, sl st in next tr, rep from * around, join with sl st in base of beg ch-7. Fasten off. *(12 ch-11 sps, 12 ch-13 sps)*

**Rnd 8:** With RS facing, join with sl st in any ch-11 sp, **beg shell** *(see Special Stitches)* in same ch sp, *(5 tr, ch 3, 5 tr) in next ch-13 sp**, **shell** *(see Special Stitches)* in next ch-11 sp, rep from * around, ending last rep at **, join with sl st in 3rd ch of beg ch-3.

**Rnd 9:** Sl st to ch-3 sp, **beg double shell** *(see Special Stitches)* in same ch sp, *tr in next tr, sk next 3 tr, tr in next tr, ch 5, (sl st, ch 9, sl st) in 2nd ch of next ch-3, ch 5, tr in next tr, sk next 3 tr, tr in next tr**, **double shell** *(see Special Stitches)* in ch-3 sp of next shell, rep from * around, ending last rep at **, join with sl st in 3rd ch of beg ch-3.

**Rnd 10:** Sl st to ch-3 sp, beg shell in same ch sp, shell in next ch-3 sp, *tr in 3rd ch of next ch-5 sp, 9 tr in next ch-9 sp, tr in 3rd ch of next ch-5 sp**, shell in each of next 2 ch-3 sps, rep from * around, ending last rep at **, join with sl st in 3rd ch of beg ch-3. *(12 pineapple bases)*

**Rnd 11:** Sl st to ch-3 sp of shell, beg shell in same ch sp, shell in ch-3 sp of next shell, *2 dc in next tr, [ch 1, sk next tr, 2 dc in next tr] 5 times**, [shell in ch-3 sp of next shell] twice, rep from * around, ending last rep at **, join with sl st in 3rd ch of beg ch-3.

**Rnd 12:** Sl st to ch-3 sp, beg shell in same ch sp, *ch 5, shell in next shell, 2 dc in next ch-1 sp, [ch 1, 2 dc in next ch-1 sp] 4 times, shell in next shell, rep from * around, join with sl st in 3rd ch of beg ch-3.

**Rnd 13:** Sl st to ch-3 sp, beg shell in same ch sp, *ch 3, sl st in 3rd ch of next ch-5 sp, ch 3, shell in next shell, 2 dc in next ch-1 sp, [ch 1, 2 dc in next ch-1 sp] 3 times**, shell in next shell, rep from * around, ending last rep at **, join with sl st in 3rd ch of beg ch-3.

**Rnd 14:** Sl st to ch-3 sp, beg shell in same ch sp, *ch 5, sl st in sl st between ch-3 sps, ch 5, shell in next shell, 2 dc in next ch-1 sp, [ch 1, 2 dc in next ch-1 sp] twice**, shell in next shell, rep from * around, ending last rep at **, join in 3rd ch of beg ch-3.

**Rnd 15:** Sl st to ch-3 sp, beg shell in same ch sp, *ch 7, sl st in sl st between ch-5 sps, ch 7, shell in next shell, 2 dc in next ch-1 sp, ch 1, 2 dc in next ch-1 sp**, shell in next shell, rep from * around, ending last rep at **, join with sl st in 3rd ch of beg ch-3.

**Rnd 16:** Sl st to ch-3 sp, beg shell in same ch sp, *ch 9, sl st in sl st between ch-7 sps, ch 9, shell in next shell, 2 dc in next ch-1 sp**, shell in next shell, rep from * around, ending last rep at **, join with sl st in 3rd ch of beg ch-3.

**Rnd 17:** Sl st to ch-3 sp, *ch 3, sk next 2 dc of same shell, 3 dc in next dc, ch 7, sl st in sl st between ch-9 sps, ch 7, 3 dc in first dc of next shell, ch 3, [shell in next shell] twice, rep from * around, join with sl st in 3rd ch of beg ch-3.

**COMPLETING FIRST SECTION**

**Row 18:** Sl st to 2nd ch of ch-3 sp, ch 4, shell in next shell, sk next 2 dc, 3 dc in next dc, ch 5, (sl st, ch 9, sl st) in sl st between ch-7 sps, ch 5, 3 dc in next dc, shell in next ch-3 sp, tr in 2nd ch of next ch-3 sp, ch 4, turn.

**Row 19:** Shell in shell, ch 3, sk next 5 dc, sl st in next dc, 9 tr in next ch-9 sp, sl st in next dc, ch 3, shell in next shell, tr in 4th ch of beg ch-4, ch 4, turn.

**Row 20:** Shell in shell, ch 3, sl st in next tr, ch 7, 3 dtr in same st, sk next 3 tr, (sl st, ch 9, sl st) in next tr, ch 7, 3 tr in same st, sk next 3 tr, sl st in next tr, ch 3, shell in next shell, tr in 4th ch of beg ch-4. Fasten off.

**COMPLETING REMAINING SECTIONS**

With RS facing, join with sl st in 2nd ch of ch-3 sp of next shell to left of last completed Section, rep rows 18–20 around for total of 12 Sections. ■

# Passionate Plum

DESIGN BY AGNES RUSSELL

This twirling pinwheel of purple pineapples is not just easy on the eyes—it's also easy to make! Rich texture and color work together to make it an eye-catching focal point for any room.

**FINISHED SIZE**
16 inches in diameter

**MATERIALS**
Size 10 crochet cotton:
300 yds bright violet
Size 8/1.50mm steel crochet hook or size needed to obtain gauge
Spray starch

**GAUGE**
8 dc = 1 inch; 3 shell rnds = 1 inch

**SPECIAL STITCHES**
**Shell:** (2 dc, ch 2, 2 dc) in indicated st or ch sp.

**Beginning shell (beg shell):** Ch 3 *(counts as first dc),* (dc, ch 2, 2 dc) in same sp as beg ch-3.

**PATTERN NOTE**
If pattern indicates shell at the beginning of round, slip stitch to next chain space and work beginning shell for first shell of the round.

## INSTRUCTIONS

**DOILY**

**Rnd 1 (RS):** Ch 5, sl st in first ch to form ring, ch 1, 12 sc in ring, join with sl st in beg sc. *(12 sc)*

**Rnd 2:** Ch 1, sc in first sc, ch 3, [sc in next sc, ch 3] around, join with sl st in beg sc. *(12 ch-3 sps)*

**Rnd 3:** Sl st in ch-3 sp, ch 1, sc in same ch sp, ch 4, [sc in next ch-3 sp, ch 4] around, join with sl st in beg sc.

**Rnd 4:** Ch 3 *(counts as first dc),* 3 dc in next ch-4 sp, ch 4, [dc in next sc, 3 dc in next ch-4 sp, ch 4] around, join with sl st in 3rd ch of beg ch-3. *(12 groups of 4 dc)*

**Rnd 5:** Sl st in next dc, ch 3, dc in each dc across dc group, 2 dc in next ch-4 sp, ch 4, [sk next dc, dc in each dc across next dc group, 2 dc in ch-4 sp, ch 4] around, join with sl st in 3rd ch of beg ch-3. *(12 groups of 5 dc)*

**Rnds 6–10:** Rep rnd 5. *(12 groups of 10 dc between each ch-4 sp at end of last rnd)*

**Rnd 11:** Sl st in next dc, ch 3, dc in each dc across dc group to last dc, 2 dc in last dc, 2 dc in next ch-4 sp, ch 4, [sk next dc, dc in each dc across dc group to last dc, 2 dc in last dc, 2 dc in next ch-4 sp, ch 4] around, join with sl st in 3rd ch of beg ch-3. *(12 groups of 12 dc between ch-4 sps)*

**Rnd 12:** Rep rnd 5. *(12 groups of 13 dc between ch-4 sps)*

**Rnd 13:** Rep rnd 11. *(12 groups of 15 dc between ch-4 sps)*

**Rnd 14:** Rep rnd 5. *(12 groups of 16 dc between ch-4 sps)*

**Rnd 15:** Rep rnd 11. *(12 groups of 18 dc between ch-4 sps)*

**Rnd 16:** Sl st in next dc, ch 2, dc in next dc *(counts as beg dc dec),* dc in each of next 13 dc, **dc dec** *(see Stitch Guide)* in next 2 dc, ch 4, (dc, ch 3, dc) in next ch-4 sp, ch 4, *sk next dc, dc dec in next 2 dc, dc in each of next 13 dc, dc dec in next 2 dc, ch 4, (dc, ch 3, dc) in next ch-4 sp, ch 4, rep from * around, join with sl st in top of beg dc dec.

**Rnd 17:** Sl st in next dc, ch 2, dc in next dc, dc in each of next 10 dc, dc dec in next 2 dc, ch 4, ({dc, ch 1} 5 times, dc) in next ch-3 sp, ch 4, *sk next dc, dc dec in next 2 dc, dc in each of next 10 dc, dc dec in next 2 dc, ch 4, ({dc, ch 1} 5 times, dc) in next ch-3 sp, ch 4, rep from * around, join with sl st in top of beg dc dec. *(12 pineapple bases)*

**Rnd 18:** Sl st in next dc, ch 2, dc in next dc, dc in each of next 7 dc, dc dec in next 2 dc, ch 4, dc in next dc, [dc in next ch-1 sp, dc in next dc] 5 times, ch 4, *sk next dc, dc dec in next 2 dc, dc in each of next 7 dc, dc dec in next 2 dc, ch 4, dc in next dc, [dc in next ch-1 sp, dc in next dc] 5 times, ch 4, rep

from * around, join with sl st in top of beg dc dec.

**Rnd 19:** Sl st in next dc, ch 2, dc in next dc, dc in each of next 4 dc, dc dec in next 2 dc, ch 4, sc in first dc of next 11-dc group, [ch 3, sc in next dc] 10 times, ch 4, *sk next dc, dc dec in next 2 dc, dc in each of next 4 dc, dc dec in next 2 dc, ch 4, sc in first dc of next 11-dc group, [ch 3, sc in next dc] 10 times, ch 4, rep from * around, join with sl st in top of beg dc dec.

**Rnd 20:** Sl st in next dc, ch 2, dc in next dc, dc dec in next 2 dc, ch 4, sc in next ch-3 sp, [ch 3, sc in next ch-3 sp] 9 times, ch 4, *sk next dc, dc dec in next 2 dc, dc in next dc, dc dec in next 2 dc, ch 4, sc in next ch-3 sp, [ch 3, sc in next ch-3 sp] 9 times, ch 4, rep from * around, join with sl st in top of beg dc dec.

**Rnd 21:** Sl st in next dc, ch 3, (dc, ch 2, dc) in same st as beg ch-3, (dc, ch 2, 2 dc) in next dc, ch 4, sc in next ch-3 sp, [ch 3, sc in next ch-3 sp] 8 times, ch 4, *sk next dc, (2 dc, ch 2, dc) in next dc, (dc, ch 2, 2 dc) in next dc, ch 4, sc in next ch-3 sp, [ch 3, sc in next ch-3 sp] 8 times, ch 4, rep from * around, join with sl st in 3rd ch of beg ch-3.

**COMPLETE PINEAPPLE**

**Row 22 (RS): Beg shell** *(see Special Stitches)* in next ch-2 sp, ch 4, sc in next ch-3 sp, [ch 3, sc in next ch-3 sp] 7 times, ch 4, **shell** *(see Special Stitches)* in next ch-2 sp, leaving rem sts unworked, turn.

**Row 23 (WS):** Shell in shell, ch 4, sc in next ch-3 sp, [ch 3, sc in next ch-3 sp] 6 times, ch 4, shell in shell, turn.

**Row 24 (RS):** Shell in shell, ch 4, sc in next ch-3 sp, [ch 3, sc in next ch-3 sp] 5 times, ch 4, shell in shell, turn.

**Row 25 (WS):** Shell in shell, ch 4, sc in next ch-3 sp, [ch 3, sc in next ch-3 sp] 4 times, ch 4, shell in shell, turn.

**Row 26 (RS):** Shell in shell, ch 4, sc in next ch-3 sp, [ch 3, sc in next ch-3 sp] 3 times, ch 4, shell in shell, turn.

**Row 27 (WS):** Shell in shell, ch 4, sc in next ch-3 sp, [ch 3, sc in next ch-3 sp] twice, ch 4, shell in shell, turn.

**Row 28 (RS):** Shell in shell, ch 4, sc in next ch-3 sp, ch 3, sc in next ch-3 sp, ch 4, shell in shell, turn.

**Row 29 (WS):** Shell in shell, ch 4, sc in next ch-3 sp, ch 4, shell in shell, turn.

**Row 30 (RS):** Shell in shell, dtr in next sc, shell in shell, fasten off.

*With RS facing and previously finished Pineapple to the right, join with sl st in next ch-2 sp of shell to the left of finished Pineapple, rep rows 22–30, rep from * until all 12 Pineapples are completed.

Starch and press Doily. ■

# Pussy Willows

DESIGN BY JOSIE RABIER

The beauty of the pineapple doily is evident in this popcorn-stitch masterpiece with an edge reminiscent of its namesake. Unique in texture and style, this piece is a wonderful addition to any decor.

ERMEDIATE

**FINISHED SIZE**
24 inches in diameter

**MATERIALS**
Size 10 crochet cotton:
700 yds ecru
Size 9/1.25mm steel crochet hook or size needed to obtain gauge

**GAUGE**
Rnds 1–3 = 2 inches in diameter

**SPECIAL STITCHES**
**Popcorn (pc):** 7 dc in indicated st, drop lp from hook, insert hook in first dc of dc group, pull dropped lp through.

**Reverse popcorn (reverse pc):** 7 dc in indicated st, drop lp from hook, insert hook from back to front through first dc of dc group, pull dropped lp through.

## INSTRUCTIONS

**DOILY**

**Rnd 1 (RS):** Ch 10, sl st in first ch to form a ring, ch 3 *(counts as first dc)*, 23 dc in ring, join with sl st in 3rd ch of beg ch-3. *(24 dc)*

**Rnd 2:** [Ch 5, sk next 2 dc, sl st in next dc] around, join with sl st in base of beg ch-5. *(8 ch-5 sps)*

**Rnd 3:** Sl st in ch-5 sp, ch 3, 5 dc in same ch sp, 6 dc in each ch-5 sp around, join with sl st in 3rd ch of beg ch-3. *(48 dc)*

**Rnd 4:** [Ch 5, sk next 2 dc, sl st in next dc] around, join with sl st in base of beg ch-5. *(16 ch-5 sps)*

**Rnd 5:** Sl st in ch-5 sp, ch 3, 4 dc in same ch sp, 5 dc in each ch-5 sp around, join with sl st in 3rd ch of beg ch-3. *(80 dc)*

**Rnd 6:** Ch 3, *sk next 3 dc, dc in next dc, ch 5**, dc in next dc, rep from * around, ending last rep at **, join with sl st in 3rd ch of beg ch-3. *(16 ch-5 sps)*

**Rnd 7:** Sl st in ch-5 sp, ch 3, 6 dc in same sp, 7 dc in each ch-5 sp around, join with sl st in 3rd ch of beg ch-3. *(112 dc)*

**Rnd 8:** Ch 3, dc in each of next 13 dc, ch 5, [dc in each of next 14 dc, ch 5] around, join with sl st in 3rd ch of beg ch-5. *(8 groups of 14 dc, 8 ch-5 sps)*

**Rnd 9:** Ch 3, dc in each of next 5 dc, *sk next 2 dc, dc in each of next 6 dc, ch 5, sl st in next ch-5 sp, ch 5**, dc in each of next 6 dc, rep from * around, ending last rep at **, join with sl st in 3rd ch of beg ch-3.

**Rnd 10:** Ch 3, dc in each of next 4 dc, *sk next 2 dc, dc in each of next 5 dc, [ch 5, sl st in next ch-5 sp] twice, ch 5**, dc in each of next 5 dc, rep from * around, ending last rep at **, join with sl st in 3rd ch of beg ch-3.

**Rnd 11:** Ch 3, dc in each of next 3 dc, *sk next 2 dc, dc in each of next 4 dc, ch 3, 3 dc in next ch-5 sp, 10 dc in next ch-5 sp, 3 dc in next ch-5 sp, ch 3**, dc in each of next 4 dc, rep from * around, ending last rep at **, join with sl st in 3rd ch of beg ch-3. *(192 dc)*

**Rnd 12:** Ch 3, dc in each of next 2 dc, *sk next 2 dc, dc in each of next 3 dc, ch 3, 3 dc in next dc, dc in each of next 14 dc, 3 dc in next dc, ch 3**, dc in each of next 3 dc, rep from * around, ending last rep at **, join with sl st in 3rd ch of beg ch-3. *(208 dc)*

**Rnd 13:** Ch 3, dc in next dc, *sk next 2 dc, dc in each of next 2 dc, ch 3, dc in each of next 10 dc, ch 5, dc in each of next 10 dc, ch 3**, dc in each of next 2 dc, rep from * around, ending last rep at **, join with sl st in 3rd ch of beg ch-3. *(192 dc)*

**Rnd 14:** Ch 3, *sk next 2 dc, dc in next dc, ch 5, dc in each of next 4 dc, sk next 2 dc, dc in each of next 4 dc, ch 5, sl st in next ch-5 sp, ch 5, dc in each of next 4 dc, sk next 2 dc, dc in each of next 4 dc, ch 5**, dc in next dc, rep from * around, ending last rep at **, join with sl st in 3rd ch of beg ch-3.

**Rnd 15:** Sl st to 3rd ch of ch-5, ch 5, *dc in each of next 3 dc, sk next 2 dc, dc in each of next 3 dc, [ch 5, sl st in next ch-5 sp] twice, ch 5, rep from * around, join with sl st in base of beg ch-5.

**Rnd 16:** Sl st to 3rd ch of ch-5, ch 5, *dc in each of next 2 dc, sk next 2 dc, dc in each of next 2 dc, [ch 5, sl st in next ch-5 sp] 3 times, ch 5, rep from * around, join with sl st in base of beg ch-5.

**Rnd 17:** Sl st to 3rd ch of ch-5, ch 5, *dc in next dc, sk next 2 dc, dc in next dc, [ch 5, sl st in next ch-5 sp] 4 times, ch 5, rep from * around, join with sl st in base of beg ch-5.

**Rnd 18:** Sl st to 3rd ch of ch-5, ch 5, *sl st in next ch-5 sp, ch 5, rep from * around, join with sl st in base of beg ch-5. *(80 ch-5 sps)*

**Rnd 19:** Sl st to 2nd ch of 4th ch-5 sp after joining, ch 3, 3 dc in same sp, 4 dc in each ch-5 sp around, join with sl st in 3rd ch of beg ch-3. *(320 dc)*

**Rnd 20:** Ch 3, dc in each of next 19 dc, ch 5, [dc in each of next 20 dc, ch 5] around, join with sl st in 3rd ch of beg ch-3. *(16 groups of 20 dc)*

**Rnd 21:** Ch 3, dc in each of next 8 dc, *sk next 2 dc, dc in each of next 9 dc, ch 5, sl st in next ch-5 sp, ch 5**, dc in each of next 9 dc, rep from * around, ending last rep at **, join with sl st in 3rd ch of beg ch-3.

**Rnd 22:** Ch 3, dc in each of next 7 dc, *sk next 2 dc, dc in each of next 8 dc, ch 3, sl st in next ch-5 sp, ch 5, sl st in next ch-5 sp, ch 3**, dc in each of next 8 dc, rep from * around, ending last rep at **, join with sl st in 3rd ch of beg ch-3. *(16 groups of 16 dc)*

**Rnd 23:** Ch 3, dc in each of next 6 dc, *sk next 2 dc, dc in each of next 7 dc, ch 3, ({**pc**—*see Special Stitches*, ch 5} twice, pc) in next ch-5 sp, ch 3**, dc in each of next 7 dc, rep from * around, ending last rep at **, join with sl st in 3rd ch of beg ch-3.

**Rnd 24:** Ch 3, dc in each of next 5 dc, *sk next 2 dc, dc in each of next 6 dc, ch 3, (pc, ch 5, pc) in each of next 2 ch-5 sps, ch 3**, dc in each of next 6 dc, rep from * around, ending last rep at **, join with sl st in 3rd ch of beg ch-3. Fasten off. *(16 groups of 12 dc, 16 groups of 4 pcs)*

#### COMPLETE FIRST SECTION

**Row 25:** With RS facing, join with sl st in 2nd ch-5 sp between pc sts, ch 4 *(counts as first tr)*, (pc, ch 5, pc) in same ch sp, ch 3, dc in each of next 5 dc, sk next 2 dc, dc in each of next 5 dc, ch 3, (pc, ch 5, pc) in next ch-5 sp, tr in same ch sp, turn.

**Row 26 (WS):** Ch 4, (**reverse pc**—*see Special Stitches*, ch 5, reverse pc) in first ch-5 sp, ch 3, dc in each of next 4 dc, sk next 2 dc, dc in each of next 4 dc, ch 3, (reverse pc, ch 5, reverse pc) in next ch-5 sp, tr in same ch sp, turn.

**Row 27 (RS):** Ch 4, (pc, ch 5, pc) in first ch-5 sp, ch 3, dc in each of next 3 dc, sk next 2 dc, dc in each of next 3 dc, ch 3, (pc, ch 5, pc) in next ch-5 sp, tr in same ch sp, turn.

**Row 28 (WS):** Ch 4, (reverse pc, ch 5, reverse pc) in first ch-5 sp, ch 3, dc in each of next 2 dc, sk next 2 dc, dc in each of next 2 dc, ch 3, (reverse pc, ch 5, reverse pc) in next ch-5 sp, tr in same ch sp, turn.

**Row 29 (RS):** Ch 4, (pc, ch 5, pc) in first ch-5 sp, ch 3, dc in next dc, sk next 2 dc, dc in next dc, ch 3, (pc, ch 5, pc) in next ch-5 sp, tr in same ch sp, turn.

**Row 30 (WS):** Ch 4, (reverse pc, ch 5, reverse pc) in each of next 2 ch-5 sps, tr in same ch sp as last pc, turn.

**Row 31 (RS):** Ch 4, pc in first ch-5 sp, ch 5, pc in next ch-5 sp, tr in same ch sp, turn.

**Row 32 (WS):** Ch 4, reverse pc in ch-5 sp, ch 4, sl st in last st. Fasten off.

#### COMPLETE NEXT SECTIONS

Rep rows 25–32 around for total of 16 completed Sections.

#### EDGING

Working in ends of rows in turning ch-4 or tr, join with sl st in turning ch-4 of row 25 of any Section, *[ch 4, 2 tr in same sp, sl st in end of next row] 15 times, sl st in turning ch-4 of next Section, rep from * around, join with sl st in base of beg ch-4. Fasten off. ■

# Sunny Pineapples

DESIGN BY DOROTHY MYERS

Stitched in the color of soft, golden sunlight, this exquisite coverlet is sized large enough to fit a twin-size bed and will add the warm, welcoming beauty of pineapples to your guest bedroom.

**FINISHED SIZE**
49 x 81 inches

**MATERIALS**
Medium (worsted) weight yarn:
56 oz/2,800 yds/1,588g yellow
Size G/6/4mm crochet hook or size needed to obtain gauge
Tapestry needle

**GAUGE**
Shell = 1¼ inches across; shell row = 1 inch

**SPECIAL STITCHES**
**Beginning shell (beg shell):** Ch 3 *(counts as first dc)*, (dc, ch 2, 2 dc) in same ch sp.
**Shell:** (2 dc, ch 2, 2 dc) in next ch sp.
**V-stitch (V-st):** (Dc, ch 3, dc) in next st.

## INSTRUCTIONS

**MOTIF**
Make 7.

**Row 1:** Ch 4, (dc, ch 3, 2 dc) in 4th ch from hook, turn. *(4 dc, 1 ch sp)*

**Row 2:** Ch 1, sl st in each of first 2 dc, sl st in first ch sp, ch 3, (dc, ch 2, 2 dc, ch 2, 2 dc) in same ch sp, turn. *(6 dc)*

**Row 3:** Ch 1, sl st in each of first 2 dc, sl st in first ch sp, **beg shell** *(see Special Stitches)*, **shell** *(see Special Stitches)* in last ch sp, turn. *(2 shells)*

**Row 4:** Ch 1, sl st in each of first 2 dc, sl st in first ch sp, beg shell, dc in next sp between shells, shell in last shell, turn. *(2 shells, 1 dc)*

**Row 5:** Ch 1, sl st in each of first 2 dc, sl st in first ch sp, beg shell, ch 1, sk last 2 dc of same shell, **V-st** *(see Special Stitches)* in next dc, ch 1, shell in last shell, turn. *(2 shells, 2 ch-1 sps, 1 V-st)*

**Row 6:** Ch 1, sl st in each of first 2 dc, sl st in first ch sp, beg shell, ch 1, 9 dc in ch sp of next V-st, ch 1, shell in last shell, turn.

**Row 7:** Ch 1, sl st in first 2 dc, sl st in first ch sp, beg shell, ch 1, sk last 2 dc of same shell, dc in next dc, [ch 1, dc in next dc] 8 times, ch 1, shell in last shell, turn.

**Row 8:** Ch 1, sl st in each of first 2 dc, sl st in first ch sp, beg shell, ch 3, sk next ch-1 sp, [sc in next ch-1 sp, ch 3] 8 times, sk next ch-1 sp, shell in last shell, turn. Fasten off. **Do not fasten off** at end of last row on last Motif made.

**AFGHAN**
**Row 1:** Ch 1, sl st in each of first 2 dc, sl st in first ch sp, beg shell, *ch 3, sk next ch-3 sp, [sc in next ch-3 sp, ch 3] 7 times, sk next ch-3 sp, shell in last shell, **do not turn***, **to join next Motif, with WS of row 8 facing, shell in first shell, rep between * once, rep from ** until all motifs are joined, turn. *(56 ch-3 sps, 14 shells)*

**Row 2:** Ch 1, sl st in each of first 2 dc, sl st in first ch sp, beg shell, *ch 3, sk next ch-3 sp, [sc in next ch-3 sp, ch 3] 6 times, sk next ch-3 sp*, **shell in each of next 2 shells, rep between * once, rep from ** across with shell in last shell, turn. *(49 ch-3 sps, 14 shells)*

**Row 3:** Ch 1, sl st in each of first 2 dc, sl st in first ch sp, beg shell, *ch 3, sk next ch-3 sp, [sc in next ch-3 sp, ch 3] 5 times, sk next ch-3 sp, shell in next shell*, **dc in next sp between shells, shell in next shell, rep between * once, rep from ** across, turn. *(42 ch-3 sps, 14 shells, 6 dc)*

**Row 4:** Ch 1, sl st in first 2 dc, sl st in first ch sp beg shell, *ch 3, sk next ch-3 sp, [sc in next ch-3 sp, ch 3] 4 times, sk next ch-3 sp, shell in next shell*, **ch 1, sk last 2 dc of same shell, V-st in next dc, ch 1, shell in next shell, rep between * once, rep between ** across, turn. *(35 ch-3 sps, 14 shells, 12 ch-1 sps, 6 V-sts)*

**Row 5:** Ch 1, sl st in each of first 2 dc, sl st in first ch sp, beg shell, *ch 3,

sk next ch-3 sp, [sc in next ch-3 sp, ch 3] 3 times, sk next ch-3 sp, shell in next shell*, **ch 1, 9 dc in next V-st, ch 1, shell in next shell, rep between * once, rep from ** across, turn. *(54 dc, 28 ch-2 sps, 14 shells, 12 ch-1 sps)*

**Row 6:** Ch 1, sl st in each of first 2 dc, sl st in first ch sp, beg shell, *ch 3, sk next ch-3 sp, [sc in next ch-3 sp, ch 3] twice, sk next ch-3 sp, shell in next shell*, **ch 1, sk last 2 dc of same shell, [dc in next dc, ch 1] 9 times, shell in next shell, rep between *, rep from ** across, turn. *(60 ch-1 sps, 21 ch-3 sps, 14 shells)*

**Row 7:** Ch 1, sl st in first 2 dc, sl st in first ch sp, beg shell, *ch 3, sk next ch-3 sp, sc in next ch-3 sp, ch 3, sk next ch-3 sp, shell in next shell*, **ch 3, sk next ch-1 sp, [sc in next ch-1 sp, ch 3] 8 times, sk next ch-1 sp, shell in next shell, rep between * once, rep from ** across, turn. *(68 ch-3 sps)*

**Row 8:** Ch 1, sl st in each of first 2 dc, sl st in first ch sp, beg shell, sk next 2 ch-3 sps, shell in next shell, *ch 3, sk next ch-3 sp, [sc in next ch-3 sp, ch 3] 7 times, sk next ch-3 sp, shell in next shell, sk next 2 ch-3 sps, shell in next shell, rep from * across, turn. *(48 ch-3 sps)*

**Row 9:** Ch 1, sl st in each of first 2 dc, sl st in first ch sp, beg shell, shell in next shell, *ch 3, sk next ch-3 sp, [sc in next ch-3 sp, ch 3] 6 times, sk next ch-3 sp, shell in each of next 2 shells, rep from * across, turn. *(42 ch-3 sps, 14 shells)*

**Row 10:** Ch 1, sl st in each of first 2 dc, sl st in first ch sp, beg shell, dc in next sp between shells, shell in next shell, *ch 3, sk next ch-3 sp, [sc in next ch-3 sp, ch 3] 5 times, sk next ch-3 sp, shell in next shell, dc in next sp between shells, shell in next shell, rep from * across, turn. *(36 ch-3 sps, 7 dc)*

**Row 11:** Ch 1, sl st in each of first 2 dc, sl st in first ch sp, beg shell, *ch 1, sk last 2 dc of same shell, V-st in next dc, ch 1, shell in next shell*, **ch 3, sk next ch-3 sp, [sc in next ch-3 sp, ch 3] 4 times, shell in next shell, rep between * once, rep from ** across, turn. *(30 ch-3 sps, 14 shells, 14 ch-1 sps, 7 V-sts)*

**Row 12:** Ch 1, sl st in first 2 dc, sl st in first ch sp, beg shell, *ch 1, 9 dc in next V-st, ch 1, shell in next shell*, **ch 3, sk next ch-3 sp, [sc in next ch-3 sp, ch 3] 3 times, sk next ch-3 sp, shell in next shell, rep between * once, rep from ** across, turn. *(63 dc, 24 ch-3 sps, 14 shells, 14 ch-1 sps)*

**Row 13:** Ch 1, sl st in each of first 2 dc, sl st in first ch sp, beg shell, *ch 1, sk last 2 dc of same shell, [dc in next dc, ch 1] 9 times, shell in next shell*, **ch 3, sk next ch-3 sp, [sc in next ch-3 sp, ch 3] twice, sk next ch-3 sp, shell in next shell, rep between * once, rep from ** across, turn. *(70 ch-1 sps, 18 ch-3 sps, 14 shells)*

**Row 14:** Ch 1, sl st in each of first 2 dc, sl st in first ch sp, beg shell, *ch 3, sk next ch-1 sp, [sc in next ch-1 sp, ch 3] 8 times, shell in next shell*, **ch 3, sk next ch-3 sp, sc in next ch-3 sp, ch 3, sk next ch-3 sp, shell in next shell, rep between * once, rep from ** across, turn. *(75 ch-3 sps, 14 shells)*

**Row 15:** Ch 1, sl st in each of first 2 dc, sl st in first ch sp, beg shell, *ch 3, sk next ch-3 sp, [sc in next ch-3 sp, ch 3] 7 times, sk next ch-3 sp, shell in next shell*, **sk next 2 ch-3 sps, shell in next shell, rep between * once, rep from ** across, turn. *(56 ch-3 sps, 14 shells)*

**Rows 16–128:** Rep rows 2–15 consecutively, ending with row 2.

**FIRST POINT**

**Row 129:** Ch 1, sl st in each of first 2 dc, sl st in first ch sp, beg shell, ch 3, sk next ch-3 sp, [sc in next ch-3 sp, ch 3] 5 times, sk next ch-3 sp, shell in next shell, leaving rem sts unworked, turn. *(6 ch-3 sps)*

**Row 130:** Ch 1, sl st in each of first 2 dc, sl st in first ch sp, beg shell, ch 3, sk next ch-3 sp, [sc in next ch-3 sp, ch 3] 4 times, sk next ch-3 sp, shell in last shell, turn. *(5 ch-3 sps, 2 shells)*

**Row 131:** Ch 1, sl st in each of first 2 dc, sl st in first ch sp, beg shell, ch 3, sk next ch-3 sp, [sc in next ch-3 sp, ch 3] 3 times, sk next ch-3 sp, shell in last shell, turn. *(4 ch-3 sps, 2 shells)*

**Row 132:** Ch 1, sl st in each of first 2 dc, sl st in first ch sp, beg shell, ch 3, sk next ch-3 sp, [sc in next ch-3 sp, ch 3] twice, sk next ch-3 sp, shell in last shell, turn. *(3 ch-3 sps, 2 shells)*

**Row 133:** Ch 1, sl st in each of first 2 dc, sl st in first ch sp, beg shell, ch 3, sk next ch-3 sp, sc in next ch-3 sp, ch 3, sk next ch-3 sp, shell in last shell, turn. *(2 shells, 2 ch-3 sps)*

**Row 134:** Ch 1, sl st in each of first 2 dc, sl st in first ch sp, beg shell, sk next 2 ch-3 sps, shell in last shell, turn.

**Row 135:** Ch 1, sl st in each of first 2 dc, sl st in first ch sp, ch 3, dc in same sp, ch 2, 2 dc in next sp between shells, ch 2, 2 dc in last shell, turn.

**Row 136:** Ch 1, sl st in each of first 2 dc, sl st in first ch sp, ch 3, dc in same sp, ch 2, 2 dc in last ch sp, turn.

**Row 137:** Ch 1, sl st in each of first 2 dc, sl st in first ch sp, ch 3, 2 dc in same sp, fasten off.

**2ND POINT**

**Row 129:** With WS of row 128 facing, join with sl st in next shell, beg shell, ch 3, sk next ch-3 sp, [sc in next ch-3 sp, ch 3] 5 times, sk next ch-3 sp, shell in next shell, leaving rem sts unworked, turn.

**Rows 130–137:** Rep rows 130–137 of first point.

**REMAINING POINTS**

For rem 5 points, rep rows 129–137 of 2nd point. ■

# Coffee-Table Topper

DESIGN BY AGNES RUSSELL

The elegance of fine crochet is captured with this beautiful coffee-table accent. This classic piece has an ageless charm that fits your decor as easily as it might have in generations past.

PERIENCED

**FINISHED SIZE**
10 x 16 inches

**MATERIALS**
Size 10 crochet cotton:
280 yds ecru
Size 7/1.65mm steel crochet hook or size needed to obtain gauge

**GAUGE**
8 dc = 1 inch; 4 rnds = 1 inch

**SPECIAL STITCHES**

**Beginning shell (beg shell):** Sl st in ch-3 sp, ch 3 *(counts as first dc)*, (dc, ch 3, 2 dc) in same ch sp.

**Shell:** (2 dc, ch 3, 2 dc) in same ch sp.

**Double shell:** ({2 dc, ch 3} twice, 2 dc) in same ch sp.

## INSTRUCTIONS

**COFFEE TABLE DOILY**

**Rnd 1:** Ch 5, sl st in first ch to form ring, ch 3 *(counts as first dc)*, 19 dc in ring, join with sl st in 3rd ch of beg ch-3. *(20 dc)*

**Rnd 2:** Ch 4 *(counts as first dc and ch 1)*, [dc in next dc, ch 1] around, join with sl st in 3rd ch of beg ch-4.

**Rnd 3:** Ch 5 *(counts as first dc and ch 2)*, [dc in next dc, ch 2] around, join with sl st in 3rd ch of beg ch-5.

**Rnd 4:** Sl st in ch-2 sp, ch 6, dc in same ch-2 sp, [(dc, ch 3, dc) in next ch-2 sp] around, join with sl st in 3rd ch of beg ch-6.

**Rnd 5: Beg shell** *(see Special Stitches)* in first ch sp, **shell** *(see Special Stitches)* in each ch-3 sp around, join with sl st in 3rd ch of beg ch-3.

**Rnd 6:** Beg shell in shell, ch 1, [shell in shell, ch 1] around, join with sl st in 3rd ch of beg ch-3.

**Rnd 7:** Beg shell in shell, ch 2, 2 dc, ch 5, 2 dc in next ch-3 sp of shell, ch 2, [shell in shell, ch 2, 2 dc, ch 5, 2 dc in next ch-3 sp of shell, ch 2] around, join with sl st in 3rd ch of beg ch-3.

**Rnd 8:** Beg shell in shell, ch 2, 10 dc in next ch-5 sp, ch 2, [shell in shell, ch 2, 10 dc in next ch-5 sp, ch 2] around, join with sl st in 3rd ch of beg ch-3.

**Rnd 9:** Beg shell in shell, ch 2, dc in next dc of 10-dc group, [ch 1, dc in next dc] 9 times, ch 2, *shell in shell, ch 2, dc in next dc of 10-dc group, [ch 1, dc in next dc] 9 times, ch 2, rep from * around, join with sl st in 3rd ch of beg ch-3.

**Rnd 10:** Beg shell in shell, ch 2, sc in next ch-1 sp, [ch 3, sc in next ch-1 sp] 8 times, ch 2, *shell in shell, ch 2, sc in next ch-1 sp, [ch 3, sc in next ch-1 sp] 8 times, ch 2, rep from * around, join with sl st in 3rd ch of beg ch-3.

**Rnd 11:** Beg shell in shell, ch 2, sc in next ch-3 sp, [ch 3, sc in next ch-3 sp] 7 times, ch 2, *shell in shell, ch 2, sc in next ch-3 sp, [ch 3, sc in next ch-3 sp] 7 times, ch 2, rep from * around, join with sl st in 3rd ch of beg ch-3.

**Rnd 12:** ***Double shell** *(see Special Stitches)* in shell, ch 2, sc in next ch-3 sp, [ch 3, sc in next ch-3 sp] 6 times,

ch 2, rep from * around, join with sl st in 3rd ch of beg ch-3.

**Rnd 13:** Beg shell in ch-3 sp, ch 2, shell in ch-3 sp, ch 2, sc in next ch-3 sp, [ch 3, sc in next ch-3 sp] 5 times, ch 2,*shell in ch-3 sp, ch 2, shell in ch-3 sp, ch 2, sc in next ch-3 sp, [ch 3, sc in next ch-3 sp] 5 times, ch 2, rep from * around, join with sl st in 3rd ch of beg ch-3.

**Rnd 14:** Beg shell in shell, shell in ch-2 sp, shell in shell, ch 2, sc in next ch-3 sp, [ch 3, sc in next ch-3 sp] 4 times, ch 2,*shell in shell, shell in ch-2 sp, shell in shell, ch 2, sc in next ch-3 sp, [ch 3, sc in next ch-3 sp] 4 times, ch 2, rep from * around, join with sl st in 3rd ch of beg ch-3.

**Rnd 15:** Beg shell in shell, ch 2, (2 dc, ch 5, 2 dc) in next shell, ch 2, shell in shell, ch 2, sc in next ch-3 sp, [ch 3, sc in next ch-3 sp] 3 times, ch 2, *◊shell in shell, ch 2, (2 dc, ch 5, 2 dc) in next shell, ch 2, shell in shell, ch 2, sc in next ch-3 sp, [ch 3, sc in next ch-3 sp] 3 times, ch 2, rep from ◊ once, **[shell in shell, ch 2] 3 times, sc in next ch-3 sp, [ch 3, sc in next ch-3 sp] 3 times, ch 2, rep from **, rep from * around, join with sl st 3rd ch of beg ch-3.

**Rnd 16:** Beg shell in shell, ch 2, 10 dc in next ch-5 sp, ch 2, shell in shell, ch 2, sc in next ch-3 sp, [ch 3, sc in next ch-3 sp] twice, ch 2, *◊shell in shell, ch 2, 10 dc in next ch-5 sp, ch 2, shell in shell, ch 2, sc in next ch-3 sp, [ch 3, sc in next ch-3 sp] twice, ch 2, rep from ◊ once, **shell in shell, ch 2, double shell in shell, ch 2, shell in shell, ch 2, sc in next ch-3 sp, [ch 3, sc in next ch-3 sp] twice, ch 2, rep from ** once, rep from * around, join with sl st in 3rd ch of beg ch-3.

**Rnd 17:** Beg shell in shell, ch 2, dc in next dc of 10-dc group, [ch 1, dc in next dc] 9 times, ch 2, shell in shell, ch 2, sc in next ch-3 sp, ch 3, sc in next ch-3 sp, ch 2,*shell in shell, ch 2, dc in next dc of 10-dc group, [ch 1, dc in next dc] 9 times, ch 2, shell in shell, ch 2, sc in next ch-3 sp, ch 3, sc in next ch-3 sp, ch 2, rep from * once, **[shell in shell, ch 2] 4 times, sc in next ch-3 sp, ch 3, sc in next ch-3 sp, ch 2, rep from ** once, rep from * once, join with sl st in 3rd ch of beg ch-3.

**Rnd 18:** Beg shell in next shell, ch 2, sc in next ch-1 sp, [ch 3, sc in next ch-1 sp] 8 times, ch 2, shell in shell, ch 2, dc in rem ch-3 sp, ch 2, *shell in next shell, ch 2, sc in next ch-1 sp, [ch 3, sc in next ch-1 sp] 8 times, ch 2, shell in shell, ch 2, dc in rem ch-3 sp, ch 2, rep from * once, **[shell in shell, ch 3, sc in next ch-2 sp, ch 3] 3 times, shell in shell, ch 2, dc in ch-3 sp, ch 2, rep from ** once, rep from * once, join with sl st in 3rd ch of beg ch-3.

#### PINEAPPLE POINTS

**Row 19:** Beg shell in shell, ch 2, sc in next ch-3 sp, [ch 3, sc in next ch-3 sp] 7 times, ch 2, shell in shell, *ch 2, (dc, ch 3, dc) in single dc at top of Pineapple, ch 2, shell in shell, ch 2, sc in next ch-3 sp, [ch 3, sc in next ch-3 sp] 7 times, ch 2, shell in shell, shell in shell, ch 2, sc in next ch-3 sp, [ch 3, sc in next ch-3 sp] 7 times, ch 2, shell in shell, *ch 2, (dc, ch 3, dc) in single dc at top of Pineapple, ch 2, shell in shell, ch 2, sc in next ch-3 sp, [ch 3, sc in next ch-3 sp] 7 times, ch 2, shell in shell, rep from * once, turn.

**Row 20:** Beg shell in shell, ch 2, sc in next ch-3 sp, [ch 3, sc in next ch-3 sp] 6 times, ch 2, shell in shell, *ch 2, shell in next ch-3 sp, ch 2, shell in shell, ch 2, sc in next ch-3 sp, [ch 3, sc in next ch-3 sp] 6 times, ch 2, shell in shell, rep from * once, turn.

**Row 21:** Beg shell in shell, ch 2, sc in next ch-3 sp, [ch 3, sc in next ch-3 sp] 5 times, ch 2, shell in shell, *ch 2, (2 dc, ch 5, 2 dc) in next shell, ch 2, shell in shell, ch 2, sc in next ch-3 sp, [ch 3, sc in next ch-3 sp] 5 times, ch 2, shell in shell, rep from * once, turn.

**Row 22:** Beg shell in shell, ch 2, sc in next ch-3 sp, [ch 3, sc in next ch-3 sp] 4 times, ch 2, shell in shell, *ch 2, 10 dc in next ch-5 sp, ch 2, shell in shell, ch 2, sc in next ch-3 sp, [ch 3, sc in next ch-3 sp] 4 times, ch 2, shell in shell, rep from * once, turn.

**Row 23:** Beg shell in shell, ch 2, sc in next ch-3 sp, [ch 3, sc in next ch-3 sp] 3 times, ch 2, shell in shell, *ch 2, dc in next dc of 10-dc group, [ch 1, dc in next dc] 9 times, ch 2, shell in shell, ch 2, sc in next ch-3 sp, [ch 3, sc in next ch-3 sp] 3 times, ch 2, shell in shell, rep from * once, turn.

**Row 24:** Beg shell in shell, ch 2, sc in next ch-3 sp, [ch 3, sc in next ch-3 sp] twice, ch 2, shell in shell, *ch 2, sc in next ch-1 sp, [ch 3, sc in next ch-1 sp] 8 times, ch 2, shell in shell, ch 2, sc in next ch-3 sp, [ch 3, sc in next ch-3 sp] twice, ch 2, shell in shell, rep from * once, turn.

**Row 25:** Beg shell in shell, ch 2, sc in next ch-3 sp, ch 3, sc in next ch-3 sp, ch 2, shell in shell, *ch 2, sc in next ch-3 sp, [ch 3, sc in next ch-3 sp] 7 times, ch 2, shell in shell, ch 2, sc in next ch-3 sp, ch 3, sc in next ch-3 sp, ch 2, shell in shell, rep from * once, turn.

**Row 26:** Beg shell in shell, ch 2, dc in next ch-3 sp, ch 2, shell in shell, *ch 2, sc in next ch-3 sp, [ch 3, sc in next ch-3 sp] 6 times, ch 2, shell in shell, ch 2, dc in next ch-3 sp, ch 2, shell in shell, rep from * once, turn.

**Row 27:** Beg shell in shell, shell in shell, ch 2, sc in next ch-3 sp, [ch 3, sc in next ch-3 sp] 5 times, ch 2, shell in shell, ch 2, shell in dc at top of Pineapple, ch 2, shell in shell, ch 2, sc in next ch-3 sp, [ch 3, sc in next ch-3 sp] 5 times, ch 2, shell in shell, shell in shell, turn.

**Row 28:** Sl st in ch-3 sp, ch 3, shell in next shell, ch 2, sc in next ch-3 sp, [ch 3, sc in next ch-3 sp] 4 times, ch 2, shell in shell, ch 2, double shell in next shell, ch 2, shell in shell, ch 2, sc in next ch-3 sp, [ch 3, sc in next ch-3 sp] 4 times, ch 2, shell in shell, dc in next shell, turn.

**Row 29:** Beg shell in shell, ch 2, sc in next ch-3 sp, [ch 3, sc in next ch-3 sp] 3 times, ch 2, shell in shell, ch 2, shell in shell, ch 3, shell in shell, ch 2, shell in shell, ch 2, sc in next ch-3 sp, [ch 3, sc in next ch-3 sp] 3 times, ch 2, shell in shell, turn.

**Row 30:** Beg shell in shell, ch 2, sc in next ch-3 sp, [ch 3, sc in next ch-3 sp] twice, [ch 2, shell in shell] twice, ch 2, shell in ch-3 sp between shells, [ch 2, shell in shell] twice, ch 2, sc in next ch-3 sp, [ch 3, sc in next ch-3 lp] twice, ch 2, shell in shell, turn.

**Row 31:** Beg shell in shell, ch 2, sc in next ch-3 sp, ch 3, sc in next ch-3 sp, [ch 2, shell in shell] twice, ch 2, double shell in next shell, [ch 2, shell in shell] twice, ch 2, sc in next ch-3 sp, ch 3, sc in next ch-3 sp, ch 2, shell in shell, turn.

**Row 32:** Beg shell in shell, ch 2, dc in ch-3 sp of Pineapple, [ch 2, shell in shell] 6 times, ch 2, dc in next ch-3 sp of Pineapple, ch 2, shell in shell, turn.

**Row 33:** Beg shell in shell, ch 2, sc in dc at top of Pineapple, ch 2, [shell in shell, ch 2, sc in next ch-2 sp, ch 2] 5 times, shell in shell, ch 2, sc in dc at top of pineapple, ch 2, shell in shell. Fasten off.

With finished Pineapple Point to your right, join with sl st in next shell before new Pineapple that has 8 ch-3 sps across. Rep rows 19–33 for 2nd section. At the end of row 33, **do not fasten off, do not turn.**

#### TRIM

Working around entire outer edge of Doily, evenly sp sc around, join with sl st in beg sc. Fasten off. ■

# Pineapple Perfection

DESIGN BY DOT DRAKE

Treat yourself to the timeless good looks of this pineapple delight! Whether it is used to welcome overnight guests or to dress up the master bedroom, this luxurious coverlet will add elegance to your home.

**FINISHED SIZE**
75 x 109 inches

**MATERIALS**
Aunt Lydia's Classic size 10 crochet cotton (400 yds per ball): 12 balls #1 white
Size G/6/4mm crochet hook or size needed to obtain gauge

**GAUGE**
Motif = 17 inches square; rnds 1 and 2 = 4 inches

**PATTERN NOTE**
Block each Motif before joining. If piece is not blocked, the pineapples will look puckered.

**SPECIAL STITCHES**

**Double crochet cluster (dc cl):** Holding last lp of each st on hook, 2 dc in ch sp, yo, pull through all lps on hook.

**Cluster shell (cl shell):** (dc cl, ch 3, dc cl) in next ch sp.

**Double shell:** ({Dc cl, ch 2} twice, dc cl) in next ch sp.

**Treble crochet cluster (tr cl):** Holding last lp of each st on hook, 2 tr in ch sp, yo, pull through all lps on hook.

**Corner:** (Tr cl, {ch 7, tr cl} twice) in next ch sp.

**First corner joining:** Tr cl in next ch sp, ch 7, tr cl in same ch sp, ch 4, sc in adjacent corner ch sp at corner of corresponding Motif, ch 4, tr cl in same ch sp on this Motif.

**2nd corner joining:** Tr cl in next ch sp, ch 4, sc in adjacent ch sp at corner of corresponding Motif, ch 4, tr cl in same ch sp on this Motif, ch 7, tr cl in same ch sp.

**2-corner joining:** Tr cl in next ch sp, ch 4, sc in adjacent ch sp at corner of corresponding Motif, ch 4, tr cl in same ch sp on this Motif, ch 4, sc in adjacent ch sp at corner of next corresponding Motif, ch 4, tr cl in same ch sp on this Motif.

**V-stitch (V-st):** (Dc, ch 3, dc) in st.

**Beginning cluster shell (beg cl shell):** Sl st in next st, sl st in first ch sp, ch 3, yo, insert hook in same ch sp, yo, pull through, yo, pull through 2 lps on hook, yo, pull through all lps on hook, ch 3, dc cl in same ch sp.

**Double crochet shell (dc shell):** (2 dc, ch 2, sl st in top of last st made, 2 dc) in ch sp.

**Side joining:** Ch 3, sc in next adjacent ch sp of corresponding Motif, ch 3, dc in next ch sp on this Motif, [ch 3, sc in next ch sp of corresponding Motif, ch 3, sc in next ch sp on this Motif] twice, ch 3, sc in next ch sp on corresponding Motif, ch 3, cl shell in next cl shell on this Motif, sk next ch sp, cl shell in next cl shell, [ch 3, sc in next ch sp of corresponding Motif, ch 3, sc in next ch sp on this Motif] twice, ch 3, sc in next ch sp of corresponding Motif, ch 3, dc in next ch sp on this Motif, ch 3, sc in next ch sp of corresponding Motif, ch 3.

**Picot V-stitch (picot V-st):** (Dc, ch 5, sl st in 3rd ch from hook, ch 2, dc) in next st.

**Picot chain (picot ch):** Ch 5, sl st in 3rd ch from hook.

**Picot shell:** (Cl, picot ch, cl) in last cl shell of same corner ch sp.

## INSTRUCTIONS

### COVERLET

***Note:*** *Using the following instructions, for* ***first row,*** *work First Motif, [work 2nd Motif] 3 times for total of 4 Motifs in first row, *for* ***next row,*** *work 2nd Motif onto bottom of first Motif made on last row, [work 3rd Motif onto bottom of Next Motif on last row and side of last Motif made on this row] 3 times, rep from * for total of 6 rows.*

### FIRST MOTIF

**Rnd 1:** Ch 5, **beg tr cl** *(see Special Stitches),* ch 3, *yo twice insert hook in same ch, yo, pull through, [yo, pull through 2 lps on hook] twice, yo, pull through all lps on hook, rep from * once, **tr cl** *(see Special Stitches)* ch 3, rep from * 6 times, join with sl st in top of beg tr cl. *(8 ch sps)*

**Rnd 2:** Sl st in first ch sp, ch 3, (dc, ch 2, sl st in top of last st made, 2 dc) in same ch sp, *ch 3, (2 dc, ch 2, sl st in top of last st made, 2 dc) in next ch sp, rep from * 6 times, ch 1, join with dc in top of first ch-3 *(joining ch sp).*

**Rnd 3:** Ch 6, dc in joining ch sp, V-st, ch 5, sl st in 3rd ch from hook, ch 2, *(dc, ch 3, dc) in center ch of next ch sp *(V-st),* ch 5, sl st in 3rd ch from hook, ch 2, rep from * around, join with sl st in 3rd ch of beg ch-6.

**Rnd 4:** Sl st in first ch sp of first V-st, ch 3 *(counts as first dc),* 8 dc in same ch sp, *ch 4, sk next 2 ch sps, **cl shell** *(see Special Stitches)* in ch sp of next V-st, ch 4, sk next 2 ch sps**, 9 dc in next ch sp, rep from * around, ending last rep at ** join with sl st in 3rd ch of beg ch-3.

**Rnd 5:** Ch 4 *(counts as dc and ch-1),* dc in next st, [ch 1, dc in next st] 7 times, *ch 3, sk next ch sp, **double shell** *(see Special Stitches)* in ch sp of next cl shell, ch 3, sk next ch sp**, dc in next st, [ch 1, dc in next st] 8 times, rep from * around, ending last rep at **, join with sl st in 3rd ch of ch-4.

**Rnd 6:** Ch 1, sc in first ch sp, [ch 3, sc in next ch sp] 7 times, *ch 4, sk next ch sp, cl shell in first ch sp of next double shell, ch 3, cl shell in next ch sp of same double shell, ch 4, sk next ch sp**, sc in next ch sp, [ch 3, sc in next ch sp] 7 times, rep from * around, ending last rep at **, join with sl st in beg sc.

**Rnd 7:** Ch 1, sc in first ch sp, [ch 3, sc in next ch sp] 6 times, *[ch 4, sk next ch sp, cl shell in ch sp of next cl shell, ch 3, dc in next ch sp, cl shell in ch sp of next cl shell, ch 4, sk next ch sp**, sc in next ch sp, [ch 3, sc in next ch sp] 6 times, rep from * around, ending last rep at **, join with sl st in beg sc.

**Rnd 8:** Ch 1, sc in first ch sp, [ch 3, sc in next ch sp] 5 times, *ch 4, sk next ch sp, cl shell in next cl shell, ch 3, sk next ch sp, **V-st** *(see Special Stitches)* in next st, ch 3, sk next ch sp, cl shell in next cl shell, ch 4, sk next ch sp**, sc in next ch sp, [ch 3, sc in next ch sp] 5 times, rep from * around, ending last rep at **, join with sl st in beg sc.

**Rnd 9:** Ch 1, sc in first ch sp, [ch 3, sc in next ch sp] 4 times, *ch 4, sk next ch sp, cl shell in next cl shell, ch 3, sk next ch sp, V-st in first st of next V-st, V-st in last st of same V-st, ch 3, sk next ch sp, cl shell in next cl shell, ch 4, sk next ch sp**, sc in next ch sp, [ch 3, sc in next ch sp] 4 times, rep from * around, ending last rep at **, join with sl st in beg sc.

**Rnd 10:** Ch 1, sc in first ch sp, [ch 3, sc in next ch sp] 3 times, *ch 4, sk next ch sp, cl shell in next cl shell, ch 3, sk next ch sp, [V-st in first st of next V-st] twice, V-st in last st of last V-st, ch 3, sk next ch sp, cl shell in next cl shell, ch 4, sk next ch sp**, sc in next ch sp, [ch 3, sc in next ch sp] 3 times, rep from * around, ending last rep at **, join with sl st in beg sc.

**Rnd 11:** Ch 1, sc in first ch sp, [ch 3, sc in next ch sp] twice, *ch 4, cl shell in next cl shell, ch 3, sk next ch sp, [V-st in first st of next V-st] 3 times, V-st in last st of last V-st, ch 3, sk next ch sp, cl shell in next cl shell, ch 4, sk next ch sp**, sc in next ch sp, [ch 3, sc in next ch sp] twice, rep from * around, ending last rep at **, join with sl st in beg sc.

**Rnd 12:** Ch 1, sc in first ch sp, ch 3, sc in next ch sp, *ch 4, cl shell in next cl shell, ch 3, sk next ch sp, [V-st in first dc of next V-st] 4 times, V-st in last st of last V-st, ch 3, sk next ch sp, cl shell in next cl shell, ch 4, sk next ch sp**, sc in next ch sp, ch 4, sc in next ch sp, rep from * around, ending last rep at **, join with sl st in beg sc.

**Rnd 13:** Ch 1, sc in first ch sp, *ch 4, sk next ch sp, cl shell in next cl shell, ch 4, sk next ch sp, [V-st in first st of next V-st] 5 times, V-st in last st of last V-st, ch 4, sk next ch sp, cl shell in next cl shell, ch 4, sk next ch sp**, sc in next ch sp, rep from * around, ending last rep at **, join with sl st in beg sc.

**Rnd 14:** Sl st in 4 chs of first ch sp, **beg cl shell** *(see Special Stitches),* *ch 7, sk next ch sp, **dc shell** *(see Special Stitches)* in ch sp of next V-st, [ch 2, dc shell in ch sp of next V-st] 5 times, ch 7, sk next ch sp, cl shell in next cl shell, ch 5, sk next 2 ch sps**, cl shell in next cl shell, rep from * around, ending last rep at **, join with sl st in top of beg cl shell.

**Rnd 15:** Beg cl shell, *[ch 7, sc in next ch sp] twice, ch 7, dc in next ch sp, ch 7, work **corner** *(see Special Stitches)* in next ch sp, ch 7, dc in next ch sp, [ch 7, sc in next ch sp] twice, ch 7, cl shell in next cl shell, sk next ch sp**, cl shell in next cl shell, rep from * around, ending last rep at **, join with sl st in beg cl shell. Fasten off.

Block Motifs *(see Pattern Note).*

**2ND MOTIF**

**(1-Sided Joining)**
**Rnds 1–14:** Rep rnds 1–14 of First Motif.

**Rnd 15:** Beg cl shell, [ch 7, sc in next ch sp] twice, ch 7, dc in next ch sp, ch 7, work **first corner joining** *(see Special Stitches)*, work **side joining** *(see Special Stitches)*, work **2nd corner joining** *(see Special Stitches)*, *ch 7, dc in next ch sp, [ch 7, sc in next ch sp] twice, ch 7, cl shell in next cl shell, sk next ch sp**, cl shell in next cl shell, [ch 7, sc in next ch sp] twice, ch 7, dc in next ch sp, ch 7, work corner in next ch sp, rep from * around, ending last rep at **, join with sl st in beg shell. Fasten off.

**3RD MOTIF**

**(2-Sided Joining)**
**Rnds 1–14:** Rep rnds 1–14 of First Motif.

**Rnd 15:** Beg cl shell, [ch 7, sc in next ch sp] twice, ch 7, dc in next ch sp, ch 7, work first corner joining, work side joining, work **2-corner joining** *(see Special Stitches)*, work side joining, work 2nd corner joining, *ch 7, dc in next ch sp, [ch 7, sc in next ch sp] twice, ch 7, cl shell in next cl shell, sk next ch sp*, cl shell in next cl shell, [ch 7, sc in next ch sp] twice, ch 7, dc in next ch sp, ch 7, work corner in next ch sp, rep between *, join with sl st in beg cl shell. Fasten off.

**EDGING**

**Rnd 1:** Working around outer edge, join with sc in first ch sp of corner at top right, for **lp**, ch 5, dc in 3rd ch from hook *(ch-2 sp and lp)*, ch 2, *◊[sc in next ch sp, lp] 10 times, 2 tr in next joining, lp*, rep between * twice, [sc in next ch sp, lp] 20 times, 2 tr in next joining, lp, rep between * 4 times◊, [sc in next ch sp, lp] 20 times, 2 tr in next joining, rep between ◊, [sc in next ch sp, lp] 9 times, join with sl st in beg sc.

**Rnd 2:** Sl st in each of next 2 chs, sl st in next lp, ch 2, yo, insert hook in same lp, yo, pull through, [yo, pull through 2 lps on hook] twice, yo, pull through all lps on hook, [ch 3, dc cl in same ch sp] 3 times *(corner)*, *[ch 5, cl shell in next lp] 42 times, ch 5, ({cl, ch 3} 3 times, cl) in next lp *(corner)*, [ch 5, cl shell in next lp] 64 times, ch 5,* ({cl, ch 3} 3 times, cl) in next ch sp *(corner)*, rep between *, join with sl st in top of beg cl.

**Rnd 3:** Beg cl shell in first ch sp of first corner, ch 2, dc in next ch sp, ch 2, cl in last ch sp of same corner, *ch 5, sk next ch sp, [cl shell in next cl shell, ch 5, sk next ch sp] across** to next corner, cl shell in first ch sp of next corner, ch 2, dc in next ch sp, ch 2, cl shell in last ch sp of same corner, rep from * around, ending last rep at **, join with sl st in top of beg cl.

**Rnd 4:** Beg cl shell, ch 2, sk next ch sp, **picot V-st** *(see Special Stitches)*, ch 2, sk next ch sp, cl shell in last cl shell of same corner, * [**picot ch** *(see Special Stitches)*, ch 2, sk next ch sp, cl shell in next cl shell] across to ch sp before next corner, picot ch, sk next ch sp**, cl shell in first cl shell of next corner, ch 2, sk next ch sp, picot V-st in next st, ch 2, sk next ch sp, cl shell in last cl of same corner, rep from * around, ending last rep at **, join with sl st in top of beg cl.

**Rnd 5:** Sl st in first ch sp, ch 2, yo, insert hook in same ch sp, yo, pull through, [yo, pull through 2 lps on hook] twice, yo, pull through all lps on hook, picot ch, cl in same ch sp *(picot shell)*, picot ch, sk next ch sp, picot V-st in first st of next picot V-st, picot ch, picot V-st in last st of same picot V-st, picot ch, sk next ch sp, for **picot shell**, (see Special Stitches), *[picot ch, picot shell in next cl shell] across to ch sp before next corner, picot ch, picot shell in first cl shell of next corner, picot ch, sk next ch sp, picot V-st in first st of next picot V-st, picot ch, picot V-st in last st of same picot V-st, picot, sk next ch sp, picot shell in last cl of same corner, rep from * twice, [picot ch, picot shell in next cl shell] across to ch sp before next corner, picot ch, join. Fasten off. ■

# Turtledoves

DESIGN BY FEROSA HAROLD

Pairs of graceful lovebirds come together in perfect harmony to create this beautiful doily that's the perfect gift for a special anniversary or a beautiful centerpiece for a bridal table any time of year.

INTERMEDIATE

**FINISHED SIZE**
13½ x 16 inches

**MATERIALS**
Aunt Lydia's Classic size 10 crochet cotton (400 yds per ball):
1 ball #1 white
Size 10/1.15mm steel crochet hook or size needed to obtain gauge
Rustproof pins
Starch

**GAUGE**
9 dc = 1 inch; 4 dc rows = 1 inch

**SPECIAL STITCHES**
**Mesh:** Ch 2, sk next 2 chs or dc, dc in next st.

**Beginning block (beg block):** Ch 3 *(counts as first dc)*, dc in each of next 3 sts.

**Block:** 2 dc in next ch sp, dc in next st, or, dc in each of next 3 sts.

**Beginning 1-block increase (beg 1-block inc):** Ch 5, dc in 4th ch from hook, dc in next ch, dc in next st.

**Ending 1-block increase (end 1-block inc):** [Yo, insert hook in base of last dc made, pull up lp, yo, pull through 1 lp on hook, {yo, pull through 2 lps on hook} twice] 3 times.

**Beginning 2-block increase (beg 2-block inc):** Ch 8, dc in 4th ch from hook, dc in each of next 4 chs, dc in next st.

**Ending 2-block increase (end 2-block inc):** [Yo, insert hook in base of last dc made, pull up lp, yo, pull through 1 lp on hook, {yo, pull through 2 lps on hook} twice] 6 times.

**Beginning 2-block decrease (beg 2-block dec):** Sl st in each of first 7 sts.

**Ending 2-block decrease (end 2-block dec):** Leave last 2 blocks unworked, turn.

**Beginning 8-block decrease (beg 8-block dec):** Sl st in each of first 25 sts.

**Ending 8-block decrease (end 8-block dec):** Leave last 8 blocks unworked, turn.

## INSTRUCTIONS

**FIRST HALF**
**Row 1 (RS):** Ch 171, dc in 4th ch from hook *(first 3 chs count as first dc)* and in each of next 5 chs, [ch 2, sk next 2 chs, dc in next ch] 52 times, dc in each of last 6 chs, turn. *(52 mesh, 4 blocks)*

**Rows 2–21:** Using Special Stitches as needed, work according to Turtle Dove Doily Chart, turn.

**Row 22: Beg block** *(see Special Stitches)*, **block** *(see Special Stitches)* 3 times, leaving rem sts unworked, **do not turn**. Fasten off. Sk next 14 sts on same row, join with sl st in next st, beg block, work according to Chart across to last 9 blocks. Fasten off. Sk next 14 sts, join with sl st in next st, beg block, block 3 times, turn. Fasten off.

**Row 23:** Sk first 4 blocks, join with sl st in first st of next block, work according to Chart, turn.

**Row 24:** Work according to Chart across, turn.

**FIRST WING SECTION**
**Row 25:** Beg block, block 12 times, leaving rem sts unworked, turn. *(13 blocks)*

**Row 26:** Beg block, block 12 times, **end 1-block inc** *(see Special Stitches)*, turn. *(14 blocks)*

**Row 27:** Beg block, block, leaving rem sts unworked. Fasten off. Sk next 11 sts on last row, join with sl st in next st, beg block, block 6 times, leaving rem block unworked, turn.

**Row 28: Beg 2-block dec** *(see Special Stitches)*, beg block, block twice, leaving rem blocks unworked, turn. Fasten off.

**FIRST HEAD SECTION**

**Row 25:** Sk next 5 sts on row 24 from First Wing Section, join with sl st in next st, beg block, block 3 times, mesh, block 3 times, leaving rem sts unworked, turn. *(7 blocks, 1 mesh)*

**Row 26:** Sl st in each of first 4 sts, beg block, block 5 times, leaving last block unworked, turn. *(6 blocks)*

**Row 27:** Sl st in each of first 4 sts, beg block, block 3 times, leaving last block unworked. Fasten off.

**2ND HEAD SECTION**

**Row 25:** Sk next 5 sts on row 24 from First Head Section, join with sl st in next st, beg block, block twice, **mesh** *(see Special Stitches)*, block 4 times, leaving rem sts unworked, turn. *(7 blocks, 1 mesh)*

**Rows 26 & 27:** Work rows 26 and 27 of First Head Section.

**2ND WING SECTION**

**Row 25:** Sk next 5 sts on row 24 from 2nd Head Section, join with sl st in next st, beg block, block 12 times, turn. *(13 blocks)*

**Row 26: Beg 1-block inc** *(see Special Stitches)*, block 13 times, turn. *(14 blocks)*

**Row 27:** Sl st in each of first 4 sts, beg block, block 6 times, leaving rem sts unworked. Fasten off. Sk next 11 sts on last row, join with sl st in next st, beg block, block, turn. Fasten off.

**Row 28:** Sk first 4 blocks, join with sl st in first st of next block, beg block, block twice, leaving rem sts unworked. Fasten off.

**2ND HALF**

Working in starting ch on opposite side of row 1, join with sl st in first ch, starting with row 2, rep First Half.

Pin to flat surface, apply starch according to manufacturer's instructions. Let dry. ■

next st] twice, sk next st, dc shell in next st;

**C.** Rep steps A and B twice, rep step A, tr shell in last st, join with sl st in 3rd ch of beg ch-3. Fasten off.

**2ND BLOCK**

**Row 1:** Ch 77, dc in 4th ch from hook, dc in each ch across, turn. *(75 dc)*

**Row 2:** Beg block, 35 mesh, block, turn.

**Rows 3–37:** Work across according to 2nd Block Chart, turn. At end of last row, **do not fasten off.**

**Edging**

**Rnd 1:** Working around outer edge, (ch 3, 2 dc) in first st, dc in each st across to last st, 3 dc in last st, evenly sp 73 dc across ends of rows, working in starting ch on opposite side of row 1, 3 dc in first ch, dc in each ch across to last ch, 3 dc in last ch, evenly sp 73 dc across ends of rows, join with sl st in 3rd ch of beg ch-3, turn. *(75 dc between each center st at corner for total of 304 dc)*

**Rnd 2:** Sl st in next st, ch 3, sk next st, dc in next st, sk next st, dc shell in next st, work the following steps to complete the rnd:

**A.** Rep steps A and B of First Block twice, rep step A of First Block;

**B.** Joining to bottom of First Block, work **joined tr shell** *(see Special Stitches)* in next st at corner, [sk next st, dc in next st] twice, sk next st, work **joined dc shell** *(see Special Stitches)* in next st;

**C.** *[Sk next st, dc in next st] twice, sk next st, work joined dc shell in next st, rep from * 4 times, sk next st, dc in next st, sk next st, **work joined dc shell in next st, [sk next st, dc in next st] twice, sk next st, rep from ** 5 times, work joined tr shell in last st at corner, join with sl st in 3rd ch of beg ch-3. Fasten off.

**3RD BLOCK**

**Row 1:** Ch 77, dc in 4th ch from hook, dc in each ch across, turn. *(75 dc)*

**Row 2:** Beg block, 35 mesh, block, turn.

**Rows 3–37:** Work across according to 3rd Block Chart, turn. At end of last row, **do not fasten off.**

**Edging**

**Rnd 1:** Working around outer edge, (ch 3, 2 dc) in first st, dc in each st across to last st, 3 dc in last st, evenly sp 73 dc across ends of rows, working in starting ch on opposite side of row 1, 3 dc in first ch, dc in each ch across to last ch, 3 dc in last ch, evenly sp 73 dc across ends of rows, join with sl st in 3rd ch of beg ch-3, turn. *(75 dc between each center st at corner for total of 304 dc)*

**Rnd 2:** Sl st in next st, ch 3, sk next st, dc in next st, sk next st, joining on side of First Block, work joined dc shell in next st, work the following steps to complete the rnd:

**A.** *[Sk next st, dc in next st] twice, sk next st, work joined dc shell in next st, rep from * 4 times, sk next st, dc in next st, sk next st, **work joined dc shell in next st, [sk next st, dc in next st] twice, sk next st, rep from ** 5 times, work joined tr shell in next st at corner, [sk next st, dc in next st] twice, sk next st, dc shell in next st;

**B.** Rep steps A and B of First Block twice, rep step A of First Block, work joined tr shell in last st at corner, join with sl st in 3rd ch of beg ch-3. Fasten off.

**4TH BLOCK**

**Row 1:** Ch 77, dc in 4th ch from hook, dc in each ch across, turn. *(75 dc)*

**Row 2:** Beg block, block, 33 mesh, 2 blocks, turn.

**Rows 3–37:** Work across according to 4th Block Chart, turn. At end of last row, **do not fasten off.**

**Edging**

**Rnd 1:** Working around outer edge, (ch 3, 2 dc) in first st, dc in each st across to last st, 3 dc in last st, evenly sp 73 dc across ends of rows, working in starting ch on opposite side of row 1, 3 dc in first ch, dc in each ch across to last ch, 3 dc in last ch, evenly sp 73 dc across ends of rows, join with sl st in 3rd ch of beg ch-3, turn. *(75 dc between each center st at corner for total of 304 dc)*

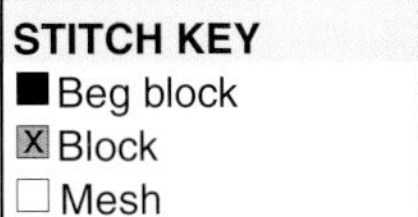

**Rnd 2:** Sl st in next st, ch 3, sk next st, dc in next st, sk next st, join on side of 2nd Block and bottom of 3rd Block, work joined dc shell in next st, work the following steps to complete the rnd:

**A.** *[Sk next st, dc in next st] twice, sk next st, work joined dc shell in next st, rep from * 4 times, sk next st, dc in next st, sk next st, **work joined dc shell in next st, [sk next st, dc in next st] twice, sk next st, rep from ** 5 times, work joined tr shell in next st at corner, [sk next st, dc in next st] twice, sk next st, dc shell in next st;

**B.** Rep steps A, B and A of First Block;

**C.** Work joined tr shell in next st at corner, [sk next st, dc in next st] twice, sk next st, work joined dc shell in next st;

**D.** *[Sk next st, dc in next st] twice, sk next st, work joined dc shell in next st, rep from * 4 times, sk next st, dc in next st, sk next st, **work joined dc shell in next st, [sk next st, dc in next st] twice, sk next st, rep from ** 5 times, work joined tr shell in last st at corner, join with sl st in 3rd ch of beg ch-3. Fasten off.

**BORDER**

**Rnd 1:** Working around outer edge of assembled Blocks, join with sc in ch sp of tr shell at top of 3rd Block, ch 8, sc in same ch sp, *ch 8, sc in ch sp of next dc shell, [ch 6, sc in ch sp of next dc shell] 5 times, ch 8, sc in ch sp of next dc shell, [ch 6, sc in ch sp of next dc shell] 5 times, [ch 8, sc in ch sp of next joined tr shell] twice, ch 8, sc in ch sp of next dc shell, [ch 6, sc in ch sp of next dc shell] 5 times, ch 8, sc in ch sp of next dc shell, [ch 6, sc in ch sp of next dc shell] 5 times, ch 8**, (sc, ch 8, sc) in ch sp of next tr shell at corner, rep from * around, ending last rep at **, join with sl st in beg sc, **turn.** *(112 ch sps)*

**STITCH KEY**
- ■ Beg block
- ☒ Block
- ☐ Mesh

**First Block Chart**

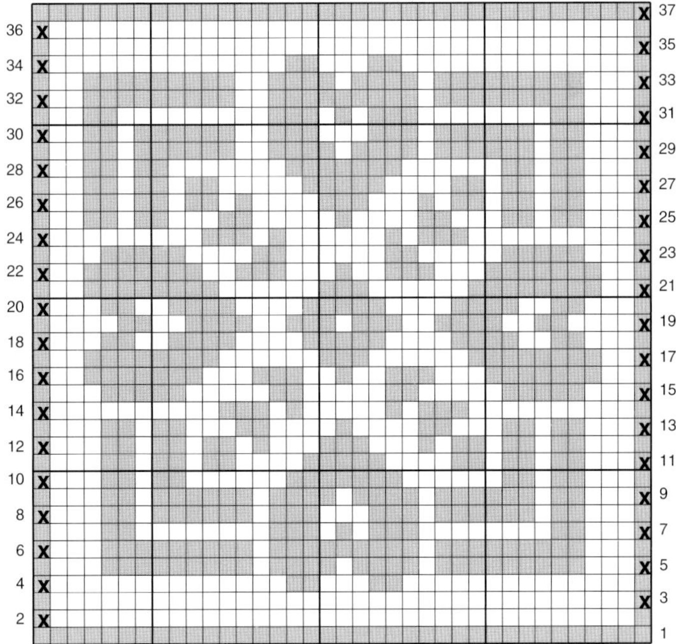

**Second Block Chart**

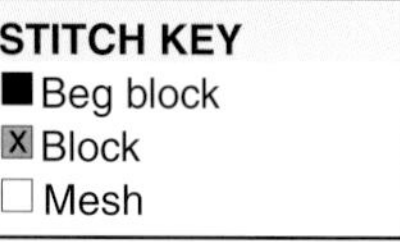

**Rnd 2:** Sl st in first ch sp, ch 3, 15 dc in same ch sp, ***small shell** *(see Special Stitches)* in next ch sp, [12 dc in next ch sp, small shell in next ch sp] twice, 16 dc in next ch sp, [small shell in next ch sp, 12 dc in next ch sp] twice, small shell in next ch sp, 16 dc in next ch sp, **large shell** *(see Special Stitches)* in next ch sp, 16 dc in next ch sp, small shell in next ch sp, [12 dc in next ch sp, small shell in next ch sp] twice, 16 dc in next ch sp, [small shell in next ch sp, 12 dc in next ch sp] twice, small shell, 16 dc in next ch sp, large shell in next ch sp**, 16 dc in next ch sp, rep from * around, ending last rep at **, join with sl st in 3rd ch of beg ch-3, turn.

**Rnd 3:** Ch 1, sc in first st, sc in next st, [ch 2, sc in each of next 2 sts] twice, small shell in next ch sp, (2 tr, ch 2, 2 tr) in next ch sp, small shell in next ch sp, work the following steps to complete the rnd:

**A.** Sc in each of next 2 sts, [ch 2, sc in each of next 2 sts] 10 times, sk next st;

**B.** Small shell, *sk next st, sc in each of next 2 sts, [ch 2, sc in each of next 2 sts] 6 times, sk next st, small shell in next ch sp, rep from *;

**C.** Sk next st, sc in each of next 2 sts, [ch 2, sc in each of next 2 sts] 8 times;

**D.** Small shell, *sk next st, sc in next 2 sts, [ch 2, sc in each of next 2 sts] 6 times, sk next st, small shell in next ch sp, rep from *;

**E.** Sk next st, sc in each of next 2 sts, [ch 2, sc in next 2 sts] 10 times;

**F.** Small shell in next ch sp, (2 tr, ch 2, 2 tr) in next ch sp, small shell in next ch sp;

**G.** Rep steps A–F 6 times;

**H.** Rep steps A–D, sk next st, [sc in each of next 2 sts, ch 2] 8 times, join with sl st in beg sc. Fasten off. ■

**STITCH KEY**
■ Beg block
☒ Block
☐ Mesh

**Third Block Chart**

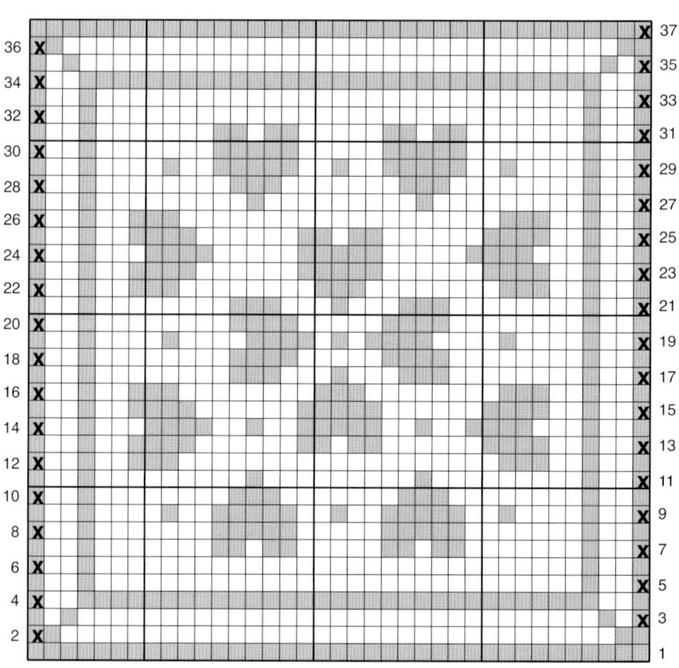

**Fourth Block Chart**

# Gothic Lattice

DESIGN BY DIANNE DRIVER

An unusual, Gothic-style border adds a melodramatic finish to the simple beauty of the center lattice design, creating an arresting contrast in style that grabs the eye wherever this piece is displayed.

ERMEDIATE

**FINISHED SIZE**
15½ inches square

**MATERIALS**
Size 10 crochet cotton:
325 yds white
Size 7/1.65mm steel crochet hook or size needed to obtain gauge
Tapestry needle
Starch

**GAUGE**
[Dc, ch 1] 5 times = 1 inch; 6 pattern rows = 1½ inches

**SPECIAL STITCHES**
**Cluster (cl):** Holding last lp of each st on hook, 3 dc in indicated st, yo, pull through all lps on hook.

**Triple picot (tr picot):** Ch 5, sl st in 5th ch from hook, ch 7, sl st in 7th ch from hook, ch 5, sl st in 5th ch from hook, sl st in same sc as first ch-5.

**INSTRUCTIONS**

**DOILY**
**Row 1:** Ch 104, dc in 6th ch from hook, [ch 1, sk next ch, dc in next ch] across, turn. *(50 ch-1 sps)*

**Row 2:** Ch 4 *(counts as first dc, ch-1)*, dc in next dc, ch 1, dc in next dc, *ch 5, sk next 2 dc, **cl** *(see Special Stitches)* in next dc, ch 5, sk next 2 dc, dc in next dc, [ch 1, dc in next dc] twice, rep from * across, ending with ch 1, dc in last st, turn.

**Row 3:** Ch 4, dc in next dc, ch 1, dc in next dc, *ch 4, sc in 5th ch of next ch-5, sk next cl, sc in first ch of next ch-5, ch 4, dc in next dc, [ch 1, dc in next dc] twice, rep from * across, ending with ch 1, dc in last st, turn.

**Row 4:** Ch 4, dc in next dc, ch 1, dc in next dc, *ch 4, sc in 4th ch of next ch-4, sc in sp between next 2 sc, sc in first ch of next ch-4, ch 4, dc in next dc, [ch 1, dc in next dc] twice, rep from * across, ending with ch 1, dc in last st, turn.

**Row 5:** Ch 4, dc in next dc, ch 1, dc in next dc, *ch 5, cl in 2nd sc, ch 5, dc in next dc, [ch 1, dc in next dc] twice, rep from * across, ending with ch 1, dc in last st, turn.

**Row 6:** Ch 4, dc in next dc, ch 1, dc in next dc, *[ch 1, sk next ch, dc in next ch] twice, ch 1, sk next ch, dc in next cl, [ch 1, sk next ch, dc in next ch] twice, sk next ch, [ch 1, dc in next dc] 3 times, rep from * across, ending with ch 1, dc in last st, turn.

**Row 7:** Ch 4, dc in next dc, [ch 1, dc in next dc] across, ending with ch 1, dc in 3rd ch of turning ch-4, turn.

**Rows 8–42:** Rep rows 2–7 consecutively, ending with row 6.

**BORDER**
**Rnd 1:** Ch 1, 3 sc in first st, sc in each st and ch sp across to last st, 3 sc in last st, working down side of piece, [sc in top of next row, sc in same row] across to end of last row, 3 sc in end of last row, sc in each ch across opposite side of starting ch, 3 sc in last ch, [sc in end of next row, sc in top of same row] across, join with sl st in beg sc, sl st in next st *(center sc of 3-sc group at corner)*, **do not turn.**

**Rnd 2:** Ch 5 *(count as first dc and ch-2)*, (dc, ch 2, dc) in same st as beg ch-5 *(corner)*, *[ch 1, sk next st, dc in next st] 49 times, ch 1, sk next st, ({dc, ch 2} twice, dc) in next st *(corner)*, [ch 1, sk next st, dc in next st] 43 times*, ch 1, sk next st, ({dc, ch 2} twice, dc) in next st *(corner)*, rep between * once, ch 1, join with sl st in 3rd ch of beg ch-5.

**Rnd 3:** Ch 23, sk next dc, sl st in next dc, *[sl st in next ch sp and next dc] twice, ch 17, sk next 5 dc, sl st in next dc, rep from * 5 times, [sl st in next ch sp and dc] twice, ch 23, sk next dc, sl st in next dc, **[sl st in next ch sp and next dc] twice, ch 17, sk next 3 dc, sl st in next dc, rep from ** 6 times*, [sl st in next ch sp and next dc] twice, ch 23, sk next dc, sl st in next dc, rep between * once, sl st in next ch, next dc and next ch.

**Rnd 4:** Ch 1, *sc in each of next 11 chs of ch-23, 3 sc in next ch, sc in each of next 11 chs, [sk next sl st, sc in next sl st, sk next sl st, sc in each of next 8 chs, 3 sc in next ch, sc in each of next 8 chs of next ch-17] 6 times, sc in each of next 11 chs of next ch-23, 3 sc in next ch, sc in each of next 11 chs, [sk next sl st, sc in next sl st, sk next sl st, sc in each of next 8 chs of next ch-17, 3 sc in next ch, sc in each of next 8 chs] 7 times, rep from * once, join with sl st in beg sc.

**Rnd 5:** Ch 12, sk next 5 sc, sc in next st, [ch 6, sk next 5 sc, sc in next st] twice, ch 12, sk next 6 sc, sc in next st, *[ch 6, sc in 6th ch of ch-12 sp just made, ch 6, sk next 9 sts, sc in next st, ch 12, sk next 9 sts, sc in next st] 6 times, ch 6, sc in 6th ch of ch-12 sp just made, ch 6, sk next 6 sts, sc in next st, [ch 6, sk next 5 sts, sc in next st] twice, ch 12, sk next 6 sts, sc in next st, [ch 6, sc in 6th ch of ch-12 sp just made, ch 6, sk next 9 sts, sc in next st, ch 12, sk next 9 sts, sc in next st] 7 times*, ch 6, sc in 6th ch of ch-12 sp just made, ch 6, sk next 6 sts, sc in next st, [ch 6, sk next 5 sts, sc in next st] twice, ch 12, sk next 6 sts, sc in next st, rep between * once, ending with ch 6, sc in 6th ch of beg ch-12, ch 6, sl st in same st as rnd 4 joining, going behind existing ch-6.

**Rnd 6:** Working in sk sc of rnd 4, sl st to first sc of rnd 5, sl st in sc, *[ch 17, sl st in next sc] twice, [ch 15, sl st in sc joining next ch-6 bars, ch 6, sl st in 6th ch of ch-15 sp just made, ch 9, sl st in next sc] 7 times*, [ch 17, sl st in next sc] twice, [ch 15, sl st in sc joining next ch-6 bars, ch 6, sl st in 6th ch of ch-15 sp just made, ch 9, sl st in next sc] 8 times, rep between * once, ending with ch 9, sl st in same st as first sl st.

**Rnd 7:** Ch 1, sk next ch, sc in each of next 7 chs of first ch-17, 3 sc in next ch, sc in each of next 7 chs, sk next ch, next sl st and next ch, sc in each of next 7 chs of next ch-17, 3 sc in next ch, sc in each of next 7 chs, *[sk next ch, next sl st and next ch, sc in each of next 8 chs, 3 sc in sl st between ch-6 bars, sc in each of next 8 chs] 7 times, [sk next ch, next sc and next ch, sc in each of next 7 chs, 3 sc in next ch, sc in each of next 7 chs] twice, [sk next ch, next sl st and next ch, sc in each of next 8 chs, 3 sc in sl st between ch-6 bars, sc in each of next 8 chs] 8 times*, [sk next ch, next sl st and next ch, sc in each of next 7 chs, 3 sc in next ch, sc in each of next 7 chs] twice, rep between * once, join with sl st in beg sc.

**Rnd 8:** Sl st in each of next 8 sts, **tr picot** *(see Special Stitches)* in same st, ch 12, sk next 16 sc, sl st in next sc, tr picot in same st, ch 12, sk next 17 sc, sl st in next sc, tr picot in same st, *[ch 12, sk next 18 sc, sl st in next sc, tr picot in same st] 6 times, ch 12, sk next 17 sc, sl st in next sc, tr picot in same st, ch 12, sk next 16 sc, sl st in next sc, tr picot in same st, ch 12, sk next 17 sc, sl st in next sc, tr picot in same st, [ch 12, sk next 18 sc, sl st in next sc, tr picot in same st] 7 times*, ch 12, sk next 17 sc, sl st in next sc, tr picot in same st, ch 12, sk next 16 sc, sl st in next sc, tr picot in same st, ch 12, sk next 17 sts, sl st in next sc, tr picot in same st, rep between * once, ch 12, join with sl st in base of first tr picot. Fasten off.

Starch and block to measurements. ■

# Wedding Roses

DESIGN BY ANN KIRTLEY

Roses are traditionally the symbol of love and romance; this afghan treasure is the perfect choice for a wedding or anniversary gift. A unique ruffled border features roses in bloom for a lovely effect.

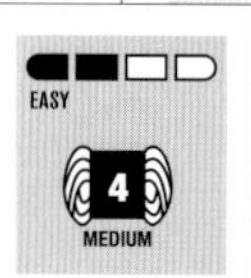


**FINISHED SIZE**
48 x 70 inches

**MATERIALS**
Medium (worsted) weight yarn:
65 oz/4,550 yds/1,950g off-white
Size G/6/4mm crochet hook or size needed to obtain gauge
Tapestry needle

**GAUGE**
19 dc = 4 inches; 9 rows = 4 inches

**SPECIAL STITCHES**

**Beginning block (beg block):** Ch 3 *(counts as first dc)*, dc in each of next 3 sts.

**Block:** Dc in each of next 3 sts.

**Mesh:** Ch 2, sk next 2 sts, dc in next st, or, ch 2, sk next ch sp, dc in next st.

## INSTRUCTIONS

**AFGHAN**

**Row 1 (RS):** Ch 195, dc in 4th ch from hook *(first 3 chs count as first dc)* and in each ch across, turn. *(193 dc)*

**Row 2: Beg block** *(see Special Stitches)*, [20 **mesh** *(see Special Stitches)*, **block** *(see Special Stitches)*] across, turn.

**Row 3:** Beg block, *8 mesh, 6 blocks, 6 mesh**, block, rep from * across, ending last rep at **, turn.

**Rows 4–127:** Using Special Stitches as needed, work according to Wedding Roses Chart, turn. At end of last row, fasten off.

**EDGING**

**Rnd 1 (RS):** Hold afghan with RS facing and row 127 at top, join with sl st in first st at upper right-hand corner, [ch 4, dc in 4th ch from hook, sk next 2 dc, sl st in next dc] across, working in ends of rows, [ch 4, dc in 4th ch from hook, sl st in base of next row] across, ch 4, dc in 4th ch from hook, working in starting ch on opposite side of row 1, sl st in first ch, [ch 4, dc in 4th ch from hook, sk next 2 chs, sl st in next ch] across, working in ends rows, ch 4, dc in 4th ch from hook, sl st in row 1, [ch 4, dc in 4th ch from hook, sl st in next row] across, join with sl st in joining sl st.

**Rnd 2:** Sl st in each of next 2 chs of next ch-4 sp, ch 1, sc in same sp, ch 3, [sc in next ch-4 sp, ch 3] around, join with sl st in beg sc.

**Rnd 3:** Sl st in next ch-3 sp, ch 4 *(counts as a tr)*, 10 tr in same ch sp, sk next ch-3 sp, *[sl st in next sc, sl st in next ch-3 sp] twice, **turn,** ({ch 3, sl st} 3 times, ch 1, turn) in same ch sp, (sc, hdc, 3 dc, hdc, sc) in ch-3 sp just made *(small petal)*, sl st in next sl st, [(sc, hdc, 3 dc, hdc, sc) in next ch-3 sp *(small petal)*, sl st in next sl st] twice, sl st in next ch-3 sp on rnd 2, turn, on this row [ch 5, working behind petals, sl st in back of next sl st] 3 times, on rnd 2, sl st in next already worked ch-3 sp, ch 1, turn, [in next ch-5 sp work (sc, hdc, 5 dc, hdc, sc) *(medium petal)*, sl st in next sl st] 3 times, sl st in next sc on rnd 2, turn, [ch 7, working behind petals, sl st in back of sl st behind next petal] 3 times, sl st in next sc, turn, [in next ch-7 sp work (sc, hdc, 7 dc, hdc, sc) *(large petal)*, sl st in next sl st] 3 times**, on rnd 2, sk next ch-3 sp, 11 tr in next ch-3 sp, sk next ch-3 sp, rep from * around, ending last rep at **, join with sl st in 4th ch of beg ch-4. Fasten off.

**Rnd 4:** Hold edging with RS facing, working in **back lps** *(see Stitch Guide)* only, join with sl st in 2nd dc on first large petal of rnd 3, *ch 7, sk next 3 dc, sl st in next dc, [ch 7, sl st in 2nd dc on next petal, ch 7, sk next 3 dc, sl st in next dc] twice, sl st in 4th tr of next 11-tr group, [ch 4, sl st in 4th ch from hook, sl st in next tr] 4 times**, sl st in 2nd dc of next petal, rep from * around, ending last rep at **, join with sl st in joining sl st. Fasten off. ■

**STITCH KEY**

● Block

□ Mesh

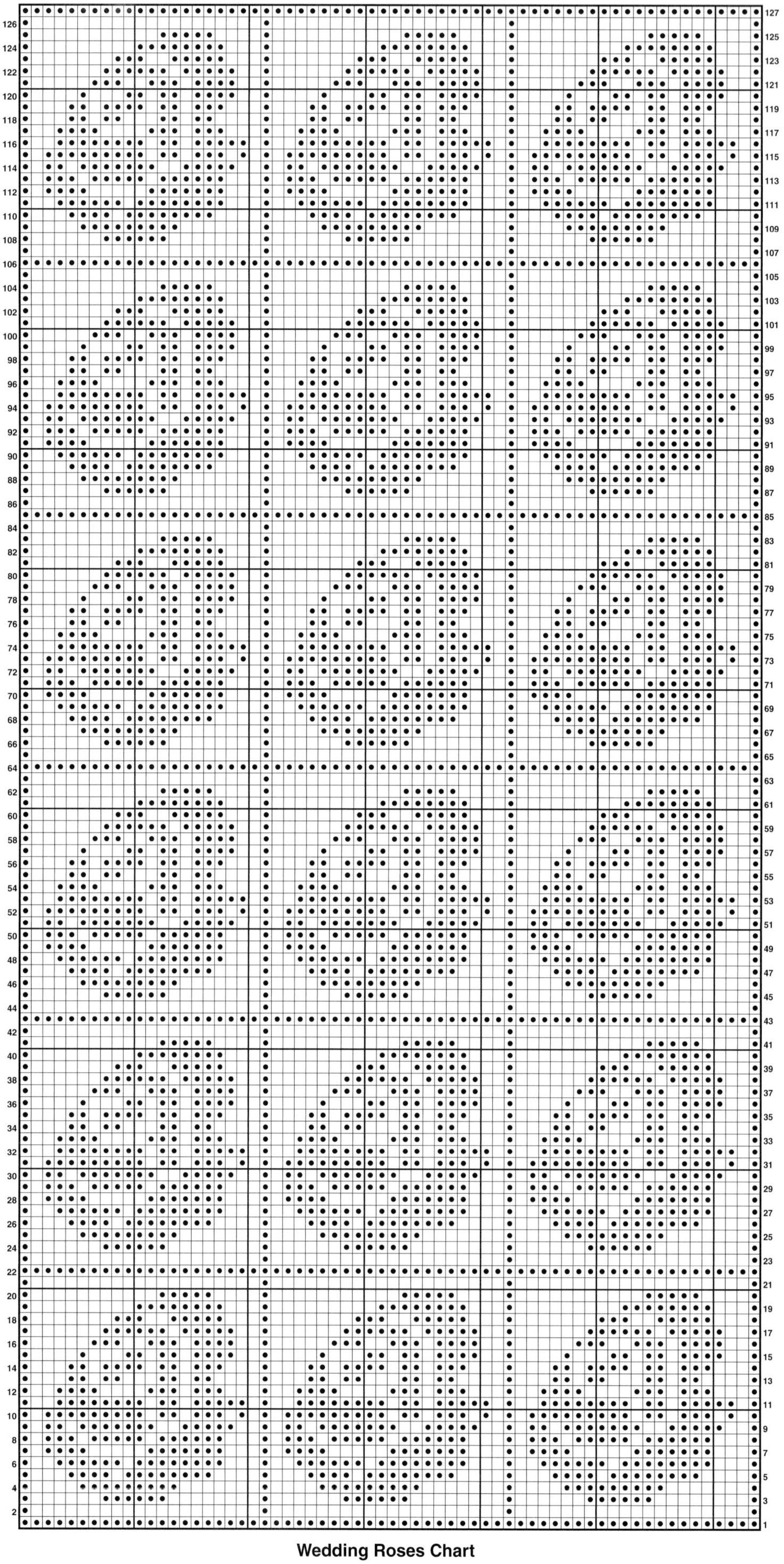

**Wedding Roses Chart**

# Loop de Loop

DESIGN BY HARTMUT HASS

Against a backdrop of lacy filet, solid stitches create a picture-perfect pattern of a large center flower nestled inside a wreath of triple-loop leaves in this impressive creation from a master of filet design.

RMEDIATE

**FINISHED SIZE**
19½ x 20 inches

**MATERIALS**
Royale Fine size 20 crochet cotton (400 yds per ball):
600 yds #201 white
Size 9/1.25mm steel crochet hook or size needed to obtain gauge
Starch

**GAUGE**
14 dc = 1 inch; 6 dc rows = 1¼ inches

**PATTERN NOTE**
Doily is crocheted from center outward.

**SPECIAL STITCHES**
**Block:** Dc in each of next 3 sts, or, 2 dc in next ch sp, dc in next st.

**Mesh:** Ch 2, sk next 2 sts, dc in next dc or ch 2, sk next ch sp, dc in next dc.

**Lacet:** Ch 3, sk next 2 sts, sc in next st, ch 3, sk next 2 sts, dc in next dc.

**Bar:** Ch 5, sk next ch sp, next sc and next ch sp, dc in next dc.

## INSTRUCTIONS

**DOILY**

**FIRST HALF**
**Row 1:** Ch 281, dc in 8th ch from hook *(beg mesh)*, dc in each of next 6 chs, [ch 2, sk next 2 chs, dc in next ch] 3 times, dc in each of next 6 chs, [ch 2, sk next 2 chs, dc in next ch] 10 times, dc in each of next 9 chs, [ch 2, sk next 2 chs, dc in next ch] 4 times, dc in each of next 12 chs, [ch 2, sk next 2 chs, dc in next ch] twice, dc in each of next 6 chs, ch 2, sk next 2 chs, dc in each of next 22 chs, ch 2, sk next 2 chs, dc in each of next 4 chs, ch 2, sk next 2 chs, dc in each of next 13 chs, ch 2, sk next 2 chs, dc in each of next 4 chs, ch 2, sk next 2 chs, dc in each of next 22 chs, ch 2, sk next 2 chs, dc in each of next 7 chs, [ch 2, sk next 2 chs, dc in next ch] twice, dc in each of next 12 chs, [ch 2, sk next 2 chs, dc in next ch] 4 times, dc in each of next 9 chs, [ch 2, sk next 2 chs, dc in next ch] 10 times, dc in each of next 6 chs, [ch 2, sk next 2 chs, dc in next ch] 3 times, dc in each of next 6 chs, ch 2, sk next 2 chs, dc in last ch, turn. *(92 mesh and blocks)*

**Row 2:** Ch 5 *(counts as first dc and ch-2)*, using Special Stitches as needed, work according to Loop de Loop Chart, across, turn.

**Rows 3–46:** Work according to Chart, as section is completed, fasten off, join with sl st as indicated and work short sections.

**2ND HALF**
**Row 1:** Working in starting ch on opposite side of row 1, join with sl st in first ch, rep row 1 of Chart.

**Rows 2–46:** Rep rows 2–46 of First Half.

Starch lightly and press. ■

Loop de Loop Chart

# Coral Reef Ripple

DESIGN BY DARLA FANTON

The color of a cool coral reef is reflected in this easy, breezy throw. It's made with soft, 100 percent cotton yarn that makes it easy to care for, and cool and comfortable for warmer weather.

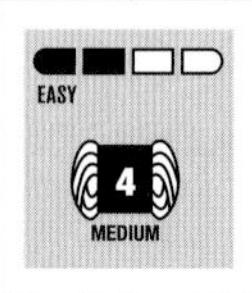

**FINISHED SIZE**
50 x 71 inches

**MATERIALS**
Medium (worsted) weight cotton yarn:
54 oz/2,700 yds/1,531g medium coral
Size G/6/4mm crochet hook or size needed to obtain gauge

**GAUGE**
4 dc = 1 inch; 2 dc rows = 1 inch

**SPECIAL STITCHES**
**Mesh:** Ch 2, sk next 2 sts, dc in next st, or, ch 2, sk next ch sp, dc in next st.

**Block:** Dc in each of next 3 sts, or, 2 dc in next ch sp, dc in next st.

**Beginning block (beg block):** Ch 3 *(counts as first dc)*, dc in each of next 3 sts.

**End increase (end inc):** *Yo, insert hook in same st as last dc made, yo, pull lp through, yo pull through 1 lp on hook *(ch-1)*, [yo, pull through 2 lps on hook] twice, working in last ch-1 made, rep from * twice.

**Beginning increase (beg inc):** Ch 5, dc in 4th ch from hook *(first 3 chs count as first dc)*, dc in next ch, dc in next st.

## INSTRUCTIONS

**AFGHAN**

**Row 1:** Ch 288, dc in 4th ch from hook, dc in each of next 2 chs *(first block)*, using Special Stitches as needed, work according to Coral Ripple Chart, turn.

**Rows 2–11:** Work according to chart, turn.

**Rows 12–101:** Rep rows 2–11 consecutively. At end of last row, fasten off. ■

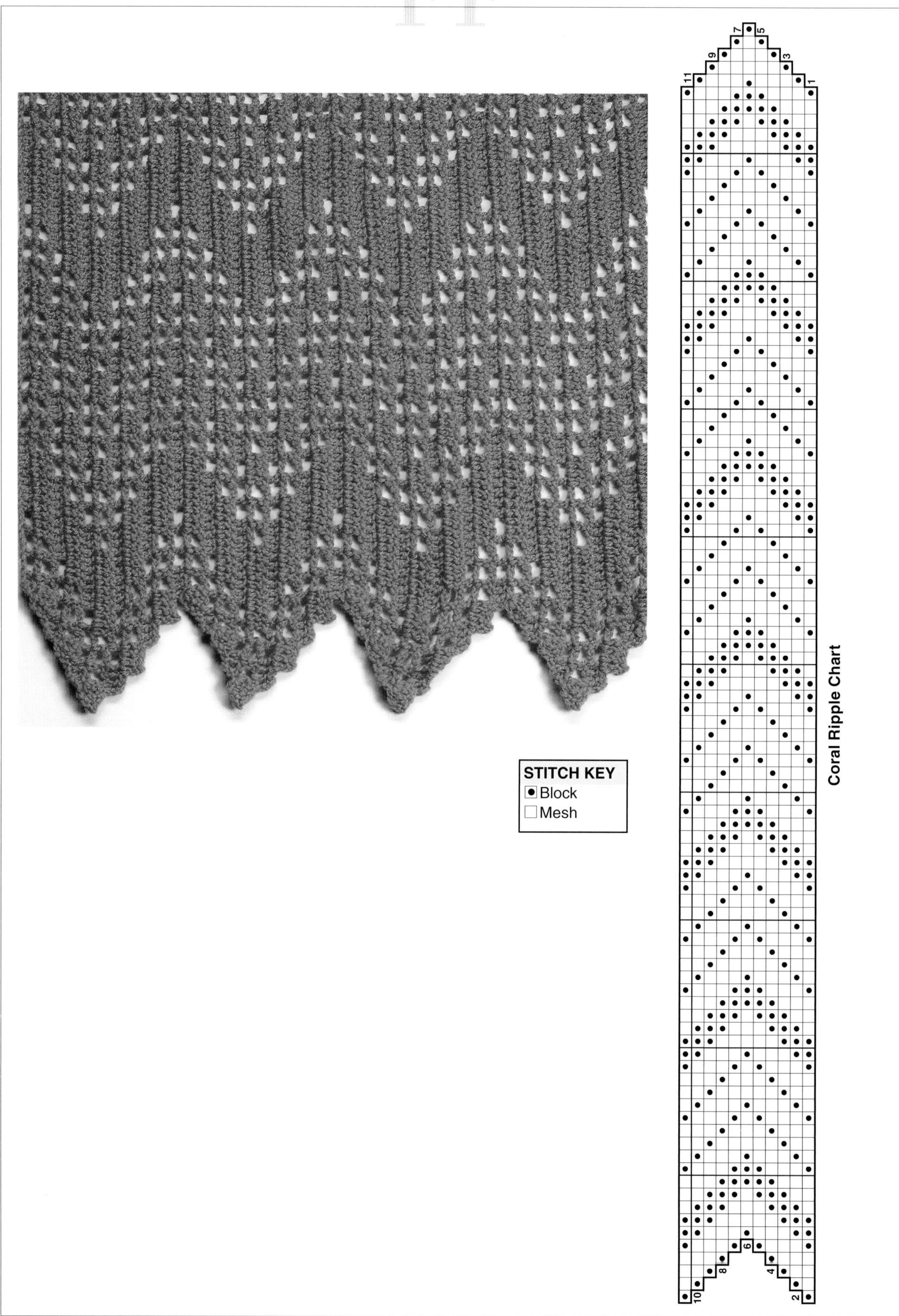
STITCH KEY
Block
Mesh
Coral Ripple Chart

# Fair Isle

DESIGN BY NANCY HEARNE

The intricate color patterns of traditional Fair Isle designs are creatively rendered in much-simpler format in this eye-catching table piece. Stitched in yarn, it would make a spectacular rug or throw.

ERMEDIATE

**FINISHED SIZE**
11½ x 15½ inches, before blocking

**MATERIALS**
Size 10 crochet cotton:
565 yds light brown
285 yds each green-gray, beige and blue
Size 7/1.65mm steel crochet hook or size needed to obtain gauge
10 yarn bobbins
Starch

**GAUGE**
13 sts = 1 inch; 9 rows = 2 inches

**PATTERN NOTES**
Wind bobbins to work color changes as follows: 5 bobbins of green-gray, 3 bobbins of blue and 2 bobbins of beige.

**Change color** *(see Stitch Guide)* in last stitch made.

Work over dropped color, carrying it in back of work to next working area.

To carry dropped color through mesh, wrap and form stitches around the dropped cotton.

Carry color through 1–3 meshes per color section per row; attach new strand of color where desired.

It is always wise to work isolated color areas with separate strands of cotton.

**SPECIAL STITCHES**

**Mesh:** Ch 2, sk next 2 sts, dc in next st or ch 2, sk next ch sp, dc in next st.

**Beginning mesh (beg mesh):** Ch 5 *(counts as first dc and ch 2)*, dc in next st.

**Popcorn (pc):** 5 dc in indicated st, drop lp from hook, insert hook in first dc of group, pull dropped lp through, ch 1 to close.

**Popcorn over mesh (pc over mesh):** Pc in next ch-2 sp, dc in next dc.

**Popcorn in popcorn (pc in pc):** Pc in top next of pc, dc in next dc.

**INSTRUCTIONS**

**DOILY**

**Row 1 (RS):** With light brown, ch 140, dc in 8th ch from hook, [ch 2, sk next 2 chs, dc in next ch] across, turn. *(45 mesh)*

**Row 2: Beg mesh** *(see Special Stitches)*, **mesh** *(see Special Stitches)* across, turn.

**Rows 3–73:** Using Special Stitches as needed, work according to Fair Isle Chart, turn. At end of last row, **do not fasten off.**

**EDGING**

**Rnd 1 (RS):** Ch 1, 2 sc in end of corner mesh, evenly sp sc around outer edge with 7 sc in each corner mesh, join with sl st in beg sc.

**Rnd 2:** Ch 3 *(counts as first dc)*, *[ch 2, sk next 2 sc, dc in next sc, pc in next sc, dc in next sc] across, pc in center corner sc, rep from * around, join with sl st in 3rd ch of beg ch-3.

**Rnd 3:** Ch 3, *ch 4, sl st in 4th ch from hook, dc in next dc, rep from * around working [dc in dc, {ch 4, sl st in 4th ch from hook} 3 times, dc in dc] at each corner, join with sl st in 3rd ch of beg ch-3. Fasten off.

Block Doily. ■

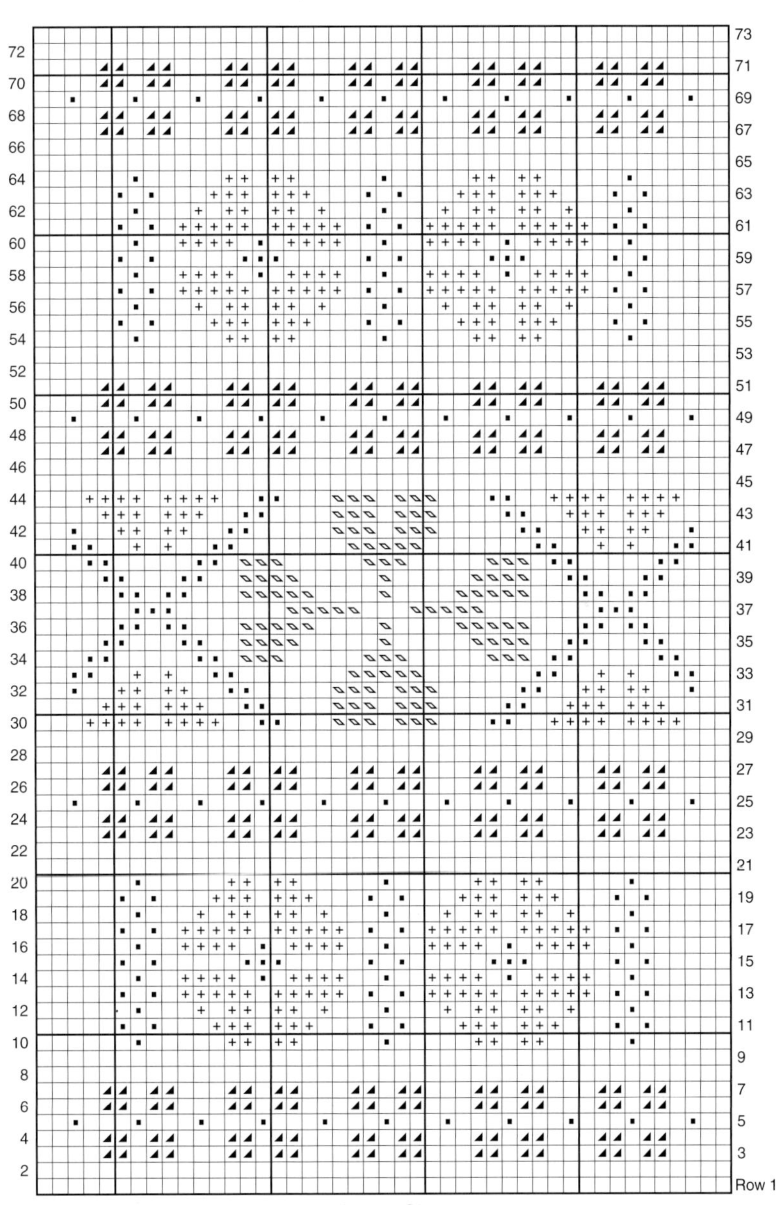


**Fair Isle Chart**

**COLOR & STITCH KEY**
- Sp (light brown)
- Pc (light brown)
- Pc (green gra )
- Pc (beige)
- Pc (antique blue)

# Bed of Roses

DESIGN BY GLENDA WINKLEMAN

Add a sweet, feminine touch to a lady's bedroom with this romantic floral throw accented with big, beautiful climbing roses. It's generously sized to fit either a single or double-size bed.

INTERMEDIATE

4 MEDIUM

**FINISHED SIZE**
61 x 79½ inches

**MATERIALS**
TLC Cotton Plus medium (worsted) weight yarn (3½ oz/186 yds/100g per skein):
18 skeins #3707 medium rose
Size F/5/3.75mm crochet hook or size needed to obtain gauge
Tapestry needle

**GAUGE**
9 dc = 2 inches; 2 dc rows = 1 inch

**PATTERN NOTE**
Work beginning mesh at beginning of each row.

**SPECIAL STITCHES**
**Mesh:** Ch 2, sk next 2 chs or dc, dc in next dc.

**Beginning mesh (beg mesh):** Ch 5, sk next 2 chs, dc in next dc.

**Block:** Dc in each of next 2 chs or dc, dc in next dc, or, dc in each of next 3 dc.

## INSTRUCTIONS

**LEFT PANEL**
**Row 1:** Ch 53, dc in 8th ch from hook, [ch 2, sk next 2 chs, dc in next ch] across, turn. *(17 dc, 16 ch sps)*

**Rows 2–32:** Using Special Stitches as needed, work according to Left Panel Chart across, turn.

**Rows 33–157:** Rep rows 8–32 consecutively.

**EDGING**
Working around entire Panel, ch 5 *(counts as first dc and ch-2 sp)*, dc in same st, 2 dc in each ch sp and dc in each st across to last st, (dc, ch 2, dc) in last st, working in ends of rows, 2 dc in first row, 3 dc in each row across to last row, 2 dc in last row, working in starting ch on opposite side of row 1, (dc, ch 2, dc) in first ch, dc in each ch and 2 dc in each ch sp across to last ch, (dc, ch 2, dc) in last ch, working in ends of rows, 2 dc in first row, 3 dc in each row across to last row, 2 dc in last row, join with sl st in 3rd ch of beg ch-5. Fasten off.

**RIGHT PANEL**
**Row 1:** Ch 53, dc in 8th ch from hook, [ch 2, sk next 2 chs, dc in next ch] across, turn. *(17 dc, 16 ch sps)*

**Rows 2–32:** Using Special Stitches as needed, work according to Right Panel Chart across, turn.

**Rows 33–157:** Rep rows 8–32 consecutively.

**EDGING**
Work same as Left Panel Edging.

**CENTER PANEL**
**Row 1:** Ch 167, dc in 8th ch from hook, [ch 2, sk next 2 chs, dc in next ch] across, turn. *(55 dc, 54 ch sps)*

**Rows 2–157:** Work according to Center Panel Chart across, turn.

**EDGING**
Work same as Left Panel Edging.

**ASSEMBLY**
Matching sts, sew Left Panel to right edge of Center Panel.

Matching sts, sew Right Panel to left edge of Center Panel. ■

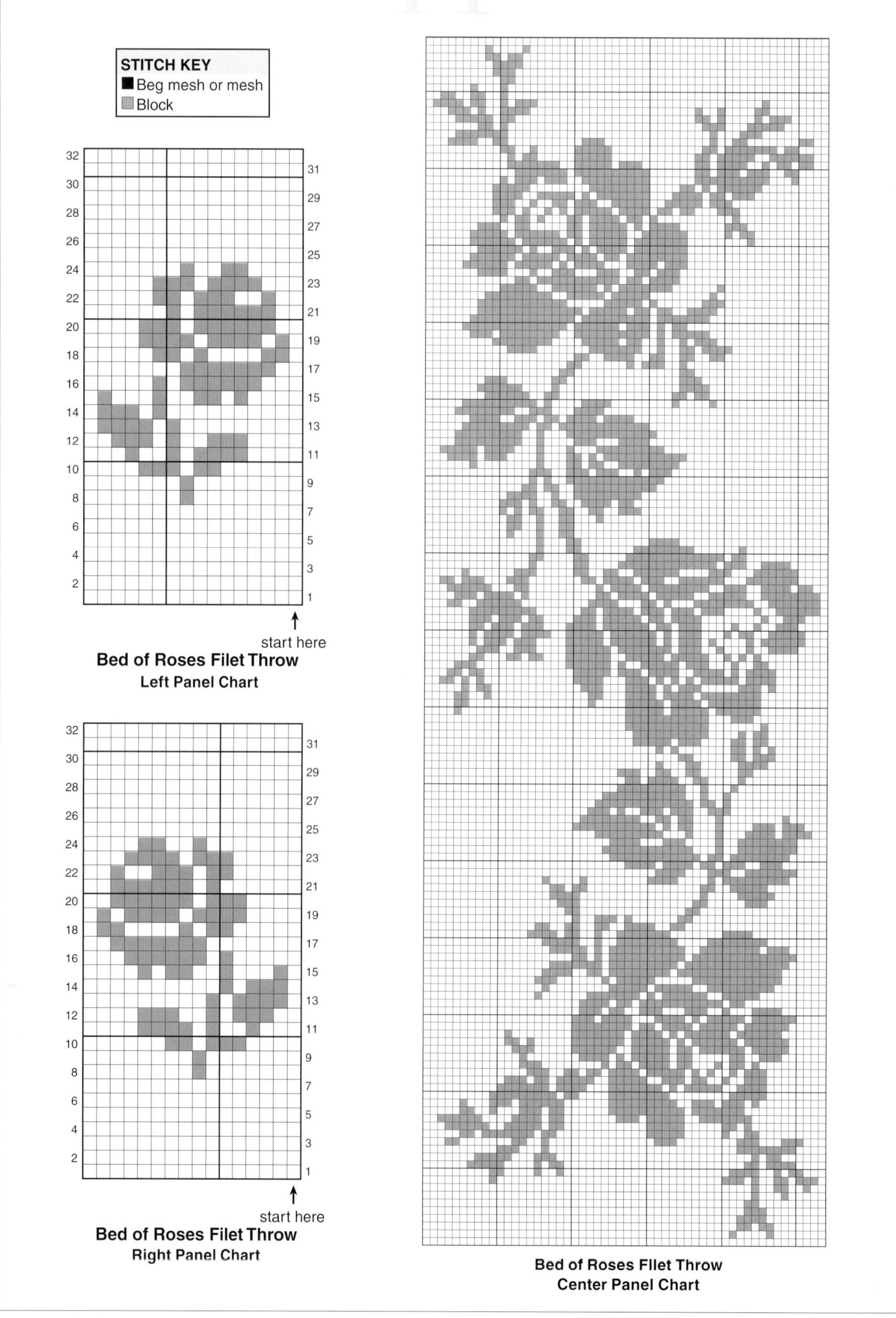


**Bed of Roses Filet Throw**
**Left Panel Chart**

**Bed of Roses Filet Throw**
**Right Panel Chart**

**Bed of Roses Filet Throw**
**Center Panel Chart**

# Rose Runner

DESIGN BY AGNES RUSSELL

"A charming picture in lavender and lace" is a phrase from an old song that perfectly describes the color and style of this stunning table runner with the look of fine, heirloom-quality threadwork.

EDIATE

**FINISHED SIZE**
15 x 40 inches

**MATERIALS**
Size 20 crochet cotton:
1,115 yds lavender
Size 11/1.10mm steel crochet hook or size needed to obtain gauge
Safety pin
Starch

**GAUGE**
7 mesh = 1½ inches; 7 rows = 1½ inches

**PATTERN NOTES**
Runner is crocheted from center outward.

After completing a few rows, attach safety pin to left edge and mark your chart with pencil on the left edge. This way you will always remember in which direction you are working as you work according to chart.

**SPECIAL STITCHES**
**Beginning block (beg block):** Ch 3 *(counts as first dc)*, dc in each of next 3 sts.

**Block:** Dc in each of next 3 sts, or, 2 dc in next ch sp, dc in next st.

**Mesh:** Ch 2, sk next 2 sts, dc in next st, or, ch 2, sk next ch sp, dc in next st.

## INSTRUCTIONS

### RUNNER

**FIRST HALF**
**Row 1 (RS):** Ch 213, dc in 4th ch from hook, dc in each of next 2 chs, [ch 2, sk next 2 chs, dc in next ch] 68 times, dc in each of last 3 chs, turn. *(2 blocks, 68 mesh)*

**Row 2: Beg block** *(see Special Stitches)*, 68 **mesh** *(see Special Stitches)*, **block** *(see Special Stitches)*, turn.

**Rows 3–100:** Using Special Stitches as needed, work according to Rose Runner Chart turn. At end of last row, fasten off.

**2ND HALF**
**Row 1 (RS):** Make sure the RS of row 1 of first half is facing, join with sl st in first ch, ch 3, dc in each of next 3 chs, 68 mesh, block, turn.

**Rows 2–100:** Rep rows 2–100 of First Half.

Starch and press. ■

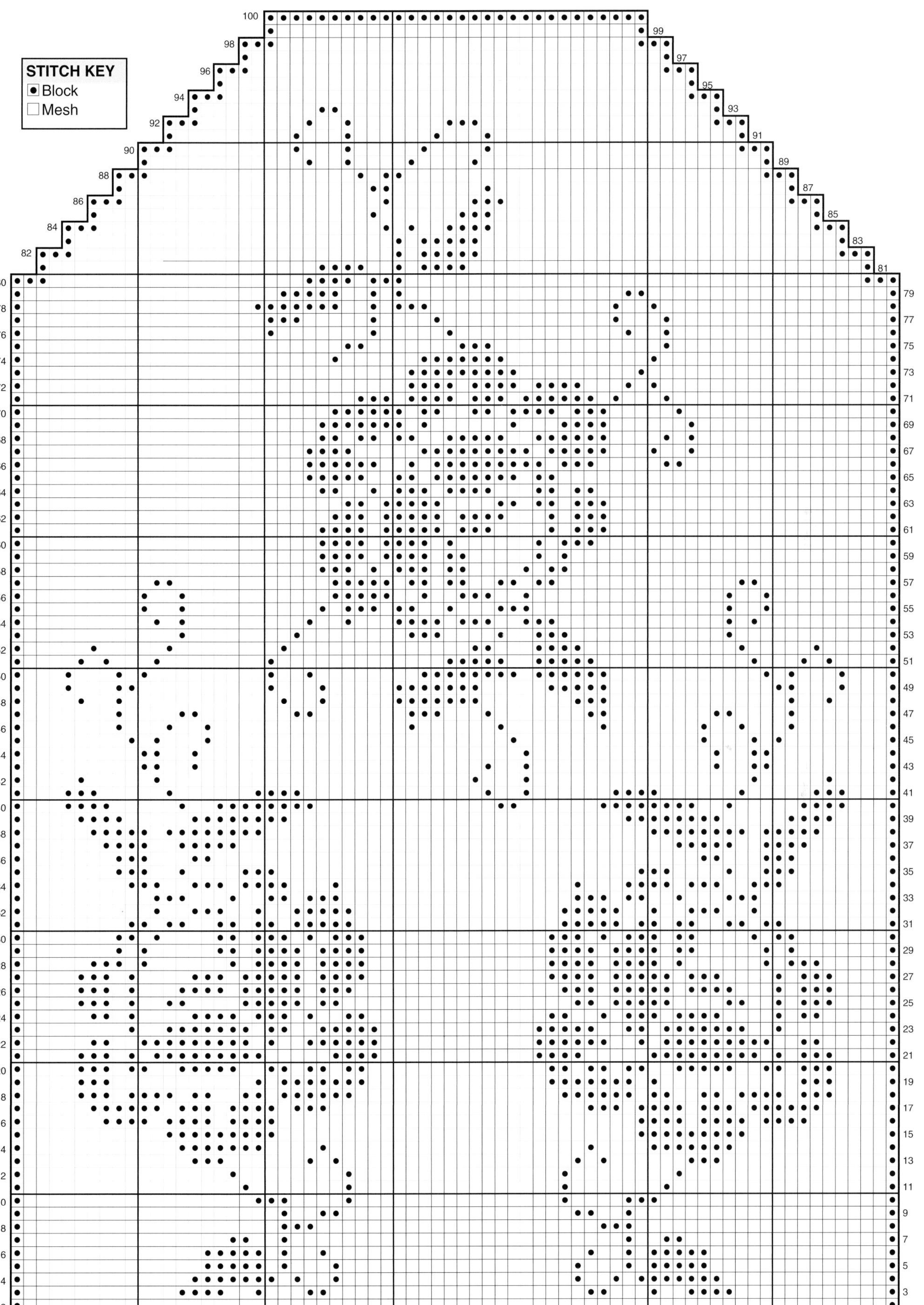


Rose Runner Chart

# Rippling Lace

DESIGN BY CHRISTINE GRAZIOSO MOODY

Medium-weight yarn highlighted with colorful shiny twists gives a lustrous tweed look to this light, airy filet ripple pattern. Deep points on each end add a look of graceful elegance.

EASY

4 MEDIUM

**FINISHED SIZE**
42 x 62 inches

**MATERIALS**
Medium (worsted) weight yarn:
24 oz/1,200 yds/680g variegated off-white with shades of green & aqua
Size I/9/5.5mm crochet hook or size needed to obtain gauge
Tapestry needle

**GAUGE**
6 dc = 2 inches; 6 dc rows = 2 inches

**SPECIAL STITCHES**
**Block:** Dc in each of next 3 sts or 2 dc in next ch sp, dc in next st.

**Mesh:** Ch 2, sk next 2 sts, dc in next st, or, ch 2, sk next ch sp, dc in next st.

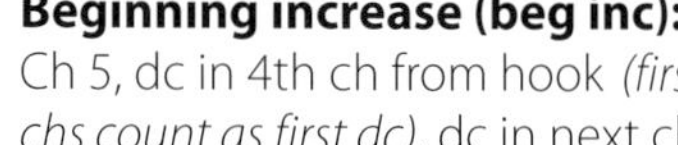

**Beginning increase (beg inc):** Ch 5, dc in 4th ch from hook *(first 3 chs count as first dc)*, dc in next ch.

**Beginning decrease (beg dec):** Sl st in each of next 4 dc, ch 3.

**Ending increase (end inc):** Tr in same st as last dc, [tr in bottom lps of last tr] twice.

**Ending decrease (end dec):** Leave last 3 sts unworked.

**INSTRUCTIONS**

**AFGHAN**
**Row 1 (RS):** Ch 195, dc in 4th ch from hook, dc in each ch across, turn. *(193 dc)*

**Row 2: Beg dec** *(see Special Stitches)*, dc in each of next 3 sts, *2 **mesh** *(see Special Stitches)*, 2 **blocks** *(see Special Stitches)*, 2 mesh**, block, rep from * across, ending last rep at **, **end inc** *(see Special Stitches)*, turn.

**Row 3: Beg inc** *(see Special Stitches)*, *2 mesh, 2 blocks, 2 mesh**, block, rep from * across, ending last rep at **, **end dec** *(see Special Stitches)*, turn.

**Rows 4–19:** Using Special Stitches as needed, work rows 4–19 according to Rippling Lace Chart, turn.

**Rows 20–60:** Rep rows 8–19 consecutively, ending last rep of with row 12.

**Row 61:** Beg dec, dc in each st across, end inc. Fasten off. ■

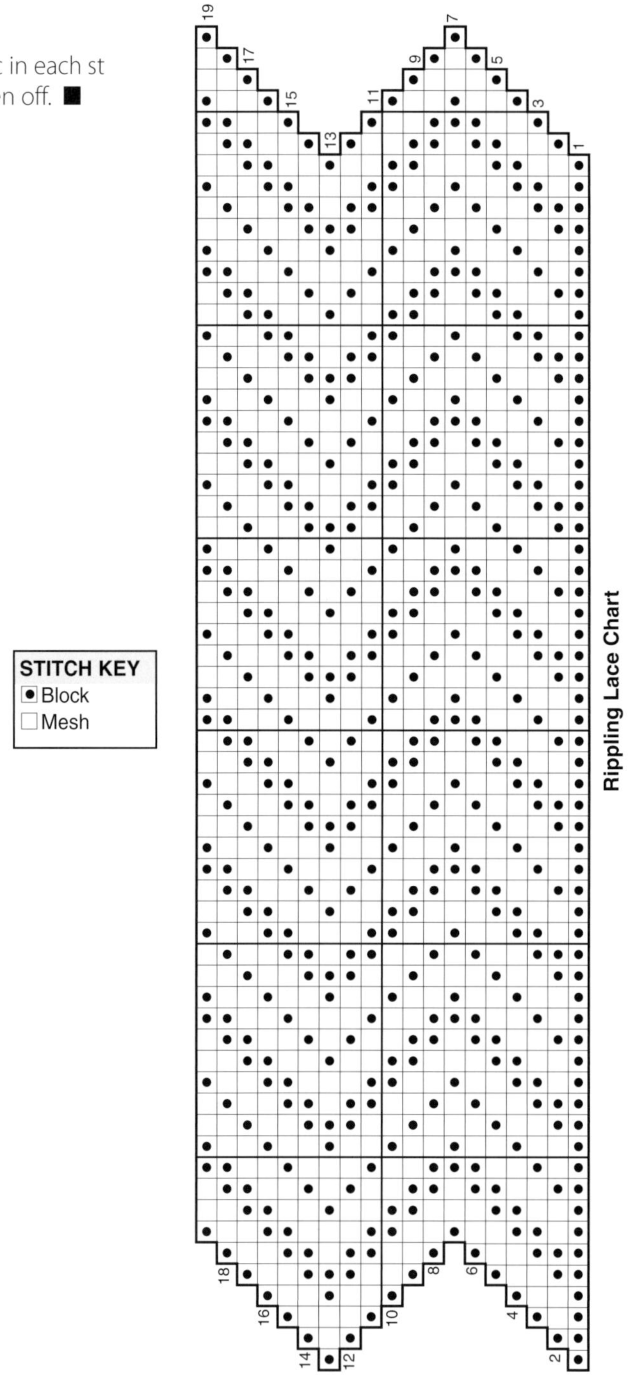

STITCH KEY
- Block
- Mesh

Rippling Lace Chart

# Shadow Box

DESIGN BY ZELDA WORKMAN

Alternating sections of lacet and traditional-style filet patterns create a shadow-box effect in the exquisite design of this stunning piece. Deep, elegant ruffles add the perfect finishing touch.

IMEDIATE

**FINISHED SIZE**
12 x 13 inches

**MATERIALS**
Royal Fine Crochet size 20 crochet cotton (400 yds per ball): 300 yds #226 natural
Size 12/1.00mm steel crochet hook or size needed to obtain gauge
Tapestry needle
Fabric stiffener
Plastic wrap
Pinning board
Rust-proof straight pins

**GAUGE**
7 block or mesh = 2 inches; 13 rows = 4 inches

**SPECIAL STITCHES**
**Block:** Tr in each of next 3 tr, or, 2 tr in next ch sp, tr in next tr.

**Beginning block (beg block):** Ch 4 *(counts as first tr)*, tr in each of next 3 tr.

**Mesh:** Ch 2, sk next ch sp, tr in next tr, or, ch 2, sk next 2 tr, tr in next tr.

**Lacet:** Ch 3, sk next 2 sts, sc in next st, ch 3, sk next 2 sts, tr in next tr.

**Bar:** Ch 5, sk next ch sp, next sc and next ch sp, tr in next tr.

**INSTRUCTIONS**

**DOILY**
**Row 1 (RS):** Ch 109, tr in 5th ch from hook *(first 4 chs count as first tr)*, tr in each ch across, turn. *(106 tr)*

**Rows 2–35:** Using Special Stitches as needed, work according to Shadow Box Chart. At the end of row 35, **do not fasten off.**

**RUFFLE**
**Rnd 1 (RS):** *Working across side edge of Doily, [ch 6, sl st at bottom of next tr or ch-4] across to corner*,

working in starting ch on opposite side of row 1, [ch 6, sk next 2 chs, sl st in next ch] across to corner, rep between * once, working across row 35, [ch 6, sk next 2 sts, sl st in next st] across, ending with sl st in corner.

**Rnds 2–5:** Sl st into center of next ch sp, ch 1, sc in same ch sp, ch 5, [sc in next ch sp, ch 5] around, join with sl st in beg sc.

At the end of rnd 5, fasten off.

**FINISHING**

Cover pinning board with plastic wrap. Saturate Doily with fabric stiffener. Solution must dry firmly enough for ruffle to hold its shape. Pin Doily to pinning board to measurements. Shape ruffles. Reshape every 1–2 hours until they are dry enough to hold their shape. Allow to dry completely before removing. ■

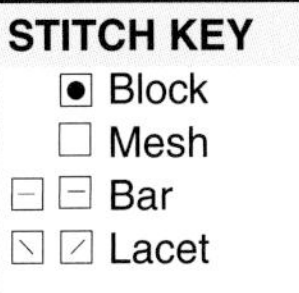


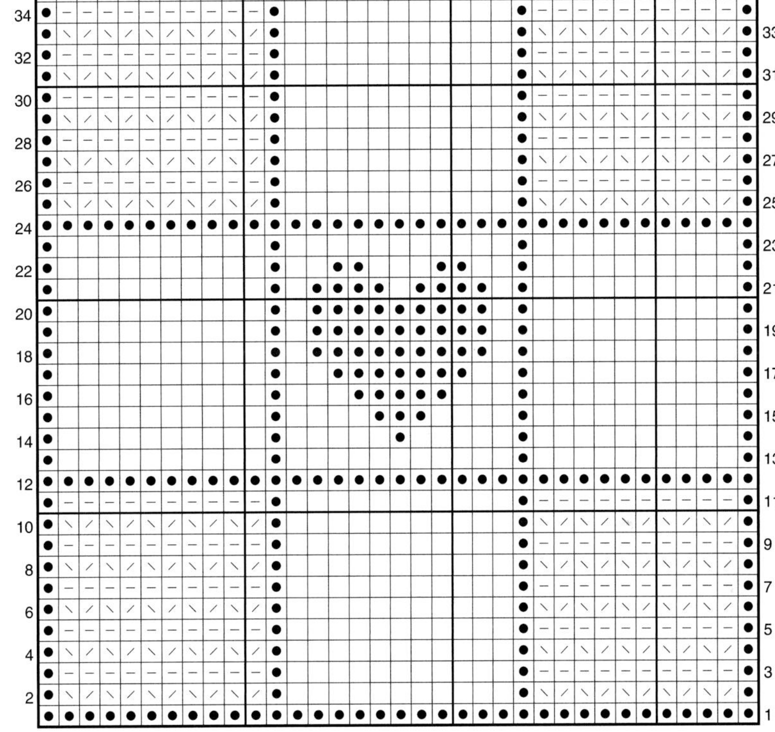

**Shadow Box Chart**

# Aran Eyelet

DESIGN BY LUCIA KARGE BUINNO

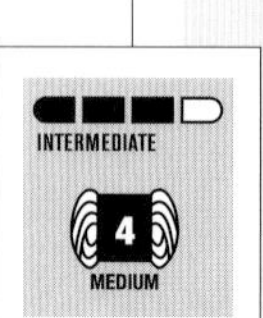


A richly textured center panel set off with lacy, eyelet-filet side panels gives both dimension and delicacy to this pretty throw that works up quickly with double-strand yarn and a large hook.

**FINISHED SIZE**
48 x 54 inches

**MATERIALS**
Medium (worsted) weight yarn:
58 oz/2,900 yds/1,644g off-white
Size N/13/9mm crochet hook or size needed to obtain gauge
Tapestry needle

**GAUGE**
**With 2 strands held tog:** 2 dc sts = 1 inch; 1 dc row = 1 inch

**PATTERN NOTES**
Entire afghan is worked with 2 strands of yarn held together.

The treble crochet used in the Center Panel gives a popcorn effect.

**SPECIAL STITCH**
**V-stitch (V-st):** (Dc, ch 1, dc) in next ch or in ch sp of next V-st.

## INSTRUCTIONS

**SIDE PANEL**
Make 2.

**Row 1:** Ch 33, dc in 4th ch from hook *(first 3 chs count as first dc)*, dc in each of next 2 chs, *ch 1, sk next 2 chs, **V-st** *(see Special Stitch)* in next ch, ch 1, sk next 2 chs*, dc in each of next 6 chs, ch 1, sk next ch, dc in each of next 6 chs, rep between *, dc in each of last 4 chs, turn. *(20 dc, 2 V-sts)*

**Row 2:** Ch 3 *(count as first dc)*, dc in each of next 3 sts, ch 1, V-st in next V-st, ch 1, sk next ch-1 sp, dc in each of next 4 sts, ch 3, sk next 2 sts, sc in next ch-1 sp, ch 3, sk next 2 sts, dc in each of next 4 sts, ch 1, V-st in next V-st, ch 1, sk next ch-1 sp, dc in each of last 4 sts, turn. *(16 dc, 2 V-sts, 2 ch-3 sps, 1 sc)*

**Row 3:** Ch 3, dc in each of next 3 sts, ch 1, V-st in next V-st, ch 1, sk next ch-1 sp, dc in each of next 2 sts, sk next 2 sts, ch 3, [sc in next ch-3 sp, ch 3] twice, sk next 2 sts, dc in each of next 2 sts, ch 1, V-st in next V-st, ch 1, dc in each of last 4 sts, turn.

**Row 4:** Ch 3, dc in each of next 3 sts, ch 1, V-st in next V-st, ch 1, sk next ch-1 sp, dc in each of next 2 sts, dc in each of next 2 chs, ch 3, sc in next ch-3 sp, ch 3, sk next 2 chs, dc in each of next 2 chs, dc in each of next 2 sts, ch 1, V-st in next V-st, ch 1, sk next ch-1 sp, dc in each of last 4 sts, turn.

**Row 5:** Ch 3, dc in each of next 3 sts, ch 1, V-st in next V-st, ch 1, sk next ch-1 sp, dc in each of next 4 sts, dc in each of next 2 chs, ch 1, sk next ch, next sc and next ch, dc in each of next 2 chs, dc in each of next 4 sts, ch 1, V-st in next V-st, ch 1, sk next ch-1 sp, dc in each of last 4 sts, turn.

**Row 6:** Ch 3, dc in each of next 3 sts, ch 1, V-st in next V-st, ch 1, sk next ch-1 sp, dc in each of next 6 sts, ch 1, sk next ch-1 sp, dc in each of next 6 sts, ch 1, V-st in next V-st, ch 1, sk next ch-1 sp, dc in each of last 4 sts, turn.

**Rows 7–50:** Rep rows 2–6 consecutively, ending with row 5. For **First Side Panel,** fasten off. For **2nd Side Panel, do not fasten off.**

**FIRST SIDE PANEL**
**Row 51:** Working in ends of rows, join with sc in row 1, sc in same row, 2 sc in each row across. Fasten off. *(100 sc)*

Do not work on opposite end of rows.

**2ND SIDE PANEL**
**Row 51:** Working in end of rows, ch 1, 2 sc in each row across. Fasten off. *(100 sc)*

Do not work on opposite end of rows.

**CENTER PANEL**
**Row 1:** Ch 30, sc in 2nd ch from hook, sc in each ch across, turn. *(29 sc)*

**Row 2:** Ch 1, sc in first st, [tr in next st, sc in next st] across, turn. *(15 sc, 14 tr)*

**Row 3:** Ch 1, sc in each sc and in each tr across, turn. *(29 sc)*

**Rows 4–87:** Rep rows 2 and 3 alternately.

**Row 88:** Working in end of rows, ch 1, sc in each of first 7 rows, 2 sc in next row, [sc in each of next 5 rows, 2 sc in next row] 12 times, sc in each of last 7 rows. Fasten off. *(100 sc)*

**Row 89:** Working on opposite side of Panel, in end of rows, join with sc in row 1, sc in each of next 6 rows, 2 sc in next row, [sc in each of next 5 rows, 2 sc in next row] 12 times, sc in each of last 7 rows. Fasten off. *(100 sc)*

### ASSEMBLY

With RS tog, working through both thicknesses, in row 89 of Center Panel and in row 51 of 1 Side Panel, with WS of pieces facing, join with sc in first st, sc in each st across. Fasten off.

Join rem pieces tog.

### EDGING

**Row 1:** Working on opposite side of starting ch on all 3 pieces, with row 1 facing, join with sc in first st, sc in each st, in end of each row and in each seam across, turn. *(97 sc)*

**Row 2:** Ch 1, sc in first st, [sk next 2 sts, 5 dc in next st, sk next 2 sts, sc in next st] across. Fasten off.

Working in last row of all 3 pieces, rep rows 1 and 2. ■

# Laura's Roses

DESIGN BY JENNIFER MCCLAIN

Satisfy your passion for uncommonly beautiful pieces with this striking yet simple afghan, suffused with the essence of true Victoriana. The vibrant colors make it a striking accent for any home.

**FINISHED SIZE**
46¾ x 59¼ inches

**MATERIALS**
Medium (worsted) weight yarn:
21 oz/1,050 yds/595g each black and light raspberry
17 oz/850 yds/481g light fuchsia
4 oz/200 yds/113g soft pink
Size G/6/4mm crochet hook or size needed to obtain gauge
Tapestry needle

**GAUGE**
Rnds 1 and 2 = 1¾ inches across

Block = 6¼ inches square

**SPECIAL STITCH**
**Berry stitch (berry st):** Insert hook in next st, yo, pull lp through, working through first lp only, ch 3, yo, pull through both lps on hook.

**INSTRUCTIONS**

**BLOCK**
Make 63.

**Rnd 1:** With soft pink, ch 2, 8 sc in 2nd ch from hook, join with sl st in beg sc. *(8 sc)*

**Rnd 2:** Ch 1, sc in first st, **berry st** *(see Special Stitch)* in same st, (sc, berry st) in each st around, join with sl st in beg sc. Fasten off. *(8 sc, 8 bs)*

**Rnd 3:** Join light raspberry with sl st in first st, ch 3, sk next st, [sl st in next st, ch 3, sk next st] around, join with sl st in beg sl st. *(8 ch-3 sps)*

**Rnd 4:** Sl st in first ch sp, ch 1, (sc, ch 2, sc) in same ch sp, ch 2, *(sc, ch 2, sc) in next ch sp, ch 2, rep from * around, join with sl st in beg sc. *(16 ch-2 sps)*

**Rnd 5:** Sl st in first ch sp, ch 1, ({sc, ch 3} twice, sc) in same ch sp, ch 3, sk next ch sp, *({sc, ch 3} twice, sc) in next ch sp, ch 3, sk next ch sp, rep from * around, join with sl st in beg sc. Fasten off.

**Rnd 6:** Working behind rnd 5, in sk ch sps of rnd 4, join light fuchsia with sc in any ch sp, ch 3, sc in same ch sp, ch 3, *(sc, ch 3, sc) in next ch sp, ch 3, rep from * around, join with sl st in beg sc.

**Rnd 7:** Sl st in first ch sp, ch 1, (sc, ch 3, sc, ch 5, sc, ch 3, sc) in same ch sp, ch 2, sk next ch sp, *(sc, ch 3, sc, ch 5, sc, ch 3, sc) in next ch sp, ch 2, sk next ch sp, rep from * around, join with sl st in beg sc.

**Rnd 8:** Ch 1, working from back to front through next ch sp on rnd 6, dc around adjacent ch-3 sp on rnd 5, ch 2, sc over next ch sps on last 2 rnds, ch 2, rep from * around, join with sl st in beg dc. Fasten off. *(8 dc, 8 sc, 16 ch-2 sps)*

**Rnd 9:** Join black with sl st in first ch sp, ch 3 *(counts as first dc)*, (dc, ch 2, 2 dc) in same ch sp, *(dc, hdc, sc) in next ch sp, 3 sc in next ch sp, (sc, hdc, dc) in next ch sp**, (2 dc, ch 2, 2 dc) in next ch sp, rep from * around, ending last rep at **, join with sl st in 3rd ch of beg ch-3. *(52 sts, 4 ch-2 sps)*

**Rnd 10:** Ch 1, sc in each st around with (sc, ch 2, sc) in each corner ch sp, join with sl st in beg sc. *(15 sc on each edge between corner ch sps)*

**Rnd 11:** Sl st in next st, ch 1, sc in same st, ch 1, sk next st, *(sc, ch 2, sc) in next comer ch sp, ch 1, sk next st, [sc in next st, ch 1, sk next st] across to next corner, rep from * around, join with sl st in beg sc. Fasten off.

**Rnd 12:** Join light raspberry with sc in any corner ch sp, (sc, ch 2, 2 sc) in same ch sp, 2 sc in each ch-1 sp across to next corner ch sp, *(2 sc, ch 2, 2 sc) in next corner ch sp, 2 sc in each ch-1 sp across to next corner ch sp, rep from * around, join with sl st in beg sc. Fasten off. *(20 sc on each side between corner ch sps)*

With light raspberry, sew Blocks tog in 7 rows of 9 Blocks each.

**BORDER**

**Rnd 1:** Join light raspberry with sc in any corner ch sp, ch 2, sc in same ch sp, sc in each st and in each ch sp on each side of seams around with (sc, ch 2, sc) in each corner ch sp, join with sl st in beg sc. Fasten off. *(154 sc on each short end, 198 sc on each long edge, 4 ch-2 sps)*

**Rnd 2:** Join black with sc in corner ch sp before 1 short end, ch 2, sc in same ch sp, *ch 2, sk next st, [**sc dec** *(see Stitch Guide)* in next 2 sts, ch 2, sk next st] across to next corner ch sp, (sc, ch 2, sc) in next corner ch sp, ch 2, sk next 2 sts, sc dec in next 2 sts, [ch 2, sk next st, sc dec in next 2 sts] across to 2 sts before next corner ch sp, ch 2, sk next 2 sts*, (sc, ch 2, sc) in next corner ch sp, rep between *, join with sl st in beg sc. Fasten off.

**Rnd 3:** Join light fuchsia with sl st in any sc, ch 1, bs in next ch sp, [sl st in next sc, ch 1, bs in next ch sp] around, join with sl st in first sl st. Fasten off.

**Rnd 4:** Working over sl sts on last rnd into sc on rnd 2, join black with sl st in any sc, ch 3, 2 dc in same sc, (sl st, ch 3, 2 dc) in each sc around, join with sl st in beg sl st. Fasten off. ■

# Pineapple Fans

REPRODUCED FROM A VINTAGE PATTERN

Unusual and unique, this square doily uses several different stitches to achieve a wonderful visual and tactile texture. Frame it on a deep contrasting color or place it on an accent table for a dazzling look.

RIENCED

**FINISHED SIZE**
21 inches square

**MATERIALS**
Size 10 crochet cotton:
572 yds white
Size 7/1.65mm steel crochet hook or size needed to obtain gauge

**GAUGE**
8 tr = 1 inch

**SPECIAL STITCHES**

**Beginning V-stitch (beg V-st):** Ch 7 *(counts as tr and ch-3)*, tr in same st.

**V-stitch (V-st):** (Tr, ch 3, tr) as indicated.

**Popcorn (pc):** 5 tr in ch sp or st indicated, drop lp from hook, insert hook in first tr of group, pull dropped lp through.

**Treble crochet cluster (tr cl):** Holding back last lp of each tr on hook, 2 tr in st indicated, yo and pull through all lps on hook.

**INSTRUCTIONS**

**DOILY**

**Rnd 1:** Ch 10, sl st in first ch to form ring, ch 4 *(counts as first tr)*, 4 tr in ring, ch 5, [5 tr in ring, ch 5] 3 times, join with sl st in 4th ch of beg ch-4.

**Rnd 2: Beg V-st** *(see Special Stitches)*, *sk next 3 tr, **V-st** *(see Special Stitches)* in next tr, (tr, ch 7, tr) in 3rd ch of next ch-5 sp *(corner)***, V-st in next tr, rep from * around, ending last rep at **, join with sl st in 4th ch of beg ch-7. *(8 V-sts)*

**Rnd 3:** Beg V-st in first st, *V-st in sp between next 2 V-sts, V-st in sp between next V-st and next tr, 7 tr in 4th ch of corner ch-7 sp *(pineapple base)***, V-st in sp between next tr of same corner and next V-st, rep from * around, ending last rep at **, join with sl st in 4th ch of beg ch-7. *(4 pineapple bases)*

**Rnd 4:** Ch 4 *(counts as first tr)*, *[V-st in sp between next 2 V-sts] twice, tr between next V-st and next pineapple base, ch 3, 2 tr in each of next 7 tr, ch 3**, tr in sp between same tr and next V-st, rep from * around, ending last rep at **, join with sl st in 4th ch of beg ch-4.

**Rnd 5:** Ch 1, sc in first st, *ch 3, sk next V-st, 4 tr in first tr of next V-st, ch 3, sc in sp between next V-st and next tr, ch 3, [tr in next tr, ch 1] 13 times, tr in next tr, ch 3**, sc in sp between next tr and next V-st, rep from * around, ending last rep at **, join with sl st in beg sc.

**Rnd 6:** Sl st in each of next 3 chs, ch 3, **tr dec** *(see Stitch Guide)* in next 3 tr, *ch 8, sk next 2 ch-3 sps, [sc in next ch-1 sp, ch 3] 12 times, sc in next ch-1 sp, ch 8, sk next 2 ch-3 sps**, tr dec in next 4 tr, rep from * around, ending last rep at **, join with sl st in beg tr dec.

**Rnd 7:** Ch 6 *(counts as first tr and ch-2)*, ({tr, ch 2} 3 times, tr) in same st, *ch 7, sk next ch-8 sp, [**pc** *(see Special Stitches)* in next ch-3 sp, ch 2] 11 times, pc in next ch-3 sp, ch 7, sk next ch-8 sp**, ({tr, ch 2} 4 times, tr) in next tr dec, rep from * around, ending last rep at **, join with sl st in 4th ch of beg ch-6.

**Rnd 8:** Ch 7, tr in next tr, ch 3, 3 tr in next tr, [ch 3, tr in next tr] twice, *ch 6, sk next ch-7 sp and next pc, sc in next ch-2 sp, [ch 3, sc in next ch-2 sp] 10 times, ch 6, sk next pc and next ch-7 sp**, [tr in next tr, ch 3] twice, 3 tr in next tr, [ch 3, tr in next tr] twice, rep from * around, ending last rep at **, join with sl st in 4th ch of beg ch-7.

**Rnd 9:** Ch 4 *(counts as first tr)*, tr in same st, *ch 3, tr in next tr, ch 3, 2 tr in next tr, 3 tr in next tr, 2 tr in next tr, ch 3, tr in next tr, ch 3, 2 tr in next tr, ch 6, sk next ch-6 sp, [pc in next ch-3 sp, ch 2] 9 times, pc in next ch-3 sp, ch 6, sk next ch-6 sp**, 2 tr in next tr, rep from * around, ending last rep at **, join with sl st in 4th ch of beg ch-4.

**Rnd 10:** Ch 4, *2 tr in next tr, ch 3, tr in next tr, ch 3, [2 tr in next tr, tr in next tr, ch 2, tr in next tr] twice, 2 tr in next tr, ch 3, tr in next tr, ch 3, 2 tr in next tr, tr in next tr, ch 6, sk next ch-6 sp, sc in next ch-2 sp, [ch 3, sc in next ch-2 sp] 8 times, ch 6, sk next ch-6 sp**, tr in next tr, rep from * around, ending last rep at **, join with sl st in 4th ch of beg ch-4.

**Rnd 11:** Ch 4, tr in each of next 2 tr, *ch 3, tr in next tr, ch 3, tr in each of next 3 tr, ch 6, tr dec in next 4 tr, ch 6, tr in each of next 3 tr, ch 3, tr in next tr, ch 3, tr in each of next 3 tr, ch 7, sk next ch-6 sp, pc in next ch-3 sp, [ch 2, pc in next ch-3 sp] 7 times, ch 7**, tr in each of next 3 tr, rep from * around, ending last rep at **, join with sl st in 4th ch of beg ch-4.

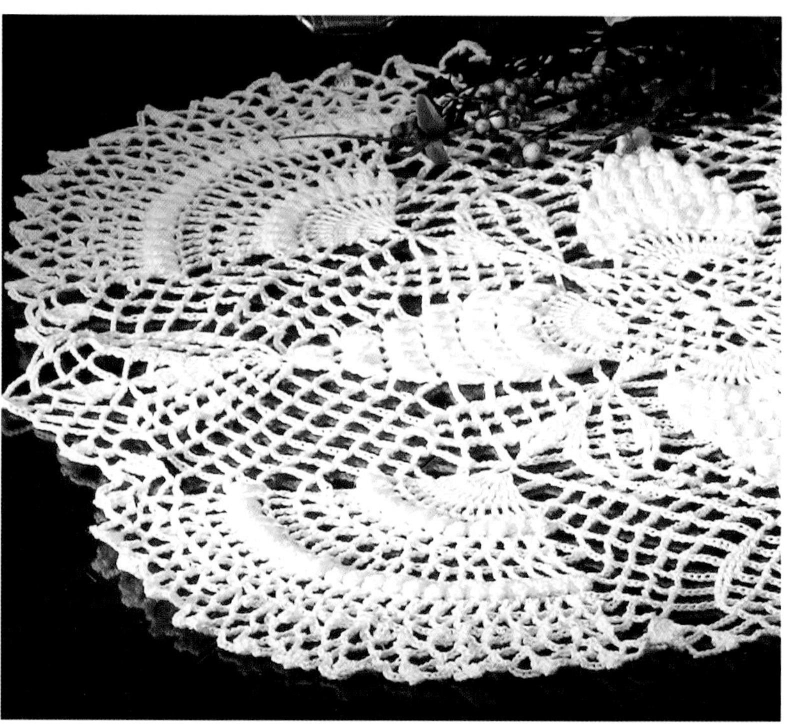

**Rnd 12:** Ch 4, tr in next tr, *ch 3, sk next tr, tr in next tr, ch 3, tr in each of next 2 tr, ch 9, sk next tr and next ch-6 sp, (sc, ch 5, sc) in next tr dec, ch 9, sk next ch-6 sp and next tr, tr in each of next 2 tr, ch 3, tr in next tr, ch 3, sk next ch-3 sp and next tr, tr in each of next 2 tr, ch 11, sk next ch-7 sp, sc in next ch-2 sp, [ch 3, sc in next ch-2 sp] 6 times, ch 11, sk next pc and next ch-7 sp**, tr in each of next 2 tr, rep from * around, ending last rep at **, join with sl st in 4th ch of beg ch-4.

**Rnd 13:** Ch 3, tr in next tr *(tr dec)*, *ch 2, tr in next tr, ch 2, tr dec in next 2 tr, ch 8, sc in next ch-9 sp, ch 4, 7 tr in next ch-5 sp *(fan base)*, ch 4, sc in next ch-9 sp, ch 8, tr dec in next 2 tr, ch 2, tr in next tr, ch 2, tr dec in next 2 tr, ch 8, sc in next ch-11 sp, ch 8, pc in next ch-3 sp, [ch 2, pc in next ch-3 sp] 5 times, ch 8, sc in next ch-11 sp, ch 8**, tr dec in next 2 tr, rep from * around, ending last rep at **, join in sl st in beg tr.

**Rnd 14:** Ch 3, tr dec in next tr and in next tr dec, *ch 8, sc in next ch-8 sp, ch 8, sk next sc and next ch-4 sp, 2 tr in each of next 7 tr, ch 8, sk next ch-4 sp and next sc, sc in next ch-8 sp, ch 8, tr dec in next tr dec, next tr and next tr dec, ch 8, [sc in next ch-8 sp, ch 8] twice, sc in next ch-2 sp, [ch 3, sc in next ch-2 sp] 4 times, ch 8, [sc in next ch-8 sp, ch 8] twice**, tr dec in next tr dec, next tr and next tr dec, rep from * around, ending last rep at **, join with sl st in beg tr dec.

**Rnd 15:** Sl st in each of next 4 chs of next ch-8 sp, ch 1, sc in same ch as last sl st made, ch 8, sc in next ch-8 sp, *ch 5, [tr in next tr, ch 1] 13 times, tr in next tr, ch 5, [sc in next ch-8 sp, ch 8] 5 times, pc in next ch-3 sp, [ch 2, pc in next ch-3 sp] 3 times**, [ch 8, sc in next ch-8 sp] 5 times, rep from * around, ending last rep at **, [ch 8, sc in next ch-8 sp] 3 times, ch 8, join with sl st in beg sc.

**Rnd 16:** Sl st in each of next 4 chs of next ch-8 sp, ch 1, sc in same ch sp, *ch 8, sk next ch-5 sp, sc in next ch-1 sp, [ch 3, sc in next ch-1 sp] 12 times, ch 8, sk next ch-5 sp, [sc in next ch-8 sp, ch 8] 4 times, 3 sc at end of next ch-8 sp, sc in next ch-2 sp, [ch 3, sc in next ch-2 sp] twice, sk next pc, 3 sc in next ch-8 sp**, [ch 8, sc in next ch-8 sp] 4 times, rep from * around, ending last rep at **, [ch 8, sc in next ch-8 sp] 3 times, ch 8, join with sl st in beg sc.

**Rnd 17:** Sl st in each of next 4 chs of next ch-8 sp, ch 1, sc in same ch-8 sp, *ch 5, pc in next ch-3 sp, [ch 2, sk next sc, pc in next ch-3 sp] 11 times, ch 5, sc in next ch-8 sp, [ch 8, sc in next ch-8 sp] 4 times, ch 8, pc in next ch-3 sp, ch 2, pc in next ch-3 sp, ch 8, sc in next ch-8 sp**, [ch 8, sc in next ch-8 sp] 4 times, rep from * around, ending last rep at **, [ch 8, sc in next ch-8 sp] 3 times, ch 8, join with sl st in beg sc.

**Rnd 18:** Sl st in each of next 5 chs of next ch-5 sp and in next pc, ch 7 *(counts as first tr and ch-3)*, *tr dec in next ch-2 sp and next pc, ch 3] 11 times, tr in next pc, ch 8, sk next ch-5 sp, sc in next ch-8 sp, [ch 8, sc in next ch-8 sp] 3 times, ch 8, 3 sc at end of next ch-8 sp, (sc, ch 3, sc) in next ch-2 sp, sk next pc, 3 sc in next ch-8 sp, [ch 8, sc in next ch-8 sp] 4 times, ch 8, sk next ch-5 sp**, tr in next pc, ch 3, rep from * around, ending last rep at **, join with sl st in 4th ch of beg ch-7.

**Rnd 19:** Ch 3, tr in next tr dec, *[ch 4, tr dec in same tr dec and next tr dec] 11 times, ch 5, sc in next ch-8 sp, [ch 8, sc in next ch-8 sp] 4 times, ch 5, sk next 3 sc, ({tr, ch 2} 4 times, tr) in next ch-3 sp, ch 5, sc in next ch-8 sp, [ch 8, sc in next ch-8 sp] 4 times, ch 5**, tr dec in next tr and next tr dec, rep from * around, ending last rep at **, join with sl st in beg tr.

**Rnd 20:** Ch 6, *[tr in next ch-4 sp, ch 2, tr in next tr dec, ch 2] 10 times, tr in next ch-4 sp, ch 2, tr in next tr dec, ch 8, sk next ch-5 sp, sc in next ch-8 sp, [ch 8, sc in next ch-8 sp] 3 times, ch 5, sk next ch-5 sp, [tr in next tr, ch 3] twice, 3 tr in next tr, [ch 3, tr in next tr] twice, ch 5, sk next ch-5 sp, sc in next ch-8 sp, [ch 8, sc in next ch-8 sp] 3 times, ch 8, sk next ch-5 sp**, tr in next tr dec, ch 2, rep from * around, ending last rep at **, join with sl st in 4th ch of beg ch-6.

**Rnd 21:** Sl st in next ch-2 sp, ch 1, sc in same ch sp, *[ch 3, sc in next ch-2 sp] 21 times, ch 3, sc in next ch-8 sp, [ch 8, sc in next ch-8 sp] 3 times, ch 5, sk next ch-5 sp, 2 tr in next tr, ch 3, tr in next tr, ch 3, 2 tr in next tr, 3 tr in next tr, 2 tr in next tr, ch 3, tr in next tr, ch 3, 2 tr in next tr, ch 5, sk next ch-5 sp, sc in next ch-8 sp, [ch 8, sc in next ch-8 sp] 3 times, ch 3**, sc in next ch-2 sp, rep from * around, ending last rep at **, join with sl st in beg sc.

**Rnd 22:** Sl st in next ch-3 sp, ch 4, 4 tr in same ch-3 sp, drop lp from hook and insert hook in 4th ch of beg ch-4, pull dropped lp through *(beg pc)*, *[ch 2, pc in next ch-3 sp] 21 times, [ch 8, sc in next ch-8 sp] 3 times, ch 5, sk next ch-5 sp, 2 tr in next tr, tr in next tr, [ch 3, tr in next tr] twice, 2 tr in next tr, ch 2, tr in next tr, 2 tr in next tr, tr in next tr, ch 2, 2 tr in next tr, tr in next tr, [ch 3, tr in next tr] twice, 2 tr in next tr, ch 5, sk next ch-5 sp, sc in next ch-8 sp, [ch 8, sc in next ch-8 sp] twice, ch 8, pc in next ch-3 sp, ch 2**, pc in next ch-3 sp, rep from * around, ending last rep at **, join with sl st in beg pc.

**Rnd 23:** Ch 7, *[tr dec in next ch-2 sp and next pc, ch 3] 21 times, tr in same pc, ch 5, sc in next ch-8 sp, [ch 8, sc in next ch-8 sp] twice, ch 5, sk next ch-5 sp, tr in each of next 3 tr, ch 3, tr in next tr, ch 3, tr in each of next 3 tr, ch 4, tr dec in next 4 tr, ch 4, tr in each of next 3 tr, ch 3, tr in next tr, ch 3, tr in each of next 3 tr, ch 5, sk next ch-5 sp, sc in next ch-8 sp, [ch 8, sc in next ch-8 sp] twice, ch 5, tr in next pc, ch 3**, tr dec in next ch-2 sp and next pc, rep from * around, ending last rep at **, tr in last ch-2 sp, join with sl st in 4th ch of beg ch-7.

**Rnd 24:** Ch 3, tr in next tr dec, *[ch 4, tr dec in same tr dec and next tr dec] 20 times, ch 4, tr dec in same tr dec and next tr, ch 8, sk next ch-5 sp, sc in next ch-8 sp, ch 8, sc in next ch-8 sp, ch 5, sk next ch-5 sp, tr in each of next 2 tr, ch 3, sk next tr and next ch-3 sp, tr in next tr, ch 3, sk next ch-3 sp and next tr, tr in each of next 2 tr, ch 8, (sc, ch 3, sc) in next tr dec, ch 8, tr in each of next 2 tr, ch 3, sk next tr and next ch-3 sp, tr in next tr, ch 3, sk next ch-3 sp and next tr, tr in each of next 2 tr, ch 5, sk next ch-5 sp, [sc in next ch-8 sp, ch 8] twice, sk next ch-5 sp, tr dec in next tr and next tr dec, ch 4**, tr dec in same tr dec and next tr dec, rep from * around, ending last rep at **, join with sl st in beg tr.

**Rnd 25:** Ch 1, sc in first st, *[ch 5, **tr cl** *(see Special Stitches)* in next tr dec, ch 5, sc in next tr dec] 10 times, ch 5, tr cl in next tr dec, ch 5, sc in next ch-8 sp, ch 9, sc in next ch-8 sp, ch 5, sk next ch-5 sp, tr dec in next 2 tr, ch 2, tr in next tr, ch 2, tr dec in next 2 tr, ch 8, sc in next ch-8 sp, ch 5, 5 tr in next ch-3 sp, ch 5, sc in next ch-8 sp, ch 8, tr dec in next 2 tr, ch 2, tr in next tr, ch 2, tr dec in next 2 tr, ch 5, sk next ch-5 sp, sc in next ch-8 sp, ch 9, sc in next ch-8 sp, ch 5, tr cl in next tr dec, ch 5**, sc in next tr dec, rep from * around, ending with last rep at **, join with sl st in beg sc.

**Rnd 26:** Ch 3, keeping last lp of each tr on hook, tr in same sc, yo and pull through 2 lps on hook *(beg tr cl)*, *[ch 5, sc in next tr cl, ch 5, tr cl in next sc] 10 times, ch 5, sc in next tr cl, ch 8, sk next ch-5 sp, 5 tr in 5th ch of next ch-9 sp, ch 8, sk next ch-5 sp, tr dec in next tr dec, next tr, and next tr dec, ch 7, sc in next ch-8 sp, ch 7, sk next sc, sc in next ch-5 sp, ch 7, tr dec in next 5 tr, ch 7, sc in next ch-5 sp, ch 7, sc in next ch-8 sp, ch 7, tr dec in next tr dec, next tr and next tr dec, ch 8, sk next ch-5 sp, 5 tr in 5th ch of next ch-9 sp, ch 8, sk next ch-5 sp, sc in next tr cl, ch 5**, tr cl in next sc, rep from * around, ending last rep at **, join with sl st in beg tr cl.

**Rnd 27:** Sl st in each of next 3 chs of next ch-5 sp, ch 1, sc in same sp, *[ch 7, sc in next ch-5 sp] 20 times, ch 7, sk next sc, sc in next ch-8 sp, ch 7, tr dec in next 5 tr, ch 8, sc in next ch-8 sp, ch 8, [sc in next ch-7 sp, ch 8] 7 times, tr dec in next 5 tr, ch 7, sc in next ch-8 sp, ch 7, sc in next ch-5 sp, ch 7**, sc in next ch-5 sp, rep from * around, ending last rep at **, join with sl st in beg sc.

**Rnd 28:** Sl st in each of next 3 chs of next ch-7 sp, ch 4, (tr, ch 3, sl st in top of tr just made, tr) in same ch sp, *[ch 5, sc in next ch-7 sp, ch 5, (2 tr, ch 3, sl st in top of tr just made, tr) in next ch-7 sp] 10 times, ch 7, sc in next ch-7 sp, ch 7, sc in next ch-8 sp, ch 7, (2 tr, ch 3, sl st in tr just made, tr) in next ch-8 sp, (ch 7, sc in next ch-8 sp) twice, ch 7, (2 tr, ch 3, sl st in top of tr just made, tr) in next ch-8 sp, [ch 7, sc in next ch-8 sp] twice, ch 7, (2 tr, ch 3, sl st in top of tr just made, tr) in next ch-8 sp, ch 7, sc in next ch-8 sp, ch 5, sc in next ch-7 sp, ch 7, (2 tr, ch 3, sl st in 4th ch from hook, tr) in next ch-7 sp, rep from * 3 times, ch 5, sc in next ch-7 sp, ch 5, join with sl st in 4th ch of beg ch-4. Fasten off. ■

TODAY'S BEST NONFICTION
SEA DRAGON HEIR
STORM CONSTANTINE

# Fisherman's Blanket

DESIGN BY ERMA FIELDER

Comfort never looked so good as in the hearty textures of this stylish Aran afghan. Snuggling up in it evokes the same comfort and deep calm of wearing your favorite sweater on a dark, dreary day.

EDIATE

4 MEDIUM

**FINISHED SIZE**
46 x 60 inches, excluding Fringe

**MATERIALS**
Medium (worsted) weight yarn:
80 oz/4,000 yds/2,268g off-white
Size N/15/10mm crochet hook or size needed to obtain gauge

**GAUGE**
7 sc = 3 inches; 7 sc rows = 3 inches

**PATTERN NOTE**
Use 2 strands of yarn held together as 1 throughout.

**SPECIAL STITCH**
**Berry stitch (berry st):** Insert hook in next st, yo, pull through st *(2 lps on hook)*, working through first lp only, ch 3, yo, pull through both lps on hook.

## INSTRUCTIONS

**CENTER**
**Row 1:** With 2 strands held tog *(see Pattern Note)*, ch 38, sc in 2nd ch from hook, sc in each ch across, turn. *(37 sc)*

**Row 2:** Ch 1, sc in first st, [**berry st** *(see Special Stitch)* in next st, sc in next st] across, turn. *(19 sc, 18 bs)*

**Row 3:** Ch 1, sc in each st across, turn.

**Rows 4–129:** Rep rows 2 and 3 alternately. At end of last row, **do not turn or fasten off.**

**FIRST SIDE PANEL**
**Row 1:** Working across side of Center, ch 1, sc in end of each row across, turn. *(129 sc)*

**Row 2:** Working this row in **front lps** *(see Stitch Guide)* only, ch 1, sc in each st across, turn.

**Row 3:** Working this row in **back lps** *(see Stitch Guide)* of row before last, ch 1, sc in each st across, turn.

**Row 4:** Ch 1, sc in each st across, **do not turn.**

**Row 5:** Working this row in front lps only, ch 1, working from left to right, **reverse sc** *(see illustration),* in each st across, **do not turn.**

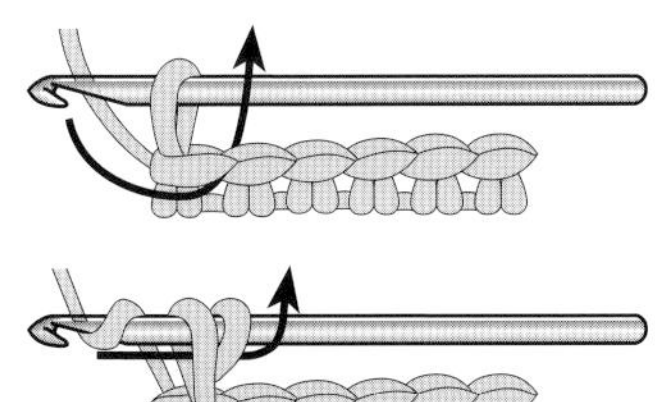

Reverse Single Crochet

**Row 6:** Rep row 3.

**Row 7:** Ch 1, sc in each st across, turn.

**Row 8:** Ch 1, sc in each of first 2 sts, *for cable, ch 3, sk next 2 unworked sts, sc in next st, **turn,** sc in each of next 3 chs, sl st in same st as ch-3, **turn,** working behind cable, sc in each of next 2 sk sts, rep from * across to last st, sc in last st, turn.

**Row 9:** Skipping cables, ch 1, sc in each of first 3 sts, [2 sc in next st, sc in next st] across, turn. *(129 sc)*

**Rows 10–13:** Rep rows 4–7.

**Rows 14 & 15:** Rep rows 2 and 3.

**Rows 16–19:** Ch 1, sc in each st across, turn.

**Row 20:** Ch 1, sc in each of first 2 sts, working around sts 3 rows below, **fptr** *(see Stitch Guide)* around 2nd st of row, sk next 4 sts, fptr around next st, sk 2 sts on last row, sc in each of next 4 sts, *working around sts 3 rows below, fptr around next st after last fptr**, sk next 4 sts, fptr around next st, sk next 2 sts on last row, sc in each of next 4 sts, rep from * across, ending last rep at **, sl st in last st on last row, turn.

**Row 21:** Ch 1, sk sl st, sc in each st across, turn.

**Rows 22 & 23:** Ch 1, sc in each st across, turn.

**Row 24:** Ch 1, fptr around 4th st on row 3 rows below *(st just above fptr on row 20)*, sk first st on last row, sc in each of next 4 sts, *working around sts 3 rows below, fptr around next st after last fptr**, sk next 4 sts, fptr around next st, sk next 2 sts on last row, sc in each of next 4 sts, rep from * across, ending last rep at **, sk next 3 sts, fptr around next st, sk next 2 sts on last row, sc in each of last 2 sts, turn.

**Rows 25–27:** Ch 1, sc in each st across, turn.

**Rows 28–35:** Rep rows 2–9.

**Rows 36–39:** Rep rows 4–7.

**Rows 40 & 41:** Rep rows 2 and 3.

**Row 42:** Ch 1, sc in each st across. Fasten off.

### 2ND SIDE PANEL

**Row 1:** With WS facing, working across opposite side of Center, join with sc in end of row 1, sc in end of each row across, turn. *(129 sc)*

**Rows 2–42:** Rep same rows of First Side Panel. At end of last row, **do not turn or fasten off.**

### EDGING

Working in ends of rows and sts across end of Blanket, ch 1, sc in each row and in each st across. Fasten off.

Working on opposite end of Blanket, join with sc in end of last row on First Side Panel, sc in each row and in each st across. Fasten off.

### FRINGE

Cut 10 strands each 12 inches in length. With all strands held tog, fold in half, insert hook in st, pull fold through, pull ends through fold, tighten. Trim ends.

Attach Fringe in every 3rd st across each short end of Blanket. ■

# Diamond Popcorn

DESIGN BY ERMA FIELDER

Accent your home with this gorgeous throw worked in tranquil, mossy green. Luxuriously textured popcorn and bullion stitches are a treat for the eyes, and the blended wool yarn provides gentle warmth in any season.

**FINISHED SIZE**
48 x 56 inches

**MATERIALS**
Patons Decor medium (worsted) weight yarn (3½ oz/210 yds/100g per skein):
14 skeins #1637 rich sage green
Size J/10/6mm crochet hook or size needed to obtain gauge

**GAUGE**
3 sc = 1 inch; 3 sc rows = 1 inch

**SPECIAL STITCHES**
**Bullion stitch (bullion st):** Insert hook in indicated st, loosely yo 9 times, yo, pull through all lps on hook, ch 1 to close.

**Popcorn (pc):** 5 dc in indicated st, drop lp from hook, insert hook in first dc of group, pull dropped lp through.

## INSTRUCTIONS

**AFGHAN**

**Row 1:** Ch 144, sc in 2nd ch from hook, sc in each of next 2 chs, dc in next ch, sc in next ch, dc in next ch, sc in each of next 2 chs, [sc in each of next 2 chs, dc in next ch, sc in next ch, dc in next ch, sc in each of next 2 chs] 19 times, sc in last ch, turn.

**Row 2:** Ch 1, sc in each st across, turn.

**Row 3:** Ch 1, sc in each of first 3 sts, *sk next 2 sts, **fpdc** *(see Stitch Guide)* around next dc on row before last, sc in 2nd sk st, working in front of fpdc and sc just made, fpdc around sk dc *(first sk st on row before last)*, sc in each of next 2 sts**, sc in each of next 2 sts, rep from * across, ending last rep at **, sc in last st, turn.

**Row 4:** Rep row 2.

**Row 5:** Ch 1, sc in each of first 2 sts, *fpdc around fpdc on row before last, sc in each of next 3 sts, fpdc around next fpdc on row before last, sc in next st**, sc in next st, rep from * across, ending last rep at **, sc in last st, turn.

**Row 6:** Rep row 2.

**Row 7:** Ch 1, sc in first st, [fpdc around next fpdc, sc in each of next 2 sts, **pc** *(see Special Stitches)* in next st, sc in each of next 2 sts, fpdc around next fpdc] across to last st, sc in last st, turn.

**Row 8:** Rep row 2.

**Row 9:** Rep row 5.

**Row 10:** Rep row 2.

**Row 11:** Ch 1, sc in each of first 3 sts, *fpdc around next fpdc, sc in next st, fpdc around next fpdc, sc in each of next 2 sts**, sc in each of next 2 sts, rep from * across, ending last rep at **, sc in last st, turn.

**Row 12:** Rep row 2.

**Row 13:** Ch 1, sc in each of first 3 sts, *sk next 2 sts, fpdc around fpdc on left side of diamond, sc in 2nd sk st, working in front of fpdc and sc just made, fpdc around fpdc on RS of diamond, sc in each of next 2 sts**, sc in each of next 2 sts, rep from * across, ending last rep at **, sc in last st, turn.

**Row 14:** Rep row 2.

**Row 15:** Ch 1, sc in each st across, **do not turn.**

**Row 16:** Ch 1, working in **front lps** *(see Stitch Guide)*, working from left to right, **reverse sc** *(see illustration)* in each st across, **do not turn.**

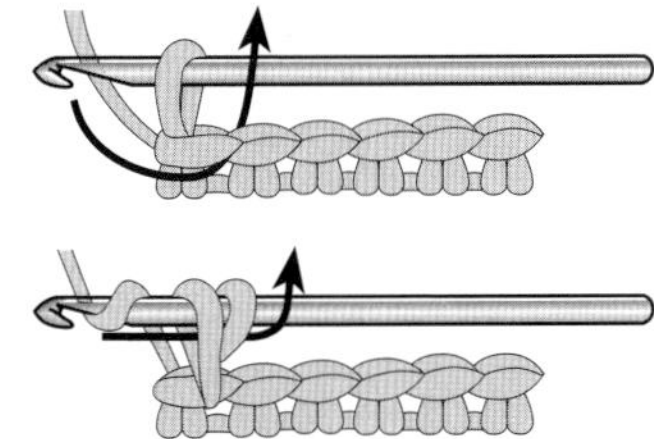

**Reverse Single Crochet**

**Row 17:** Working in **back lps** *(see*

*Stitch Guide)* of row 15, sc in each st across, **do not turn.**

**Row 18:** Rep row 16.

**Row 19:** Working in back lps only of row 17, sc in each st across, turn.

**Row 20:** Ch 1, sc in each st across, turn.

**Row 21:** Ch 3, dc in each st across, turn.

**Row 22:** Ch 3, [fpdc around next st, **bpdc** *(see Stitch Guide)* around next st] across to last st, dc in last st, turn.

**Row 23:** Ch 1, [sc in next st, **bullion st** *(see Special Stitches)* in next st] across to last 2 sts, sc in each of last 2 sts, turn.

**Rows 24–26:** Rep rows 20–22.

**Row 27:** Rep row 15.

**Row 28:** Rep row 16.

**Row 29:** Ch 1, working in back lps only of row 27, sc in each st across, turn.

**Row 30:** Rep row 16.

**Row 31:** Working in back lps only of row 29, sc in each st across, turn.

**Row 32:** Rep row 2.

**Row 33:** Ch 1, sc in each of first 3 sts, *dc in next st, sc in next st, dc in next st, sc in each of next 2 sts**, sc in each of next 2 sts, rep from * across, ending last rep at **, sc in last st, turn.

**Rows 34–45:** Rep rows 2–13.

**Rows 46–165:** Rep rows 4–13 consecutively.

**Row 166:** Rep row 2.

**Rows 167 & 168:** Rep rows 15 and 16.

**Row 169:** Working in back lps only of row 167, sc in each st across, **do not turn**.

**Row 170:** Rep row 16.

**Row 171:** Working in back lps only of row 169, sc in each st across, turn.

**Rows 172–180:** Rep rows 20–28.

**Row 181:** Working in back lps only of row 179, sc in each st across, **do not turn.**

**Row 182:** Rep row 16.

**Row 183:** Working in back lps only of row 181, sc in each st across, turn.

**Rows 184–197:** Rep rows 32–45.

**EDGING**

**Rnd 1:** Ch 1, evenly sp sc around, working 3 sc in each corner, join with sl st in beg sc.

**Rnd 2:** Ch 1, sc in first st, 5 dc in next st, sc in next st *(corner)*, *sk next 2 sts, 5 dc in next st, sk next 2 sts, sc in next st, rep from * around, join with a sl st in beg sc. Fasten off. ■

# Flora

DESIGN BY JOSIE RABIER

Past meets present in this stunning layered doily, creating a look that will never go out of style. No matter if it is used to accent a vase or centerpiece or to create a focal point, this doily will fit any decor.

INTERMEDIATE

**FINISHED SIZE**
20½ x 18 inches

**MATERIALS**
Size 10 crochet cotton:
650 yds cream
Size 7/1.65mm steel crochet hook or size needed to obtain gauge

**GAUGE**
Rnds 1–3 = 2⅜ inches in diameter

**SPECIAL STITCHES**

**Beginning treble split decrease (beg tr split dec):** Ch 3, holding back last lp of each st on hook, tr in next st, sk next st, tr in each of next 2 sts, yo, pull through all lps on hook, ch 1 to close.

**Treble split decrease (tr split dec):** Holding back last lp of each st on hook, tr in each of next 2 sts, sk next st, tr in each of next 2 sts, yo, pull through all lps on hook, ch 1 to close.

**Beginning popcorn (beg pc):** Ch 4 *(counts as first tr)*, 6 tr in same st, drop lp from hook, insert hook in 4th ch of beg ch-4, pick up dropped lp, pull through 4th ch of beg ch-4, ch 1 to close.

**Popcorn (pc):** 7 tr in indicated st, drop lp from hook, insert hook in first tr of tr group, pick up dropped lp, pull through first tr on hook, ch 1 to close.

INSTRUCTIONS

**DOILY BASE**

**CENTER**

**Row 1 (RS):** Ch 6, (tr, 5 dc, tr, dtr) in 6th ch from hook, turn.

**Row 2:** Ch 5, tr in same st, 5 dc in next tr, dc in each of next 5 dc, 5 dc in next tr, (tr, dtr) in 5th ch of ch-6, turn.

**Row 3:** Ch 5, tr in same st, sk next tr, dc in each of next 15 dc, sk next tr, (tr, dtr) in 5th ch of turning ch-5.

**Row 4:** Ch 5, tr in same st, 5 dc in next tr, dc in each of next 15 dc,

5 dc in next tr, (tr, dtr) in 5th ch of turning ch-5, turn.

**Rows 5–18:** Ch 5, tr in same st, sk next tr, dc in each of next 25 dc, sk next tr, (tr, dtr) in 5th ch of turning ch-5, turn.

**Row 19:** Ch 5, tr in same st, sk next tr, **dc dec** *(see Stitch Guide)* in next 5 dc, dc in each of next 15 dc, dc dec in next 5 dc, sk next tr, (tr, dtr) in 5th ch of turning ch-5, turn.

**Row 20:** Ch 5, tr in same st, sk next dc dec, dc in each of next 15 dc, sk next dc dec, (tr, dtr) in 5th ch of turning ch-5, turn.

**Row 21:** Ch 5, tr in same st, sk next tr, dc dec in next 5 dc, dc in each of next 5 dc, dc dec in next 5 dc, (tr, dtr) in 5th ch of turning ch-5, turn.

**Row 22:** Ch 5, tr in same st, sk next tr, dc dec in next 5 dc, (tr, dtr) in 5th ch of turning ch-5, **do not turn.**

**BORDER**

**Rnd 23: Now working in rnds,** sl st under tr, working over (tr, dtr) at end of each row, *5 hdc over both end sts, rep from * around, join with sl st in beg hdc. *(220 hdc)*

**Rnd 24: Beg tr split dec** *(see Special Stitches)*, ch 7, ***tr split dec** *(see Special Stitches)*, ch 7, rep from * around, join with sl st in top of beg tr split dec. *(44 tr split dec)*

**Rnd 25:** Sl st in ch-7 sp, ch 1, 10 hdc in same ch sp, 10 hdc in each of next 2 ch-7 sps, 5 hdc in each of next 16 ch-7 sps, 10 hdc in each of next 6 ch-7 sps, 5 hdc in each of next 16 ch-7 sps, 10 hdc in each of last 3 ch-7 sps, join with sl st in beg hdc.

**Rnd 26:** Beg tr split dec, ch 5, *tr split dec, ch 5, rep from * around, join with sl st in top of beg tr split dec.

**Rnd 27:** Ch 10, dc in next tr split dec, ch 7, *dc in next tr split dec, ch 7, rep from * around, join with sl st in 3rd ch of beg ch-10.

**Rnds 28 & 29:** Ch 10, *dc in next dc, ch 7, rep from * around, join with sl st in 3rd ch of beg ch-10.

**Rnd 30:** Ch 4, 8 tr in same st, *sl st in 4th ch of next ch-7 sp, [ch 7, sl st in 4th ch of next ch-7 sp] 3 times**, 9 tr in next dc, rep from * around, ending last rep at **, join with sl st in 4th ch of beg ch-4.

**Rnd 31: Beg pc** *(see Special Stitches)* in same st as joining, *[ch 5, sk next tr, **pc** *(see Special Stitches)* in next tr] 4 times, sl st in 4th ch of next ch-7 sp, [ch 7, sl st in 4th ch of next ch-7 sp] twice**, pc in next tr, rep from * around, ending last rep at **, join with sl st in top of beg pc.

**Rnd 32:** Sl st in ch-5 sp, ch 4, 5 tr in same ch sp, *[ch 3, 6 tr in next ch-5 sp] 3 times, sl st in 4th ch of next ch-7 sp, ch 7, sl st in 4th ch of next ch-7 sp**, 6 tr in next ch-5 sp, rep from * around, ending last rep at **, join with sl st in 4th ch of beg ch-4.

**Rnd 33:** Ch 3, **tr dec** *(see Stitch Guide)* in next 5 sts, ch 5, sl st in next ch-3 sp, *ch 5, tr dec in next 6 sts, [ch 5, sl st in next ch-3 sp, ch 5, tr dec in next 6 sts] twice, ch 3, sl st in 4th ch of next ch-7 sp, ch 3**, tr dec in next 6 sts, rep from * around, ending last rep at **, join with sl st in top of beg tr dec.

**Rnd 34:** *[Ch 5, sl st in same st, ch 7, sl st in sl st between next 2 ch-5 sps, ch 7, sl st in top of next tr dec] 3 times, ch 5, sl st in same st, ch 5, sl st in sl st between next 2 ch-3 sps, ch 5**, sl st in top of next tr dec, rep from * around, ending last rep at **, join with sl st in base of beg ch-5. Fasten off.

**INNER RUFFLE**

With RS facing, working over end sts of Doily Center rows, join with sl st in end st of any row closest to you, *ch 7, 3 dtr in same st**, sl st in end st of next row, rep from * around, ending last rep at **, join with sl st in base of beg ch-7. Fasten off.

**OUTER RUFFLE**

**Rnd 1:** With RS facing, join with sl st in any ch-5 sp between tr split dec on rnd 26, ch 4 *(counts as first tr)*, 6 tr in same ch sp, 7 tr in each ch-5 sp around, join with sl st in 4th ch of beg ch-4. *(392 tr)*

**Rnd 2:** *Ch 7, tr split dec, ch 5, sl st in top of tr split dec, ch 7 **, sl st in each of next 2 tr, rep from * around, ending last rep at**, sl st in next tr, join with sl st in base of beg ch-7. Fasten off. ■

# Roses & Leaves

DESIGN BY CATHERINE PEITER

Breathtakingly gorgeous in its lacy finery and intricate design, this creamy, off-white doily edged in petal pink roses and sage green leaves adds an aura of soft beauty wherever you place it.

ERMEDIATE

**FINISHED SIZE**
13¾ inches in diameter

**MATERIALS**
Size 20 crochet cotton:
 120 yds ecru
 90 yds each sage and pink
Size10/1.15mm steel crochet hook
 or size needed to obtain gauge

**GAUGE**
Rnds 1–3 of Doily = 1¼ inches across

Rose = 1¼ inches across

Leaf =1½ inches long

**SPECIAL STITCHES**
**V-stitch (V-st):** (Tr, ch 3, tr) in st or ch sp.

**Beginning treble crochet cluster (beg tr cl):** Ch 4, *yo twice, insert hook in st or ch sp, yo, pull lp through, [yo, pull through 2 lps on hook] twice, rep from *, yo, pull through all lps on hook.

**Treble crochet cluster (tr cl):** Yo twice, insert hook in st or ch sp, yo, pull lp through, [yo, pull through 2 lps on hook] twice, leaving last lp of st on hook, *yo twice, insert hook in same st or ch sp, yo, pull lp through, [yo, pull through 2 lps on hook] twice, leaving last lp of st on hook, rep from * number of times needed for number of tr in cl, yo, pull through all lps on hook.

**INSTRUCTIONS**

**ROSE**
Make 15.

**Rnd 1:** With pink, ch 5, sl st in first ch to form ring, ch 4 *(counts as dc and ch-1)*, [dc in ring, ch 1] 5 times, join with sl st in 3rd ch of beg ch-4. *(6 dc, 6 ch sps)*

**Rnd 2:** Ch 1, for **petals**, (sc, hdc, dc, hdc, sc) in each ch sp around, join with sl st in beg sc. *(6 petals)*

**Rnd 3:** Working behind petals, ch 1, **bpsc** *(see Stitch Guide)* around ch 3 at beg of rnd 1, ch 3, *bpsc around next st on rnd 1, ch 3, rep from * around, join with sl st in beg sc. *(6 ch sps)*

**Rnd 4:** Ch 1, for **petals**, (sc, hdc, 3 dc, hdc, sc) in each ch sp around, join with sl st in beg sc.

**Rnd 5:** Working behind petals, ch 1, bpsc around first sc on rnd 3, ch 4, [bpsc around next sc on rnd 3, ch 4] around, join with sl st in beg sc.

**Rnd 6:** Ch 1, for **petals,** (sc, hdc, 5 dc, hdc, sc) in each ch around, join with sl st in beg sc. Fasten off.

**LEAF**
Make 15.

**Row 1:** With sage, ch 11, sc in 2nd ch from hook, sc in each of next 8 chs, 3 sc in last ch, working on opposite side of ch, sc in each of next 7 chs leaving last 2 chs unworked, turn. *(19 sc)*

**Rows 2–8:** Working these rows in **back lps** *(see Stitch Guide)*, ch 1, sc in each st across to center st of 3-sc group, 3 sc in center st, sc in each st across leaving last 2 sts unworked, turn.

**Row 9:** Ch 1, sc in each st across to center st of 3-sc group, sc in center st leaving rem sts unworked. Fasten off.

**DOILY**

**Rnd 1:** With ecru, ch 6, sl st in first ch to form ring, ch 3 *(counts as first dc)*, 14 dc in ring, join with sl st in 3rd ch of beg ch-3. *(15 dc)*

**Rnd 2:** Ch 5, [dc in next st, ch 2] around, join with sl st in 3rd ch of beg ch-5. *(15 dc, 15 ch sps)*

**Rnd 3:** Ch 6, sk next ch sp, [dc in next st, ch 3, sk next ch sp] around, join with sl st in 3rd ch of beg ch-6.

**Rnd 4:** Sl st in first ch sp, **beg tr cl** *(see Special Stitches)*, ch 4, sk next st, *3-**tr cl** *(see Special Stitches)*, ch 4, sk next st, rep from * around, join with sl st in beg tr cl. *(15 cl)*

**Rnd 5:** Ch 1, sc in first ch sp, [ch 8, sc in next ch sp] 14 times, ch 4, join with tr in first sc *(ch-4 and tr count as last ch-8 sp)*.

**Rnd 6:** Ch 1, sc in last ch sp made, ch 8, [sc in next ch sp, ch 8] around, join with sl st in beg sc.

**Rnd 7:** (Sl st, ch 4, 2 tr, ch 3, 3 tr) in first ch sp (*ch-4 counts as first tr)*, (3 tr, ch 3, 3 tr) in each ch sp around, join with sl st in 4th ch of beg ch-4. *(90 tr)*

**Rnd 8:** Ch 7, sc in next ch sp, [ch 7, sc in sp between next 2 tr groups, ch 7, sc in next ch sp] around, ch 3, sk last 3 sts, join with tr in first ch of beg ch-7.

**Rnd 9:** [Ch 7, sc in next ch sp] around, ch 3, join with tr in first ch of beg ch-7.

**Rnd 10:** (Ch 7, tr) in same ch sp, ch 5, sc in next ch sp, ch 5, ***V-st** *(see Special Stitches)* in next ch sp, ch 5, sc in next ch sp, ch 5, rep from * around, join with sl st in 4th ch of beg ch-7.

**Rnd 11:** (Sl st, ch 4, 2 tr) in first ch sp, *[ch 7, sk next ch sp, sc in next sc, ch 7, sk next ch sp*, 3 tr in next V-st] 14 times, rep between *, join with sl st in 4th ch of beg ch-4.

**Rnd 12:** Ch 4, tr in same st, tr in next st, 2 tr in next st, *[ch 7, sk next ch sp, sc in next st, ch 7, sk next ch sp*, 2 tr in next st, tr in next st, 2 tr in next st] 14 times, rep between *, join with sl st in 4th ch of beg ch-4.

**Rnd 13:** Ch 4, tr in next st, V-st in next st, tr in each of next 2 sts, *[ch 4, sc in next ch sp, ch 5, sc in next ch sp, ch 4*, tr in each of next 2 sts, V-st in next st, tr in each of next 2 sts] 14 times, rep between *, join with sl st in 4th ch of beg ch-4.

**Rnd 14:** Sl st in each of next 2 sts, ch 1, sc in next ch sp, *[ch 7, sk next ch sp, V-st in next ch-5 sp, ch 7, sk next ch sp*, sc in next ch sp] 14 times, rep between *, join with sl st in beg sc.

**Rnd 15:** Ch 1, sc in first st, *[ch 8, sk next ch sp, 3 tr in next V-st, ch 8, sk next ch sp*, sc in next st] 14 times, rep between *, join with sl st in beg sc.

**Rnd 16:** Ch 1, sc in first st, *[ch 8, sk next ch sp, 2 tr in next st, tr in next st, 2 tr in next st*, ch 8, sk next ch sp, sc in next st] 14 times, rep between *, ch 4, join with tr in beg sc.

**Rnd 17:** Ch 1, sc in last ch sp made, *[ch 5, sc in next ch sp, ch 4, tr in each of next 2 sts, V-st in next st, tr in each of next 2 sts, ch 4*, sc in next ch sp] 14 times, rep between *, join with sl st in beg sc.

**Rnd 18:** (Sl st, ch 7, tr) in first ch sp, *ch 4, sc in next ch sp, ch 4, sk next 3 sts, (2-tr cl, ch 4, 2-tr cl) in next ch sp, ch 4, sk next 3 sts, sc in next ch sp, ch 4**, V-st in next ch sp, rep from * around, ending last rep at **, join with sl st in 4th ch of beg ch-7.

**Rnd 19:** (Sl st, ch 4, 2 tr) in first ch sp, *ch 5, sk next ch sp, tr in next st, ch 5, sk next ch sp, (sc, ch 3, sc) in ch sp of next shell, ch 5, sk next ch sp, tr in next st, ch 5, sk next ch sp**, 3 tr in next V-st, rep from * around, ending last rep at **, join with sl st in 4th ch of beg ch-4.

**Rnd 20:** Ch 4, tr in same st, *tr in next st, 2 tr in next st, ch 5, sk next ch sp, sc in next st, ch 5, sk next ch sp, shell in next ch sp, ch 5, sk next ch sp, sc in next st, ch 5, sk next ch sp**, 2 tr in next st, rep from * around, ending last rep at **, join with sl st in 4th ch of beg ch-4.

**Rnd 21:** Ch 4, *tr in next st, V-st in next st, tr in each of next 2 sts, ch 5, sk next ch sp, sc in next st, ch 5, sk next ch sp, shell in next shell, ch 5, sk next ch sp, sc in next st, ch 5, sk next ch sp**, tr in next st, rep from * around, ending last rep at **, join with sl st in 4th ch of beg ch-4. Fasten off.

**Rnd 22:** Join sage with sc in first st, sc in each of next 2 sts, 3 sc in next ch sp, sl st in any center dc of any Rose petal, *[3 sc in same ch sp, sc in each of next 3 sts, ch 5, sk next ch sp, dtr in next st, ch 1, sl st in center dc of next petal on same Rose, ch 1, (sc, ch 3, sc) in same dtr, ch 1, sl st in 3rd st of row 9 on 1 Leaf, ch 1, sc in same dtr, ch 5, sc in next st, 3 sc in next ch sp, sl st in center st of 3-sc group on same Leaf, 3 sc in same ch sp, sc in next st, ch 5, sk next ch sp, dtr in next st, ch 1, sl st in 3rd st of row 8 on same Leaf, ch 1, (sc, ch 3, sc) in same dtr, ch 1**, sl st in center dc of any petal on next Rose, ch 1, sc in same dtr, ch 5, sc in each of next 3 sts, 3 sc in next ch sp, sl st in center dc of next petal on same Rose, rep from * around, ending last rep at **, sl st in center st of next petal on first worked Rose, ch 1, sc in same dtr, ch 5, join with sl st in beg sc. Fasten off. ■

# French Braid

DESIGN BY TAMMY HILDEBRAND

Raised horizontal post stitches and chunky yarn in the colors of Southwestern spices and creamy ivory create the elegant look of a French braid in this lovely afghan stitched in easy-to-make panels.

**FINISHED SIZE**
42 x 65 inches

**MATERIALS**
Lion Brand Chunky bulky (chunky) weight yarn (4 oz/155 yds/113g per skein):
9 skeins #99 fisherman
Lion Brand Homespun bulky (chunky) weight yarn (6 oz/185 yds/170g per skein):
4 skeins #342 southwestern
Size Q/16mm crochet hook or size needed to obtain gauge
Tapestry needle

**GAUGE**
Panel = 9 inches wide; 4 dc = 3 inches

**PATTERN NOTE**
Project is worked holding 2 strands of yarn together throughout.

**SPECIAL STITCH**
**Join:** Ch 1, drop lp from hook, insert hook in center ch of corresponding ch-3 sp, pull dropped lp through, ch 1.

## INSTRUCTIONS

**PANEL**
Make 5.

**CENTER**
**Foundation row:** With southwestern, ch 75, dc in 4th ch from hook *(first 3 chs count as first dc)*, dc in each rem ch across. Fasten off. *(73 dc)*

**Rnd 1 (RS):** Join fisherman with a sc in first st, **fpdc** *(see Stitch Guide)* around next st, sc in next st, [fpdc around next st, sc in next st] across to end, work 3 sc over post of last st, working on opposite side of foundation ch, sc in first ch, [fpdc around next st, sc in next st] across to end, work 3 sc over post of last st, join with sl st in beg sc, **do not turn**.

**Rnd 2:** Ch 3 *(counts as first dc)*, 2 dc in same st, dc in each of next 71 sts, 3 dc in next st, [dc in next st, 3 dc in next st] twice, dc in each of next 71 sts, [3 dc in next st, dc in next st] twice, join with sl st in 3rd ch of beg ch-3. Fasten off.

**Rnd 3:** Join southwestern with a sc in center st at either end of Panel, 2 sc in same st, sc in each of next 3 sts, 3 sc in next st, sc in each of next 2 sts, [fpdc around next st, sc in next st] 35 times, sc in next st, [3 sc in next st, sc in each of next 3 sts] twice, 3 sc in next st, sc in each of next 2 sts, [fpdc around next st, sc in next st] 35 times, sc in next st, 3 sc in next st, sc in each of next 3 sts, join with sl st in beg sc. Fasten off.

**FIRST STRIP**
**Rnd 4:** Join fisherman with a sc in center st at either end of Panel, *[3 sc in next st, sk next st] twice, sk next st, 3 sc in next st, [sk next st, (sc, ch 3, sc) in next st] 37 times, sk next st, 3 sc in next st, sk next 2 sts, 3 sc in next st, sk next st, 3 sc in next st*, sc in next st, rep between *, join with sl st in beg sc. Fasten off.

**JOINING REMAINING STRIPS**
**Rnd 4:** Join fisherman with a sc in center st at either end of strip, [3 sc in next st, sk next st] twice, sk next st, 3 sc in next st, [sk next st, (sc, **join**—*see Special Stitch,* sc) in next st] 37 times, sk next st, 3 sc in next st, sk next 2 sts, 3 sc in next st, sk next st, 3 sc in next st, sc in next st, [3 sc in next st, sk next st] twice, sk next st, 3 sc in next st, [sk next st, (sc, ch 3, sc) in next st] 37 times, sk next st, 3 sc in next st, sk next 2 sts, 3 sc in next st, sk next st, 3 sc in next st, join with sl st in beg sc. Fasten off. ■

# Mint Frosting

DESIGN BY RENA STEVENS

**The name says it all in the luscious, fluffy texture of this divine crème de menthe concoction stitched in super-soft, brushed, bulky yarn. Spiral fringe adds an unusual and charming touch.**

5 BULKY

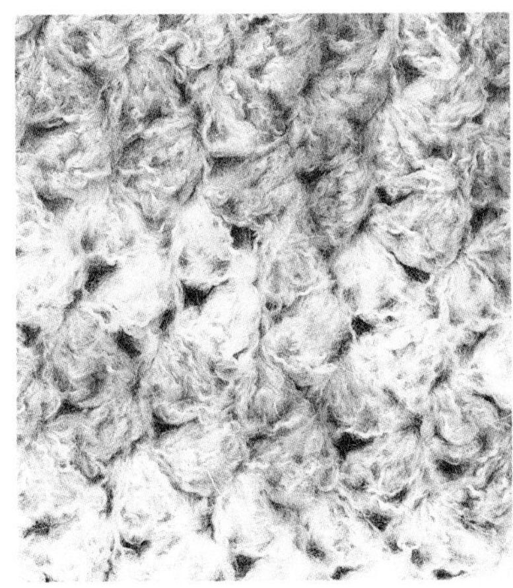

**FINISHED SIZE**
42 x 60 inches

**MATERIALS**
Patons Divine bulky (chunky) weight yarn (3½ oz/142 yds/100g per skein):
5 skeins each #06006 icicle white and #06206 frosted green
Size P/15/10mm crochet hook or size needed to obtain gauge
Yarn needle

**GAUGE**
4 pattern rep = 7½ inches

**PATTERN NOTES**
For wider Afghan, every 3 additional chains on starting chain will add approximately 2 inches.

For longer Afghan, add additional rows in middle of design as indicated in instructions below.

For **color change** *(see Stitch Guide)*, change color in last stitch made.

**INSTRUCTIONS**

**AFGHAN**
**Row 1 (RS):** With icicle white, ch 72 loosely, 2 dc in 3rd ch from hook, [sk next 2 chs, (sc, 2 dc) in next ch] across to last 3 chs, sk next 2 chs, sc in last ch, turn. *(24 sc)*

**Row 2:** Ch 1 loosely, 2 dc in first sc, [sk next 2 dc, (sc, 2 dc) in next sc] across to last 3 sts, sk next 2 dc, sc in top of end ch, turn.

**Rows 3–7:** Rep row 2, changing to frosted green in last st on row 7.

**Rows 8 & 9:** With frosted green, rep row 2.

**Rows 10 & 11:** With icicle white, rep row 2.

**Rows 12–21:** With frosted green, rep row 2.

**Rows 22 & 23:** With icicle white, rep row 2.

**Rows 24 & 25:** With frosted green, rep row 2.

**Rows 26–47:** With icicle white, rep row 2.

**Rows 48–65:** Rep rows 8–25.

**Rows 66–72:** With icicle white, rep row 2.

**Row 73:** Ch 1, sc in first st, [ch 2, sk next 2 dc, sc in next sc] across, ending last rep with sc in last st. Fasten off.

**Row 74 (RS):** Working in starting ch on opposite side of row 1, join icicle white with sl st in end ch, ch 1, sc in same ch as beg ch-1, [ch 2, sk next 2 chs, sc in next ch] across. Fasten off.

**SPIRAL EDGING**
With WS facing, join frosted green with sl st in first sc, ch 1, sc in first ch-2 sp, *[ch 9, 4 sc in 2nd ch from hook, 4 sc in each of next 6 chs, sk last ch, sc in same ch-2 sp] twice, sc in next ch-2 sp**, rep from * around, ending last rep at **. Fasten off.

Rep Spiral Edging on opposite end of Afghan. ■

# Cotton Candy

DESIGN BY BRENDA STRATTON

Pink ruffles and dainty stitches produce a sugar-sweet doily in the mouth-watering shade of a favorite town-fair tidbit. Use it to decorate a precious little girl's room or keep it for your own très chic parlour!

EASY

**FINISHED SIZE**
10½ inches in diameter

**MATERIALS**
Aunt Lydia's Classic Crochet size 10 crochet cotton (350 yds per ball): 300 yds #401 orchid pink
Size 6/1.80mm steel crochet hook or size needed to obtain gauge
Starch

**GAUGE**
8 dc = 1 inch; 2 dc rnds = 5/8 inch

**SPECIAL STITCHES**
**Beginning shell (beg shell):** Ch 3 *(counts as first dc)*, (dc, ch 2, 2 dc) in next st or ch sp.

**Shell:** (2 dc, ch 2, 2 dc) in next st or ch sp.

## INSTRUCTIONS

**DOILY**

**Rnd 1 (RS):** Ch 6, sl st in first ch to form ring, ch 4 *(counts as first tr)*, 23 tr in ring, join with sl st in 4th ch of beg ch-4. *(124 tr)*

**Rnd 2:** Ch 1, sc in first st, ch 5, sk next tr, [sc in next tr, ch 5, sk next tr] around, join with ch 3, dc in beg sc to form last ch-5 sp. *(12 ch-5 sps)*

**Rnd 3:** Sl st in ch-5 sp, **beg shell** *(see Special Stitches)* in same ch-5 sp, **shell** *(see Special Stitches)* in each ch-5 sp around, join with sl st in 3rd ch of beg ch-3. *(12 shells)*

**Rnd 4:** Sl st in ch-2 sp of beg shell, ch 1, sc in same ch-2 sp, ch 6, [sc in next ch-2 sp of shell, ch 6] 10 times, sc in next ch-2 sp of shell, join with ch 2, tr in beg sc to form last ch sp. *(12 ch-6 sps)*

**Rnd 5:** Ch 3 *(counts as first dc)*, 3 dc in same ch sp, 7 dc in each of next 11 ch-6 sps, 3 dc in same ch sp as beg 4-dc, join with sl st in 3rd ch of beg ch-3. *(84 dc)*

**Rnd 6:** Ch 1, sc in first st, ch 6, sc in sp between 7-dc groups, ch 6, sk next 3 dc, [sc in next dc, ch 6, sc in sp between 7-dc groups, ch 6, sk next 3 dc] 23 times, join with sl st in beg sc. *(24 ch-6 sps)*

**Rnd 7:** Sl st in ch-6 sp, beg shell in same ch sp, shell in each of next 23 ch-6 sps, join with sl st in 3rd ch of beg ch-3. *(24 shells)*

**Rnd 8:** Sl st in ch-2 sp of shell, ch 1, sc in same ch-2 sp, ch 6, [sc in next ch-2 sp of next shell, ch 6] 22 times, sc in next ch-2 sp of next shell, join with ch 2, tr in beg sc forming last ch sp. *(24 ch-6 sps)*

**Rnd 9:** Ch 3, 2 dc in same sp, 6 dc in each of next 23 ch-6 sps, 3 dc in same ch sp as beg 3-dc, join with sl st in 3rd ch of beg ch-3. *(144 dc)*

**Rnd 10:** Ch 3, dc in each of next 10 dc, 2 dc in next dc, [dc in each of next 11 dc, 2 dc in next dc] 11 times, join with sl st in 3rd ch of beg ch-3. *(156 dc)*

**Rnd 11:** Ch 3, dc in each dc around, join with sl st in 3rd of beg ch-3.

**Rnd 12:** Ch 3, dc in each of next 11 dc, 2 dc in next dc, [dc in each of next 12 dc, 2 dc in next dc] 11 times, join with sl st in 3rd ch of beg ch-3, **do not fasten off.** *(168 dc)*

**OUTER RUFFLE**

**Rnd 1:** Ch 1, sc in first st, ch 5, sk next 2 dc, [sc in next dc, ch 5, sk next 2 dc] around, join with sl st in beg sc. *(56 ch-5 sps)*

**Rnd 2:** Sl st in next ch-5 sp, ch 4 *(counts as first tr)*, 8 tr in same ch-5 sp, sc in next ch-5 sp, [9 tr in next ch-5 sp, sc in next ch-5 sp] around, join with sl st in beg sc. *(28 groups 9-tr)*

**Rnd 3:** Sl st in each of next 2 tr, ch 4, 3 tr in same st, [ch 1, sk next tr, 4 tr in next tr] twice, ch 4, sc in next sc, ch 4, *sk next 2 tr, 4 tr in next tr, [ch 1, sk next tr, 4 tr in next tr] twice, ch 4, sc in next sc, ch 4, rep from * around, join with sl st in 4th ch of beg ch-4.

**Rnd 4: Dc dec** *(see Stitch Guide)* in first 4 tr, [ch 3, sc in next ch-1 sp, ch 3, dc dec in next 4 tr] twice, ch 3, [sc in next ch-4 sp, ch 3] twice, *[dc dec in next 4 tr, ch 3, sc in next ch-1 sp, ch 3] twice, dc dec in next 4 tr, [ch 3, sc in next ch-4 sp] twice, ch 3, rep from * around, join with sl st in top of beg dc dec. Fasten off.

**INNER RUFFLE**

**Rnd 1:** Join with sl st in any sk sc of rnd 8, ch 1, sc in same sc, ch 5, *(sc, ch 3, sc) in next sc of rnd 8, ch 5, rep from * around, ending with sc in same sc as first sc, ch 3, join with sl st in beg sc. *(24 ch-5 sps)*

**Rnd 2:** Sl st in ch-5 sp, ch 4, 8 tr in same ch-5 sp, sc in next ch-3 sp, [9 tr in next ch-5 sp, sc in next ch-3 sp] around, join with sl st in 4th ch of beg ch-4. *(24 groups 9-tr)*

**Rnds 3 & 4:** Rep rnds 3 and 4 of Outer Ruffle.

Starch with heavy starch. Let air dry. ■

# Vintage Denim

DESIGN BY CHRISTINE GRAZIOSO MOODY

Add warmth and charm to your country home with this lovely throw stitched in a muted shade of blue. Crocheted with a size I crochet hook and medium-weight yarn, it works up in a jiffy for lasting comfort.

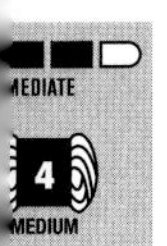

**FINISHED SIZE**
43 x 57 inches

**MATERIALS**
Red Heart Super Saver medium (worsted) weight yarn (7 oz/364 yds/198g per skein):
6 skeins #382 country blue
Size I/9/5.5mm crochet hook or size needed to obtain gauge
Tapestry needle

**GAUGE**
Rows 1–5 = 2½ inches
Panel = 3¾ inches wide

**SPECIAL STITCHES**
**Single crochet cluster (sc cl):** [Insert hook in indicated st, yo, pull up lp, yo, pull through 1 lp on hook] 3 times, yo, pull through all lps on hook.

**Back post treble crochet decrease (bptr dec):** Yo twice, insert hook around post of 2nd sc, yo, pull up lp, [yo, pull through 2 lps on hook] twice, 2 lps rem on hook, sk next sc, sk next sc cl, sk next sc, yo twice, insert hook around post of next sc, yo, pull up lp, [yo, pull through 2 lps on hook] twice, yo, pull through all lps on hook.

## INSTRUCTIONS

### AFGHAN

**PANELS**
Make 12.

**Row 1:** Ch 164 loosely, sc in 2nd ch from hook and in each of next 2 chs, [**sc cl** *(see Special Stitches)* in next ch, sc in each of next 3 chs] across, turn. *(40 sc cls)*

**Row 2 (RS):** Ch 3, dc in each st across, turn. Row 2 is bottom edge.

**Row 3:** Ch 1, sc in next dc, sc cl in next dc, sc in next dc, [**bptr dec** *(see Special Stitches)*, sk next dc, sc in next dc, sc cl in next dc, sc in next dc] across, turn.

**Row 4:** Ch 3, dc in each st across, turn.

**Row 5:** ***Note:*** *Work bptr dec around bptr dec of row 3.* Ch 1, sc in next dc, bptr around bptr dec 2 rows below, sk next dc, sc in next dc, sc cl in next dc, sc in next dc, [work bptr dec 2 rows below, sk next dc, sc in next dc, sc cl in next dc, sc in next dc] across, ending with bptr around bptr dec 2 rows below, sk next dc, sc in last dc, turn.

**PANEL BORDER**
Ch 3, 2 dc in same st, dc in each st across, 3 dc in last sc, 3 dc in dc of row 4, 2 dc in sc of row 3, 3 dc in dc of row 2, 3 dc in beg ch of row 1, dc in each ch across, 3 dc in beg ch, 3 dc in dc of row 2, 2 dc in sc of row 3, 3 dc in dc of row 4, join with sl st in 3rd ch of beg ch-3. Fasten off.

**ASSEMBLY**
With WS and bottom edges tog, whipstitch from bottom edge to top edge.

Join rem Panels in same manner until all 12 Panels are joined.

**BORDER**
Join with sc in any dc, sc in each dc around, working **sc dec** *(see Stitch Guide)* in each joining, join with sl st in beg sc. Fasten off. ■

# Study in Stitch Work

DESIGN BY KATHLEEN STUART

Show off your talent for needlework with this gorgeous afghan. Pale pink heather panels worked in a variety of deliciously textured stitches create an interesting study in dimensional crochet.

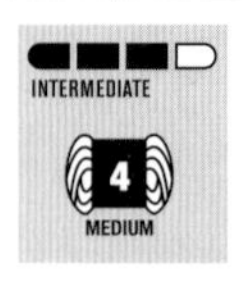


**FINISHED SIZE**
46 x 60 inches

**MATERIALS**
Lion Brand Wool-Ease medium (worsted) weight yarn (3 oz/197 yds/85g per skein):
13 skeins #104 blush heather
Size K/10½/6.5mm crochet hook or size needed to obtain gauge
Yarn needle

**GAUGE**
10 sc = 3 inches; 12 sc rows = 3 inches

**SPECIAL STITCH**
**Popcorn (pc):** 4 dc in indicated st, drop lp from hook, insert hook in first dc of dc group, pull dropped lp through, ch 1 to close.

## INSTRUCTIONS

**HEART PANEL**
Make 2.

**Row 1 (WS):** Ch 18, sc in 2nd ch from hook, sc in each ch across, turn. *(17 sc)*

**Row 2 (RS):** Ch 3 *(counts as first dc)*, dc in each of next 7 sts, **pc** *(see Special Stitch)* in next st, dc in each of last 8 sts, turn. *(17 sts)*

**Row 3:** Ch 1, sc in each st across, turn.

**Row 4:** Ch 3, dc in each of next 5 sts, pc in next st, dc in each of next 3 sts, pc in next st, dc in each of last 6 sts, turn.

**Row 5:** Rep row 3.

**Row 6:** Ch 3, dc in each of next 3 sts, pc in next st, dc in each of next 7 sts, pc in next st, dc in each of last 4 sts, turn.

**Row 7:** Rep row 3.

**Row 8:** Ch 3, dc in next st, pc in next st, dc in each of next 11 sts, pc in next st, dc in each of last 2 sts, turn.

**Row 9:** Rep row 3.

**Row 10:** Ch 3, dc in next st, pc in next st, dc in each of next 5 sts, pc in next st, dc in each of next 5 sts, pc in next st, dc in each of last 2 sts, turn.

**Row 11:** Rep row 3.

**Row 12:** Ch 3, dc in each of next 3 sts, pc in next st, dc in next st, pc in next st, dc in each of next 3 sts, pc in next st, dc in next st, pc in next st, dc in each of last 4 sts.

**Row 13:** Rep row 3.

**Rows 14–125:** Rep rows 6–13 consecutively. *(15 hearts completed)*

**EDGING**

**Rnd 126:** Ch 1, 3 sc in corner st, evenly sp sc across each side, working 3 sc in each corner, join with sl st in beg sc. Fasten off.

**SEDGE STITCH PANEL**

Make 2.

**Row 1:** Ch 36, sk 2 chs *(counts as first sc)*, (hdc, dc) in next ch, [sk next 2 chs, (sc, hdc, dc) in next ch] across to last 3 chs, sk next 2 chs, sc in last ch, turn.

**Row 2:** Ch 1 *(counts as first sc)*, (hdc, dc) in first st, [sk next dc and hdc, (sc, hdc, dc) in next sc] across to last 3 sts, sk next dc and next hdc, sc in last ch, turn.

**Rows 3–125:** Rep row 2. At end of row 125, **do not turn.**

**EDGING**

**Rnd 126:** Ch 1, 3 sc in corner st, evenly sp sc across each side, working 3 sc in each corner st, join with sl st in beg sc. Fasten off.

**CROSSED CABLE PANEL**

**Row 1:** Ch 30, sc in 2nd ch from hook, sc in each ch across, turn. *(29 sc)*

**Row 2:** Ch 3, dc in each st across, turn. *(29 dc)*

**Row 3:** Ch 1, sc in first st, **fptr** *(see Stitch Guide)* around 4th st from beg 2 rows below *(sc row)*, *sk st on working row directly behind fptr, sc in next st, fptr around 2nd sc before previous fptr 2 rows below *(X made)*, sk st on working row directly behind fptr, sc in next st**, fptr in 4th sc from previous fptr 2 rows below, rep from * across, ending last rep at **, turn. *(7 crossed cables)*

**Row 4:** Rep row 2.

***Note:*** *In pattern row 5, fptr sts are worked around post of fptr below as indicated. Each fptr row worked the fptr sts are crossed, forming an X.*

**Row 5:** Ch 1, sc in first st, fptr around 4th st from beg 2 rows below, *sk st directly behind fptr on working row, sc in next st, fptr in 2nd st before previous fptr 2 rows below *(X made)*, sk st directly behind fptr on working row, sc in next st**, fptr in 4th st from previous fptr 2 rows below, rep from * across, ending last rep at **, turn. *(7 crossed cables)*

**Rows 6–125:** Rep rows 4 and 5 alternately. At the end of row 125, **do not turn.**

**EDGING**

**Rnd 126:** Ch 1, 3 sc in corner st, evenly sp sc across each side, working 3 sc in each corner st, join with sl st in beg sc. Fasten off.

**JOINING**

Join Panels left to right, Heart Panel, Sedge Stitch Panel, Crossed Cable Panel at center, Sedge Stitch Panel and Heart Panel.

Holding WS of Panels tog and working in **back lps** *(see Stitch Guide)* only, join with sl st, ch 1, working from left to right, **reverse sc** *(see illustration)* in each st across. Fasten off.

Join rem Panels in same manner. ■

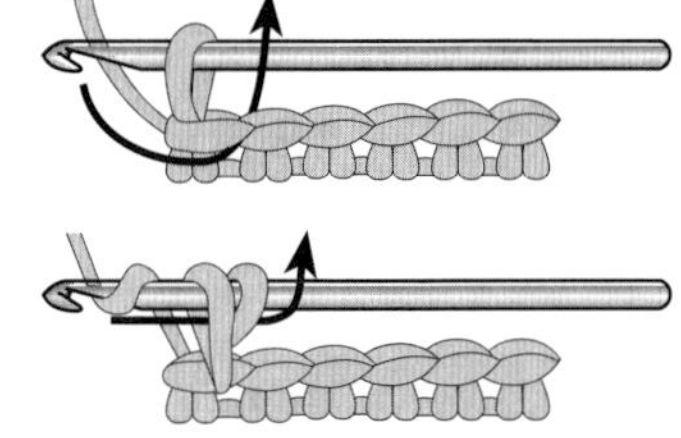

**Reverse Single Crochet**

# Curly Qs

DESIGN BY JO ANN MAXWELL

ERMEDIATE

Equally suitable for a Victorian, contemporary or rustic country home, this stunning, cotton doily bridges many decorating styles. It is sure to become a spectacular focal point wherever you place it.

**FINISHED SIZE**
25 inches across

**MATERIALS**
Size 10 crochet cotton:
800 yds white
Size 5/1.90mm steel hook or size needed to obtain gauge

**GAUGE**
Rnds 1–4 = 3½ inches across

**SPECIAL STITCHES**
**Shell:** (2 dc, ch 2, 2 dc) in next st or ch sp.

**Beginning shell (beg shell):** Ch 3 *(counts as first dc)*, (dc, ch 2, 2 dc) in same st or ch.

**Picot:** Ch 3, sl st in top of last st made.

**Small curlicue:** Ch 12, 4 dc in 4th ch from hook, 4 dc in each ch across.

**Large curlicue:** Ch 14, 4 dc in 4th ch from hook, 4 dc in each ch across.

**INSTRUCTIONS**

**DOILY**

**Rnd 1:** Ch 8, sl st in first ch to form ring, ch 3 *(counts as first dc)*, 2 dc in same ch, 3 dc in each ch around, join with sl st in 3rd ch of beg ch-3. *(24 dc)*

**Rnd 2:** Ch 6 *(counts as first tr and ch-2)*, (tr, ch 2) in each st around, join with sl st in 4th ch of beg ch-6. *(24 tr, 24 ch sps)*

**Rnd 3:** Ch 3, dc in each st and in each ch around, join with sl st in 3rd ch of beg ch-3. *(72 dc)*

**Rnd 4: Beg shell** *(see Special Stitches)* in first st, sk next 2 sts, *__shell__ *(see Special Stitches)* in next st, sk next 2 sts, rep from * around, join with sl st in 3rd ch of beg ch-3. *(24 shells)*

**Rnd 5:** Sl st in next st, sl st in next ch sp, ch 1, sc in same ch sp, **picot** *(see Special Stitches)*, ch 5, [sc in ch sp of next shell, picot, ch 5] around, join with sl st in beg sc.

**Rnd 6:** Sl st in each of next 3 chs, beg shell, ch 1, [shell in center ch of next ch-5, ch 1] around, join with sl st in 3rd ch of beg ch-3.

**Rnd 7:** Sl st in next st, sl st in next ch sp, ch 1, sc in same ch sp, picot, ch 7, [sc in next shell, picot, ch 7] around, join with sl st in beg sc.

**Rnd 8:** Sl st in next 4 chs, ch 12, *dtr in center ch of next ch-7, ch 7, rep from * around, join with sl st in 5th ch of beg ch-12.

**Rnd 9:** Beg shell, ch 2, sc in next ch sp, ch 2, [shell in next st, ch 2, sc in next ch sp, ch 2] around, join with sl st in 3rd ch of beg ch-3.

**Rnd 10:** Sl st in next st, sl st in next ch sp, ch 1, sc in same ch sp, ***small curlicue** *(see Special Stitches)*, ch 4, sc in next sc, picot, ch 4, drop lp from hook, twist curlicue 4 or 5 times, insert hook in end of curlicue, pull dropped lp through, ch 1**, sc in next shell, rep from * around, ending last rep at **, join with sl st in beg sc.

**Rnd 11:** Working this rnd in **back lps** *(see Stitch Guide)* only, ch 8, dtr in same st, ch 9, sk next curlicue, *(dtr, ch 3, dtr) in next sc, ch 9, sk next curlicue, rep from * around, join with sl st in 5th ch of beg ch-8.

**Rnd 12:** Sl st in each of next 2 chs, beg shell, *ch 1, sc in next ch-9 sp, ch 1, shell in 5th ch of same ch-9, ch 1, sc in same ch sp, ch 1**, shell in 2nd ch of next ch-3, rep from * around, ending last rep at **, join with sl st in 3rd ch of beg ch-3.

**Rnds 13–15:** Rep rows 7–9.

**Rnd 16:** Sl st in next st, sl st in next ch sp, ch 1, sc in same ch sp, **large curlicue** *(see Special Stitches)*, ch 4, sc in next sc, picot, ch 4, [sc in next shell, large curlicue, ch 4, sc in next sc, picot, ch 4] around, join with sl st in beg sc. Fasten off.

**Rnd 17:** Twist first curlicue 6 or 7 times, join with sc in tip of same curlicue, ch 8, [twist next curlicue 6 or 7 times, sc in tip of same curlicue, ch 8] around, join with sl st in beg sc.

**Rnd 18:** Beg shell, ch 3, sc in next ch sp, ch 3, [shell in next sc, ch 3, sc in next ch sp, ch 3] around, join with sl st in 3rd ch of beg ch-3.

**Rnd 19:** Sl st in next st, sl st in next ch sp, ch 1, sc in same ch sp, picot, ch 9, [sc in next shell, picot, ch 9] around, join with sl st in beg sc.

**Rnd 20:** Sl st in each of next 5 chs of next ch-9, ch 14, [dtr in 5th ch of next ch-9, ch 9] around, join with sl st in 5th ch of beg ch-14.

**Rnd 21:** Beg shell, ch 3, sc in next ch sp, ch 3, [shell in next st, ch 3, sc in next ch sp, ch 3] around, join with sl st in 3rd ch of beg ch-3.

**Rnd 22:** Sl st in next st, sl st in next ch sp, ch 1, sc in same ch sp, *large curlicue, ch 4, sc in next sc, picot, ch 4, drop lp from hook, twist curlicue 6 or 7 times, insert hook in end of curlicue, pull dropped lp through, ch 1**, sc in next shell, rep from * around, ending last rep at **, join with sl st in beg sc.

**Rnds 23 & 24:** Rep rnds 11 and 12.

**Rnd 25:** Sl st in next st, sl st in next ch sp, ch 3, 6 dc in same ch sp, *ch 1, sc in next ch-1 sp, ch 4, sc in next shell, picot, ch 4, sk next sc, sc in next ch-1 sp, ch 1**, 7 dc in next shell, rep from * around, ending last rep at **, join with sl st in 3rd ch of beg ch-3.

**Rnd 26:** Sl st in each of next 3 sts, beg shell in same st, *ch 5, sc in next picot, tr in next dc, [ch 3, tr in next dc] 6 times, sc in next picot, ch 5**, shell in 4th dc of next 7-dc group, rep from * around, ending last rep at **, join with sl st in 3rd ch of beg ch-3.

**Rnd 27:** Sl st in next st, sl st in next ch sp, ch 3, 8 dc in same ch sp, sc in next ch-5 sp, dc in next tr, dc in next 24 chs or tr, sc in next ch-5 sp, [9 dc in next shell, sc in next ch-5 sp, dc in next tr, dc in next 24 chs or tr, sc in next ch-5 sp] around, join with sl st in 3rd ch of beg ch-3.

**Rnd 28:** Ch 1, sc in first st, ch 5, sk next 3 sts, sc in next st, picot, ch 5, sk next 3 sts, sc in next st, sc in next dc, [ch 5, sk next 2 sts, sc in next st] 8 times, *sc in next dc, ch 5, sk next 3 sts, sc in next st, picot, ch 5, sk next 3 sts, sc in next st, sc in next dc, [ch 5, sk next 2 sts, sc in next st] 8 times, rep from * around, join with sl st in beg sc. Fasten off. ■

# Cockscomb

DESIGN BY JOSIE RABIER

Pamper yourself with this visually stunning doily that is just the right accent for any surface. Opulent textures, stunning beauty and a unique edging highlight this elegant doily stitched in the pineapple tradition.

INTERMEDIATE

**FINISHED SIZE**
18 inches in diameter

**MATERIALS**
Grandma's Best size 10 crochet cotton:
650 yds white
Size 7/1.65mm steel crochet hook or size needed to obtain gauge
Starch

**GAUGE**
8 dc = 1 inch; 3 dc rnds = 1 inch

**SPECIAL STITCHES**

**Front post treble crochet cluster (fptr cl):** Holding back last lp of each tr on hook, fptr around each of next 4 fptr, yo, pull through all 5 lps on hook, ch 1 to close.

**Cluster (cl):** Holding last lp of each st on hook, 4 tr in specified st or ch sp, yo, pull through all lps on hook.

**Beginning split cluster (beg split cl):** Holding back last lp of each st, dc in next dc, sk next 2 dc, dc in each of next 2 dc, yo, pull through all lps on hook.

**Split cluster (split cl):** Holding back last lp of each st, dc in each of next 2 dc, sk next 2 dc, dc in each of next 2 dc, yo, pull through all lps on hook.

## INSTRUCTIONS

**DOILY**

**Rnd 1 (RS):** Ch 8, sl st in first ch to form ring, ch 3 *(counts as first dc)*, 31 dc in ring, join with sl st in 3rd ch of beg ch-3. *(32 dc)*

**Rnd 2:** Ch 3, dc in next dc, ch 2, [dc in each of next 2 dc, ch 2] around, join with sl st in 3rd ch of beg ch-3.

**Rnd 3:** Sl st in ch-2 sp, ch 3, 4 dc in same ch-2 sp, *ch 3, sl st in next ch-2 sp, ch 3**, 5 dc in next ch-2 sp, rep from * around, ending last rep at **, join with sl st in 3rd ch of beg ch-3. *(8 groups 5-dc)*

**Rnd 4:** Ch 2, **dc dec** *(see Stitch Guide)* in next 4 dc, *ch 5, dc in sl st, ch 5**, dc dec in next 5 dc, rep from * around, ending last rep at **, join with sl st in top of beg dc dec. *(16 ch-5 sps)*

**Rnd 5:** Sl st in ch-5 sp, ch 3, 6 dc in same ch sp, 7 dc in each ch-5 sp around, join with sl st in 3rd ch of beg ch-3. *(112 dc)*

**Rnd 6:** Ch 1, sc in first dc, sc in each of next 2 dc, *3 sc in next dc**, sc in each of next 6 dc, rep from * around, ending last rep at **, sc in each of last 3 dc, join with sl st in beg sc. *(144 sc)*

**Rnd 7:** Ch 1, sc in each sc around, join with sl st in beg sc.

**Rnd 8:** Ch 3, dc in next sc, *2 **fptr** *(see Stitch Guide)* around 4th dc of 7-dc group of rnd 5 directly below, dc in each of next 2 sc of this rnd, (dc, ch 3, dc) in next sc, dc in each of next 2 sc, 2 fptr around same dc as previous 2 fptr**, dc in each of next 4 sc, rep from * around, ending last rep at **, dc in each of last 2 sc, join with sl st in 3rd ch of beg ch-3.

**Rnd 9:** Sl st in next dc, ch 3, *fptr around each of next 2 fptr, 7 tr in next ch-3 sp, fptr around each of next 2 fptr, dc in next dc, sk next 2 dc**, dc in next dc, rep from *

around, ending last rep at **, join with sl st in 3rd ch of beg ch-3.

**Rnd 10:** Sl st in first tr of next 7-tr group, ch 3, dc in same st, *2 dc in each of next 6 tr, **fptr cl** *(see Special Stitches),* dc in each of next 3 tr, (dc, ch 3, dc) in next tr, dc in each of next 3 tr, fptr cl**, 2 dc in next tr, rep from * around, ending last rep at **, join with sl st in 3rd ch of beg ch-3.

**Rnd 11:** Ch 3, dc in each of next 6 dc, *ch 5, dc in each of next 7 dc, sk next fptr cl, [**cl** *(see Special Stitches)* in next dc, ch 5, sl st in next dc, ch 5] twice, cl in next ch-3 sp, [ch 5, sl st in next dc, ch 5, cl in next dc] twice, ch 1, sk next fptr cl**, dc in each of next 7 dc, rep from * around, ending last rep at **, join with sl st in 3rd ch of beg ch-3.

**Rnd 12:** Sl st in each of 6 dc, next ch-5 sp and in next dc, ch 3, dc in each of next 6 dc, *ch 5, sk first cl, sl st in next cl, [ch 5, sl st in next cl] twice, ch 5, sk next cl, dc in each of next 7 dc, ch 5, sl st in next ch-5 sp, ch 5**, dc in each of next 7 dc, rep from * around, ending last rep at **, join with sl st in 3rd ch of beg ch-3.

**Rnd 13:** Ch 3, dc in each of next 6 dc, *sl st in next ch-5 sp, [ch 5, sl st in next ch-5 sp] 3 times, dc in each of next 7 dc, [ch 5, sl st in next ch-5 sp] twice, ch 5**, dc in each of next 7 dc, rep from * around, ending last rep at **, join with sl st in 3rd ch of beg ch-3.

**Rnd 14:** Ch 3, dc in each of next 6 dc, *sl st in next ch-5 sp, [ch 5, sl st in next ch-5 sp] twice, dc in each of next 7 dc, ch 5, sl st in next ch-5 sp, 7 dc in next ch-5 sp, sl st in next ch-5 sp, ch 5**, dc in each of next 7 dc, rep from * around, ending last rep at **, join with sl st in 3rd ch of beg ch-3.

**Rnd 15:** Ch 3, dc in each of next 6 dc, *sl st in next ch-5 sp, ch 5, sl st in next ch-5 sp, dc in each of next 7 dc, ch 5, sl st in next ch-5 sp, 2 dc in each of next 7 dc, sl st in next ch-5 sp, ch 5**, dc in each of next 7 dc, rep from * around, ending last rep at **, join with sl st in 3rd ch of beg ch-3.

**Rnd 16:** Ch 3, dc in each of next 6 dc, *sl st in next ch-5 sp, dc in each of next 7 dc, ch 5, sl st in next ch-5 sp, dc in each of next 14 dc, sl st in next ch-5 sp, ch 5**, dc in each of next 7 dc, rep from * around, ending last rep at **, join with sl st in 3rd ch of beg ch-3.

**Rnd 17:** Ch 3, dc in each of next 5 dc, *sk next 2 dc, dc in each of next 6 dc, ch 5, sl st in next ch-5 sp, dc in each of next 2 dc, [ch 2, dc in each of next 2 dc] 6 times, sl st in next ch-5 sp, ch 5**, dc in each of next 6 dc, rep from * around, ending last rep at **, join with sl st in 3rd ch of beg ch-3.

**Rnd 18:** Ch 3, dc in each of next 4 dc, *sk next 2 dc, dc in each of next 5 dc, ch 5, sl st in next ch-5 sp, dc in each of next 2 dc, [ch 3, dc in each of next 2 dc] 6 times, sl st in next ch-5 sp, ch 5**, dc in each of next 5 dc, rep from * around, ending last rep at **, join with sl st in 3rd ch of beg ch-3.

**Rnd 19:** Ch 3, dc in each of next 3 dc, *sk next 2 dc, dc in each of next 4 dc, ch 5, sl st in next ch-5 sp, [dc in next dc, ch 3, dc in next dc] 7 times, sl st in next ch-5 sp, ch 5**, dc in each of next 4 dc, rep from * around, ending last rep at **, join with sl st in 3rd ch of beg ch-3.

**Rnd 20:** Ch 3, dc in each of next 2 dc, *sk next 2 dc, dc in each of next 3 dc, ch 5, sl st in next ch-5 sp, 5 dc in each of next 7 ch-3 sps, sl st in next ch-5 sp, ch 5**, dc in each of next 3 dc, rep from * around, ending last rep at **, join with sl st in 3rd ch of beg ch-3.

**Rnd 21:** Ch 2, **beg split cl** *(see Special Stitches),* *ch 5, sl st in next ch-5 sp, [2 **fpdtr** *(see Stitch Guide),* around each of next 2 dc of rnd 18, dc in each of next 2 dc of rnd, 5 tr in next dc, dc in each of next 2 dc, 2 fpdtr around same dc as previous 2 fpdtr] 7 times, sl st in next ch-5 sp, ch 5**, **split cl** *(see Special Stitches),* rep from * around, ending last rep at **, join with sl st in top of beg split cl.

**Rnd 22:** Sl st in 3rd ch of next ch-5 sp, ◊fpdc *[sk next around each of next 2 fpdtr, *[sk next st, (sl st, ch 5, tr) in next st] 3 times, sk next st, sl st in next st**, fpdc around each of next 4 fpdtr*, rep between * 5 times, rep from * to **, fpdc around each of next 2 fpdtr, sl st in 3rd ch of next ch-5 sp, sl st in each of next 2 chs, sl st in next split cl, sl st in each of next 3 chs, rep from ◊ 7 times, fasten off.

Starch lightly and press. ■

# Wild Orchids

DESIGN BY DEBRA CALDWELL

Sparkle and shine with this exquisitely delicate beaded doily. Stitched in size 30 thread, it's beautifully exotic and reminiscent of wild Hawaiian orchids, transporting you to beautiful beaches and warm breezes.

RMEDIATE

**FINISHED SIZE**
14½ inches in diameter

**MATERIALS**
DMC Cebelia size 30 crochet cotton (282 yds per ball):
1 ball each #001 white and #553 violet
Size 9/1.25mm steel crochet hook or size needed to obtain gauge
.23-oz containers size 11/0 orchid #4-39 glass beads from Creative Beginnings: 6

**GAUGE**
Rnds 1 and 2 = 1 inch in diameter

**SPECIAL STITCHES**
**V-stitch (V-st):** (Dc, ch 2, dc) in indicated ch sp or st.

**Shell:** (2 dc, ch 2, 2 dc) in indicated ch sp or st.

**Bead:** Slide bead up to hook.

**Beaded half double crochet (bhdc):** Yo, insert hook in indicated st or ch sp, yo, pull up lp, bead, yo, pull through all lps on hook, pushing bead to RS of work.

**Picot:** Ch 3, sl st in 3rd ch from hook.

## INSTRUCTIONS

**DOILY**

**Rnd 1 (RS):** With violet, ch 6, sl st in first ch to form ring, ch 4 *(counts as first dc and ch-1)*, [dc in ring, ch 1] 11 times, join with sl st in 3rd ch of beg ch-4. *(12 ch-1 sps)*

**Rnd 2:** Sl st in first ch-1 sp, ch 3 *(counts as first dc)*, dc in same ch sp, ch 2, [2 dc in next ch sp, ch 2] around, join with sl st in 3rd ch of beg ch-3. *(12 dc groups)*

**Rnd 3:** Ch 3, 2 dc in next st, ch 7, [dc in next dc, 2 dc in next dc, ch 7] around, join with sl st in 3rd ch of beg ch-3. *(12 dc groups)*

**Rnd 4:** Sl st in next dc, ch 1, sc in same st, *ch 3, sc in next ch-7 sp, ch 3**, sc in center dc of next dc group, rep from * around, ending last rep at **, join with sl st in beg sc.

**Rnd 5:** Ch 1, sc in first st, *ch 3, (sc, ch 5, sc) in next sc, ch 3**, sc in next sc, rep from * around, ending last rep at **, join with sl st in beg sc. Fasten off.

**Rnd 6:** With RS facing, join white with sl st in any ch-5 sp, ch 9 *(counts as first dc and ch-6)*, [**V-st** *(see Special Stitches)* in next ch-5 sp, ch 6] around, ending with (dc, ch 2) in same ch sp as beg ch-9, join with sl st in 3rd ch of beg ch-9.

**Rnd 7:** Ch 3, dc in same st, *ch 4, 2 dc in next dc, ch 2, dc in next ch sp, ch 2**, 2 dc in next dc, rep from * around, ending last rep at **, join with sl st in 3rd ch of beg ch-3.

**Rnd 8:** Ch 3, *2 dc in next dc, ch 2, 2 dc in next dc, dc in next dc, ch 2, V-st in next dc, ch 2**, dc in next dc, rep from * around, ending last rep at **, join with sl st in 3rd ch of beg ch-3.

**Rnd 9:** Ch 3, dc in next dc, *2 dc in next dc, ch 1, 2 dc in next dc, dc in each of next 2 dc, ch 2, **shell** *(see Special Stitches)* in ch sp of next V-st, ch 2, sk next ch sp**, dc in each of next 2 dc, rep from * around, ending last rep at **, join with sl st in 3rd ch of beg ch-3. Fasten off.

**Rnd 10:** With RS facing, join violet with sl st in any dc immediately to the left of any ch-1 sp, ch 3, *dc in each of next 3 dc, 2 dc in next ch sp, dc in each of next 2 dc, 3 dc in next ch sp, dc in each of next 2 dc, 2 dc in next ch sp, dc in each of next 4 dc, ch 5, sk ch-1 sp**, dc in next dc, rep from * around, ending last rep at **, join with sl st in 3rd ch of beg ch-3. Fasten off.

**Rnd 11:** String all orchid beads onto white, with WS facing, join white with sl st in any ch-5 sp, ch 2 *(counts as first hdc)*, 2 **bhdc** *(see Special Stitches)* in same ch sp, *ch 6, (hdc, 2 bhdc) in center dc of next dc group above rnd 9 shell, ch 6**, (hdc, 2 bhdc) in next ch-5 sp, rep from * around, ending last rep at **, join with sl st in 2nd ch of beg ch-2. *(24 groups of hdc and 2 bhdc)*

**Rnd 12:** Sl st in next st, ch 2, *bhdc in next st, 2 bhdc in next ch sp, ch 6, sk next hdc**, hdc in next st, rep from * around, ending last rep at **, join with sl st in 2nd ch of beg ch-2. *(24 groups of hdc and 3 bhdc)*

**Rnd 13:** Sl st in next st, ch 2, *bhdc in each st across to next ch sp, 3 bhdc in next ch sp, ch 6, sk next hdc**, hdc in next st, rep from * around, ending last rep at **, join with sl st in 2nd ch of beg ch-2. *(24 groups of hdc and 5 bhdc)*

**Rnd 14:** Rep rnd 13. *(24 groups of hdc and 7 bhdc)*

**Rnd 15:** Sl st in next st, ch 2, *bhdc in each st across to next ch sp, 3 bhdc in next ch sp, ch 4, sk next hdc**, hdc in next st, rep from * around, ending last rep at **, join with sl st in 2nd ch of beg ch-2. *(24 groups of hdc and 9 bhdc)*

**Rnd 16:** Sl st in next st, ch 2, *bhdc in each st across to next ch sp, 3 bhdc in next ch sp, ch 2, sk next hdc**, hdc in next st, rep from * around, ending last rep at **, join with sl st in 2nd ch of beg ch-2. *(24 groups of hdc and 11 bhdc)*

**Rnd 17:** Sl st in next st, ch 2, *bhdc in each of next 9 sts, ch 4, sk next ch

in 3rd ch of beg ch-3. Fasten off. *(80 dc, 4 shells)*

**Rnd 17:** Join light plum with sl st in any corner ch-2 sp, beg shell, *sk next 2 sts, 2 dc in next st, ch 1, working behind 2 dc just made, 2 dc in 2nd sk st, [sc in next ch-1 sp, sk next 3 sts, 2 dc in next st, ch 1, working behind 2 dc just made, 2 dc in 2nd sk st], sc in next ch-1 sp, sk next 3 sts, 2 dc in next st, ch 1, working behind 2 dc just made, 2 dc in 3rd sk st, rep between [ ], sc in next ch-1 sp, sk next 2 sts, 2 dc in next st, ch 1, working behind 2 dc just made, 2 dc in 2nd sk st**, shell in next ch-2 sp, rep from * around, ending last rep at **, join with sl st in 3rd ch of beg ch-3. Fasten off. *(80 dc, 16 sc, 4 shells)*

**Rnd 18:** Sl st in next st, sl st in next ch sp, beg shell, *sk next 2 sts, 2 dc in next st, ch 1, working behind 2 dc just made, 2 dc in 2nd sk st, [sc in next ch-1 sp, sk next 3 sts, 2 dc in next st, ch 1, working behind 2 dc just made, 2 dc in 2nd sk st] 4 times, sc in next ch-1 sp, sk next 2 sts, 2 dc in next st, ch 1, working behind 2 dc just made, 2 dc in 2nd sk st**, shell in next ch-2 sp, rep from * around, ending last rep at **, join with sl st in 3rd ch of beg ch-3. Fasten off. *(96 dc, 20 sc, 4 shells)*

**Rnd 19:** Join cream in any corner

ch-2 sp, beg shell, *dc in next st, **fpdc** *(see Stitch Guide)* around next st, [sk next st, sc in next st, sc in next ch-1 sp, sc in next st, sk next st, fpdc around next sc] 5 times, sk next st, sc in next st, sc in next ch-1 sp, sc in next st, sk next st, fpdc around next dc, dc in next st**, shell in next corner ch-2 sp, rep from * around, ending last rep at **, join with sl st in 3rd ch of beg ch-3. *(72 sc, 28 fpdc, 8 dc, 4 shells)*

**Rnd 20:** Ch 1, sc in each st around with (sc, ch 2, sc) in each corner ch-2 sp, join with sl st in beg sc. Fasten off. *(33 sc on each side between corner ch-2 sps)*

With cream, sew Motifs WS tog in 4 rows of 5 Motifs each.

### EDGING

**Rnd 1:** Join cream with sc in any st, sc in each st and in each ch sp on each side of seams around with (sc, ch 2, sc) in each corner ch-2 sp, join with sl st in beg sc. Fasten off. *(140 sc across each short end between corner ch sps, 175 sc on each long edge between corner ch sps)*

**Rnd 2:** Join dark plum in any corner ch-2 sp, beg shell, *ch 1, sk next 2 sts, sc in next st, [sk next 2 sts, 2 dc in next st, ch 1, working behind 2 dc just made, 2 dc in 2nd sk st, sk next st, sc in next st] across to last 2 sts before next corner ch sp, ch 1, sk next 2 sts**, shell in next corner ch-2 sp, rep from * around, ending last rep at **, join with sl st in 3rd ch of beg ch-3.

**Rnd 3:** Sl st in next st, sl st in next ch sp, beg shell, *sk next ch-1 sp, 2 dc in next sc, ch 1, working behind 2 dc just made, 2 dc in sk ch-1 sp, sc in next ch sp, [sk next 3 sts, 2 dc in next dc, ch 1, working behind 2 dc just made, 2 dc in 2nd sk st, sc in next ch-1 sp] across to last sc on this side, sk next sc, 2 dc in next ch-1 sp, ch 1, working behind 2 dc just made, 2 dc in sk sc**, shell in next corner ch sp, rep from * around, ending last rep at **, join with sl st in 3rd ch of beg ch-3. Fasten off. ■

# Simply White

DESIGN BY DIANE STONE

Relaxed elegance is the theme of this lovely piece. A ring of winter white flowers with pearl centers outside a double ruffle edged in silver makes this candle doily delicate as a snowflake.

INTERMEDIATE

**FINISHED SIZE**
11½ inches in diameter

**MATERIALS**
Size 10 crochet cotton:
200 yds white
30 yds silver lamé thread
Size 7/1.65mm steel crochet hook or size needed to obtain gauge
Sewing needle
Sewing thread
12 white 6mm pearl beads

**GAUGE**
Rnds 1–3 = 2 inches

**SPECIAL STITCHES**

**Beginning popcorn (beg pc):** Ch 4, 4 tr in same st, drop lp from hook, insert hook in top of ch-4, pull dropped lp through.

**Popcorn (pc):** 5 tr in next st or ch sp, drop lp from hook, insert hook in top of first tr of group, pull dropped lp through.

**Picot:** Ch 6, sc in 3rd ch from hook, hdc in next ch, ch 2.

**INSTRUCTIONS**

**DOILY**

**Rnd 1:** With white, wrap crochet cotton around finger twice to form a ring, ch 3 *(counts as first dc)*, 15 dc in ring, pull tightly to close ring, join with sl st in 3rd ch of beg ch-3. *(16 dc)*

**Rnd 2:** Ch 3, dc in same st, 2 dc in each st around, join with sl st in 3rd ch of beg ch-3. *(32 dc)*

**Rnd 3:** Ch 3, 2 dc in next st, [dc in next st, 2 dc in next st] around, join with sl st in 3rd ch of beg ch-3. *(48 dc)*

**Rnd 4:** Ch 3, dc in next st, 2 dc in next st, [dc in each of next 2 sts, 2 dc in next st] around, join with sl st in 3rd ch of beg ch-3. *(64 dc)*

**Rnd 5:** Ch 3, dc in each of next 2 sts, 2 dc in next st, [dc in each of next 3 sts, 2 dc in next st] around, join with sl st in 3rd ch of beg ch-3. *(80 dc)*

**Rnd 6:** Working in **back lps** *(see Stitch Guide)*, ch 3, dc in each of next 3 sts, 2 dc in next st, [dc in each of next 4 sts, 2 dc in next st] around, join with sl st in 3rd ch of beg ch-3. *(96 dc)*

**Rnd 7:** Ch 1, sc in first st, [ch 3, sk next st, sc in next st] around, join with dc in beg sc forming last ch sp.

**Rnd 8:** Ch 1, sc in last ch sp made, [ch 3, sc in next ch sp] around, join with dc in beg sc.

**Rnds 9 & 10:** Ch 1, sc in last ch sp made, [ch 4, sc in next ch sp] around, join with ch 1, dc in beg sc.

**Rnd 11:** Ch 1, sc in last ch sp made, [ch 5, sc in next ch sp] around, join with ch 2, dc in beg sc.

**Rnd 12:** Ch 1, sc in last ch sp made, ch 5, [sc in next ch sp, ch 5] around, join with sl st in beg sc. Fasten off.

**FIRST FLOWER MOTIF**

**Rnd 1:** Form a ring with white, ch 1, 8 sc in ring, pull tightly to close ring, join with sl st in beg sc. *(8 sc)*

**PETALS**

**Rnd 2: Beg pc** *(see Special Stitches)*

in first st, [ch 5, **pc** *(see Special Stitches)* in next st] around, join with ch 2, dc in beg pc forming last ch sp.

**Rnd 3:** Ch 1, (sc, ch 3, sc) in last ch sp made, ch 2, sc in any ch-5 sp on last rnd of Doily, ch 2, [(sc, ch 3, sc) in center ch of next ch sp on Flower Motif, ch 5] around, join with sl st in beg sc. Fasten off.

#### JOINED FLOWER MOTIF

Make 10.

**Rnds 1 & 2:** Work same as rnds 1 and 2 of First Flower Motif.

**Rnd 3:** Ch 1, (sc, ch 3, sc) in last ch sp made, ch 2, sk next 3 ch sps on last rnd of Doily, sc in next ch-5 sp on Doily, ch 2, (sc, ch 3, sc) in center ch of next ch sp on this Motif, ch 5, (sc, ch 3, sc) in next ch sp, ch 2, sc in corresponding ch-5 sp on last Flower Motif, ch 2, [(sc, ch 3, sc) in center ch of next ch sp on this Motif, ch 5] around, join with sl st in beg sc. Fasten off.

#### LAST FLOWER MOTIF

**Rnds 1 & 2:** Work same as rnds 1 and 2 of First Flower Motif.

**Rnd 3:** Ch 1, (sc, ch 3, sc) in last ch sp made, ch 2, sk next 3 ch sps on last rnd of Doily, sc in next ch-5 sp on Doily, ch 2, (sc, ch 3, sc) in center ch of next ch sp on this Motif, ch 5, (sc, ch 3, sc) in center ch of next ch sp, ch 2, sc in corresponding ch-5 sp on Last Flower Motif, ch 2, [(sc, ch 3, sc) in center ch of next ch sp on Flower Motif, ch 5] 3 times, (sc, ch 3, sc) in center ch of next ch sp, ch 2, sc in corresponding ch sp of First Flower Motif, ch 2, (sc, ch 3, sc) in center ch of next ch sp, ch 5, join with sl st in beg sc. Fasten off.

#### EDGING

Working in unworked ch-5 sps around outer edge, join with sc in first ch-5 sp to left of side joining, ch 3, sc in same ch sp, *[**picot** *(see Special Stitches)*, (sc, ch 3, sc) in center ch of next ch-5 sp] twice, ch 8, sc in 2nd ch from hook, hdc in next ch, dc in next ch, ch 3**, (sc, ch 3, sc) in center ch of next ch-5 sp on next Flower Motif, rep from * around, ending last rep at **, join with sl st in beg sc. Fasten off.

Sew 1 bead to center of each Flower Motif.

#### FILL-IN

Working in the 3 sk ch-5 sps on last rnd of Doily between Flower Motifs, join with sc in center ch of first ch-5 sp, (dc, ch 3, sl st in top of last dc just made, ch 1) 3 times in center ch of next ch-5 sp, sc in center ch of last ch-5 sp. Fasten off.

Work in each sp between Flower Motifs.

#### RUFFLE

**Rnd 1:** Working in **front lps** *(see Stitch Guide)* of rnd 5 on Doily, join with sl st in any st, ch 4 *(counts as dc and ch-1)*, (dc, ch 1, dc) in next st, ch 1, [dc in next st, ch 1, (dc, ch 1, dc) in next st, ch 1] around, join with sl st in 3rd ch of beg ch-4. *(120 dc)*

**Rnd 2:** Ch 5 *(counts as first tr and ch-1)*, [tr in next st, ch 1] around, join with sl st in 4th ch of beg ch-5. Fasten off.

**Rnd 3:** Join silver lamé with sc in any ch sp, ch 4, [sc in next ch sp, ch 4] around, join with sl st in beg sc. Fasten off. ■

# White Pines

DESIGNS BY MARGRET WILLSON

Lacy, white doilies highlighted with rings of charming Christmas trees that are worked into the design as you stitch, bring to mind a pristine pine forest blanketed in new-fallen snow.

INTERMEDIATE

**FINISHED SIZES**
Large Doily: 13 inches in diameter

Small Doily: 7½ inches in diameter

**MATERIALS**
Size 10 crochet cotton:
400 yds white
Size 6/1.80mm steel crochet hook or size needed to obtain gauge

**GAUGE**
5 dc = ½ inch; 4 dc = 1 inch

**SPECIAL STITCHES**
**Beginning shell (beg shell):** (Ch 3, dc, ch 1, 2 dc) in indicated st or ch sp.

**Shell:** (2 dc, ch 1, 2 dc) in indicated st or ch sp.

**Beginning large shell (beg large shell):** (Ch 3, 2 dc, ch 1, 3 dc) in indicated st or ch sp.

**Large shell:** (3 dc, ch 1, 3 dc) in indicated st or ch sp.

## INSTRUCTIONS

**LARGE DOILY**
**Rnd 1:** Ch 5, sl st in first ch to form ring, ch 3, dc in ring, ch 1, [2 dc in ring, ch 1] 7 times, join with sl st in 3rd ch of beg ch-3. *(16 dc, 8 ch sps)*

**Rnd 2:** Sl st in next st, sl st in next ch sp, **beg shell** *(see Special Stitches)* in same sp, **shell** *(see Special Stitches)* in each ch sp around, join with sl st in 3rd ch of beg ch-3. *(8 shells)*

**Rnd 3:** Sl st in next st, sl st in next ch sp, **beg large shell** *(see Special Stitches)* in same sp, **large shell** *(see Special Stitches)* in ch sp of each shell around, join with sl st in 3rd ch of beg ch-3. *(8 large shells)*

**Rnd 4:** Ch 1, sc back in sp between last shell and first shell, 9 dc in first shell, [sc in sp between last worked shell and next shell, 9 dc in next shell] around, join with sl st in beg sc. *(8 sc, 8 dc groups)*

**Rnd 5:** Ch 9 *(counts as first tr and ch-5)*, sc in center st of next dc group, ch 5, [tr in next sc, ch 5, sc in center st of next dc group, ch 5] around, join with sl st in 4th ch of beg ch-9. *(16 ch sps, 8 tr, 8 sc)*

**Rnd 6:** Ch 3, dc in same st, ch 4, 2 dc in next sc, ch 4, [2 dc in next tr, ch 4, 2 dc in next sc, ch 4] around, join with sl st in 3rd ch of beg ch-3. *(32 dc, 16 ch sps)*

**Rnd 7:** Ch 3, dc in same st, 2 dc in next st, ch 3, [2 dc in each of next 2 sts, ch 3] around, join with sl st in 3rd of beg ch-3. *(64 dc, 16 ch sps)*

**Rnd 8:** Ch 3, dc in same st, dc in each of next 2 sts, 2 dc in next st, ch 2, [2 dc in next st, dc in each of next 2 sts, 2 dc in next st, ch 2] around, join with sl st in 3rd ch of beg ch-3. *(96 dc, 16 ch sps)*

**Rnd 9:** Ch 3, dc in same st, *dc in each of next 4 sts, 2 dc in next st, ch 1**, 2 dc in next st, rep from * around, ending last rep at **, join with sl st in 3rd ch of beg ch-3. *(128 dc, 16 ch sps)*

**Rnd 10:** Ch 3, dc in each st and in each ch sp around, join with sl st in 3rd ch of beg ch-3. *(144 dc)*

**Rnd 11:** Sl st in each of next 2 sts, ch 6 *(counts as first dc and ch-3 sp)*, sk next 2 sts, [dc in next st, ch 3, sk next 2 sts] around, join with sl st in 3rd ch of beg ch-3. *(48 dc, 48 ch sps)*

**Rnd 12:** Sl st in next ch sp, beg shell, sk next ch sp, shell in next dc, sk next ch sp, [shell in next ch sp, sk next ch sp, shell in next dc, sk next ch sp] around, join with sl st in 3rd ch of beg ch-3. *(32 shells)*

**Rnd 13:** Sl st in next st, sl st in next ch sp, beg large shell, large shell in each shell around, join with sl st in 3rd ch of beg ch-3. *(32 large shells)*

**Rnd 14:** Rep rnd 4. *(32 sc, 32 dc groups)*

**Rnd 15:** Ch 7 *(counts as first tr and ch-3)*, sc in center st of next dc group, ch 3, [tr in next sc, ch 3, sc in center st of next dc group, ch 3] around, join with sl st in 4th ch of beg ch-7. *(64 ch sps, 32 tr, 32 sc)*

**Rnd 16:** Beg shell in same st, shell in each sc and in each tr around, join with sl st in 3rd ch of beg ch-3. *(64 shells)*

**Rnds 17–19:** Sl st in next st, sl st in next ch sp, beg shell in same ch sp, shell in each shell around, join with sl st in 3rd ch of beg ch-3.

**Rnd 20:** Sl st in next st, sl st in next ch sp, ch 3, dc in same ch sp, ch 7, sk next shell, [2 dc in next shell, ch 7, sk next shell] around, join with sl st in 3rd ch of beg ch-3. *(64 dc, 32 ch sps)*

**Rnd 21:** Ch 3, dc in same st, 2 dc in next st, ch 6, [2 dc in each of next 2 sts, ch 6] around, join with sl st in 3rd of beg ch-3. *(128 dc, 32 ch sps)*

**Rnd 22:** Ch 3, dc in same st, dc in each of next 2 sts, 2 dc in next st, ch 4, [2 dc in next st, dc in each of next 2 sts, 2 dc in next st, ch 4] around, join with sl st in 3rd ch of beg ch-3. *(192 dc, 32 ch sps)*

**Rnd 23:** Ch 3, dc in same st, *dc in each of next 4 sts, 2 dc in next st, ch 2**, 2 dc in next st, rep from * around, ending last rep at **, join with sl st in 3rd ch of beg ch-3. *(256 dc, 32 ch sps)*

**Rnd 24:** Ch 3, dc in same st, *dc in each of next 6 sts, 2 dc in next st, ch 1**, 2 dc in next st, rep from * around, ending last rep at **, join with sl st in 3rd ch of beg ch-3. *(320 dc, 32 ch sps)*

**Rnd 25:** Ch 3, dc in each st around, join with sl st in 3rd ch of beg ch-3. *(320 dc)*

**Rnd 26:** Sl st in each of next 3 sts, ch 6 *(counts as first dc and ch-3)*, sk next 2 dc, dc in next st, ch 3, sk next 3 sts, dc in sp between last sk st and next st, ch 3, sk next 3 sts, [dc in next st, ch 3, sk next 2 sts, dc in next st, ch 3, sk next 3 sts, dc in sp between last sk st and next st, ch 3, sk next 3 sts] around, join with sl st in 3rd ch of beg ch-6. *(96 dc, 96 ch sps)*

**Rnd 27:** Sl st in next ch sp, beg large shell, sk next ch sp, large shell in next dc, sk next ch sp, [large shell in next ch sp, sk next ch sp, large shell in next dc, sk next ch sp] around, join with sl st in 3rd ch of beg ch-3. *(64 large shells)*

**Rnd 28:** Ch 1, sc back into sp between last shell and first shell, 9 dc in first shell, [sc in sp between last worked shell and next shell, 9 dc in next shell] around, join with sl st in beg sc. Fasten off.

**SMALL DOILY**

**Rnds 1–14:** Work rnds 1–14 of Large Doily. Fasten off at end of last rnd. ■

# Snowflake Rose

DESIGN BY CAROL ALEXANDER

Lush, multilayered, beaded roses adorn large, lacy snowflake-style motifs that join as you go to create a stunning holiday throw or an exquisite home accent to dress up your decor any time of year.

**FINISHED SIZE**
50 x 70 inches

**MATERIALS**
Red Heart Super Saver medium (worsted) weight yarn (7 oz/364 yds/198g per skein):
6 skeins #316 soft white
3 skeins #376 burgundy
2 skeins #633 dark sage
Size G/6/4mm crochet hook or size needed to obtain gauge
Sewing needle
Red sewing thread
59 ivory 6mm pearl beads

**GAUGE**
4 dc = 1 inch; 2 dc rows = 1 inch
Motif is 10 inches in diameter

**SPECIAL STITCHES**

**Extended double crochet (edc):** Yo, insert hook in next st, yo, pull lp through, yo, pull through 1 lp on hook, [yo, pull through 2 lps on hook] twice.

**Cluster (cl):** Yo 3 times, insert hook in next ch sp, yo, pull lp through, [yo, pull through 2 lps on hook] 3 times, *yo 3 times, insert hook in same ch sp, yo, pull lp through, [yo, pull through 2 lps on hook] 3 times, rep from *, yo, pull through all lps on hook.

**Single crochet picot (sc picot):** Ch 2, sc in top of last cl made.

**Picot:** Ch 3, sl st in 3rd ch from hook.

## INSTRUCTIONS

### FIRST ROW

#### FIRST MOTIF

**Rnd 1:** With burgundy, ch 4, sl st in first ch to form ring, ch 6 *(counts as first edc and ch-2 sp)*, [**edc** *(see Special Stitches)* in ring, ch 2] 7 times, join with sl st in 4th ch of beg ch-6. *(8 edc, 8 ch sps)*

**Rnd 2:** Working around top of post of each edc, for **large petals**, (sc, ch 1, 5 tr, ch 1, sc) around front of **post** *(see Stitch Guide)* of each st around, join with sl st in beg sc. *(8 petals)*

**Rnd 3:** Working around same posts in front of large petals, for **small petals**, (sc, 3 dc, sc) around post of each st around, join with sl st in beg sc. Fasten off. Sew 1 bead to center of flower.

**Rnd 4:** For **leaves,** working behind petals, join dark sage with sl st in any ch-2 sp of rnd 1, (ch 4, **cl**—*see Special Stitches*, **sc picot**—*see Special Stitches*, ch 4, sl st) in same ch sp, (sl st, ch 4, cl, sc picot, ch 4, sl st) in each ch-2 sp around, join with sl st in beg sl st. *(8 leaves)*

**Rnd 5:** Ch 1, working behind leaves,

sl st in center bottom of first leaf, ch 3, [sl st in center bottom of next leaf, ch 3] around, join with sl st in beg sl st. Fasten off. *(8 ch sps)*

**Rnd 6:** Join soft white with sl st in any ch sp, ch 3, dc in same ch sp and in **back lp** *(see Stitch Guide)* of 2nd tr on corresponding large petal at same time, dc in same ch sp on last row, ch 4, [dc in next ch sp, dc in same ch sp and in back lp of 2nd tr on next large petal at same time, dc in same ch sp on last row, ch 4] around, join with sl st in 3rd ch of beg ch-3. *(8 dc groups, 8 ch sps)*

**Rnd 7:** Ch 3, 2 dc in next st, dc in next st, ch 4, sk next ch sp, [dc in next st, 2 dc in next st, dc in next st, ch 4,

**FINISHED SIZE**
22 x 37 inches

**MATERIALS**
DMC Cebelia size 20 crochet cotton (405 yds per ball):
3 balls white
Size 6/1.80mm steel crochet hook or size needed to obtain gauge

**GAUGE**
14 dc = 1 inch; 5 mesh = 1 inch
5 dc rows = 1 inch

**PATTERN NOTES**
Each half of this piece is crocheted in sections. Work according to chart, fastening off and rejoining where indicated to complete these sections.

Work a begininng block at beginning of each row or each time you rejoin for a new section.

**SPECIAL STITCHES**
**Block:** Dc in each of next 3 chs or sts, or, 2 dc in next ch sp, dc in next st.

**Mesh:** Ch 2, sk next 2 chs or sts, dc in next st or ch, or, ch 2, sk next ch sp, dc in next st.

**Beginning block (beg block):** Ch 3, dc in each of next 3 sts.

**Beginning 1-block increase (beg 1-block inc):** Ch 5, dc in 4th ch from hook, dc in last ch, dc in next st.

**Ending 1-block increase (end 1-block inc):** Yo, insert hook in bottom of last st, yo, pull through, yo, pull through 1 lp on hook *(ch-1),* [yo, pull through 2 lps on hook] twice *(dc completed),* *yo, insert hook in last ch-1 made, yo, pull through, yo, pull through 1 lp on hook, [yo, pull through 2 lps on hook] twice, rep from *.

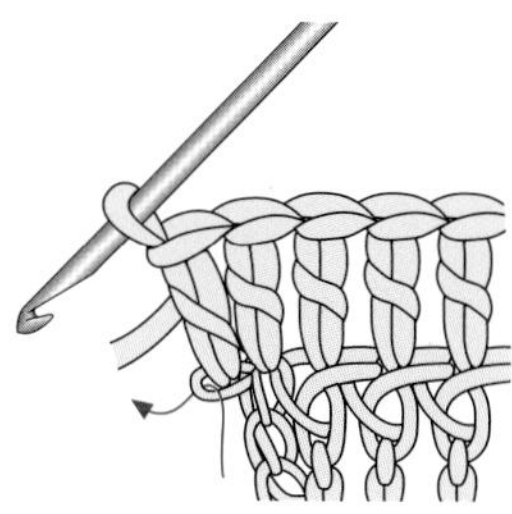

**Ending 2-block increase (end 2-block inc):** Yo, insert hook in bottom of last st, yo, pull through, yo, pull through 1 lp on hook *(ch-1),* [yo, pull through 2 lps on hook] twice *(dc completed),* *yo, insert hook in last ch-1 made, yo, pull through, yo, pull through 1 lp on hook, [yo, pull through 2 lps on hook] twice, rep from * 4 times.

**Beginning 2-block increase (beg 2-block inc):** Ch 8, dc in 4th ch from hook, dc in each of last 4 chs, dc in next st.

**Beginning 3-block increase (beg 3-block inc):** Ch 11, dc in 4th ch from hook, dc in each of last 7 chs, dc in next st.

**Ending 3-block increase (end 3-block inc):** Yo, insert hook in bottom of last st, yo, pull through, yo, pull through 1 lp on hook *(ch-1),* [yo, pull through 2 lps on hook] twice *(dc completed),* *yo, insert hook in last ch-1 made, yo, pull through, yo, pull through 1 lp on hook, [yo, pull through 2 lps on hook] twice, rep from * 7 times.

**Ending 4-block increase (end 4-block inc):** Yo, insert hook in bottom of last st, yo, pull through, yo, pull through 1 lp on hook *(ch-1),* [yo, pull through 2 lps on hook] twice *(dc completed),* *yo, insert hook in last ch-1 made, yo, pull through, yo, pull through 1 lp on hook, [yo, pull through 2 lps on hook] twice, rep from * 10 times.

**Beginning 1-block decrease (beg 1-block dec):** Sl st in each of first 4 sts.

**Beginning 2-block decrease (beg 2-block dec):** Sl st in each of first 7 sts.

**Beginning 3-block decrease (beg 3-block dec):** Sl st in each of first 10 sts.

**Lacet:** Ch 3, sk next 2 sts or ch sp, sc in next st, ch 3, sk next 2 sts or ch sp, dc in next st.

**Bar:** Ch 5, sk next 2 ch sps, dc in next st.

**Join with dc:** Place slip knot on hook, yo, insert hook in st, yo, pull lp through, [yo, pull through 2 lps on hook] twice.

## INSTRUCTIONS

**FIRST SIDE**
**Row 1:** Ch 255, dc in 4th ch from hook, dc in each of next 2 chs *(first block completed),* for row 1 of First Side chart, 10 **blocks** *(see Special Stitches),* 5 **mesh** *(see Special Stitches),* 5 blocks, 6 mesh, 5 blocks, 4 mesh, 4 blocks, 20 mesh, 8 blocks, 3 mesh, block, 2 mesh, 6 blocks, 2 mesh, 2 blocks, turn. *(42 blocks, 42 mesh)*

**Rows 2–94:** Using Special Stitches as needed, work according to chart, turn, joining and fastening off where indicated.

At end of row 23, turn and fasten off. Place slip knot on hook, ch 24, **join with dc** *(see Special Stitches)* in first st, work according to chart, turn. Last part of row 25 will be worked in chs. This adds 6 blocks and 2 mesh to row.

**2ND SIDE**
**Row 95:** For row 95 of 2nd Side chart, working in starting ch on opposite side of row 1 on First Side, with WS facing, join with sl st in ch of last st on 7th block, beg block, 4 blocks, 4 mesh, 3 blocks, 7 mesh, 3 blocks, 8 mesh, 5 blocks, 14 mesh, 6 blocks, mesh, 5 blocks, 2 mesh, [block, mesh] twice, 6 blocks, 2 mesh, 2 blocks, turn.

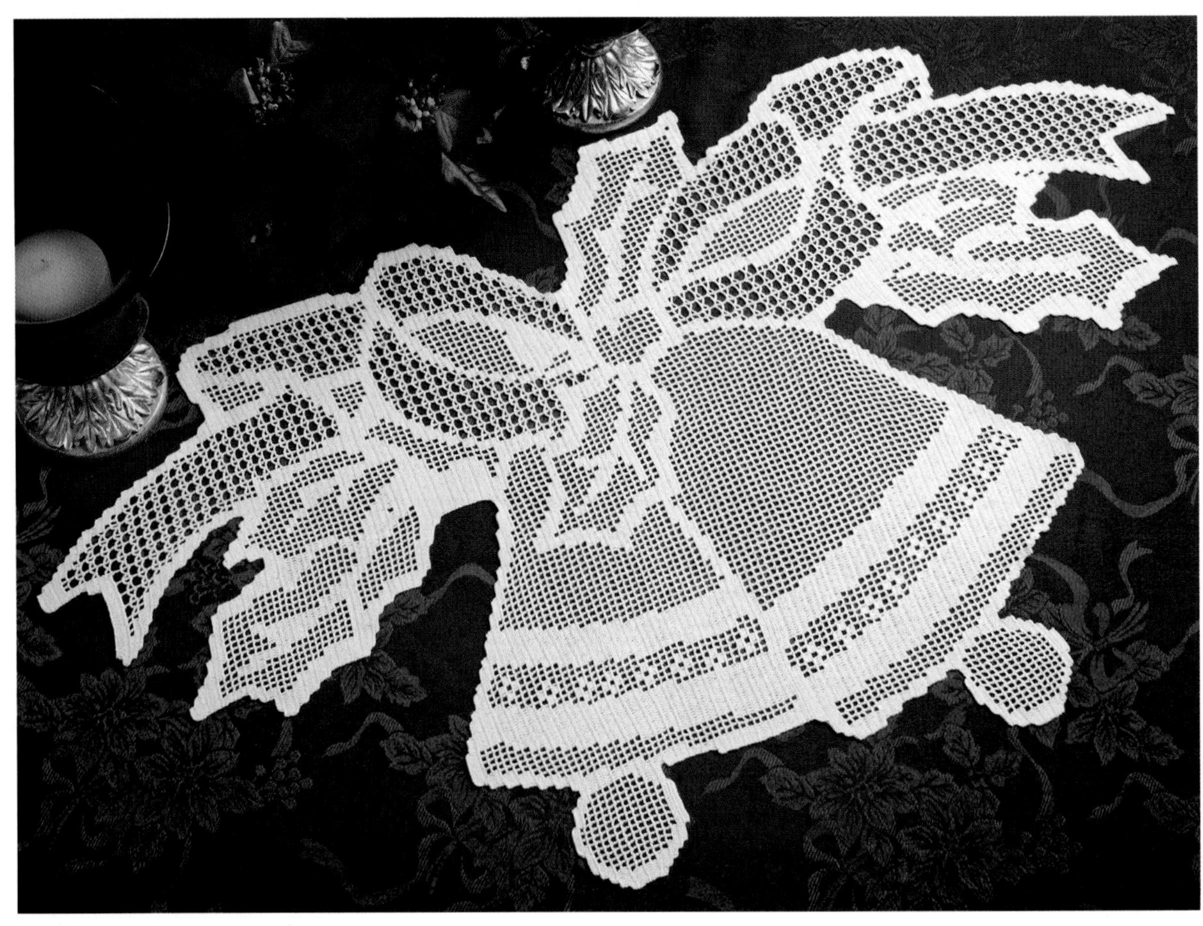

**Rows 96–185:** Using Special Stitches as needed, work according to chart, turn, joining and fastening off where indicated.

At end of row 113, ch 32, dc in 4th ch from hook, dc in next 28 chs, dc in next st, complete row 114 according to chart. This adds 10 blocks to row.

Block as desired. ■

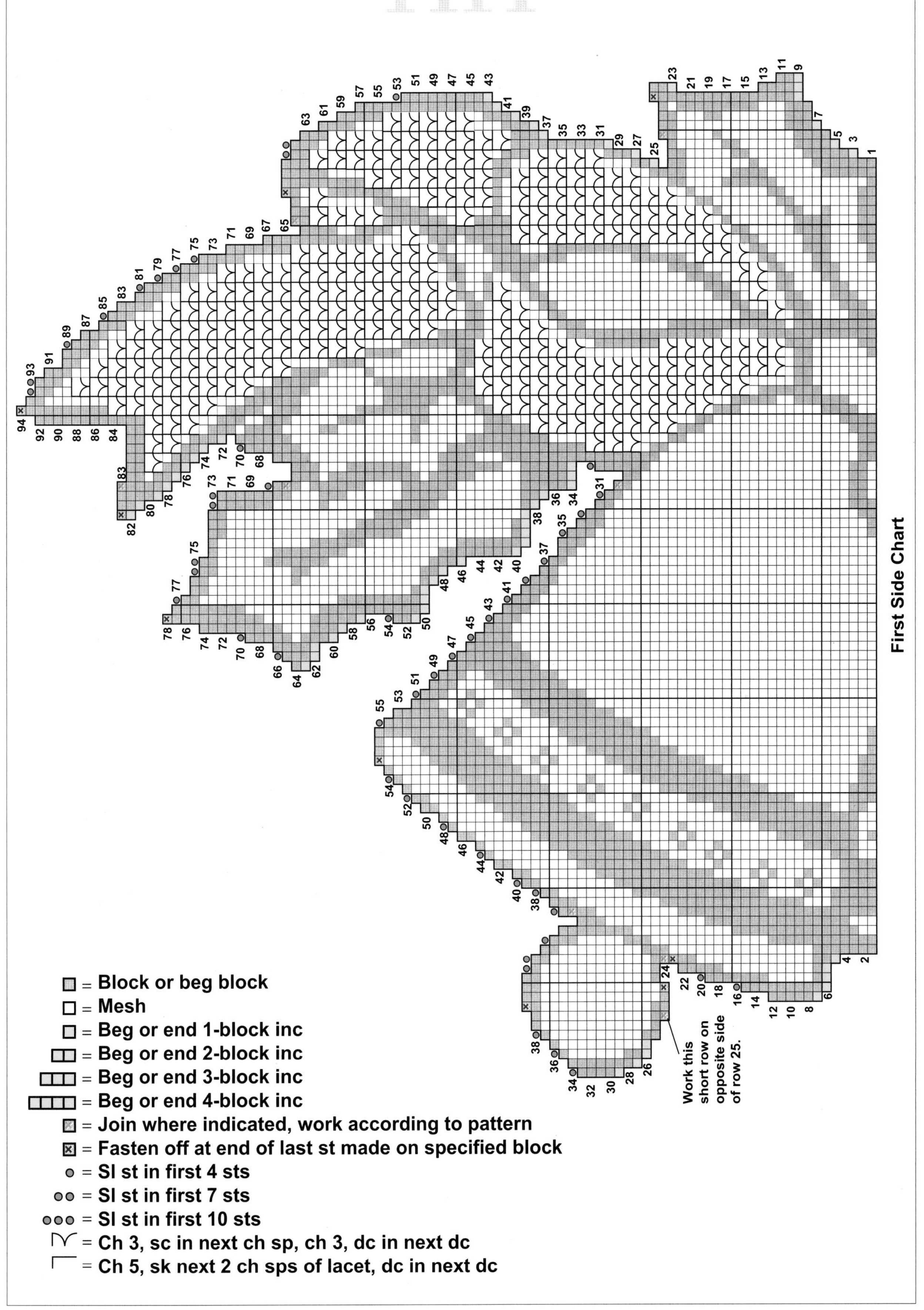
First Side Chart
Work this short row on opposite side of row 25.
= Block or beg block
= Mesh
= Beg or end 1-block inc
= Beg or end 2-block inc
= Beg or end 3-block inc
= Beg or end 4-block inc
= Join where indicated, work according to pattern
= Fasten off at end of last st made on specified block
= Sl st in first 4 sts
= Sl st in first 7 sts
= Sl st in first 10 sts
= Ch 3, sc in next ch sp, ch 3, dc in next dc
= Ch 5, sk next 2 ch sps of lacet, dc in next dc

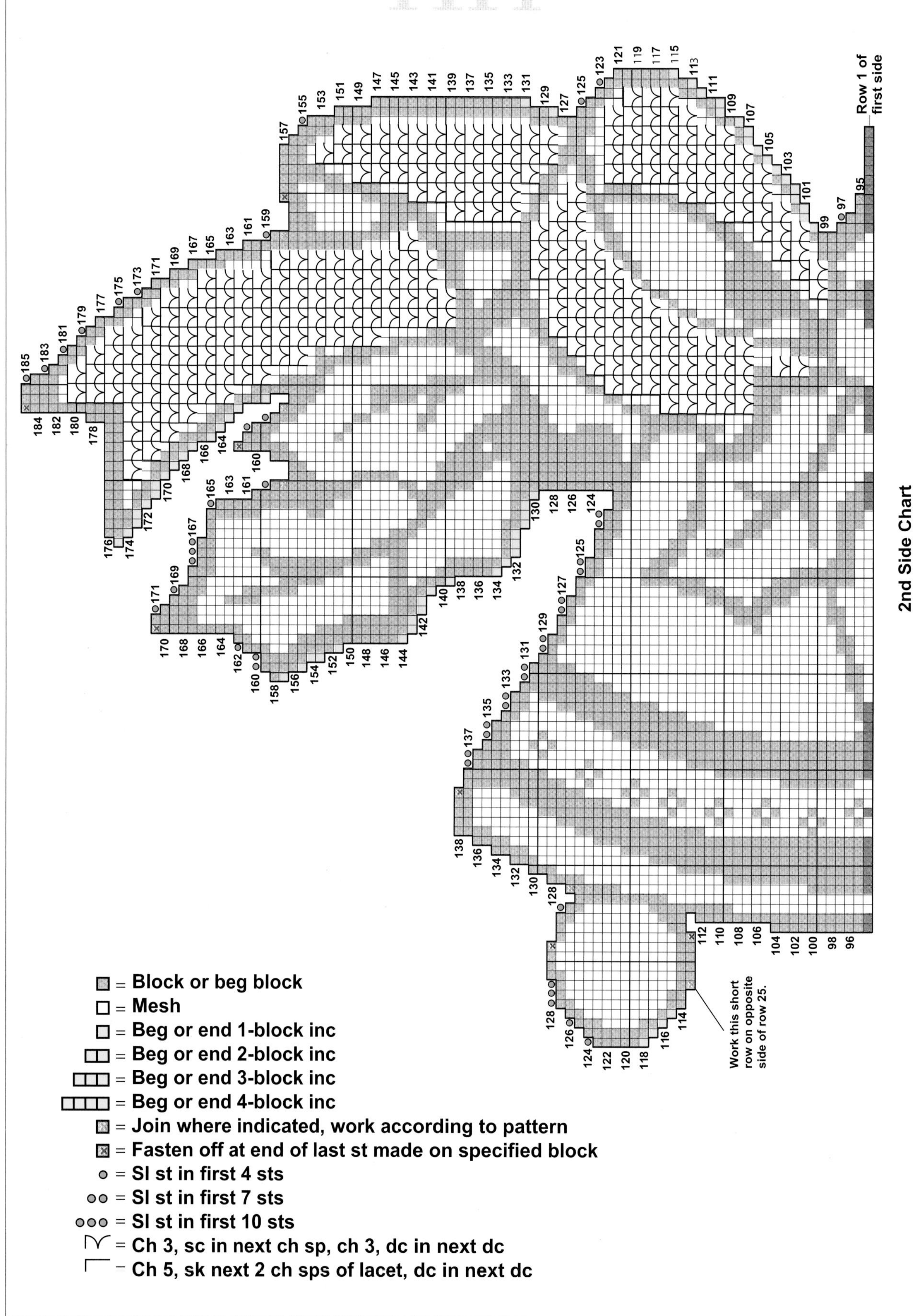
2nd Side Chart
Row 1 of first side
Work this short row on opposite side of row 25.
= Block or beg block
= Mesh
= Beg or end 1-block inc
= Beg or end 2-block inc
= Beg or end 3-block inc
= Beg or end 4-block inc
= Join where indicated, work according to pattern
= Fasten off at end of last st made on specified block
= Sl st in first 4 sts
= Sl st in first 7 sts
= Sl st in first 10 sts
= Ch 3, sc in next ch sp, ch 3, dc in next dc
= Ch 5, sk next 2 ch sps of lacet, dc in next dc

# Santas & Snowmen

DESIGNS BY ELEANOR MILES-BRADLEY

These whimsical throws featuring jolly Santas and cheery snowmen are sure to garner smiles from your holiday guests. The colorful patterns are cross-stitched on simple, single crochet motifs.

RMEDIATE

4 MEDIUM

**SANTAS THROW**

**FINISHED SIZE**
44 x 61 inches

**MATERIALS**
Medium (worsted) weight yarn:
42 oz/2,100 yds/1,191g emerald green
16 oz/800 yds/454g each red and white
3½ oz/175 yds/99g each black, off-white and pink
¼ oz/12½ yds/7g each yellow and blue
Size G/6/4mm crochet hook or size needed to obtain gauge
Tapestry needle

**GAUGE**
4 sc = 1 inch; 4 sc rows = 1 inch

**PATTERN NOTE**
Each square on Chart equals 1 sc.

Using cross-stitch *(see illustration)*, embroider each Motif according to Santa Chart.

Using cross-stitch *(see illustration on page 212)*, embroider each Motif according to Snowman Chart.

**INSTRUCTIONS**

**THROW**

**MOTIF**
Make 9.

**Row 1:** With green, ch 38, sc in 2nd ch from hook and in each ch across, turn. *(37 sc)*

**Rows 2–60:** Ch 1, sc in each st across, turn. At end of last row, **do not turn.**

**Rnd 61:** Working around outer edge, ch 1, sc in each st and in end of each row around with 3 sc in each corner, join with sl st in beg sc. Fasten off.

**EDGING**
**Rnd 1:** Join white with sc in any center corner st, ch 2, sc in same st as first sc, sc in each st around with (sc, ch 2, sc) in each center corner st, join with sl st in beg sc, **turn.** Fasten off.

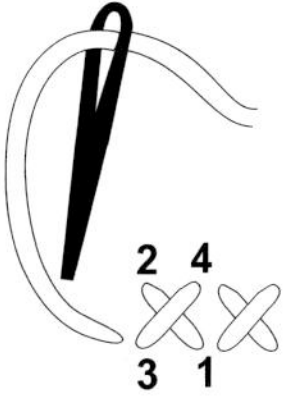


**Cross-Stitch**

**Rnd 2:** Join red with sl st in any corner ch sp, ch 4 *(counts as first tr)*, (tr, ch 2, 2 tr) in same ch sp, tr in each st around with (2 tr, ch 2, 2 tr) in each corner ch sp, join with sl st in 4th ch of beg ch-4, turn. Fasten off.

**Rnd 3:** Join white with sc in any corner ch sp, ch 2, sc in same ch sp as first sc, sc in each st around with (sc, ch 2, sc) in each corner ch sp, join with sl st in beg sc, turn. Fasten off.

**Rnd 4:** Join green with sl st in any corner ch sp, ch 4, (tr, ch 2, 2 tr) in same ch sp, tr in each st around with (2 tr, ch 2, 2 tr) in each corner ch sp, join with sl st in 4th ch of beg ch-4, turn. Fasten off.

**Rnd 5:** Join white with sc in any corner ch sp, 2 sc in same ch sp as first sc, sc in each st around with 3 sc in each corner ch sp, join with sl st in beg sc. Fasten off.

With white, sew **back lps** *(see Stitch Guide)* on Motifs tog 3 Motifs wide and 3 Motifs long. Block.

**BORDER**

**Rnd 1:** With WS facing, join white with sc in any center corner st, ch 2, sc in same st as first sc, sc in each st and in each seam around with (sc, ch 2, sc) in each center corner st, join with sl st in beg sc, turn.

**Rnd 2:** Ch 1, sc in each of first 3 sts, ch 2, sl st in 3rd ch from hook, [sc in each of next 3 sts, ch 2, sl st in 3rd ch from hook] around with 3 sc in each corner ch sp, join with sl st in beg sc. Fasten off.

**SNOWMEN THROW**

**FINISHED SIZE**

49 x 58 inches

**MATERIALS**

Medium (worsted) weight yarn:
- 40 oz/2,000 yds/1,134g blue
- 16 oz/800 yds/454g white
- 3½ oz/175 yds/99g each brown, red, green, orange and black

Size G/6/4mm crochet hook or size needed to obtain gauge

Tapestry needle

**GAUGE**

4 sc = 1 inch; 4 sc rows = 1 inch

**INSTRUCTIONS**

**THROW**

**MOTIF**

Make 9.

**Row 1:** With blue, ch 43, sc in 2nd ch from hook and in each ch across, turn. *(42 sc)*

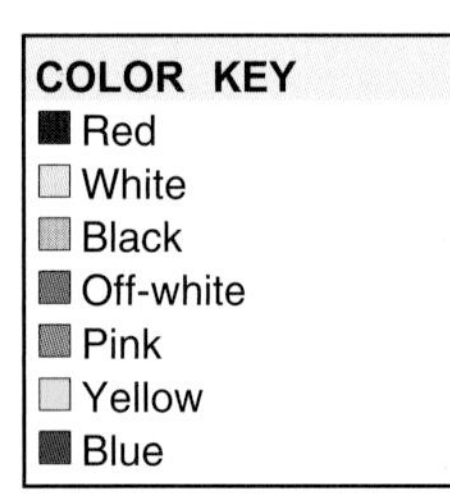

Santa Chart

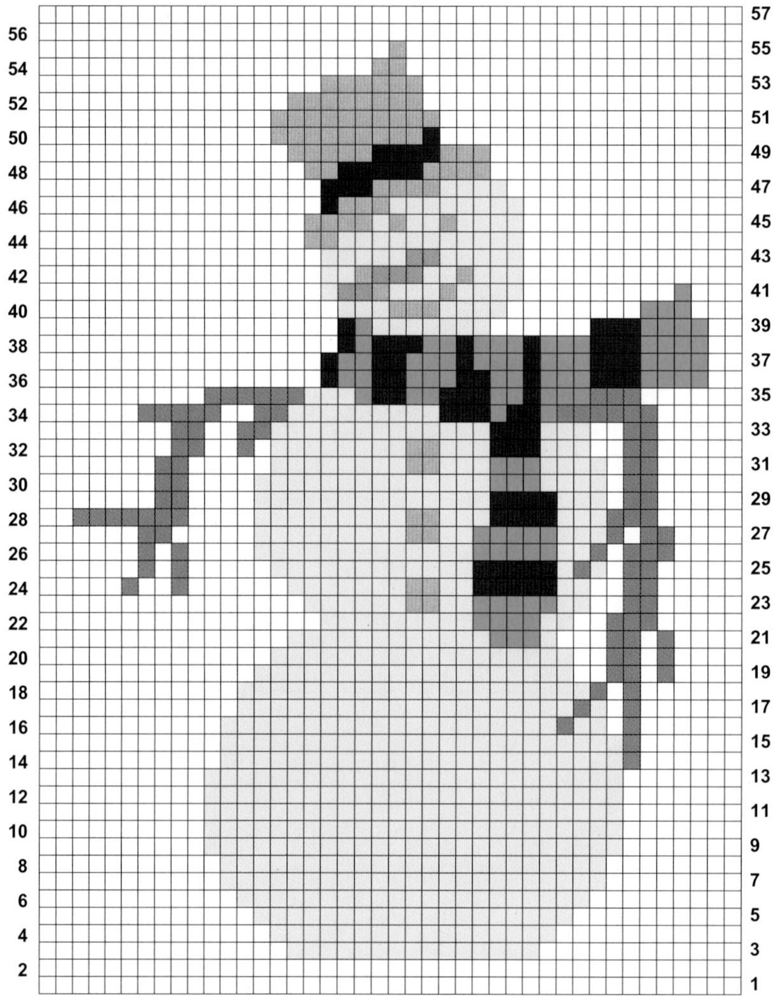


**Snowmen Chart**

**Rows 2–57:** Ch 1, sc in each st across, turn. At end of last row, **do not turn.**

**Rnd 58:** Working around outer edge, ch 1, sc in each st and in end of each row around with 3 sc in each corner, join with sl st in beg sc. Fasten off.

**EDGING**

**Rnd 1:** Join white with sc in any center corner st, ch 2, sc in same st, sc in each st around with (sc, ch 2, sc) in each center corner st, join with sl st in beg sc, turn. Fasten off.

**Rnd 2:** Join green with sl st in any corner ch sp, ch 4, (tr, ch 2, 2 tr) in same ch sp, tr in each st around with (2 tr, ch 2, 2 tr) in each corner ch sp, join with sl st in top of ch-4, turn. Fasten off.

**Rnd 3:** Join white with sc in any corner ch sp, ch 2, sc in same ch sp as first sc, sc in each st around with (sc, ch 2, sc) in each corner ch sp, join with sl st in beg sc, turn. Fasten off.

**Rnd 4:** Join red with sl st in any corner ch sp, ch 4, (tr, ch 2, 2 tr) in same ch sp, tr in each st around with (2 tr, ch 2, 2 tr) in each corner ch sp, join with sl st in 4th ch of beg ch-4, turn. Fasten off.

**Rnd 5:** Join white with sc in any corner ch sp, 2 sc in same ch sp as first sc, sc in each st around with 3 sc in each corner ch sp, join with sl st in beg sc. Fasten off.

With white, sew **back lps** *(see Stitch Guide)* on Motifs tog 3 Motifs wide and 3 Motifs long. Block.

**BORDER**

**Rnd 1:** With WS facing, join white with sc in any center corner st, (ch 2, sc) in same st, sc in each st and in each seam around with (sc, ch 2, sc) in each center corner st, join with sl st in beg sc, turn.

**Rnd 2:** Ch 1, sc in each of first 3 sts, ch 2, sl st in 2nd ch from hook, [sc in each of next 3 sts, ch 2, sl st in 2nd ch from hook] around with 3 sc in each ch sp, join with sl st in beg sc. Fasten off. ■

# Winter Roses

DESIGN BY AGNES RUSSELL

Plush scarlet roses take center stage in a web of lacy, white pineapple leaves in this sparkling yuletide doily. Silver-accented metallic thread adds the perfect touch of glitz and glitter.

INTERMEDIATE

**FINISHED SIZE**
17½ inches in diameter

**MATERIALS**
Size 10 crochet cotton:
75 yds myrtle green
Size 10 metallic crochet cotton:
350 yds white/silver
75 yds scarlet/silver
Size 7/1.65mm steel crochet hook or size needed to obtain gauge
Spray starch

**GAUGE**
3 shell rnds = 1 inch

**SPECIAL STITCHES**

**Beginning shell (beg shell):** Sl st across to ch sp, (ch 3, dc, ch 3, 2 dc) in ch sp.

**Shell:** (2 dc, ch 3, 2 dc) in indicated st or ch sp.

**Beginning double shell (beg double shell):** (Ch 3, dc, {ch 3, 2 dc} twice) in indicated st or ch sp.

**Double shell:** (2 dc, {ch 3, 2 dc} twice) in indicated st or ch sp.

## INSTRUCTIONS

**DOILY**

**Rnd 1:** With white/silver, ch 5, sl st in first ch to form ring, ch 3 *(counts as first dc)*, dc in ring, ch 3, [2 dc in ring, ch 3] 7 times, join with sl st in 3rd ch of beg ch-3.

**Rnd 2: Beg shell** *(see Special Stitches)*, **shell** *(see Special Stitches)* in each of next 7 ch-3 sps, join with sl st in 3rd ch of beg ch-3.

**Rnd 3:** Beg shell, ch 4, [shell in ch sp of next shell, ch 4] around, join with sl st in 3rd ch of beg ch-3. Fasten off.

**Rnd 4:** Join myrtle green with sl st in any ch-3 sp of shell, (ch 3, dc, ch 3, 2 dc) in same ch sp, ch 2, [dc in next ch-4 sp, ch 2] 6 times, *shell in shell, ch 2, [dc in ch 4 sp, ch 2] 6 times, rep from * around, join with sl st in 3rd ch of beg ch-3, pull up lp of myrtle green, remove hook, **do not fasten off.**

**Rnd 5:** *Join scarlet/silver with sl st in 2nd ch-2 sp to the left of shell, ch 1, (sc, 6 dc, sc) in ch-2 sp, (sc, 6 dc, sc) in each of next 4 ch-2 sps, pull up a lp, remove hook, insert hook in first sc of first petal, pick up dropped lp and pull through st on hook, ch 1, **fasten off**, rep from * 7 times. *(8 flowers)*

**Rnd 6:** Pick up dropped lp of myrtle green, beg shell in shell, [ch 5, sc in next ch-2 sp] twice, ch 5, *shell in shell, [ch 5, sc in next ch-2 sp] twice, ch 5, rep from * around, join with sl st in 3rd ch of beg ch-3. Fasten off.

**Rnd 7:** Join white/silver with sl st in any ch-3 sp of shell, (ch 3, dc, ch 3, 2 dc) in same ch sp, [ch 3, sc in next ch-5 sp] 3 times, ch 3, *shell in shell, [ch 3, sc in next ch-5 sp] 3 times, ch 3, rep from * around, join with sl st in 3rd ch of beg ch-3.

**Rnd 8: Beg double shell** *(see Special Stitches)* in shell, [ch 3, sc in next ch-3 sp] 4 times, ch 3, ***double shell** *(see Special Stitches)* in shell, [ch 3, sc in next ch-3 sp] 4 times, ch 3, rep from * around, join with sl st in 3rd ch of beg ch-3.

**Row 9 (RS):** Now working in rows, beg shell in shell in first ch sp of double shell, ch 2, shell in next ch sp, turn.

**Row 10:** Beg shell in shell, ch 2, 5 dc in ch-2 sp, ch 2, shell in shell, turn.

**Row 11:** Beg shell in shell, ch 2, dc in first dc of 5-dc group, [ch 1, dc in next dc] 4 times, ch 2, shell in shell, turn.

**Row 12:** Beg shell in shell, ch 2, sc in next ch-1 sp, [ch 3, sc in next ch-1 sp] 3 times, ch 2, shell in shell, turn.

**Row 13:** Beg shell in shell, ch 2, sc in next ch-3 sp, [ch 3, sc in next ch-3 sp] twice, ch 2, shell in shell, turn.

**Row 14:** Beg shell in shell, ch 2, sc in next ch-3 sp, ch 3, sc in next ch-3 sp, ch 2, shell in shell, turn.

**Row 15:** Beg shell in shell, ch 2, sc in next ch-3 sp, ch 2, shell in shell, turn.

**Row 16:** Beg double shell in shell, ch 2, double shell in shell, turn.

**Row 17:** Double shell in shell, ch 2, [shell in shell, ch 2] twice, double shell in shell, turn.

**Row 18:** Beg shell in shell, [ch 2, shell in shell] 5 times. Fasten off.

**Next rows:** *With finished pineapple to the right, join white/silver with sl st in first ch-3 sp of double shell, rep rows 9–18, rep from * 6 times. *(8 pineapples)*

At the end of last pineapple, turn, **do not fasten off.**

**Rnd 19: Now working in rnds,** sl st into ch-3 sp of shell, beg shell in shell, ch 2, 5 dc in next ch-3 sp of shell, ch 2, [shell in shell, ch 2] twice, 5 dc in ch-3 sp of shell, ch 2, shell in shell, ch 2, working across next 6-shell section,* shell in shell, ch 2, 5 dc in next ch-3 sp of shell, ch 2, [shell in shell, ch 2] twice, 5 dc in ch-3 sp of shell, ch 2, shell in shell, ch 2, working across next 6-shell section, rep from * across, continue to rep across each section until all 8 sections are completed, join with sl st in 3rd ch of beg ch-3.

**Rnd 20:** Beg shell in shell, ch 2, dc in first dc of 5-dc group, [ch 1, dc in next dc] 4 times, ch 2, shell in shell, ch 2, *shell in shell, ch 2, dc in first dc of 5-dc group, [ch 1, dc in next dc] 4 times, ch 2, shell in shell, ch 2, rep from * around, join with sl st in 3rd ch of beg ch-3.

**Rnd 21:** Beg shell in shell, ch 2, sc in next ch-1 sp, [ch 3, sc in next ch-1 sp] 3 times, ch 2, shell in shell, ch 2, *shell in shell, ch 2, sc in next ch-1 sp, [ch 3, sc in next ch-1 sp] 3 times, ch 2, shell in shell, ch 2, rep from * around, join with sl st in 3rd ch of beg ch-3.

**Row 22 (RS): Now working in rows,** beg shell in shell, ch 2, sc in next ch-3 sp, [ch 3, sc in next ch-3 sp] twice, ch 2, shell in shell, turn.

**Row 23 (WS):** Beg shell in shell, ch 2, sc in next ch-3 sp, ch 3, sc in next ch-3 sp, ch 2, shell in shell, turn.

**Row 24 (RS):** Beg shell in shell, ch 2, sc in rem ch-3 sp, ch 2, shell in shell, turn.

**Row 25 (WS):** Beg shell in next shell, shell in next shell. Fasten off.

**Next rows:** *With finished pineapple to the right, join white with sl st in next unworked ch-3 sp of shell, rep rows 22–25, rep from * around.

At the end of the 16th pineapple, turn, **do not fasten off.**

### TRIM

**Rnd 26 (RS):** Sl st into ch-3 sp of shell, ch 1, *sc in ch-3 sp of shell, ch 4, sc in next ch-3 sp of shell, [ch 4, sc over dc at side edge of shell] 4 times, ch 4, sc over ch-2 sp, [ch 4, sc over dc at side edge of shell] 4 times, ch 4, rep from * around entire outer edge, join with sl st in beg sc. Fasten off.

**Rnd 27 (RS):** Join myrtle green with sl st in any ch-4 sp, (ch 1, sc, ch 3, dc) in same ch-4 sp, (sc, ch 3, dc) in each ch-4 sp around, join with sl st in beg sc. Fasten off. ■

# Heavenly Angels

DESIGN BY RUBY GATES

A host of heavenly angels, highlighted in sparkling gold, brings inspiration and beauty to this divine throw. Gold-edge crosses symbolize the message of peace and faith celebrated during this season.

INTERMEDIATE

4 MEDIUM

**FINISHED SIZE**
53 x 61 inches

**MATERIALS**
Medium (worsted) weight yarn:
80 oz/4,000 yds/2,268g white
10½ oz/525 yds/298g light rose
Size 10 metallic crochet cotton:
700 yds gold
Sizes C/2/2.75mm and G/6/4mm crochet hooks or size needed to obtain gauge

**GAUGE**
**Size G hook:** 4 sc = 1 inch; 4 sc rows = 1 inch

**SPECIAL STITCHES**
**Cluster (cl):** Holding back last lp of each st on hook, 4 dc in next st, yo, pull through all lps on hook.

**Single crochet V-stitch (sc V-st):** (Sc, ch 2, sc) in ch sp or st specified in instructions.

**1-corner joining:** Sc in ch-2 sp at corner of this Motif, ch 1, drop lp from hook, insert hook in corresponding ch-2 sp at corner of previous Motif, pull dropped lp through ch sp, ch 1, sc in same ch-2 sp on this Motif.

**Chain-2 space joining (ch-2 sp joining):** Ch 1, sk next st on this Motif, drop lp from hook, insert hook in corresponding ch-2 sp of previous Motif, pull dropped lp through ch-2 sp, ch 1, sc in next st on this Motif.

**2-corner joining:** Sc in ch-2 sp at corner of this Motif, ch 1, drop lp from hook, insert hook in corresponding ch-2 sp of previous Motif, pull dropped lp through ch-2 sp, ch 1, insert hook in corresponding ch-2 sp of adjacent Motif, pull dropped lp through ch sp, ch 1, sc in same ch-2 sp on this Motif.

**Shell:** (2 dc, ch 3, 2 dc) in next st or ch sp specified in instructions.

## INSTRUCTIONS

**FIRST ROW**

**FIRST ANGEL MOTIF**
**Row 1:** With size G hook and white, ch 62, sc in 2nd ch from hook and in each ch across, turn. *(61 sc)*

**Rows 2–5:** Ch 1, sc in each st across, turn.

**Row 6:** Ch 1, sc in each of first 21 sts, ***cl** *(see Special Stitches)* in next st, sc in next st, rep from * 5 times, sc in each st across, turn.

**Rows 7–75:** Ch 1, using Special Stitches as needed, work across according to corresponding rows on Angel Chart, turn. At end of last row, **do not turn.**

**Rnd 76:** Working around outer edge, ch 1, sc in end of first 75 rows, ch 2, working in rem lps on opposite side of starting ch, sc in each ch across, ch 2, sc in end of last 75 rows, ch 2, working across row 75, sc in each st across, ch 2, join with sl st in beg sc. Fasten off. *(272 sc)*

**BODY TRIM**
**Rnd 1:** With RS of Motif facing, with 2 strands of metallic crochet cotton held tog and size C hook, working between sts around Angel, join with sc at bottom of Angel, sc between each of next 2 sts around Angel to first sc, join with sl st in beg sc.

**Rnd 2:** Ch 1, **sc V-st** *(see Special Stitches)* in each st around, join with sl st in beg sc. Fasten off.

**HALO TRIM**
Beg at 1 end of Halo, rep rnds 1 and 2 of Angel Body Trim.

**ANGEL MOTIF BORDER**
**Rnd 1:** With RS of Motif facing, with size G hook and 1 strand of light rose and 2 strands of metallic crochet cotton held tog, join with sc in first ch-2 sp at top right hand corner of rnd 76, ch 2, sc in same ch-2 sp, sc in each st around with sc V-st in each ch-2 sp at corner, join with sl st in beg sc. *(63 sc across top and bottom between corner ch sps, 77 sc across each side between corner ch sps, total 280 sc)*

**Rnd 2:** Ch 1, sc in each st around with sc V-st in each ch-2 sp at corner, join with sl st in beg sc. *(65 sc across each top and bottom, 79 sc across each side, total 284 sc)*

**Rnd 3:** Ch 1, sc in first st, ch 2, sk next st, sc V-st in ch-2 sp, *ch 2, sk next st, [sc in next st, ch 2, sk next st] across to next ch-2 sp at corner, sc V-st in ch-2 sp at corner, rep from * twice, ch 2, sk next st, [sc in next st, ch 2, sk next st] around, join with sl st in beg sc. Fasten off.

**FIRST CROSS MOTIF**
**Row 1:** With size G hook and white, ch 62, sc in 2nd ch from hook and in each ch across, turn. *(61 sc)*

**Rows 2–7:** Ch 1, sc in each st across, turn.

**Row 8:** Ch 1, sc in each of first 28 sts, [cl in next st, sc in next st] 3 times, sc in each st across, turn.

**Rows 9–75:** Ch 1, work across according to corresponding rows on Cross Chart, turn. At end of last row,
**do not turn.**

**Rnd 76:** Working around outer edge, ch 1, sc in end of first 75 rows, ch 2, working in rem lps on opposite side of starting ch, sc in each ch across, ch 2, sc in end of last 75 rows, ch 2, working across row 75, sc in each st across, ch 2, join with sl st in beg sc. Fasten off. *(272 sc)*

**CROSS TRIM**
Starting at bottom of Cross, rep Angel Body Trim.

**CROSS MOTIF BORDER**
**Rnds 1–2:** Rep rnds 1 and 2 of Angel Motif Border.

**Rnd 3:** Ch 1, sc in first st, ch 2, sk next st, with WS tog, starting at bottom of last Motif and top of this Motif, work **1-corner joining** *(see Special Stitches)*, work **ch-2 sp joining** *(see Special Stitches)* across to st before next corner ch-2 sp, ch 1, sk next st on this Motif, drop lp from hook, insert hook in corresponding ch-2 sp of previous Motif, pull dropped lp through ch-2 sp, ch 1, work 1-corner joining, *ch 2, sk next st, [sc in next st, ch 2, sk next st] across to next ch-2 sp at corner, sc V-st in ch-2 sp at corner, rep from *, ch 2, sk next st, [sc in next st, ch 2, sk next st] around, join with sl st in beg sc. Fasten off.

To join rem Motifs, rep rnd 3 of Cross Motif Border, working 1-corner joining, 2 corner joining, and ch-2 sp joinings number of times needed to join Motifs.

Alternating Motifs, make 3 rows of 3 Motifs as shown in photo.

**EDGING**
**Rnd 1:** With RS of work facing, working around entire outer edge, with size G hook, join white with sc in ch-2 sp at right corner, ch 2, sc in same ch sp, 2 sc in ch-2 sp and sc in each joined ch sp around with sc V-st in each corner ch sp, join with sl st in beg sc. *(204 sc across top and bottom, 246 sc across each side, total of 900 sc, 4 ch-2 sps)*

**Rnd 2:** (Sl st, ch 3, dc, ch 3, 2 dc) in first ch-2 sp, sk next 3 sts, sc in next st, ◊*sk next 2 sts, **shell** *(see Special Stitches)* in next st, sk next 2 sts, sc in next st*, rep between * 32 times, sk next 2 sts, shell, sk next 3 sts, sc in next st, rep between * 40 times, sk next 2 sts◊, shell in next ch-2 sp, rep between ◊, join with sl st in 3rd ch of beg ch-3.

**Rnd 3:** Sl st in next st, (sl st, ch 4) in first ch-3 sp, (ch 1, dc) 8 times in same ch-3 sp, **sc in next sc, *dc in next ch-3 sp, (ch 1, dc) 5 times in same ch-3 sp, sc in next sc, rep from * across to next corner***, dc in next ch-3 sp, (ch 1, dc) 8 times in same ch-3 sp**, rep between ** around, ending last rep at ***, join with sl st in 3rd ch of beg ch-4. Fasten off.

**Rnd 4:** With size C hook and 2 strands of metallic crochet cotton held tog, sk all sc, join with sc in last ch-1 sp, sc in next ch-1 sp, **sc V-st in next dc, [sc V-st in next ch-1 sp, sc V-st in next dc] 6 times, *sc in each of next 2 ch-1 sps, sc V st in next dc, [sc V-st in next ch-1 sp, sc V-st in next dc] 3 times, rep from * across to corner***, sc in each of next 2 ch-1 sps, rep from ** around, ending last rep at ***, join with sl st in beg sc. Fasten off. ■

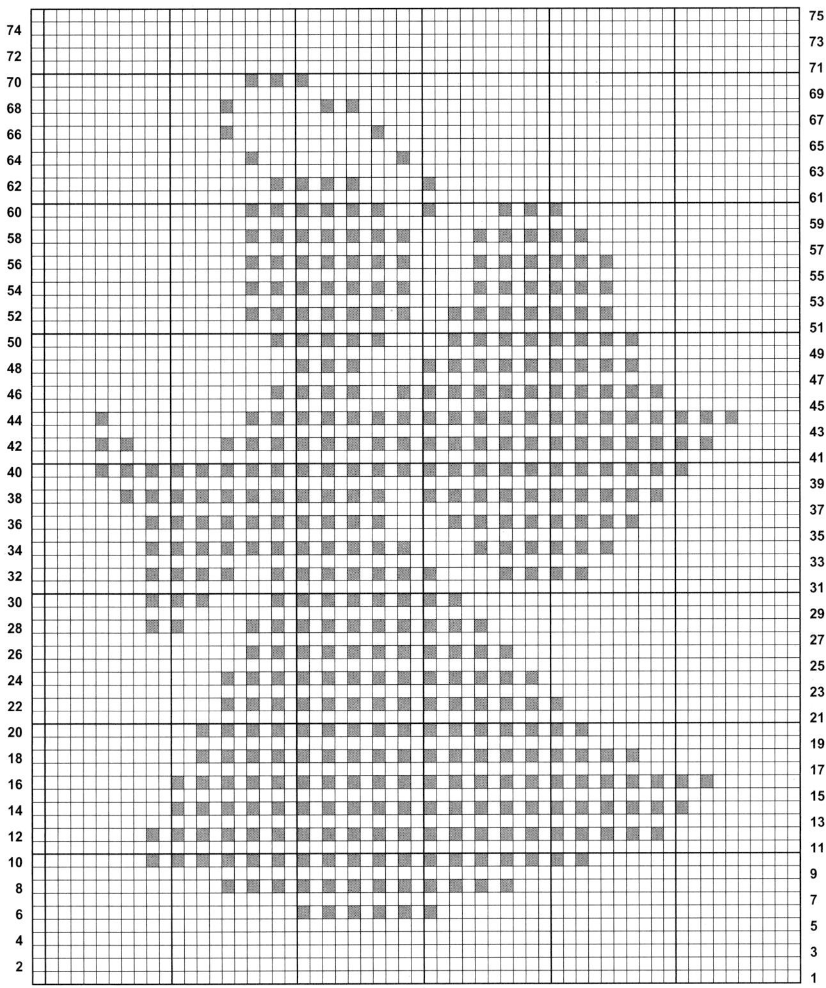


**Heavenly Angels**
**Angel Chart**

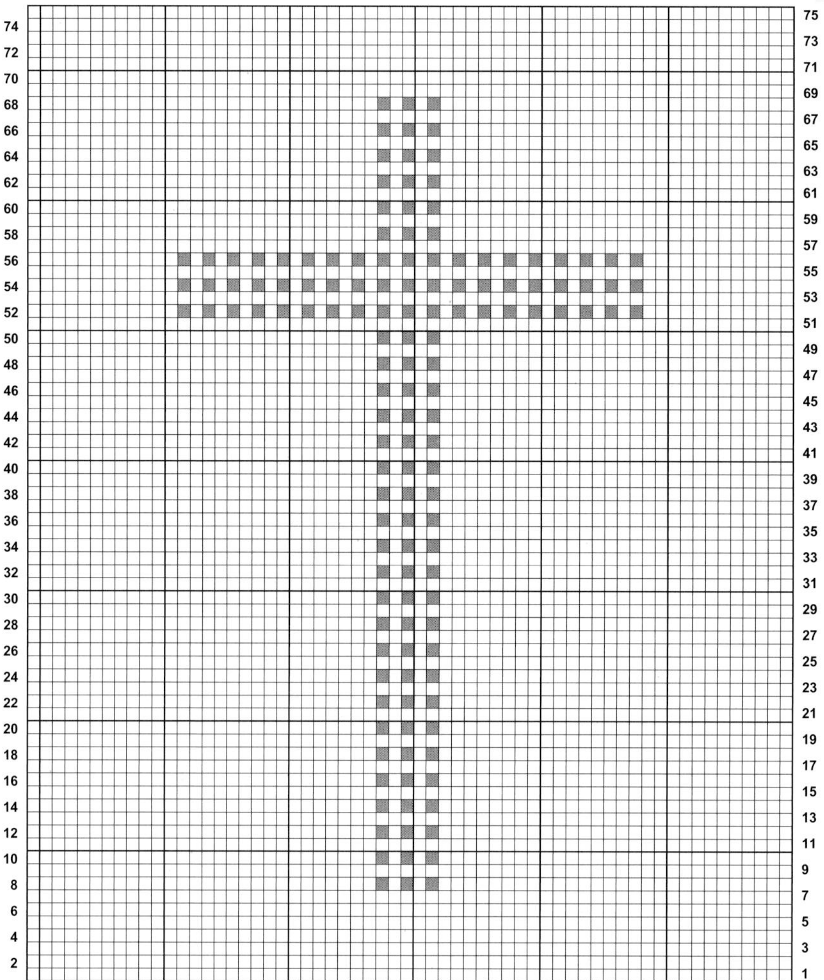

Heavenly Angels
Cross Chart

# Holiday Snowfall

DESIGN BY KATHRYN CLARK

The seven different snowflake designs featured in this stunning throw give testament to the old adage that no two snowflakes are like. All motif edges connect as you go, so no sewing is needed.

INTERMEDIATE

2 FINE

**FINISHED SIZE**
51 x 51 inches

**MATERIALS**
Fine (sport) weight yarn:
30 oz/2,700 yds/851g white
25 oz/2,250 yds/709g blue
Size E/4/3.5mm crochet hook or size needed to obtain gauge

**GAUGE**
Snowflake = ¾ inches across
Motif rnds 1–3 = 2¾ inches across

**PATTERN NOTE**
Label each Snowflake as it is completed.

**SPECIAL STITCHES**
**Picot:** Sl st in **back lp** *(see Stitch Guide)* and left bar of last sc made *(see illustration).*

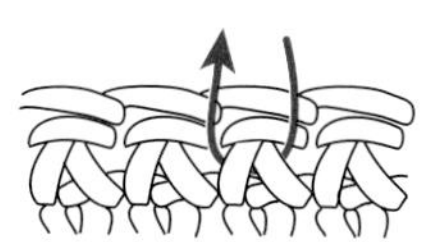

Back strands of sc, shown from back of sts

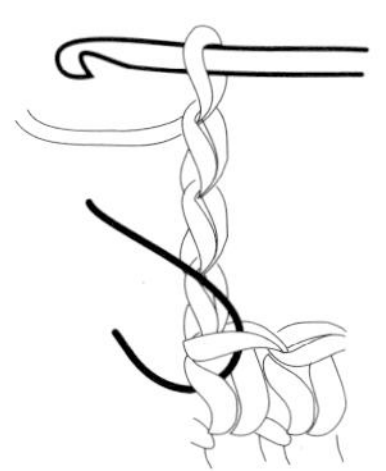

Back Loop Left Bar

**Joining:** Drop lp from hook, with RS of both pieces facing, insert hook in corresponding tr or dc on adjacent Motif, pick up dropped lp, pull through st, sl st in top of last st made on this Motif.

## INSTRUCTIONS

**SNOWFLAKE NO. 1**
Make 15.

**Rnd 1:** With white, ch 6, sl st in first ch to form ring, [sc in ring, ch 2] 6 times, join with sl st in beg sc. *(6 ch sps)*

**Rnd 2:** Ch 1, *sc in sc, [ch 3, **picot** *(see Special Stitches)*] twice, (hdc, dc) in next ch sp, ch 6, sc in 4th ch from hook, ch 5, picot *(corner completed)*, ch 4, picot, sl st in each of next 2 chs of ch-6, sl st in last dc made, hdc in same ch sp as dc, rep from * around, join with sl st in beg sc. Fasten off. *(6 corners)*

**SNOWFLAKE NO. 2**
Make 15.

With white, ch 6, sl st in first ch to form ring, ch 10, sc in 4th ch from hook, ch 5, picot *(corner completed)*, ch 4, picot, sl st in each of next 4 chs of ch-10, *[dc in ring, ch 3, sl st in 2nd ch from hook, ch 1*, dc in ring, ch 7, sc in 4th ch from hook, ch 5, picot *(corner completed)*, ch 4, picot, sl st in each of next 3 chs of ch-7, sl st in last dc made] 5 times, rep between *, join with sl st in 3rd ch of beg ch-10. Fasten off. *(6 corners)*

**SNOWFLAKE NO. 3**
Make 14.

With white, ch 6, sl st in first ch to form ring, ch 10, sc in 4th ch from hook, ch 5, picot *(corner completed)*, ch 4, picot, ch 3, [dc in ring, ch 3, sl st in last dc made, dc in ring, ch 7, sc in 4th ch from hook, ch 5, picot *(corner completed)*, ch 4, picot, ch 3]

5 times, dc in ring, ch 3, sl st in last dc made, join with sl st in 3rd ch of beg ch-10. Fasten off. *(6 corners)*

**SNOWFLAKE NO. 4**

Make 15.

With white, ch 6, sl st in first ch to form ring, ch 1, *sc in ring, ch 3, sc in ring, [ch 5, sc in 4th ch from hook] twice, ch 5, picot *(corner completed)*, ch 4, picot, sl st in next ch, (sl st, ch 4, sl st) in back lp and left bar of next sc, sl st in next ch, rep from * 5 times, join with sl st in beg sc. Fasten off. *(6 corners)*

**SNOWFLAKE NO. 5**

Make 15.

**Rnd 1:** With white, ch 6, sl st in first ch to form ring, ch 1, [2 sc in ring, ch 3, picot] 6 times, join with sl st in beg sc. *(12 sc)*

**Rnd 2:** Ch 6, sl st in 4th ch from hook, [ch 7, sc in 4th ch from hook, ch 5, picot *(corner completed)*, ch 4, picot, sl st in next ch of ch-7, ch 2, sk next sc on rnd 1, dc in next sc, ch 3, sl st in last dc made] 5 times, ch 7, sc in 4th ch from hook, ch 5, picot *(corner completed)*, ch 4, picot, sl st in next ch of ch-7, ch 2, sk last sc on rnd 1, join with sl st in 3rd ch of beg ch-6. Fasten off. *(6 corners)*

**SNOWFLAKE NO. 6**

Make 15.

**Rnd 1:** With white, ch 6, sl st in first ch to form ring, ch 4 *(counts as first dc and ch-1 sp)*, [dc in ring, ch 1] 11 times, join with sl st in 3rd ch of beg ch-4. *(12 ch sps)*

**Rnd 2:** Ch 1, *(sc, ch 3, sc) in next ch sp, sc in next ch sp, ch 6, sc in 4th ch from hook, ch 5, picot *(corner completed)*, ch 4, picot, sl st in each of next 2 chs of ch-6, sc in same ch sp on rnd 1, rep from * 5 times, join with sl st in beg sc. Fasten off. *(6 corners)*

**SNOWFLAKE NO. 7**

Make 15.

**Rnd 1:** With white, ch 6, sl st in first ch to form ring, ch 4 *(counts as first sc and ch-3)*, [sc in ring, ch 3] 5 times, join with sl st in first ch of beg ch-4. *(6 ch sps)*

**Rnd 2:** Sl st in next ch, [sc in next ch sp, ch 3, picot, ch 8, sc in 4th ch from hook, ch 5, picot *(corner completed)*, ch 4, picot, sl st in next ch of ch-8, ch 3] 6 times, join with sl st in beg sc. Fasten off. *(6 corners)*

**MOTIF**

Make 1 for each Snowflake.

**Rnd 1:** With blue, ch 6, sl st in first

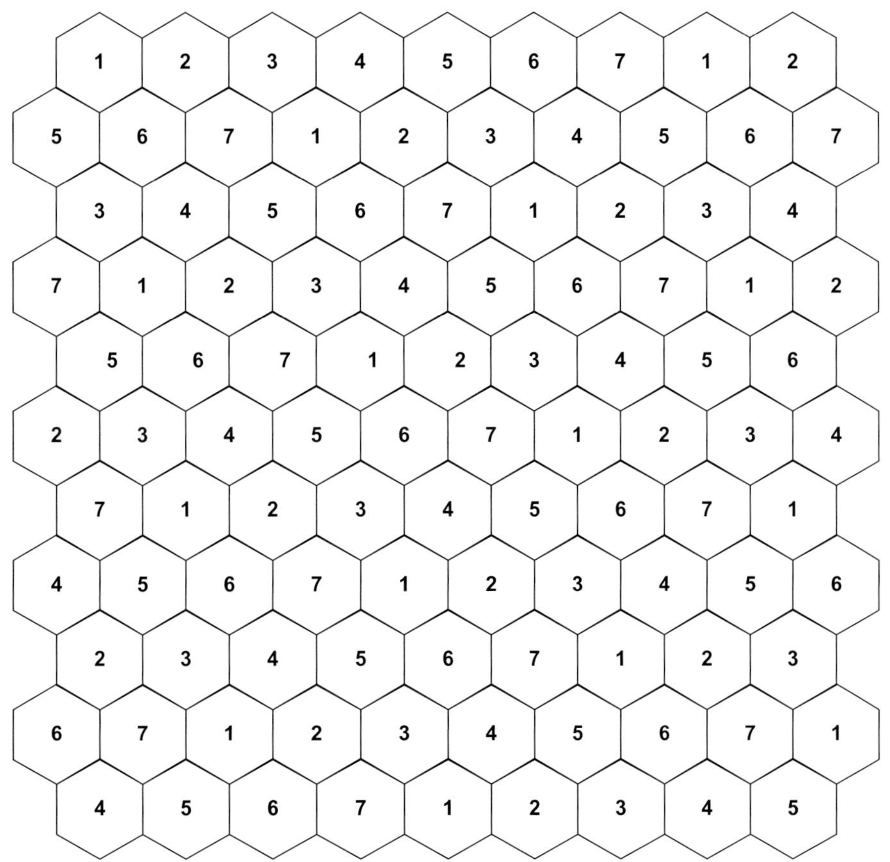


**Holiday Snowfall Assembly Diagram**

ch to form ring, ch 3 *(counts as first dc)*, 11 dc in ring, join with sl st in 3rd ch of beg ch-3. *(12 dc)*

**Rnd 2:** Ch 3, dc in same st, dc in next st, [3 dc in next st, dc in next st] 5 times, dc in same st as beg ch-3, join with sl st in 3rd ch of beg ch-3. *(24 dc)*

**Rnd 3:** Ch 3, dc in same st, dc in each of next 3 sts, [3 dc in next st, dc in each of next 3 sts] 5 times, dc in same st as beg ch-3, join with sl st in 3rd ch of beg ch-3. *(36 dc)*

**Rnd 4:** Ch 3, dc in same st, dc in each of next 5 sts, [3 dc in next st, dc in each of next 5 sts] 5 times, dc in same st as beg ch-3, join with sl st in 3rd ch of beg ch-3. *(48 dc)*

**Rnd 5:** Ch 1, for joining sc, with RS of both pieces facing, insert hook in any corner on Snowflake and in first st on rnd 4 at same time, complete as sc, ch 2, sk next st on rnd 4, [sc in next st, ch 2, sk next st] 3 times, *work joining sc, ch 2, sk next st on rnd 4, [sc in next st, ch 2, sk next st] 3 times, rep from * 4 times, join with sl st in beg sc. *(24 ch sps)*

**Rnd 6:** Ch 1, *sc in joining sc *(corner st)*, ch 3, [sc in next ch sp, ch 3] 4 times, rep from * around, join with sl st in beg sc. Fasten off. *(30 ch sps)*

**ASSEMBLY**

Work Motif Borders positioning Snowflakes to match numbers shown on assembly diagram.

**MOTIF BORDER NO. 1**

Make 1.

Join white with sl st in ch sp to the right of any corner st on first Motif, (ch 2, hdc, 2 dc) in same ch sp, tr in corner st, (2 dc, 2 hdc) in next ch sp, *sc in next ch sp, (hdc, 3 dc, hdc) in next ch sp, sc in next ch sp, (2 hdc, 2 dc) in next ch sp, tr in corner st, (2 dc, 2 hdc) in next ch sp, rep from * 4 times, sc in next ch sp, (hdc, 3 dc, hdc) in next ch sp, sc in next ch sp, join with sl st in 2nd ch of beg ch-2. Fasten off. *(6 tr, 42 dc)*

**MOTIF BORDER NO. 2**

**JOINS ON 1, 2 OR 3 SIDES.**

Join white with sl st in ch sp to the right of any corner st, (ch 2, hdc, 2 dc) in same ch sp, *to join side, tr in corner st, work **joining** *(see Special Stitches)*, (2 dc, 2 hdc) in next ch sp, sc in next ch sp, (hdc, 2 dc, work joining, dc, hdc) in next ch sp, sc in next ch sp, (2 hdc, 2 dc) in next ch sp, tr in corner st, work joining, rep from * once or twice as needed to join according to assembly diagram, **to complete rnd, (2 dc, 2 hdc) in next ch sp, sc in next ch sp, (hdc, 3 dc, hdc) in next ch sp, sc in next ch sp, (2 hdc, 2 dc) in next ch sp, tr in corner st, rep from ** around to last 4 ch sps, (2 dc, 2 hdc) in next ch sp, sc in next ch sp, (hdc, 3 dc, hdc) in next ch sp, sc in next ch sp, join with sl st in 2nd ch of beg ch-2. Fasten off. *(6 tr, 42 dc)*

Rep Motif Border No. 2 until all Motifs are joined according to assembly diagram.

**BORDER**

**Rnd 1:** Working around outer edge of assembled Motifs, join white with sc in 2nd st past any joined tr, *(ch 2, sc) in each st around to next joined tr, sk next joined tr, sc in next st on next Motif, ch 2, rep from * around, join with sl st in beg sc.

**Rnds 2–4:** Sl st in next ch sp, ch 1, sc in same ch sp, ch 2, [sc in next ch sp, ch 2] around, join with sl st in beg sc.

**Rnd 5:** Ch 1, (sc, ch 2, sc) in each ch sp around, join with sl st in beg sc. Fasten off. ■

# Holly Berries

DESIGN BY ANNE HALLIDAY

Plush, textured stitches and luscious, super bulky yarn create the cozy comfort and delightful dimension in this luxurious throw that will make a great holiday gift for a family member or special friend.

**FINISHED SIZE**
39½ x 63½ inches, excluding Fringe

**MATERIALS**
Red Heart Light & Lofty super bulky (super chunky) weight yarn (6 oz/140 yds/170g per skein): 6 skeins each #9632 pine and #9376 wine
Size K/10½/6.5mm crochet hook or size needed to obtain gauge

**GAUGE**
With 2 strands yarn held tog: 6 sts = 4 inches; 5 pattern rows = 2 inches

**PATTERN NOTES**
Leave 8 inches of yarn at beginning and end of each row to be worked into Fringe.

Hold 2 strands same-color yarn together throughout.

**SPECIAL STITCH**
**Cluster (cl):** Ch 3, yo, insert hook in 3rd ch from hook, yo, pull lp through, yo, pull through 2 lps on hook, yo, insert hook in same ch, yo, pull lp through, yo, pull through 2 lps on hook, yo, pull through all lps on hook.

## INSTRUCTIONS

**THROW**
**Row 1 (RS):** With pine, ch 186, sc in 2nd ch from hook, [ch 1, sk next ch, sc in next ch] across, turn. Fasten off. *(93 sc, 92 ch sps)*

**Row 2:** Join wine with sc in first st, [ch 3, sk next ch sp, next st and next ch sp, sc in next st] across, turn. Fasten off. *(47 sc, 46 ch sps)*

**Row 3:** Join pine with sc in first st, *ch 1, working in front of next ch sp, dc in next sk st on row before last, ch 1, sc in next sc on last row, rep from * across, turn. Fasten off. *(93 sts, 92 ch sps)*

**Rows 4–7:** Rep rows 2 and 3 alternately.

**Row 8:** Join wine with sc in first st, [ch 3, sk next ch sp, next st and next ch sp, sc in next st] twice, *[**cl** *(see Special Stitch)*, sk next ch sp, next st and next ch sp, sc in next st] twice, [ch 3, sk next ch sp, next st and next ch sp, sc in next st] twice, rep from * across, turn. Fasten off.

**Row 9:** Join pine with sc in first st, [ch 1, working in front of next ch sp, dc in next sk st on row before last,

ch 1, sc in next st on last row] twice, *[ch 1, working behind next cl, dc in next sk dc on row before last, ch 1, sc in next sc] twice, [ch 1, working in front of next ch sp, dc in next sk dc on row before last, ch 1, sc in next sc on last row] twice, rep from * across, turn. Fasten off.

**Rows 10–13:** Rep rows 8 and 9 alternately.

**Row 14:** Join wine with sc in first st, [ch 3, sk next ch sp, next st and next ch sp, sc in next st] across, turn. Fasten off.

**Row 15:** Join pine with sc in first st, *ch 1, working in front of next ch sp, dc in next sk st on row before last, ch 1, sc in next sc on last row, rep from * across, turn. Fasten off.

**Rows 16–21:** Rep rows 14 and 15 alternately.

**Rows 22–89:** Rep rows 8–21 consecutively, ending with row 19. At end of last row, **do not turn.** Fasten off.

**Row 90:** With RS facing, join pine with sl st in first st, sl st in next ch sp, [ch 1, sl st in next ch sp] across to last st, sl st in last st. Fasten off.

**Row 91:** Working in starting ch on opposite side of row 1, join pine with sl st in first ch, sl st in next ch, [ch 1, sl st in next sk ch] across to last ch, sl st in last ch. Fasten off.

**FRINGE**

For each Fringe, cut 1 strand 16 inches in length. Fold strand in half, insert hook in end of row, pull fold through, pull ends through fold including 8-inch end at end of row; tighten. Trim ends.

Matching row colors, attach 1 Fringe in end of each row on short ends of Afghan. ■

# Yuletide Welcome

DESIGN BY L.V. JOHNSON

Pineapples have long been known as a symbol of gracious hospitality, and this large, lacy table centerpiece creates the perfect accent to welcome guests to your holiday celebrations.

INTERMEDIATE

**FINISHED SIZE**
21 inches in diameter

**MATERIALS**
Size 10 crochet cotton:
575 yds white
Size 8/1.50mm steel crochet hook or size needed to obtain gauge.

**GAUGE**
10 sts = 1 inch; bullion st = 5/8 inch tall

**PATTERN NOTE**
A (double treble crochet, chain 1) can be substituted for the bullion stitch if desired.

**SPECIAL STITCHES**
**Bullion stitch (bullion st):** Yo 20 times, insert hook in st, yo, pull lp through st, yo, pull through all lps on hook at same time *(if pulling through all lps is difficult, try pulling hook through 1 or 2 lps at a time until all lps have been worked off)*, ch 1. If making this st for the first time, practice before starting instructions.

**Shell:** 3 bullion sts in next sc, ch 3, sk next sc, 3 bullion sts in next sc.

**Bullion stitch shell (bullion st shell):** (Bullion st, ch 1) 6 times in st or ch.

## INSTRUCTIONS

**CENTERPIECE**
**Rnd 1:** Ch 7, sl st in first ch to form ring, ch 4, 38 tr in ring, join with sl st in 4th ch of beg ch-4. *(38 tr)*

**Rnd 2:** Ch 7, **bullion st** *(see Special Stitches)* in each st around, join with sl st in beg bullion st.

**Rnd 3:** *Ch 6, sk next 2 bullion sts, sc in next sp between bullion sts, [ch 6, sk next bullion st, sc in next sp between bullion st] twice, rep from * around to last st, ch 6, join with sl st in joining sl st of last rnd. *(28 ch sps)*

**Rnds 4–6:** Sl st across to center of first ch sp, [ch 6, sc in next ch sp] around, join with sl st in base of beg ch sp.

**Rnd 7:** Sl st to center of first ch sp, *13 tr in next ch sp, sc in next ch lp, [ch 6, sc in next ch lp] twice, rep from * around, joining with sl st in sl st before first tr.

**Rnd 8:** [Ch 7, bullion st in each of next 13 tr, ch 7, sc in next ch sp, ch 6, sc in next ch sp] around, ch 7, join with sl st in beg bullion st.

**Rnd 9:** *Ch 5, [sc in next sp between bullion sts, ch 5] 12 times, sk next ch sp, 3 bullion sts in next ch sp, ch 5, sc in next bullion st, rep from * around, join with sl st in base of beg ch-5.

**Rnd 10:** Sl st to center of first ch sp, *[ch 5, sc in next ch sp] 11 times, ch 5, sc in each of next 3 bullion sts, ch 5, sk next ch sp, sc in next ch sp, rep from * around, join with sl st in base of beg ch-5.

**Rnd 11:** Sl st to center of first ch sp, *[ch 5, sc in next ch sp] 10 times, ch 5, bullion st in each of next 3 sc, ch 5, sk next ch sp, sc in next ch sp, rep from * around, join with sl st in base of beg ch-5.

**Rnd 12:** Sl st to center of first ch sp, *[ch 5, sc in next ch sp] 9 times, ch 5, sc in each of next 3 bullion sts, ch 5, sk next ch sp, sc in next ch sp, rep from * around, join with sl st in base of beg ch-5 sp.

**Rnd 13:** Sl st to center of first ch sp, *[ch 5, sc in next ch sp] 8 times, ch 5, bullion st in each of next 3 sc, ch 5, sk next ch sp, sc in next ch sp, rep from * around, join with sl st in base of beg ch-5.

**Rnd 14:** Sl st to center of first ch sp, *[ch 5, sc in next ch sp] 7 times, sc in each of next 3 bullion sts, ch 5, sk next ch sp, sc in next ch sp, rep from * around, join with sl st in base of beg ch-5.

**Rnd 15:** Sl st to center of first ch sp, *[ch 5, sc in next ch sp] 6 times, ch 8, bullion st in each of next 3 sc, ch 8, sk next ch sp, sc in next ch sp, rep from * around, join with sl st in base of beg ch-5.

**Rnd 16:** Sl st to center of first ch sp, *[ch 5, sc in next ch sp] 5 times, ch 8, sc in each of next 3 bullion sts, ch 8, sk next ch sp, sc in next ch sp, rep from * around, join with sl st in base of beg ch-5.

**Rnd 17:** Sl st to center of first ch sp, *[ch 5, sc in next ch sp] 4 times, ch 8, 3 bullion sts in next sc, ch 5, sk next sc, 3 bullion sts in next sc, ch 8, sk next ch sp, sc in next ch sp, rep from * around, join with sl st in base of beg ch-5.

**Rnd 18:** Sl st to center of first ch sp, *[ch 5, sc in next ch sp] 3 times, ch 8, sc in each of next 3 bullion sts, sl st in each of next 5 chs, sc in each of next 3 bullion sts, ch 8, sk next ch sp, sc in next ch sp, rep from * around, join with sl st in base of beg ch-5.

**Rnd 19:** Sl st to center of first ch sp, *[ch 5, sc in next ch sp] twice, ch 8, bullion st in each of next 3 sc, ch 4, 13 tr in next ch-5 sp of previous row, ch 4, bullion st in each of next 3 sc, ch 8, sk next ch sp, sc in next ch sp, rep from * around, join with sl st in base of beg ch-5.

**Rnd 20:** Sl st to center of first ch sp, *ch 5, sc in next ch sp, ch 8, sc each of in next 3 bullion sts, ch 7, bullion st in each of next 13 tr, ch 7, sc in each of next 3 bullion sts, ch 8, sk next ch sp, sc in next ch sp, rep from * around, join with sl st in base of beg ch-5.

**Rnd 21:** Sl st to center of ch sp, ch 11, ****shell** *(see Special Stitches)*, ch 5, sc in top of ch-7, [ch 5, sc in next sp between bullion sts] 12 times, ch 5, shell, ch 8, sk next ch sp**, *dc in next ch sp, ch 8, rep between **, rep from * around, join with sl st in 3rd ch of beg ch-11.

**Rnd 22:** Sl st in each of next 8 chs, *sc in each st and sl st in each ch across shell, ch 5, sk next ch sp, sc in next ch sp, [ch 5, sc in next ch sp] 11 times, ch 5, sc in each st and sl st in each ch across shell, ch 11, rep from * around, join with sl st in beg sc on first shell, **turn,** sl st back to center of ch-11 to start next rnd, **turn.**

**Rnd 23:** *◊Bullion st in each of next 3 sc on next shell, ch 5, sk next 3 sl sts, bullion st in each of next 3 sc on same shell◊, ch 6, sk next ch sp, sc in next ch sp, [ch 5, sc in next ch sp] 10 times, ch 6, rep between ◊, sc in next ch-11 sp, rep from * around, join with sl st in last sl st before beg bullion st, turn. Fasten off.

### FIRST POINT

**Row 24:** Working in rows, sk first 3 bullion sts and next 5 chs, join with sc in next bullion st, sc in each of next 2 bullion sts, ch 6, sk next ch sp, sc in next ch sp, [ch 5, sc in next ch sp] 9 times, ch 6, sc in each of last 3 bullion sts, turn.

**Row 25:** Ch 7, bullion st in each of first 3 sc, ch 6, sk next ch sp, sc in next ch sp, [ch 5, sc in next ch sp] across to next ch-6 sp, ch 6, bullion st in each of last 3 sc, turn.

**Row 26:** Ch 1, sc in each of first 3 bullion sts, ch 6, sk next ch sp, sc in next ch sp, [ch 5, sc in next ch sp] across to next ch-6 sp, ch 6, sc in each of last 3 bullion sts, turn.

**Rows 27–31:** Rep rows 25 and 26 alternately, ending with row 25.

**Row 32:** Ch 1, sc in each of first 3 bullion sts, ch 6, sk next ch sp, sc in next ch sp, ch 5, sc in next ch sp, ch 6, sc in each of last 3 bullion sts, turn.

**Row 33:** Ch 7, bullion st in each of first 3 sc, ch 6, sk next ch sp, sc in next ch sp, ch 6, bullion st in each of last 3 sc, turn.

**Row 34:** Ch 1, sc in each of first 3 bullion sts, ch 11, sc in each of last 3 bullion sts, turn.

**Row 35:** Ch 7, bullion st in each of first 3 sc, sc in center of ch-11, bullion st in each of last 3 sc, **do not turn,** working down ends of rows, [ch 7, sc in end of next sc row] 6 times, turn. Fasten off.

### 2ND–7TH POINTS

Sk first 3 bullion sts and next 5 chs on next Pineapple, work same as First Point.

**Do not turn or fasten off** at the end of the 7th Point.

### BORDER

**Rnd 36:** *Ch 1, **bullion st shell** *(see Special Stitches)* in 5th ch of next ch-5 on rnd 23, ch 1, sc in sc worked over center of ch-11 on rnd 22, ch 1, bullion st shell in first ch of next ch-5 on rnd 23, ch 1, [sc in end of next sc row, ch 1, bullion st shell in end of next sc row, ch 1] 3 times, sc in top of first bullion st on row 35, ch 1, bullion st shell in sc worked over center of ch-11 on row 34, ch 1, sc in last bullion st on row 35, ch 1, [bullion st shell in next sc row, ch 1, sc in next sc row, ch 1] 3 times, rep from * around.

**Rnd 37:** Sc in next ch-1 and in next bullion st, sc in next sp between bullion sts, [ch 5, sc in next sp between bullion sts] 4 times, ch 3, *sc in next sc, sc in sp between first and 2nd bullion st on next bullion st shell, [ch 5, sc in next sp between bullion sts] 4 times, ch 3, rep from * around, join with sl st in beg sc. Fasten off. ■

# Vintage Poinsettias

DESIGN BY DIANE STONE

The old-fashioned look of Christmases past is reflected in this beautiful, vintage-style doily that will add a touch of gracious elegance to your holiday celebrations wherever it is displayed.

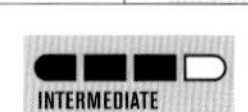


**FINISHED SIZE**
14 inches in diameter

**MATERIALS**
Size 10 crochet cotton:
100 yds ecru
80 yds red
50 yds green
1 skein gold embroidery floss
Size 6/1.80mm steel crochet hook or size needed to obtain gauge

**GAUGE**
Rnds 1–2 = 2 inches across

**SPECIAL STITCHES**
**Popcorn (pc):** 6 dc in indicated st or ch, drop lp from hook, insert hook in first st of dc group, pull dropped lp through st.

**Petal:** Ch 5, sl st in 2nd ch from hook, sc in next ch, hdc in next ch, dc in last ch.

**Cross-stitch (cross-st):** Sk next st, tr in next st, ch 3, sl st in 3rd ch from hook, working behind last tr, tr in sk st.

**Picot:** Ch 4, sl st in 2nd ch from hook, sc in next ch, hdc in last ch.

## INSTRUCTIONS

**FLOWER**
Make 8.

**Rnd 1:** With 6 strands of floss held tog as 1, ch 2, 12 sc in 2nd ch from hook, join with sl st in beg sc. Fasten off. *(12 sc)*

**Rnd 2:** Join red with sl st in first st, **petal** *(see Special Stitches)*, sk next st, [sl st in next st, petal, sk next st] around, join with sl st in beg sl st. *(6 petals)*

**Rnd 3:** Working behind last rnd, sl st in first sk st on rnd 1, petal, [sl st in next sk st on rnd 1, petal] around, join with sl st in beg sl st. Fasten off. *(6 petals)*

**DOILY**
**Rnd 1:** With ecru, ch 4, 11 dc in 4th ch from hook, join with sl st in 3rd ch of beg ch-3. *(12 dc, counting sk 3 chs as 1 dc)*

**Rnds 2 & 3:** Ch 3 *(counts as first dc)*, dc in same st, 2 dc in each st around, join with sl st in 3rd ch of beg ch-3. *(48 dc at end of last rnd)*

**Rnd 4:** Ch 7, sl st in 3rd ch from hook, working behind ch-7 just made, tr in last st of last rnd, [**cross-st** *(see Special Stitches)*] around, join with sl st in 4th ch of beg ch-7. Fasten off. *(24 cross-sts)*

**Rnd 5:** Working in sps between cross-sts, join ecru with sc in any sp, ch 7, [sc in next sp, ch 7] around, join with sl st in beg sc. *(24 ch sps)*

**Rnd 6:** Sl st in each of next 4 chs, ch 3, 6 dc in same ch sp, (sc, ch 3, sc) in 4th ch of next ch-7, [7 dc in 4th ch of next ch-7, (sc, ch 3, sc) in 4th ch of next ch-7] around, join with sl st in 3rd ch of beg ch-3. *(84 dc, 24 sc, 12 ch-3 sps)*

**Rnd 7:** Sl st in each of next 3 dc, ch 1, sc in same st, ch 7, sc in next ch-3 sp, ch 7, [sc in 4th st of next dc group, ch 7, sc in next ch-3 sp, ch 7] around, join with sl st in beg sc. *(24 ch sps)*

**Rnd 8:** Sl st in each of next 3 chs, ch 1, sc in same ch sp, ch 7, [sc in next ch sp, ch 7] around, join with sl st in beg sc. *(24 sc, 24 ch sps)*

**Rnd 9:** Ch 1, *sc in first ch of next ch-7, [ch 3, sk next ch, sc in next ch] 3 times, rep from * around, join with sl st in beg sc. Fasten off. *(96 sc, 72 ch sps)*

**Rnd 10:** Sk first ch sp on last rnd, join ecru with sc in next ch sp, ch 3, sc in same ch sp, *[ch 7, sk next 2 ch sps, (sc, ch 3, sc) in next ch sp] twice, ch 3, sl st in tip of any petal on rnd 3 of 1 Flower, ch 3, sk next 2 ch sps on last rnd**, (sc, ch 3, sc) in next ch sp, rep from * around, ending last rep at **, join with sl st in beg sc. Fasten off. *(48 sc, 24 ch-3 sps, 16 ch-7 sps, 8 joinings)*

**Rnd 11:** Join green with sc in first ch-7 sp, *ch 7, sc in next ch-7 sp, ch 4, sc in tip of petal on rnd 2 of next Flower, [ch 3, sc in tip of next petal on rnd 3 of Flower, ch 3, sc in tip of next petal on rnd 2 of Flower] 5 times, ch 4**, sc in next ch-7 sp on last rnd, rep from * around, ending last rep at **, join with sl st in beg sc. *(80 ch-3 sps, 64 sc, 16 ch-7 sps, 16 ch-4 sps)*

**Rnd 12:** Sl st in each of next 4 chs, ch 1, (sc, ch 3, sc) in same ch, *ch 7, sk next ch-4 sp, sc in next ch-3 sp, ch 3, sc in next ch sp, [**picot** *(see Special Stitches)*, (sc, ch 3, sc) in next ch sp on last rnd] 6 times, picot, sc in next ch-3 sp on last rnd, ch 3, sc in next ch sp, ch 7, sk next ch-4 sp**, (sc, ch 3, sc) in 4th ch of next ch-7 sp, rep from * around, ending last rep at **, join with sl st in beg sc. Fasten off. *(144 sc, 72 ch-3 sps, 56 picots, 16 ch-7 sps)*

**Rnd 13:** Join ecru with sc in first ch-7 sp, *[ch 5, sc in next ch sp] 9 times, ch 3, **pc** *(see Special Stitches)* in next ch-3 sp, ch 3**, sc in next ch-7 sp, rep from * around, ending last rep at **, join with sl st in beg sc. *(80 sc, 72 ch-5 sps, 16 ch-3 sps, 8 pc)*

**Rnd 14:** Sl st in each of next 2 chs of next ch-5, ch 1, sc in same ch sp, *[ch 5, (sc, ch 3, sc) in next ch-5 sp] 7 times, ch 5, sc in next ch-5 sp, ch 3, pc in 3rd ch of next ch-3, ch 3, pc in first ch of next ch-3, ch 3**, sc in next ch-5 sp, rep from * around, ending last rep at **, join with sl st in beg sc. *(128 sc, 80 ch-3 sps, 64 ch-5 sps, 16 pc)*

**Rnd 15:** Sl st in each of next 2 chs of next ch-5, ch 1, sc in same ch sp, *[ch 5, (sc, ch 3, sc) in next ch-5 sp] 6 times, ch 5, sc in next ch-5 sp, ch 3, sk next ch-3 sp, pc in next ch-3 sp between pc on last rnd, ch 3, sk next ch-3 sp**, sc in next ch-5 sp, rep from * around, ending last rep at **, join with sl st in beg sc. *(112 sc, 64 ch-3 sps, 56 ch-5 sps, 8 pc)*

**Rnd 16:** Sl st in each of next 2 chs of next ch-5, ch 1, sc in same ch sp, *ch 5, (sc, ch 3, sc) in next ch-5 sp, ch 7, (sc, ch 3, sc) in next ch-5 sp, ch 7, (pc, ch 5, sl st in 2nd ch from hook, sc in next ch, hdc in next ch, ch 1, pc) in 3rd ch of next ch-5, [ch 7, (sc, ch 3, sc) in next ch sp] twice, ch 5, sc in next ch sp, ch 3, sk next 2 ch sps and pc**, sc in next ch-5 sp, rep from * around, ending last rep at **, join with sl st in beg sc. Fasten off. *(72 sc, 40 ch-3 sps, 32 ch-7 sps, 24 ch-5 sps, 16 pc, 8 ch-1 sps, 8 sl sts, 8 hdc)* ■

# Christmas Flowers

DESIGN BY CAROLYN CHRISTMAS

Festive red flowers bloom in pretty procession across lacy, white panels bordered in rich forest green in this bright and beautiful throw. It works up quickly with double-strand yarn and large hook.

INTERMEDIATE

4 MEDIUM

**FINISHED SIZE**
54 x 62 inches

**MATERIALS**
Medium (worsted) weight yarn:
35 oz/1,750 yds/992g red
18 oz/900 yds/510g white
3 oz/150 yds/85g each green and yellow
Size P/15/10mm crochet hook or size needed to obtain gauge

**GAUGE**
**With 2 strands yarn held tog:** rnds 1–2 = 4 inches in diameter; 3 dc = 2 inches; 2 dc rows = 3 inches

**PATTERN NOTE**
Hold 2 strands same-color yarn together throughout..

**SPECIAL STITCHES**
**Picot:** Ch 3, sl st in 3rd ch from hook.

**Popcorn (pc):** 5 dc in next sc, drop lp from hook, insert hook in top of first dc, pull dropped lp through.

## INSTRUCTIONS

**SIDE STRIP**
Make 2.

**FIRST BLOCK**
**Rnd 1:** With 2 strands of yellow held tog as 1 *(see Pattern Note)*, ch 2, 8 sc in 2nd ch from hook, join with sl st in beg sc. Fasten off. *(8 sc)*

**Rnd 2:** Join red with sl st in any st, ch 3, 4 dc in same st, drop lp from hook, insert hook in top of ch-3, pull dropped lp through *(beg pc completed)*, ch 2, **pc** *(see Special Stitches)* in next st, ch 2, (pc, ch 2) in each st around, join with sl st in top of beg pc. Fasten off. *(8 pc)*

**Rnd 3:** Join green with sl st in any ch-2 sp, ch 1, (sc, **picot**—*see Special Stitches*, sc) in same ch-2 sp, *sc in top of next pc, (sc, picot, sc) in next ch-2 sp, rep from * around, sc in last pc, join with sl st in beg sc. Fasten off. *(24 sc, 8 picots)*

**Rnd 4:** Working behind picots, join white with sc in first sc after any picot, sc in each of next 2 sc, ch 1, [sc in each of next 3 sc, ch 1] around, join with sl st in beg sc.

**Rnd 5:** Ch 1, sc in first st, [ch 3, sk next st or ch, sc in next st] around, ch 1, join with dc in first sc forming last ch sp. *(16 ch-sps)*

**Rnd 6:** Ch 1, sc in last ch sp made, ch 5, sc in same ch sp, *ch 3, [sc in next ch-3 sp, ch 3] 3 times**, (sc, ch 5, sc) in next ch sp, rep from * around, ending last rep at **, join with sl st in beg sc. Fasten off.

**2ND BLOCK**
**Rnds 1–5:** Rep rnds 1–5 of First Block.

**Rnd 6:** Ch 1, sc in last ch sp made, ch 2, sl st in any ch-5 sp on last Block made, ch 2, sc in joining sp on 2nd Block, [ch 1, sl st in next ch-3 sp on last Block, ch 1, sc in next ch-3 sp on 2nd Block] 4 times, ch 2, sl st in next ch-5 sp on last Block, ch 2, sc in same ch-5 sp on 2nd Block, *ch 3, [sc in next ch-3 sp, ch 3] 3 times**, (sc, ch 5, sc) in next ch-3 sp, rep from *, around, ending last rep at **, join with sl st in beg sc. Fasten off.

#### 3RD–7TH BLOCKS
Working on side of Block opposite last joined edge, rep 2nd Block.

### EDGING

#### PANELS
**Row 1:** Working across 1 long edge of 1 Side Strip, join red with sl st in bottom right corner sp, ch 3, dc in same ch sp, 2 dc in each ch sp across ending with 2 dc in corner ch sp at end of Side Strip, turn.

**Rows 2–7:** Ch 3, dc in each dc across, turn. At end of last row, fasten off.

Beg at top left corner ch sp and working across rem long edge of Side Strip, rep rows 1–7.

#### ASSEMBLY
To join Side Strips, hold Strips WS tog, matching sts, join red with sl st in first st on first Side, sl st in first st on 2nd Side, [sl st in next st on first Side, sl st in next st on 2nd Side] across. Fasten off.

#### BORDER
**Rnd 1:** Working around outer edge, join red with sc in first st of last Edging row on either Side, 2 sc in same st, sc around all edges, working 2 sc in end of each dc row, 2 sc in each ch sp of Blocks, sc in each dc along sides and 3 sc in each corner, join with sl st in first sc. Fasten off.

***Note:*** *On next rnd, it may be necessary to sk 1 more or fewer sts than indicated before corners to place (sc, ch 3, sc) in center st of each corner.*

**Rnd 2:** Join yellow with sc in center sc at any corner, ch 3, sc in same corner, [ch 2, sk next 2 sts, sc in next st] around with (sc, ch 3, sc) in center st of each corner, join with sl st in beg sc. Fasten off.

**Rnd 3:** Join red in sl st in first corner ch-3 sp, ch 3 *(counts as first dc)*, 4 dc in same ch sp, 3 dc in each ch-2 sp around with 5 dc in each corner, join with sl st in 3rd ch of beg ch-3. Fasten off.

**Rnd 4:** Join green with sl st in 3rd dc of 5-dc group at any corner, (ch 4, dc, ch 1, dc) in same st, *ch 1, sk next 2 sts, sc in next sp between 3-dc groups, [ch 1, sk next st, dc in next st, ch 1, sk next st, sc in next sp between 3-dc groups] across to next corner, ch 1**, (dc, ch 1, dc, ch 1, dc) in center dc of 5-dc group at corner, rep from * around, ending last rep at **, join with sl st in 3rd ch of beg ch-4. Fasten off.

**Rnd 5:** Join white with sl st in first dc of any corner, (ch 3, picot, dc) in same st, sk all ch-1 sps, (dc, picot, dc) in each of next 2 dc, *hdc in each ch-1 sp, sc in each sc and (dc, picot, dc) in each dc across to next corner**, sk all ch-1 sps, (dc, picot, dc) in each of next 3 dc at corner, rep from * around, ending last rep at **, join with sl st 3rd ch of beg ch-3. Fasten off. ■

# O Tannenbaum

DESIGN BY CAROL DECKER

Create a festive table setting with this gorgeous red lace tablecloth highlighted with dainty green Christmas trees. This elegant thread creation is sure to become a treasured family heirloom.

EXPERIENCED

**FINISHED SIZE**
63 x 89 inches

**MATERIALS**
Size 10 crochet cotton:
 10,150 yds red
 1,400 yds green
 45 yds brown
Size 7/1.65mm steel crochet hook or size needed to obtain gauge
Stitch markers

**GAUGE**
Rnds 1–3 of Flower Motif: 1¼ inches across; 9 dc = 1 inch; 5 dc rows = 1 inch

Motif = 4 inches square

**SPECIAL STITCH**
**Picot:** Ch 3, sl st in third ch from hook.

## INSTRUCTIONS

**SIDE PATTERNS**
***Note:*** *Side Patterns are used to work rnd 10 of each Motif according to Chart.*

**Side A** *(red line on Chart)*: Join with sc in corner ch sp, (ch 1, dc, tr, ch 3, tr, dc, ch 1, sc) in same ch sp, *(dc, ch 2, sc, ch 3, sc) in next ch sp, sc in next ch sp, dc in next ch sp, ch 6, sc in next ch sp, **picot** *(see Special Stitch)*, ch 3, (sc, ch 1, 2 dc, ch 2, 2 dc, ch 1, sc) in next ch sp, ch 3, sc in next ch sp, picot, ch 6, dc in next ch sp, sc in next ch sp, (sc, ch 3, sc, ch 2, dc) in next ch sp*.

**Side B** *(blue line on Chart)*: Join with sc in corner ch-6 sp, (ch 1, dc, tr, ch 1) in same ch sp, sc in corner ch-3 sp on last Motif, (ch 1, tr, dc, ch 1, sc) in same ch sp on this Motif, *(dc, ch 1) in next ch sp, dc in next ch-2 sp on last Motif, (ch 1, sc, ch 3, sc) in same ch sp on this Motif, sc in next ch sp, dc in next ch sp, ch 2, 2 tr in ch-6 sp of last Motif, ch 2, sc in next ch sp, picot, ch 3, (sc, ch 1, 2 dc, ch 1) in next ch sp, drop lp from hook, insert hook in corresponding ch sp on last Motif and pull lp through, (ch 1, 2 dc, ch 1, sc) in same ch sp on this Motif, ch 3, sc in next ch sp, picot, ch 2, 2 tr in ch-6 sp on this Motif, ch 2, dc in next ch sp, sc in next ch sp, (sc, ch 3, sc, ch 1) in next ch sp, dc in ch-2 sp on last Motif, ch 1, dc in same ch sp on this Motif, (sc, ch 1, dc, tr, ch 1) in next corner ch sp, sc in corner ch-3 sp on last Motif, (ch 1, tr, dc, ch 1, sc) in same ch sp on this Motif*.

**Side C** *(purple lines on Chart):* Join with sc in corner ch-6 sp, (ch 1, dc, tr, ch 1) in same ch sp, sc in corner ch-3 sp on last Motif, (ch 1, tr, dc, ch 1, sc) in same ch sp on this Motif, *(dc, ch 1) in next ch sp, dc in next ch-2 sp on last Motif, (ch 1, sc, ch 3, sc) in last ch sp on this Motif, sc in next ch sp, dc in next ch sp, ch 2, 2 tr in ch-6 sp of last Motif, ch 2, sc in next ch sp, picot, ch 3, (sc, ch 1, 2 dc, ch 1) in next ch sp, drop lp from hook, insert hook in corresponding ch sp on last Motif and pull lp through, (ch 1, 2 dc, ch 1, sc) in same ch sp on this Motif, ch 3, sc in next ch sp, picot, ch 2, 2 tr in ch-6 sp on last Motif, ch 2, dc in next ch sp, sc in next ch sp, (sc, ch 3, sc, ch 1) in next ch sp, dc in ch-2 sp on last Motif, ch 1, dc in same ch sp on this Motif, (sc, ch 1, dc, tr, ch 1) in next corner ch sp, sc in corner ch-3 sp on last Motif, (ch 1, tr, dc, ch 1, sc) in same ch sp on this Motif, rep from *.

**Side D** *(green line on Chart):* (Dc, ch 1, sc, ch 3, sc) in next ch sp, sc in next ch sp, dc in next ch sp,

ch 3 *(mark for Tree)*, dc around last dc made, ch 3, sc in next ch sp, picot, ch 3, (sc, ch 1, 2 dc, ch 2, 2 dc, ch 1, sc) in next ch sp, ch 3, sc in next ch sp, picot, ch 3, dc in next ch sp, ch 3 *(mark for Tree)*, dc around last dc made, sc in next ch sp, (sc, ch 3, sc, ch 2, dc) in next ch sp, (sc, ch 1, dc, tr, ch 3, tr, dc, ch 1, sc) in next ch sp.

**Side E** *(orange line on Chart)*: ◊Join with sc in corner ch-6 sp, (ch 1, dc, tr, ch 1) in same ch sp, sc in corner ch-3 sp on other Motif, (ch 1, tr, dc, ch 1, sc) in same ch sp on this Motif, *(dc, ch 1) in next ch sp, dc around trtr of Bottom of Tree fill-in, (ch 1, sc, ch 3, sc) in same ch sp on this Motif, sc in next ch sp, dc in next ch sp, ch 2, dc in first point on tree, ch 2, (sc, picot) in next ch sp, ch 3, (sc, ch 1, 2 dc, ch 1) in next ch sp, drop lp from hook, insert hook in next point on tree and pull dropped lp through, (ch 1, 2 dc, ch 1, sc) in same ch sp on this Motif, ch 3, (sc, picot) in next ch sp, ch 2, dc in next point on tree, ch 3, dc in next ch sp, sc in next ch sp, (sc, ch 3, sc, ch 1) in next ch sp, tr in next point on tree, ch 1, dc in same ch sp on this Motif, (sc, ch 1, dc, tr, ch 1) in next ch sp, sc in corner ch-3 sp on last Motif, (ch 1, tr, dc, ch 1, sc) in same ch sp on this Motif◊, rep from *.

## INSTRUCTIONS

***Notes***: *Beg at center, work in rnds. Work Motifs as needed according to Chart.*

### CENTER

#### MOTIF A

**Rnd 1:** With red, ch 5, sl st in first ch to form ring, ch 4 *(counts as first dc and ch-1 sp)*, (dc in ring, ch 1) 7 times, join with sl st in 3rd ch of ch-4. *(8 ch sps)*

**Rnd 2:** Sl st in first ch sp, ch 1, sc in same ch sp, ch 4, [sc in next ch sp, ch 4] around, join with sl st in beg sc.

**Rnd 3:** (Sl st, ch 1, sc, {ch 1, dc} twice, ch 1, sc) in first ch sp, (sc, {ch 1, dc} twice, ch 1, sc) in each ch sp around, join with sl st in beg sc. *(8 petals)*

**Rnd 4:** Working behind last rnd, ch 2 *(does not count as st)*, [dc in next ch sp on rnd 1, ch 5] around, join with sl st in top of beg dc.

**Rnd 5:** Ch 1, *(sc, ch 1, dc, tr) in next ch sp, tr in center ch sp of next petal on rnd 3, (tr, dc, ch 1, sc) in same ch sp, rep from * around, join with sl st in beg sc.

**Rnd 6:** Sl st in next ch, sl st in next 2 sts, ch 1, sc around next tr, [ch 10, sc around center tr on next petal] 7 times, join with ch 4, trtr in first sc forming last ch sp.

**Rnd 7:** Ch 3, (2 dc, ch 3, 3 dc) in ch sp just made, *ch 5, (3 dc, ch 3, 3 dc) in next ch sp, rep from * around, join with trtr in top of trtr on last rnd forming last ch sp.

**Rnd 8:** (Ch 3, tr, ch 3, sc, ch 3, tr, dc) in ch sp just made, ch 3, (sc, ch 3, sc) in next ch sp, ch 3, *(dc, tr, ch 3, sc, ch 3, tr, dc) in next ch sp, ch 3, (sc, ch 3, sc) in next ch sp, ch 3, rep from * around, join with sl st in first ch of beg ch-3.

**Rnd 9:** Sl st in each of next 2 chs, sl st in next st, ch 1, *for **corner**, sc in next ch sp, ch 3, dc in sc just made, ch 3, dc around last dc made, ch 6, dc around last dc made, [ch 3, dc around last dc made] twice, sc in next ch sp, ch 3, dc in next ch sp, ch 6, sk next ch sp, **dc dec** *(see Stitch Guide)* in next 2 ch sps, sc in same ch sp last worked in, ch 4, sc in next ch sp, insert hook in same ch sp, yo, pull through, yo, insert hook in next ch sp, yo, pull through, yo, pull through 2 lps on hook, yo, pull through all lps on hook, ch 6, sk next ch sp, dc in next ch sp, ch 3, rep from * around, join with sl st in beg sc. Fasten off.

**Rnd 10:** Work Side A *(see Side Patterns)*, ◊(sc, ch 1, dc, tr, ch 3, tr, dc, ch 1, sc) in next ch sp, rep between * of Side A, rep from ◊ around, join with sl st in beg sc. Fasten off.

#### MOTIF B

**Rnds 1–9:** Rep rnds 1–9 of Motif A on Center.

**Rnd 10:** Work Side Pattern B, ◊work between * of Side Pattern A, (sc, ch 1, dc, tr, ch 3, tr, dc, ch 1, sc) in next ch sp, rep from ◊ once, rep between * of Side Pattern A, join with sl st in beg sc. Fasten off.

Rep Motif B twice for a total of 4 Motifs in Center according to Chart.

Work the rem Tablecloth in rnds according to Chart.

**MOTIF C**

**Rnds 1–9:** Rep rnds 1–9 of Motif A on Center.

**Rnd 10:** Work Side B, rep Side A between *, (sc, ch 1, dc, tr, ch 3, tr, dc, ch 1, sc) in next ch sp, work Side D, rep Side A between *, join with sl st in beg. Fasten off.

**MOTIF D**

**Rnds 1–9:** Rep rnds 1–9 of Motif A on Center.

**Rnd 10:** Work Side C, rep Side A between *, (sc, ch 1, dc, tr, ch 3, tr, dc, ch 1, sc) in next ch sp, work Side D, join with sl st in beg sc. Fasten off.

**MOTIF E**

**Rnds 1–9:** Rep rnds 1–9 of Motif A on Center.

**Rnd 10:** Work Side B, rep between * on Side A, work Side D, join with sl st in beg sc. Fasten off.

**MOTIF F**

**Rnds 1–9:** Rep rnds 1–9 of Motif A on Center.

**Rnd 10:** Work Side C, work Side D, rep between * on Side D, join with sl st in beg sc. Fasten off.

**MOTIF G**

**Rnds 1–9:** Rep rnds 1–9 of Motif A on Center.

**Rnd 10:** Work Side E, work between * on Side A, (sc, ch 1, dc, tr, ch 3, tr, dc, ch 1, sc) in next ch sp, rep between * on Side A, join with sl st in beg sc. Fasten off.

**MOTIF H**

**Rnds 1–9:** Rep rnds 1–9 of Motif A on Center.

**Rnd 10:** Work Side C, rep between * on Side A, (sc, ch 1, dc, tr, ch 3, tr, dc, ch 1, sc) in next ch sp, rep between * on Side A, join with sl st in beg sc. Fasten off.

**TREE MOTIF**

**First Tree**

**Row 1:** Join green with sc in first marked ch sp on the right, turn. *(1 sc)*

**Row 2:** Ch 3 *(counts as first dc)*, 2 dc in same sc, turn. *(3 dc)*

**Row 3:** Ch 3, dc in same st, 2 dc in each st across, turn. *(6 dc)*

**Row 4:** Ch 3, dc in same st, 2 dc in next st, dc in each of next 2 sts, 2 dc in each of last 2 sts, turn. *(10 dc)*

**Row 5:** Ch 1, sl st in each of first 2 sts, sl st in next dc, ch 3, dc in same st, dc in each of next 4 sts, 2 dc in next st leaving rem sts unworked, turn. *(8 dc)*

**Row 6:** Ch 3, dc in same st, dc in each of next 6 sts, 2 dc in last st, turn. *(10 dc)*

**Row 7:** Ch 3, dc in same st, 2 dc in next st, dc in each of next 6 sts, 2 dc in each of the last 2 sts, turn. *(14 dc)*

**Row 8:** Sl st in each of first 3 sts, sl st in next st, ch 3, dc in same st, dc in each of next 6 sts, 2 dc in next st leaving rem sts unworked, turn. *(10 dc)*

**Row 9:** Ch 3, dc in same st, dc in each of next 8 sts, 2 dc in last st, turn. *(12 dc)*

**Row 10:** Ch 3, dc in same st, 2 dc in next st, dc in each of next 8 sts, 2 dc in each of last 2 sts, turn. *(16 dc)*

**Row 11:** Ch 1, sl st in each of first 3 sts, sl st in next st, ch 3, dc in same st, dc in each of next 8 sts, 2 dc in next st leaving rem sts unworked, turn. *(12 dc)*

**Row 12:** Ch 3, dc in same st, dc in each of next 10 sts, 2 dc in next st, turn. *(14 dc)*

**Row 13:** Ch 3, dc in same st, dc in each of next 12 sts, 2 dc in last st, turn. *(16 dc)*

**Row 14:** (Ch 3, dc) in first st, 2 dc in next st, dc in each of next 12 sts, 2 dc in each of last 2 sts. Fasten off. *(20 dc)*

**Row 15:** For **trunk**, sk first 8 sts, join brown with sl st in next st, ch 3, dc in each of next 3 sts leaving rem sts unworked, turn. *(4 dc)*

**Row 16:** Ch 3, dc in each st across, turn. Fasten off.

**2nd Tree**

**Row 1:** Join green with sc in next marked ch sp on the right, turn. *(1 sc)*

**Row 2:** Ch 3 *(counts as first dc)*, 2 dc in same sc, turn. *(3 dc)*

**Rows 3–9:** Rep rows 3–9 of First Tree.

**Row 10:** Ch 3, dc in same st, 2 dc in next st, dc in each of next 8 sts, 2 dc in each of last 2 sts, tr in corresponding st on last Tree, turn. *(16 dc)*

**Rows 11–13:** Rep rows 11–13 of First Tree.

**Row 14:** Ch 3, dc in same st, 2 dc in next st, dc in each of next 12 sts, 2 dc in each of last 2 sts, sl st in corresponding st on last Tree, turn. Fasten off.

**Rows 15 & 16:** Rep rows 15 and 16 of First Tree.

Rep Trees across according to Chart.

**For top fill-in** between Trees on rnd 3 *(see red X on Chart)*, ◊with RS and top of Tree facing, join red with sc in first ch-3 sp on Motif after First Tree of 1 side, *ch 6, dtr in next ch-2 sp on Motif, ch 1, dc in end of row 4 on Tree, ch 2, dc in top of last dtr, ch 3, dc around last dc made, ch 4, dc in next point on Tree, ch 2, trtr around tr connecting Trees, ch 2, dc in next point on next Tree, ch 4, dc around corresponding dc on first side, [ch 3, dc in last dc] twice, dc in next point on Tree, ch 1, dtr in same ch-2 sp on Motif, ch 6, sc in next ch sp after picot◊**, ch 3, sl st around dc above Tree, ch 3, sc in next ch sp, ch 7, dtr over Motif joining, rep from * across top of Trees ending last rep at **. Fasten off.

Rep on each strip of Trees.

**Bottom of Trees**

**Row 1:** Working across bottom of Trees *(see pink dotted line on Chart)*, ◊with WS facing and red crochet cotton, yo 4 times, insert hook in bottom point of First Tree, yo, pull through, [yo, pull through 2 lps on hook] 5 times *(trtr completed)*, *ch 6, dc in top of trtr, ch 3, dc in ch-6 sp, ch 3, dc in last dc, sc in next dc on Tree Trunk, ch 3, sk next 2 sts, sc in next st, ch 6, dtr in ch sp between Trees, ch 5, dc in last dtr, dtr in same sp between Trees as last dtr, ch 6, sc in next dc on Tree Trunk, ch 3, sk next 2 sts, sc in next st, ch 3, dc in last sc, ch 6, dc in last dc**, (dtr, ch 5, dtr) between next 2 Trees, rep from * across, ending last rep at **, dtr in last point on Tree, turn.

**Row 2:** ◊(Sl st, sc, ch 1, dc, tr, ch 3, tr, dc, ch 1, sc) in first ch-6 sp, *(dc, ch 2, sc, ch 3, sc) in next ch sp, sc in next ch sp, dc in next ch sp, ch 6, (sc, picot) in next ch sp, ch 3, (sc, ch 1, 2 dc, ch 2, 2 dc, ch 1, sc) in next ch-5 sp, ch 3, (sc, picot) in next ch sp, ch 6, dc in next ch sp, sc in next ch sp, (sc, ch 3, sc, ch 2, dc) in next ch sp, (sc, ch 1, dc, tr, ch 3, tr, dc, ch 1, sc) in next ch sp◊**, ch 2, sc in next ch sp, ch 2, (sc, ch 1, dc, tr, ch 1) in next ch sp, sc in last ch-3 sp made, (ch 1, tr, dc, ch 1, sc) in same ch sp as last tr made, rep from * across ending last rep with **. Fasten off.

For Bottom of Trees and top fill-in between Trees for rnd 7, work between ◊ on Bottom of Trees and top fill-in between Trees for rnd 2.

**MOTIF I**

**Rnds 1–9:** Rep rnds 1–9 of Motif A on Center.

**Rnd 10:** Rep Side E between ◊ and ◊, rep Side B between *, rep Side A between *, (sc, ch 1, dc, tr, ch 3, tr, dc, ch 1, sc) in next ch sp, rep Side A between *, join with sl st in beg sc. Fasten off.

**MOTIF J**

**Rnds 1–9:** Rep rnds 1–9 of Motif A on Center.

**Rnd 10:** Rep Side C, rep Side E between ◊, rep Side A between *, join. Fasten off.

**EDGING**

**Rnd 1:** Working around outer edge, with green, join with dc in any corner ch-3 sp, ◊[ch 3, dc around last dc made, dc in same ch-3 sp] 4 times, *ch 3, 2 dc in next ch-2 sp, ch 3, sk next ch-3 sp, 2 dc in next ch-3 sp, ch 3, sk next ch sp and next picot, 2 dc in ch sp after next picot, ch 3, dc in next ch sp, [ch 3, dc around last dc made] 3 times, dc in same ch sp on Motif, ch 3, 2 dc in ch sp before next picot, ch 3, sk next ch sp, 2 dc in next ch sp, ch 3, sk next ch sp, 2 dc in next ch-2 sp, ch 3**, 2 dc in next joined ch sp, [ch 3, dc around last dc made] 3 times, 2 dc in next joined ch sp, rep from * across to next corner ch-3 sp, ending last rep at ** ◊◊, dc in next ch sp, rep from ◊ around ending last rep at ◊◊, join with sl st in top of first dc. Fasten off.

**Rnd 2:** Join red with sc in last ch-3 sp, ch 3, (sc, picot) in next ch sp, ch 3, (sc, picot) in next ch sp, ◊ch 5, sl st in 3rd ch from hook, ch 2, (sc, picot) in next ch sp, ch 3, (sc, picot) in next ch sp, ch 2, sc in next ch sp, ch 3, (sc, picot) in next ch sp, ch 4, (sc, picot) in next ch sp, ch 3, sc in next ch sp, ch 2, *[sc in next ch sp, picot, ch 3] twice, (sc, picot) in next ch sp, ch 2, sc in next ch sp, ch 3, (sc, picot) in next ch sp, ch 4, (sc, picot) in next ch sp, ch 3◊◊, sc in next ch sp, ch 2, rep from * across to first ch sp of next corner, (sc, picot) in next ch sp, ch 3, (sc, picot) in next ch sp, rep from ◊ around, ending last rep at ◊◊, join with sl st in beg sc. Fasten off. ■

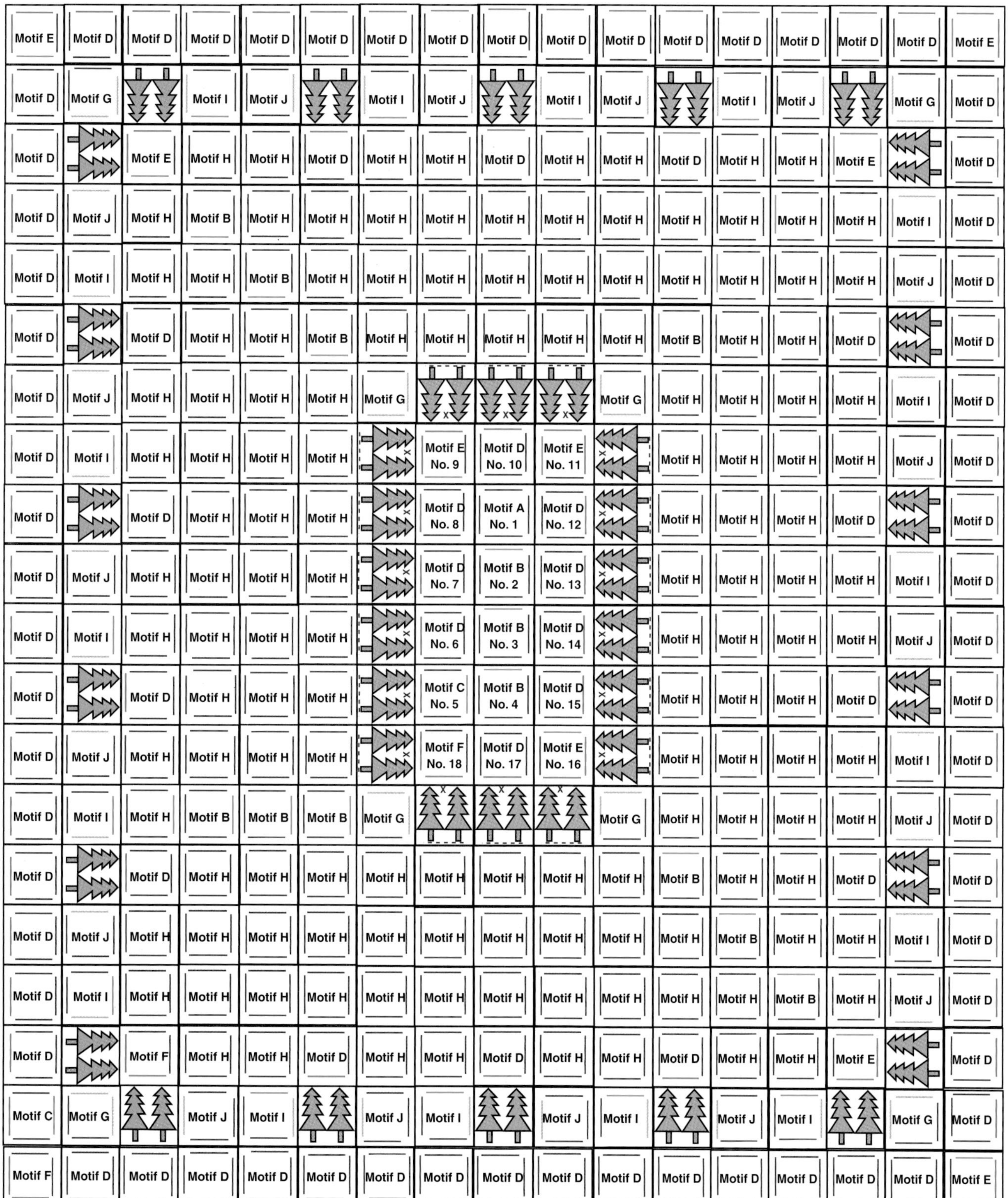

| Motif E | Motif D | Motif D | Motif D | Motif D | Motif D | Motif D | Motif D | Motif D | Motif D | Motif D | Motif D | Motif D | Motif D | Motif D | Motif D | Motif E |
|---|---|---|---|---|---|---|---|---|---|---|---|---|---|---|---|---|
| Motif D | Motif G | | Motif I | Motif J | | Motif I | Motif J | | Motif I | Motif J | | Motif I | Motif J | | Motif G | Motif D |
| Motif D | | Motif E | Motif H | Motif H | Motif D | Motif H | Motif H | Motif D | Motif H | Motif H | Motif D | Motif H | Motif H | Motif E | | Motif D |
| Motif D | Motif J | Motif H | Motif B | Motif H | Motif H | Motif H | Motif H | Motif H | Motif H | Motif H | Motif H | Motif H | Motif H | Motif H | Motif I | Motif D |
| Motif D | Motif I | Motif H | Motif H | Motif B | Motif H | Motif H | Motif H | Motif H | Motif H | Motif H | Motif H | Motif H | Motif H | Motif H | Motif J | Motif D |
| Motif D | | Motif D | Motif H | Motif H | Motif B | Motif H | Motif H | Motif H | Motif H | Motif H | Motif B | Motif H | Motif H | Motif D | | Motif D |
| Motif D | Motif J | Motif H | Motif H | Motif H | Motif H | Motif G | | | | Motif G | Motif H | Motif H | Motif H | Motif H | Motif I | Motif D |
| Motif D | Motif I | Motif H | Motif H | Motif H | Motif H | | Motif E No. 9 | Motif D No. 10 | Motif E No. 11 | | Motif H | Motif H | Motif H | Motif H | Motif J | Motif D |
| Motif D | | Motif D | Motif H | Motif H | Motif H | | Motif D No. 8 | Motif A No. 1 | Motif D No. 12 | | Motif H | Motif H | Motif H | Motif D | | Motif D |
| Motif D | Motif J | Motif H | Motif H | Motif H | Motif H | | Motif D No. 7 | Motif B No. 2 | Motif D No. 13 | | Motif H | Motif H | Motif H | Motif H | Motif I | Motif D |
| Motif D | Motif I | Motif H | Motif H | Motif H | Motif H | | Motif D No. 6 | Motif B No. 3 | Motif D No. 14 | | Motif H | Motif H | Motif H | Motif H | Motif J | Motif D |
| Motif D | | Motif D | Motif H | Motif H | Motif H | | Motif C No. 5 | Motif B No. 4 | Motif D No. 15 | | Motif H | Motif H | Motif H | Motif D | | Motif D |
| Motif D | Motif J | Motif H | Motif H | Motif H | Motif H | | Motif F No. 18 | Motif D No. 17 | Motif E No. 16 | | Motif H | Motif H | Motif H | Motif H | Motif I | Motif D |
| Motif D | Motif I | Motif H | Motif B | Motif B | Motif B | Motif G | | | | Motif G | Motif H | Motif H | Motif H | Motif H | Motif J | Motif D |
| Motif D | | Motif D | Motif H | Motif H | Motif H | Motif H | Motif H | Motif H | Motif H | Motif H | Motif B | Motif H | Motif H | Motif D | | Motif D |
| Motif D | Motif J | Motif H | Motif H | Motif H | Motif H | Motif H | Motif H | Motif H | Motif H | Motif H | Motif H | Motif B | Motif H | Motif H | Motif I | Motif D |
| Motif D | Motif I | Motif H | Motif H | Motif H | Motif H | Motif H | Motif H | Motif H | Motif H | Motif H | Motif H | Motif H | Motif B | Motif H | Motif J | Motif D |
| Motif D | | Motif F | Motif H | Motif H | Motif D | Motif H | Motif H | Motif D | Motif H | Motif H | Motif D | Motif H | Motif H | Motif E | | Motif D |
| Motif C | Motif G | | Motif J | Motif I | | Motif J | Motif I | | Motif J | Motif I | | Motif J | Motif I | | Motif G | Motif D |
| Motif F | Motif D | Motif D | Motif D | Motif D | Motif D | Motif D | Motif D | Motif D | Motif D | Motif D | Motif D | Motif D | Motif D | Motif D | Motif D | Motif E |

**O Tannenbaum Chart**

# Snowflakes & Snowmen

DESIGN BY CAROL DECKER

Cheerful little scarf-adorned snowmen create a fun, festive border around a center panel of lacy snowflakes. This colorful, eye-catching table runner is sure to capture everyone's holiday fancy!

EXPERIENCED

**FINISHED SIZE**
22½ x 44 inches

**MATERIALS**
Royale Classic Crochet size 10 crochet cotton (350 yds per ball):
- 4 balls #487 dark royal
- 2 balls #201 white
- 1 ball #12 black

Aunt Lydia's Classic Crochet size 10 crochet cotton:
- 100 yds #431 pumpkin

Royale Fine Crochet size 20 crochet cotton (400 yds per ball):
- 1 ball #201 white

Coats Opera size 20 crochet cotton (442 yds per ball):
- 10 yds each of assorted colors for scarf

Sizes 8/1.50mm, 7/1.65mm and 6/1.80mm steel crochet hooks or size needed to obtain gauge
Embroidery needle
Beads:
- 108 black 4mm
- 54 black 6mm

Stitch markers

**GAUGE**
**With size 8 hook and size 20 crochet cotton:** Each Snowflake is 1¾ inches across

**PATTERN NOTE**
Snowmen are optional.

**SPECIAL STITCHES**
**Picot:** Ch 3, sl st in top of last st made.

**Double crochet cluster (dc cl):** Holding back last lp of each st on hook, 2 dc in next st or ch sp, yo, pull through all lps on hook.

**Treble crochet cluster (tr cl):** Holding back last lp of each st on hook, 2 tr in next st or ch sp, yo, pull through all lps on hook.

**Join with double crochet (join with dc):** Yo, insert hook in st or ch sp, yo, pull lp through, yo, complete as dc

## INSTRUCTIONS

**SNOWMEN**
Make 18.

**LOWER BODY**
**Rnd 1:** Thread 1 black 6mm bead on white size 10 crochet cotton, with size 6 hook, ch 4, sl st in first ch to form ring, ch 1, 6 sc in ring, **do not join rnds**. Mark first st. *(6 sc)*

**Rnd 2:** 2 sc in each st around. *(12 sc)*

**Rnd 3:** [2 sc in next st, sc in next st] around. *(18 sc)*

**Rnd 4:** Sc in each of next 4 sts, 2 sc in next st, sc in each of next 2 sts, 2 sc in next st, sc in each of next 2 sts, pull up bead, [sc in each of next 2 sts, 2 sc in next st] twice, sc in each of last 2 sts. *(22 sc)*

**Rnd 5:** [Sc in each of next 3 sts, 2 sc in next st, sc in next st, 2 sc in next st, sc in each of next 2 sts, 2 sc in next st, sc in next st, 2 sc in next st] twice. *(30 sc)*

**Rnd 6:** Sc in each of next 5 sts, 2 sc in next st, sc in each of next 6 sts, 2 sc in next st, sc in each of next 7 sts, 2 sc in next st, sc in each of next 6 sts, 2 sc in next st, sc in each of next 2 sts. *(34 sc)*

**Rnd 7:** *Sc in each of next 5 sts, [2

sc in next st, sc in each of next 2 sts] 3 times, rep from *. *(42 sc)*

**Rnd 8:** Sc in each of next 8 sts, 2 sc in next st, sc in each of next 6 sts, 2 sc in next st, sc in each of next 13 sts, 2 sc in next st, sc in each of next 6 sts, 2 sc in next st, sc in each of next 5 sts. *(46 sc)*

**Rnd 9:** Sc in each of next 7 sts, 2 sc in next st, sc in each of next 3 sts, 2 sc in next st, sc in each of next 2 sts, 2 sc in next st, sc in each of next 3 sts, 2 sc in next st, sc in each of next 4 sts, sc in each of next 7 sts, 2 sc in next st, sc in each of next 3 sts, 2 sc in next st, sc in each of next 2 sts, 2 sc in next st, sc in each of next 3 sts, 2 sc in next st, sc in each of next 3 st, join with sl st in first sc. Fasten off.

#### MIDDLE BODY

**Rnd 1:** Thread 2 black 6mm beads on white size 10 crochet cotton, with size 6 hook, ch 4, sl st in first ch to form ring, ch 1, 6 sc in ring, **do not join rnds.** Mark first st. *(6 sc)*

**Rnd 2:** Pull up 1 bead, 2 sc in each st around. *(12 sc)*

**Rnd 3:** [2 sc in next st, sc in next st] around. *(18 sc)*

**Rnd 4:** Sc in each of next 4 sts, 2 sc in next st, sc in each of next 2 sts, 2 sc in next st, sc in each of next 2 sts, pull up bead, [sc in each of next 2 sts, 2 sc in next st] twice, sc in each of next 2 sts. *(22 sc)*

**Rnd 5:** [Sc in each of next 3 sts, 2 sc in next st, sc in next st, 2 sc in next st, sc in each of next 2 sts, 2 sc in next st, sc in next st, 2 sc in next st] twice. *(30 sc)*

**Rnd 6:** Sc in each of next 5 sts, 2 sc in next st, sc in each of next 6 sts, 2 sc in next st, sc in each of next 7 sts, 2 sc in next st, sc in each of next 6 sts, 2 sc in next st, sc in each of next 2 sts. *(34 sc)*

**Rnd 7:** Sc in each of next 5 sts, [2 sc in next st, sc in each of next 2 sts] 4 times, mark center 5 sts on rnd 9 on bead end of Lower Body for joining sts, drop lp from hook, insert hook in first of marked sts on Lower Body and pull lp through, sc in next st on Middle Body, [drop lp from hook, insert hook in next marked st, pull lp through, hdc in next st on Middle Body] 5 times, sc in next st on Middle Body, [2 sc in next st, sc in each of next 2 sts] 3 times, 2 sc in next st, sc in next st, join with sl st in beg sc. Fasten off.

#### HEAD

**Rnd 1:** Thread 6 black 4mm beads on white size 10 crochet cotton, with size 6 hook, ch 4, sl st in first ch to form ring, ch 1, 6 sc in ring, **do not join rnds.** Mark first st. *(6 sc)*

**Rnd 2:** 2 sc in each st around. *(12 sc)*

**Rnd 3:** 2 sc in next st, sc in next st, pull up bead, [2 sc in next st, sc in next st] 4 times, 2 sc in next st, pull up bead, sc in last st. *(18 sts)*

**Rnd 4:** Sc in each of next 4 sts, 2 sc in next st, sc in each of next 3 sts, pull up bead, sc in same st as last sc, sc in next st, [sc in next st, pull up bead, sc in next st] 3 times, sc in same st as last sc, sc in each of next 2 sc, 2 sc in next st, sc in next st. *(22 sc)*

**Rnd 5:** [Sc in each of next 3 sts, 2 sc in next st, sc in next st, 2 sc in next st, sc in each of next 2 sts, 2 sc in next st, sc in next st, 2 sc in next st] twice. *(30 sc)*

**Rnd 6:** Sc in each of next 5 sts, 2 sc in next st, sc in each of next 6 sts, 2 sc in next st, sc in each of next 2 sts, hdc in next st, mark 3 sts of rnd 7 on Middle Body for joining, drop lp from hook, insert hook in first marked st, pull lp through, hdc in next st on Head, [drop lp from hook, insert hook in next marked st, pull lp through, hdc in next st on Head] twice, sc in each of next 2 sts on Head, 2 sc in next st, sc in each of next 6 sts, 2 sc in next st, sc in next st, join with sl st in beg sc. Fasten off.

#### SCARF

**Row 1:** With size 7 hook and size 20 crochet cotton in desired color, ch 5, working in **front lps** only *(see Stitch Guide)*, hdc in 3rd ch from hook and in each ch across **changing color** *(see Stitch Guide)* in last st made to next color, turn. *(4 hdc)*

**Rows 2–6:** Working over dropped color, ch 2, hdc in each st across changing color in last st made, turn.

**Row 7:** Ch 2, **hdc dec** *(see Stitch Guide)* in next 2 sts, hdc in last st changing color in last st, turn. *(3 hdc)*

**Rows 8–15:** Rep row 2.

**Row 16:** Ch 2, 2 hdc in next st, hdc in each st across changing color in last st, turn. *(4 hdc)*

**Rows 17–19:** Rep row 2. At end of last row, fasten off.

#### FRINGE

Cut 20 strands of matching colors each 2 inches in length, with 2 strands held tog, fold in half, insert hook in st, pull fold through, pull all ends through fold, tighten.

Attach Fringe in each st across both short ends of Scarf. Trim ends.

#### NOSE

**Row 1:** With size 6 hook and pumpkin crochet cotton, ch 2, sc in 2nd ch from hook, turn. *(1 sc)*

**Rows 2–4:** Ch 1, sc in st, turn.

**Row 5:** Ch 1, Fasten off.

Sew Nose to Head between beads of eyes and mouth as shown in photo.

#### HAT

**Row 1:** With size 6 hook and black, ch 2, sl st in each of center 8 sts across top of Head, turn. *(8 sl sts, 2 chs)*

**Row 2:** Ch 3, sc in 2nd ch from hook and in each ch and st across, turn. *(12 sc)*

**Row 3:** Ch 1, sc in each st across, turn.

**Row 4:** Sl st in each of first 2 sts, ch 1, sc in each of next 8 sts leaving rem sts unworked, turn. *(8 sc)*

**Rows 5 & 6:** Ch 1, 2 sc in first st, sc in each st across, turn. *(9 sc, 10 sc)*

**Row 7:** Ch 1, sc in each st across, turn. Fasten off.

Wrap and tack Scarf around neck.

**SNOWFLAKE**

**MOTIF A**

**Rnd 1:** With size 8 hook and white size 20 crochet cotton, ch 5, sl st in first ch to form ring, ch 9 *(counts as dc and ch 6)*, [dc in ring, ch 6] 5 times, join with sl st in 3rd ch of ch-9. *(6 dc, 6 ch-6 sps)*

**Rnd 2:** (Sl st, ch 3, dc, ch 4, sc, ch 4, 2 dc) in first ch sp, (2 dc, ch 4, sc, ch 4, 2 dc) in each ch sp around, join with sl st in 3rd ch of beg ch 3. *(30 sts, 12 ch sps)*

**Rnd 3:** Sl st in next st, (sl st, sc, **picot**—*see Special Stitches*, ch 5) in next ch-4 sp, **tr dec** *(see Stitch Guide)* in same ch sp worked in and in next ch-4 sp, (picot, ch 5, sc, picot) in same ch-4 sp worked in, [(sc, picot, ch 5) in next ch-4 sp, tr dec in same ch sp worked in and in next ch-4 sp, (picot, ch 5, sc, picot) in same ch-4 sp worked in] around, join with sl st in beg sc. Fasten off. *(18 sts, 12 ch sps)*

**Rnd 4:** With size 7 hook, **join** dark royal **with dc** *(see Special Stitches)* in first ch-5 sp, dc in same ch-5 sp, ch 7, 2 dc in next ch-5 sp, ch 5, [2 dc in next ch-5 sp, ch 7, 2 dc in next ch sp, ch 5] around, join with sl st in top of first dc. *(24 dc, 12 ch sps)*

**Rnd 5:** Sl st in next st, (sl st, ch 3, dc, ch 2, **tr cl**—*see Special Stitches*, ch 3, 2 dc) in first ch-7 sp, ch 4, (sc, picot) in next ch-5 sp, [ch 4, (2 dc, ch 2, tr cl, ch 3, 2 dc) in next ch-7 sp, ch 4, (sc, picot) in next ch-5 sp] around, join with sl st in 3rd ch of beg ch-3. Fasten off.

**MOTIF B**

**Rnds 1–4:** Rep rnds 1–4 of Motif A.

**Rnd 5:** Sl st in next st, (ch 3, dc, ch 2, tr cl) in first ch-7 sp, ch 1, dc in tr cl on corresponding Motif, sl st in top of last tr cl made on this Motif, ch 2, 2 dc in same ch-7 sp on this Motif, ch 1, 2 dc in next ch-4 sp on corresponding Motif, ch 1, (sc, picot) in next ch-5 sp on this Motif, ch 1, 2 dc in next ch-4 sp on corresponding Motif, ch 1, (2 dc, ch 2, tr cl) in next ch-7 sp, ch 1, dc in tr cl on corresponding Motif, ch 1, sl st in top of last tr cl made on this Motif, ch 2, 2 dc in same ch-7 sp, ch 4, (sc, picot) in next ch-5 sp, [ch 4, (2 dc, ch 2, tr cl, ch 3, 2 dc) in next ch-7 sp, ch 4, (sc, picot) in next ch-5 sp] around, join with sl st in 3rd ch of beg ch-3. Fasten off.

**MOTIF C**

**Rnds 1–4:** Rep rnds 1–4 of Motif A.

**Rnd 5:** Sl st in next st, (ch 3, dc, ch 2, tr cl) in first ch-7 sp, ch 1, dc in tr cl on corresponding Motif, sl st in top of last tr cl made on this Motif, ch 2, 2 dc in same ch-7 sp on this Motif, *ch 1, 2 dc in next ch-4 sp on corresponding Motif, ch 1, (sc, picot) in next ch-5 sp on this Motif, ch 1, 2 dc in next ch-4 sp on corresponding Motif, ch 1, [(2 dc, ch 2, tr cl) in next ch-7 sp, ch 1, dc in tr cl on corresponding Motif, ch 1, sl st in top of last tr cl made on this Motif, ch 2, 2 dc in same ch-7 sp, rep from *, ch 4, (sc, picot) in next ch-5 sp, [ch 4, (2 dc, ch 2, tr cl, ch 3, 2 dc) in next ch-7 sp, ch 4, (sc, picot) in next ch-5 sp] around, join with sl st in 3rd ch of beg ch-3. Fasten off.

**MOTIF D**

**Rnds 1–4:** Rep rnds 1–4 of Motif A.

**Rnd 5:** Sl st in next st, (ch 3, dc, ch 2, tr cl) in first ch-7 sp, ch 1, dc in tr cl on corresponding Motif, sl st in top of last tr cl made on this Motif, ch 2, 2 dc in same ch-7 sp on this Motif, *ch 1, 2 dc in next ch-4 sp on corresponding Motif, ch 1, (sc, picot) in next ch-5 sp on this Motif, ch 1, 2 dc in next ch-4 sp on corresponding Motif, ch 1, (2 dc, ch 2, tr cl) in next ch-7 sp, ch 1, dc in tr cl on corresponding Motif, ch 1, sl st in top of last tr cl made on this Motif, ch 2, 2 dc in same ch-7 sp, rep from * twice, ch 4, (sc, picot) in next ch-5 sp, [ch 4, (2 dc, ch 2, tr cl, ch 3, 2 dc) in next ch-7 sp, ch 4, (sc, picot) in next ch-5 sp] around, join with sl st in 3rd ch of beg ch-3. Fasten off.

Work and join Motifs according to Assembly Diagram.

**FILL-IN MOTIF**

**Row 1:** With size 7 hook, join dark royal with sc in ch-2 sp before joining *(see assembly diagram)*, ch 5, 2 dc in next ch-4 sp, ch 6, 2 dc in next ch-4 sp, ch 5, sc in next ch sp after joining, ch 3, sc in next ch-4 sp, turn.

**Row 2:** Ch 5, (sc, picot) in ch-5 sp, ch 3, (2 dc, ch 2, tr cl, ch 2, 2 dc) in ch-6 sp, ch 3, (sc, picot) in ch-5 sp, ch 5, sc in next ch-4 sp on next Motif, ch 2, dc in next ch-4 sp, turn.

**Row 3:** Ch 3, (**dc cl**—*see Special Stitches*, ch 3, dc cl) in ch-5 sp, ch 5, sc in next ch-2 sp, ch 2, sc in next ch-2 sp, ch 5, (dc cl, ch 3, dc cl) in ch-5 sp, ch 2, tr in next ch-4 sp on Motif, picot, turn.

**Row 4:** Ch 6, (sc, ch 3, 2 dc) in ch-5 sp, ch 1, sk next ch sp, (2 dc, ch 3, sc) in next ch-5 sp, ch 6, (sc, picot) in next ch sp, ch 3, dc in next ch sp on next Motif, turn.

**Row 5:** Ch 3, (2 dc, ch 2, 2 tr, ch 2, 2 dc) in ch-6 sp, ch 3, sc in next ch-1 sp, ch 3, (2 dc, ch 2, 2 tr, ch 2, 2 dc) in next ch-6 sp, ch 3, sc around tr, ch 3, sc in next ch-2 sp on Motif. Fasten off.

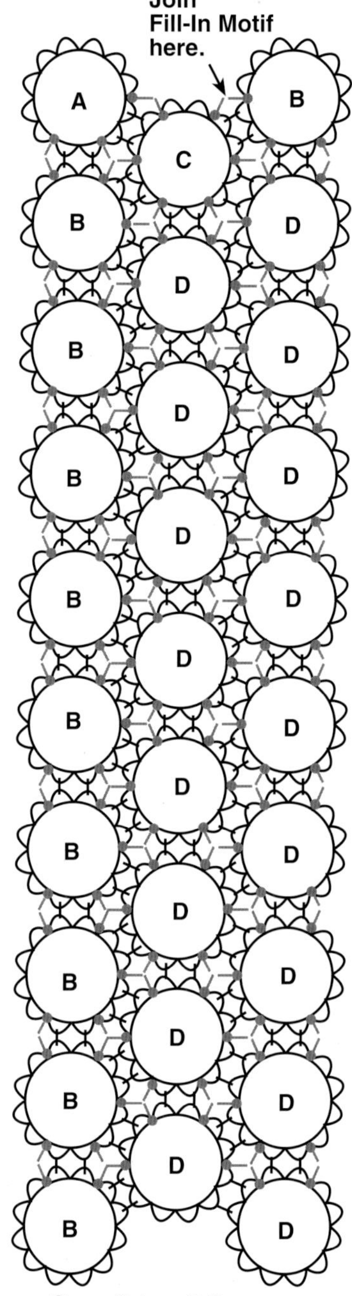


Snowflakes & Snowmen Runner Assembly Diagram

Work Fill-in Motif on other end of Motifs, at end of last row, **do not fasten off.**

**BORDER**

**Rnd 1:** Working around outer edge, picot, ch 3, sc in next ch-3 sp, ch 3, [(dc cl, ch 3, dc cl) in next ch-4 sp, ch 3] twice, sc in next ch-2 sp, ch 2, sc in next ch-3 sp, ch 3, [(dc cl, ch 3, dc cl) in next ch-4 sp, ch 3] twice, mark first ch-3 sp between cls in this rep for corner, sc in next ch-2 sp, ch 2, sc in next ch-3 sp, ch 3, (dc cl, ch 3, dc cl) in next ch-4 sp, ch 3, *(sc, picot) in next ch sp, sl st in next ch, sl st in each of next 2 dc, sl st in next ch sp, ch 1, tr in next unworked ch-2 sp on next Motif, ch 2, dc in sc of last-made picot, (dc, ch 2, tr cl, ch 2, 2 dc) in next tr sp just made, ch 2, (sc, picot) in next ch sp, ch 3, (dc cl, ch 3, dc cl) in next ch-4 sp, ch 3, sc in next ch-2 sp, ch 2, sc in next ch-3 sp, ch 3, (dc cl, ch 3, dc cl) in next ch-4 sp, ch 3*, rep between * 8 times to next corner, **(dc cl, ch 3, dc cl) in next ch-4 sp, ch 3, sc in next ch sp, ch 2, sc in next ch sp, ch 3, [(dc cl, ch 3, dc cl) in next ch-4 sp, ch 3] twice, sc in next ch sp, ch 2, (sc, picot) in next ch sp, ch 3, dc cl around joining, ch 3, sc in next ch sp, ch 2, sc in next ch sp, [ch 3, dc cl in next ch sp] twice, ch 3, sc in next ch sp, ch 2, sc in next ch sp, ch 3, sk next ch sp, dc cl in next ch sp, ch 3**, (sc, picot) in next ch sp, ch 2, sc in next ch sp, ch 3, [(dc cl, ch 3, dc cl) in next ch-4 sp, ch 3] twice, sc in next ch sp, ch 2, sc in next ch sp, ch 3, [(dc cl, ch 3, dc cl) in next ch-4 sp, ch 3] twice, sc in next ch sp, ch 2, sc in next ch sp, ch 3, rep between * 9 times to next corner, rep between **, join with sl st in sc of beg picot. Fasten off.

**Rnd 2:** Join with dc in marked corner ch sp, ch 5, sk next ch sp, dc in same corner ch sp, ch 5, sk next ch-3 sp, 2 dc in next ch-3 sp, ch 5, 2 sc in next ch sp, ch 5, sk next ch-3 sp, 2 dc in next ch-3 sp, sk next 2 ch sps, *ch 5, 2 tr in next ch-2 sp, ch 5, 2 tr in next ch sp, ch 5, sk next 2 ch sps, 2 dc in next ch sp between cls, ch 5, sk next ch sp, 2 sc in next ch sp, ch 5, sk next ch sp, 2 dc in next sp between cls*, rep between * 8 times, **ch 5, sk next ch sp, (dc, ch 5, dc) in next ch sp between cls, [ch 5, sk next ch sp, 2 sc in next ch sp between cls] twice, [ch 5, sk next ch sp, 2 dc in next ch sp] 3 times, [ch 5, sk next ch sp, 2 tr in next ch sp] twice, [ch 5, sk next ch sp, 2 dc in next ch sp] 3 times, [ch 5, sk next ch sp, 2 sc in next ch sp] twice**, ch 5, sk next ch sp, (dc ch 5, dc) in next ch sp between cls for corner, ch 5, sk next ch sp, 2 dc in next ch sp, ch 5, 2 sc in next ch sp, ch 5, sk next ch sp, 2 dc in next ch sp, rep between * 9 times, rep between **, join with dtr in first dc forming last ch sp.

**Rnd 3:** Ch 5, (tr, ch 1) 3 times in last ch sp made, tr in same ch sp, ch 3, (sc, picot) in corner ch sp, ch 3, *({tr, ch 1} 4 times, tr) in next ch sp, ch 3, (sc, picot) in next ch sp**, ch 3, rep from * around, ending last rep at **, join with dc in 4th ch of beg ch-5.

**Rnd 4:** Ch 2, dc in next ch-1 sp, *[ch 3, sc in next ch-1 sp] twice, ch 3, **dc dec** *(see Stitch Guide)* in next 2 ch sps**, ch 4 *(work ch 5 in corners)*, dc dec in next 2 ch sps, rep from * around, ending last rep at **, join with tr in beg dc forming last ch sp.

**Rnd 5:** (Sl st, ch 3, 2 dc) in last ch sp made, ch 3, sc in next ch sp, (sc, ch 3, sc) in next ch sp between sc, sc in next ch sp, **ch 3, (2 dc, ch 5, 2 dc) in corner ch-5 sp**, *ch 3, sc in next ch sp, (sc, ch 3, sc) in next ch sp, sc in next ch sp, ch 3, 3 dc in next ch sp*, rep between * around with rep between ** for each corner, join with dc in top of beg ch-3 forming last ch sp.

**Rnd 6:** (Sl st, ch 3, dc) in last ch sp made, [ch 5, 2 dc in next ch sp] around with (ch 5, dc, ch 5, dc) in each corner ch sp, ch 5, join with sl st in 3rd ch of beg ch-3.

**Rnd 7:** Sl st in next st, (sl st, ch 5, {tr, ch 1} 3 times, tr) in next ch sp, ch 3, *(sc, picot) in next ch sp**, ch 3, ({tr, ch 1} 4 times, tr) in next ch sp, ch 3, rep from * around having picot in corner ch sp and ending last rep at **, join with sl st in 4th ch of ch-5.

**Rnds 8–27:** Rep rnds 4–7 consecutively.

**Rnds 28 & 29:** Rep rnds 4 and 5.

**Rnd 30:** Sl st in next st, (sl st, ch 5, {tr, ch 1} 4 times, tr) in next ch sp, *ch 2, (sc, picot) in next ch sp, ch 2, **({tr, ch 1} 5 times, tr) in next ch sp*, rep between * across to corner, ch 3, sc in corner ch sp, ch 3, beg rep again at ** and continue across to next corner and work as established around, ch 3, (sc, picot) in next ch sp, ch 3, join with sl st in 4th ch of first ch-5. Fasten off.

**TRIM**

**Rnd 31:** With size 7 hook, join white size 10 crochet cotton with sc in first ch-1 sp of group, picot, *ch 1, (sc, picot) in next ch-1 sp*, rep between * 3 times, **ch 4, ◊(sc, picot) in next ch-1 sp, rep between * 4 times**, rep between ** to corner, ch 3, (sc, picot) in corner sc, ch 3, beg rep again at ◊ and continue across to next corner and work as established around, ch 4, join with sl st in beg sc. Fasten off.

Sew Snowmen to Runner, 7 on each long side and 2 on each short end. ■

# Peppermint Stripes

DESIGN BY MARY BECKER

Narrow stripes of red and green worked together bring to mind a favorite confection of Christmas celebrations. Creamy panels accented with delicate bobbles set them off to perfection.

**FINISHED SIZE**
48 x 60 inches, excluding Fringe

**MATERIALS**
Bernat Super Value medium (worsted) weight yarn (8 oz/445 yds/225g per skein):
- 5 skeins #07414 natural
- 1 skein each #07513 scarlet and #07506 hunter green

Size I/9/5.5mm crochet hook or size needed to obtain gauge

**GAUGE**
3 dc = 1 inch

**SPECIAL STITCHES**
**Extended sc (esc):** Pull up lp in indicated st, yo, pull through 1 lp on hook, yo, pull through both lps on hook.

**Mini bobble:** Pull up lp in indicated st, [yo, pull through 1 lp] 4 times, yo, pull through both lps on hook.

## INSTRUCTIONS

**THROW**
**Row 1 (RS):** With natural, ch 181, dc in 4th ch from hook *(first 3 chs count as first dc)* and in each ch across, turn. *(179 dc)*

**Row 2:** Working in **back lps** *(see Stitch Guide)* only this row, ch 1, sc in each st across, turn.

**Row 3:** Working in rem lps of row 1, ch 3 *(counts as first dc)*, dc in each st across, turn.

**Row 4:** Ch 1, sc in back lp of first st, [sc in **front lp** *(see Stitch Guide)* of next st, sc in back lp of next st] across, turn.

**Row 5:** Ch 1, sc in each of first 3 sts, [**mini bobble** *(see Special Stitches)* in next st, sc in each of next 3 sts] across, turn.

**Row 6:** Rep row 4.

**Row 7:** Ch 3, dc in each st across, turn.

**Row 8:** Rep row 2.

**Row 9:** Rep row 3.

**Row 10:** Rep row 7, turn. Fasten off.

**Row 11:** With RS facing, join scarlet with sc in first st, sc in each of next 2 sts, [sk next 2 sts, (tr, dc, ch 1, dc, tr) in next st, sk next 2 sts, sc in each of next 3 sts] across, turn. Fasten off.

**Row 12:** With WS facing, join hunter green with sl st in first st, ch 3, dc in each of next 2 sts, [ch 1, (**esc**—*see Special Stitches*, sc, esc) in next ch-1 sp, ch 1, sk next dc and next tr, dc in each of next 3 sc] across, turn. Fasten off.

**Row 13:** With RS facing, join scarlet with sc in first st, ch 1, [(esc, sc, esc) in next ch-1 sp, ch 1] across, ending with sc in last st, turn. Fasten off.

**Row 14:** With WS facing, join natural with sl st in first st, ch 3, dc in each st across, being sure to insert hook under 2 top lps of each ch-1 and not into ch-1 sp, turn.

**Row 15:** Rep row 7, turn.

**Rows 16–23:** Rep rows 2–9.

**Rows 24–121:** Rep rows 10–23 consecutively 7 times. At end of last row, fasten off.

**FRINGE**
Cut 5 strands of natural each 18 inches in length, fold in half. Pull fold through st, pull ends through fold. Pull to tighten.

Attach Fringe 3 inches apart on each short end. Trim ends. ■

# Chapeaus

DESIGN BY EDNA HOWELL

Remember how excited you were to get a new bonnet each spring and how hard it was to pick just the right one? Now you can stitch a bonnet in every color—and you won't have to wait for spring!

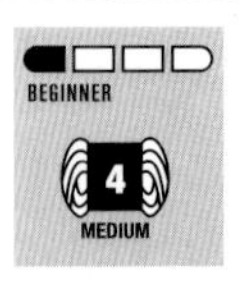


**FINISHED SIZE**
55 x 71 inches

**MATERIALS**
Medium (worsted) weight yarn:
40½ oz/2,025 yds/1,148g black
24 oz/1,200 yds/680g assorted scrap colors
Size H/8/5mm crochet hook or size needed to obtain gauge
Yarn needle
Sewing needle
Black sewing thread

**GAUGE**
7 sc = 2 inches; 7 dc = 2 inches

Motif = 7½ inches square

**SPECIAL STITCHES**
**Shell:** (Hdc, 3 dc, hdc) in indicated st.

**Beginning shell (beg shell):** Ch 2 *(counts as first hdc)*, (3 dc, hdc) in same st as beg ch-2.

**Picot:** Ch 3, sc in 3rd ch from hook.

## INSTRUCTIONS

**MOTIF**
Make 63.

**Rnd 1 (RS):** Beg at crown with first scrap color, ch 2, 6 sc in 2nd ch from hook, **do not join rnds**. *(6 sc)*

**Rnd 2:** 2 sc in each sc around. *(12 sc)*

**Rnd 3:** [Sc in next sc, 2 sc in next sc] 6 times. *(18 sc)*

**Rnd 4:** [Sc in each of next 2 sc, 2 sc in next sc] around. *(24 sc)*

**Rnd 5:** Sc in each of next 23 sc, join with sl st in beg sc. Fasten off.

**TIES**
**Rnd 6:** With 2nd scrap color, ch 25, join ch to any sc on crown of hat with a sc, sc in each of next 23 sts, ch 25. Fasten off.

**BRIM**
**Rnd 7:** Join first scrap color with a sl st in first sc of rnd 6, ch 5 *(counts as first dc and ch 2)*, dc in same st, sk next sc, [(dc, ch 2, dc) in next sc, sk next sc] 11 times, make sure Ties are on RS of Motif, join with sl st in 3rd ch of beg ch-5.

**Rnd 8:** Sl st into ch-2 sp, **beg shell** *(see Special Stitches)* in same ch-2 sp, ch 1, [**shell** *(see Special Stitches)* in next ch-2 sp, ch 1] 11 times, join with sl st in 2nd ch of beg ch-2. Fasten off.

**Rnd 9:** Sk next 4 shells on hat Brim after joining of rnd 8, sk next shell, join black with sl st in next ch-1 sp, ch 5 *(counts as first tr and ch-1)*, tr in same st *(for corner)*, *[ch 5, hdc in next ch-1 sp] twice, ch 5**, (tr, ch 1, tr) in next ch-1 sp *(for corner)*, rep from * around, ending last rep at **, join with sl st in 4th ch of beg ch-5.

**Rnd 10:** Sl st into ch-1 sp, ch 3 *(counts as first dc)*, (2 dc, ch 3, 3 dc) in same ch-1 sp, *[4 dc in each of next 3 ch-5 sps**, (3 dc, ch 3, 3 dc) in next corner ch-1 sp, rep from * around, ending last rep at **, join with sl st in 3rd ch of beg ch-3. *(72 dc)*

**Rnd 11:** Ch 3, dc in each of next 2 dc, *(3 dc, ch 2, 3 dc) in next ch-3 sp**, dc in each of next 18 dc, rep from * around, ending last rep at **, dc in each of last 15 dc, join with sl st in 3rd ch of ch-3. *(96 dc)*

**Rnd 12:** Ch 1, sc in each of first 6 sc, *3 sc in next corner ch-2 sp**, sc in each of next 24 sts, rep from * around, ending last rep at **, sc in each of last 18 sts, join with sl st in beg sc. Fasten off. *(108 sc)*

**BOWS**
Tie left Tie over right Tie, then make Bow approximately 2½ inches wide. Adjust lengths of the Ties to about 1½ inches.

With sewing needle and thread, sew ends of the Ties to Motif between rnds 10 and 11, directly

under Bow, approximately 1¼ inches apart.

**ASSEMBLY**

With black, making sure all hats are placed in the same direction and working through **back lps** *(see Stitch Guide)* only, beg in center sc of first corner and ending in center sc of next corner, whipstitch Motifs tog to form 7 vertical strips of 9 Motifs each. Whipstitch strips tog in same manner.

**BORDER**

**Rnd 1:** Join black with sl st in center corner sc of Motif on upper right side of throw, (ch 3, 2 dc) in same st, *dc in each of next 194 sts, 3 dc in center st of next corner, dc in each of next 250 sts*, 3 dc in center st of next corner, rep between *, join with sl st in 3rd ch of beg ch-3. *(900 dc)*

**Rnd 2:** Ch 1, sc in first st, **picot** *(see Special Stitches)*, sk next dc, [sc in next dc, picot, sk next dc] around, join with sl st in beg sc. Fasten off. ■

# Primrose Path

DESIGN BY DOT DRAKE

Pastel primroses in cornflower blue and soft yellow with spring green leaves adorn this lovely lace doily. Appealing colors and a unique shape make it a beautiful accent for a dainty bedroom.

EXPERIENCED

**FINISHED SIZE**
15 inches square

**MATERIALS**
Size 10 crochet cotton:
150 yds each white and mint green
50 yds each blue and yellow
Size 7/1.65mm steel crochet hook or size needed to obtain gauge

**GAUGE**
Rnds 1–3 = 1¾ inches across

**SPECIAL STITCHES**
**Join:** Ch 1, sc in corresponding ch sp on other Motif, ch 1.

**3-double crochet cluster (3-dc cl):** Holding back last lp of each st, 3 dc in ch sp indicated, yo, pull through all lps on hook.

**4-double crochet cluster (4-dc cl):** Holding back last lp of each st, 4 dc in ch sp indicated, yo, pull through all lps on hook.

**Picot:** Ch 3, sl st in top of last st made.

## INSTRUCTIONS

**FLOWER MOTIF**
**Rnd 1:** With white, ch 7, sl st in first ch to form ring, ch 1, 16 sc in ring, join with sl st in beg sc. *(16 sc)*

**Rnd 2:** Ch 8 *(counts as first dc and ch-5 sp)*, sk next 3 sts, [dc in next st, ch 5, sk next 3 sts] around, join with sl st in 3rd ch of beg ch-8. Fasten off. *(4 ch sps)*

**Rnd 3:** Join blue with sc in any ch sp, (hdc, 3 dc, sc, 3 dc, hdc, sc) in same ch sp, [(sc, hdc, 3 dc, sc, 3 dc, hdc, sc) in each ch sp] around, join with sl st in **back strands of beg sc** *(see illustration)*. *(4 petals)*

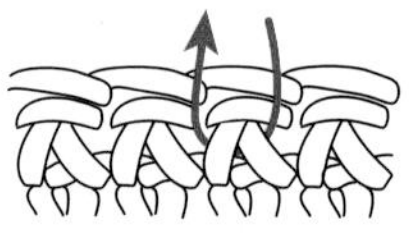

Back strands of sc, shown from back of sts

**Rnd 4:** Working behind petals, ch 6, [sc in back strands of first sc on next petal, ch 6] around, join with sl st in first ch of beg ch-6. *(4 ch sps)*

**Rnd 5:** Ch 1, [(sc, ch 5, 9 dtr, ch 5, sc) in each ch sp] around, join with sl st in beg sc. Fasten off. *(4 petals)*

**Rnd 6:** Join white with sc in first ch-5 sp of first petal, 5 sc in same sp, *sc in each of next 3 sts, (sc, ch 3, sc) in each of next 3 sts, sc in each of next 3 sts, 6 sc in next ch-5 sp**, 6 sc in next ch-5 sp of next petal, rep from * around, ending last rep at **, join with sl st in beg sc. Fasten off. *(24 sc on each petal)*

**Rnd 7:** Working behind petals, join green with sc in base of center dtr of any 9-dtr group on rnd 5, ch 7, [sc in base of center dtr of next 9-dtr group on rnd 5, ch 7] around, join with sl st in beg sc. *(4 ch sps)*

**Rnd 8:** Ch 1, (4 sc, ch 13, 4 sc) in each of first 3 ch sps, 9 sc in last ch sp, join with sl st in beg sc. *(33 sc, 3 ch-13 sps)*

**Row 9:** Now working in rows, sl st in each of next 3 sts, ch 1, (2 sc, 2 hdc, 15 dc, 2 hdc, 2 sc) in next ch-13 sp, [sk next st, sl st in each of next 6 sts, sk next st, (2 sc, 2 hdc, 15 dc, 2 hdc, 2 sc) in next ch-13 sp] twice, sl st in next st, leaving rem sts unworked, turn. *(23 sts in each ch-13 sp)*

**Row 10:** Ch 1, *sc in first sc of 23-st group, ch 4, sk next 2 sts, dc in next st, [ch 2, sk next st, dc in next st] 3 times, ch 2, sk next st, (dc, ch 3, dc) in next st, [ch 2, sk next st, dc in next st] 4 times, ch 4, sk next 2 sts, sc in next st**, sk next sl st, sl st in each of next 4 sts, sk next sl st; rep from * around, ending last rep at **, turn. *(33 ch sps, 30 dc)*

**Rnd 11: Now working rnds,** ch 1, *4 sc in next ch-4 sp, [(sc, ch 3, sc) in next dc, 2 sc in next ch sp] 4 times, sc in next dc, (3 sc, ch 3, 3 sc) in next ch-3 sp, sc in next dc, [2 sc

in next ch sp, (sc, ch 3, sc) in next dc] 4 times, 4 sc in next ch-4 sp, sk next sl st, sl st in each of next 2 sl sts, sk next sl st, rep from *, 4 sc in next ch-4 sp, [(sc, ch 3, sc) in next dc, 2 sc in next ch sp] 4 times, sc in next dc, (3 sc, ch 3, 3 sc) in next ch-3 sp, sc in next dc, [2 sc in next ch sp, (sc, ch 3, sc) in next dc] 4 times, 4 sc in next ch-4 sp, sl st in each unworked st around, join with sl st in beg sc. Fasten off.

Work and **join** *(see Special Stitches)* Flower Motifs according to black dots on Assembly Diagram in flower colors indicated on Diagram.

**TREFOIL FILLER**

With white, ch 7, sl st in first ch to form ring, ch 1, 3 sc in ring, **turn,** ch 10, sl st in first sc made, **turn,** 8 sc in ch-10 sp just made, join in ch-3 sp of Flower Motif indicated by red dot on diagram, 8 sc in same ch-10 sp, 4 sc in beg ring, **turn,** ch 10, sl st in 2nd sc of last 4-sc group in ring, **turn,** 8 sc in ch-10 sp just made, sk next 4 ch-3 sps on Flower Motifs, dc in each of next 2 ch-3 sps indicated by blue dots on diagram, 8 sc in same ch-10 sp, 4 sc in beg ring, **turn,** ch 10, sc in 2nd sc of last 4-sc group in ring, **turn,** 8 sc in ch 10 sp just made, sk next 4 ch-3 sps on Flower Motifs, join in next ch-3 sp indicated by purple dot on diagram, 8 sc in same ch-10 sp, (2 sc, ch 3, 2 sc) in beg ring, join with sl st in beg sc. Fasten off.

Work and join Trefoil Fillers according to Assembly Diagram.

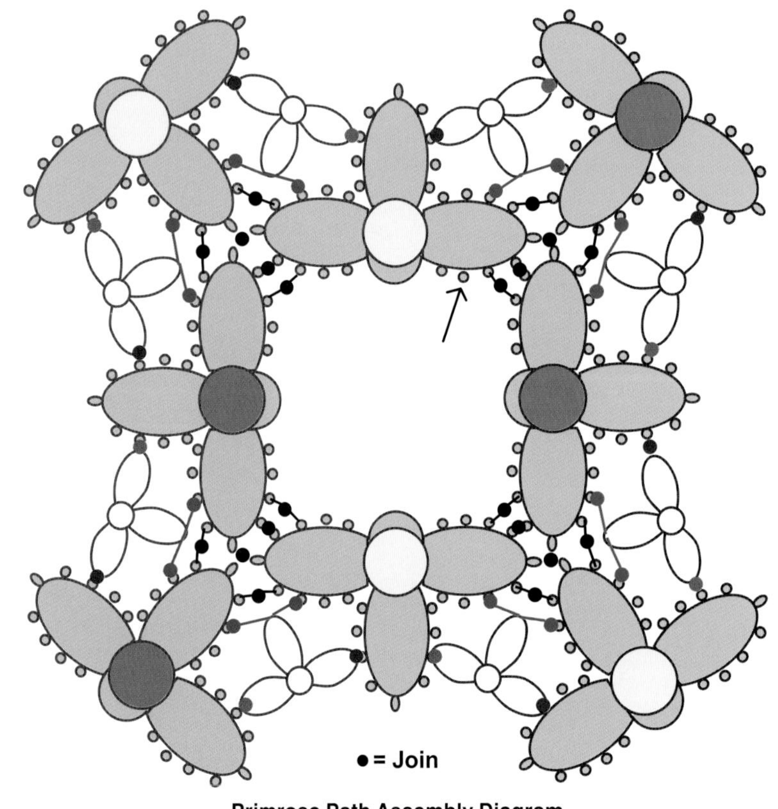

**Primrose Path Assembly Diagram**

**CENTER**

**Rnd 1:** With white, ch 7, sl st in first ch to form ring, ch 1, 16 sc in ring, join with sl st in beg sc. *(16 sc)*

**Rnd 2:** Ch 1, sc in first st, ch 3, sk next st, [sc in next st, ch 3, sk next st] around, join with sl st in beg sc. *(8 ch sps)*

**Rnd 3:** Sl st in next ch sp, ch 3, **3-dc cl** *(see Special Stitches)* in same ch sp, [ch 7, **4-dc cl** *(see Special Stitches)* in next ch sp] around, join with ch 3, tr in top of beg cl forming last ch sp. *(8 cls, 8 ch sps)*

**Rnd 4:** Ch 3, 4 dc in ch sp just made, ch 7, [5 dc in center ch of next ch-7, ch 7] around, join with sl st in 3rd ch of beg ch-3. *(8 dc groups, 8 ch sps)*

**Rnd 5:** Sl st in each of next 2 sts, ch 8 *(counts as first dc and ch-5 sp),* dc in same st, *ch 5, (sc, **picot**—*see Special Stitches*) in next ch sp, ch 5, dc in center st of next 5-dc group, ch 5, (sc, picot) in next ch sp, ch 5**, (dc, ch 5, dc) in center st of next 5-dc group, rep from * around, ending last rep at **, join with sl st in 3rd ch of beg ch-8. *(12 dc, 8 picots)*

**Rnd 6:** Sl st in each of 3 chs, ch 1, sc in same ch sp, ch 3, sc in ch sp on Flower Motifs indicated by arrow on assembly diagram, *ch 3, sc in next ch sp on Center, ch 3, sc in next ch sp on Flower Motifs, ch 3, sc in next ch sp on Center, ch 3, sc in Center st of next 9-st group on Flower Motifs, ch 3, sc in next ch sp on Center**, [ch 3, sc in next ch sp on Flower Motifs, ch 3, sc in next ch sp on Center] twice, ch 3, sc in next unworked ch sp on Flower Motifs, rep from * around, ending last rep at **, ch 3, sc in next ch sp on Flower Motifs, ch 3, sc in next ch sp on Center, ch 3, sc in next ch sp on Flower Motifs, ch 3, join with sl st in beg sc. Fasten off.

#### OUTER BORDER

**Rnd 1:** Join white with sc in ch-3 sp of 1 Trefoil Filler before 1 corner Flower Motif, *ch 10, sc in next unworked ch-3 sp of next corner Flower Motif, [ch 7, sc in next ch-3 sp] 5 times, ch 7, sc in center st of next 9-st group, [ch 7 sc in next ch-3 sp] 6 times, ch 10, sc in ch-3 sp of next Trefoil Filler, ch 10, sc in next ch-3 sp of next Flower Motif, [ch 7, sc in next ch-3 sp] twice**, ch 10, sc in next ch-3 sp of next Trefoil Filler, rep from * around, ending last rep at **, join with ch 5, dtr in beg sc forming last ch sp. *(72 ch sps)*

**Rnd 2:** Ch 1, sc last ch sp made, picot, [ch 7, sc in next ch sp, picot] around, join with ch 3, tr in beg sc forming last ch sp.

**Rnd 3:** Ch 10 *(counts as first dc and ch-7 sp)*, dc in next ch sp, [ch 7, dc in next ch sp] twice, *ch 5, (4-dc cl, {ch 7, 4-dc cl} twice) in next ch sp, ch 5, dc in next ch sp, [ch 7, dc in next ch sp] 6 times, ch 5, (4-dc cl, {ch 7, 4-dc cl} twice) in next ch sp, ch 5, dc in next ch sp**, [ch 7, dc in next ch sp] 8 times, rep from * around, ending last rep at **, [ch 7, dc in next ch sp] 4 times, ch 7, join with sl st in 3rd ch of beg ch-10. *(72 ch-7 sps, 16 ch-5 sps)*

**Rnd 4:** Ch 1, 6 sc in each ch-7 sp, and 5 sc in each ch-5 sp around, join with sl st in beg sc. *(512 sc)*

**Rnd 5:** Ch 2 *(counts as first hdc)*, hdc in each st around with 2 hdc in last st, join with sl st in 2nd ch of beg ch-2. *(513 hdc)*

**Rnd 6:** Ch 1, sc in each of first 3 sts, picot, [sc in each of next 3 sts, picot] around, join with sl st in beg sc. Fasten off. ■

# Flower Wheel

DESIGN BY KATHERINE ENG

**This eye-catching, creatively designed doily is a perfect inspiration for picking up your crochet hook and thread, and then stitching! A sweet little treasure, it's perfect for adding color and style to a difficult-to-decorate nook.**

EASY

**FINISHED SIZE**
12 inches in diameter

**MATERIALS**
Size 10 crochet cotton:
150 yds white
25 yds each lilac, blue and green
Size 7/1.65mm steel crochet hook or size needed to obtain gauge

**GAUGE**
Rnds 1–4 = 2 inches

**SPECIAL STITCHES**
**Beginning cluster (beg cl):** Ch 4, holding back last lp of each st on hook, 3 dc in indicated st, yo, pull through all lps on hook.

**Cluster (cl):** Holding back last lp of each st on hook, 4 dc in indicated st yo, pull through all lps on hook.

**V-stitch (V-st):** (Dc, ch 2, dc) in indicated st.

**Shell:** (2 dc, ch 2, 2 dc) in indicated st.

## INSTRUCTIONS

**DOILY**

**Rnd 1:** With lilac, ch 4, sl st in first ch to form ring, ch 1, 8 sc in ring, join with sl st in beg sc. *(8 sc)*

**Rnd 2: Beg cl** *(see Special Stitches)* in first st, ch 3, [**cl** *(see Special Stitches)* in next sc, ch 3] around, join with sl st in top of beg cl. Fasten off. *(8 flower petals)*

**Rnd 3:** Join green with sc in any ch sp, 4 sc in same ch sp, ch 1, [5 sc in next ch-3 sp, ch 1] around, join with sl st in beg sc. *(40 sc)*

**Rnd 4:** Ch 1, sc in each sc and in each ch-1 sp around, join with sl st in beg sc. *(48 sc)*

**Rnd 5:** Ch 1, sc in first sc, ch 3, sk next sc, [sc in next sc, ch 3, sk next sc] around, join with sl st in beg sc. Fasten off. *(24 ch-3 sps)*

**Rnd 6:** Join blue with sc in any ch-3 sp, ch 4, cl in next ch-3 sp, ch 4, [sc in next ch-3 sp, ch 4, cl in next ch-3 sp, ch 4] around, join with sl st in beg sc. Fasten off. *(12 cls)*

**Rnd 7:** Join white with sc in any ch sp to right of cl, ch 1, sc in next ch sp, ch 6, [sc in next ch sp, ch 1, sc in next ch sp, ch 6] around, join with sl st in beg sc.

**Rnd 8:** Ch 3 *(counts as first dc)*, 2 dc in next ch-1 sp, dc in next sc, 6 dc in next ch-6 sp, [dc in next sc, 2 dc in next ch-1 sp, dc in next sc, 6 dc in next ch-6 sp] around, join with sl st in 3rd ch of beg ch-3.

**Rnd 9:** Ch 1, sc in first st, ch 1, sk next dc, [sc in next dc, ch 1, sk next dc] around, join with sl st in beg sc.

**Rnd 10:** Sl st in first ch-1 sp, ch 1, (sc, ch 3, sc) in same ch sp, sc in next ch-1 sp, [(sc, ch 3, sc) in next ch-1 sp, sc in next ch-1 sp] around, join with sl st in beg sc.

**Rnd 11:** Sl st in first ch-3 sp, ch 5 *(counts as first dc and ch-2)*, dc in same ch sp, ch 2, [**V-st** *(see Special Stitches)* in next ch-3 sp, ch 2] around, join with sl st in 3rd ch of beg ch-5. *(30 V-sts)*

**Rnd 12:** Ch 3 *(counts as first dc)*, 2 dc in ch-2 sp, [dc in next dc, 2 dc in next ch-2 sp] around, join with sl st in 3rd ch of beg ch-3.

**Rnd 13:** Ch 1, sc in first st, ch 1, sk next dc, [sc in next dc, ch 1, sk next dc] around, join with sl st in beg sc.

**Rnd 14:** Sl st in first ch-1 sp, ch 1, (sc, ch 3, sc) in same ch sp, sc in next ch-1 sp, [(sc, ch 3, sc) in next ch-1 sp, sc in next ch-1 sp] around, join with sl st in beg sc.

**Rnd 15:** Sl st in first ch-3 sp, ch 5 *(counts as first dc and ch-2)*, dc in same ch sp, ch 2, [V-st in next ch-3 sp, ch 2] around, join with sl st in 3rd ch of beg ch-5. *(45 V-sts)*

**Rnd 16:** Ch 3 *(counts as first dc)*, 2 dc in ch-2 sp, [dc in next dc, 2 dc in next ch-2 sp] around, join with sl st in 3rd ch of beg ch-3.

**Rnd 17:** Ch 1, sc in first st, ch 1, sk next dc, [sc in next dc, ch 1, sk next dc] around, join with sl st in beg sc.

**Rnd 18:** Sl st in first ch-1 sp, ch 1, (sc, ch 3, sc) in same ch-1 sp, sc in next ch-1 sp, ch 1, sc in next ch-1 sp, [(sc, ch 3, sc) in next ch-1 sp, sc in next ch-1 sp, ch 1, sc in next ch-1 sp] around, join with sl st in beg sc. Fasten off.

**Rnd 19:** Join blue with sc in any ch-3 sp, **shell** *(see Special Stitches)* in next ch-1 sp, [sc in next ch-3 sp, shell in next ch-1 sp] around, join with sl st in beg sc. Fasten off.

**Rnd 20:** Join green with sc in ch sp of any shell, shell in next sc, [sc in ch sp of next shell, shell in next sc] around, join with sl st in beg sc. Fasten off.

**Rnd 21:** Join lilac with sc in any sc, ch 2, (sc, ch 3, sc) in ch sp of next shell, ch 2, [sc in next sc, ch 2, (sc, ch 3, sc) in ch sp of next shell, ch 2] around, join with sl st in beg sc.

**Rnd 22:** Ch 1, sc in first st, ch 2, (sc, ch 3, sc) in next ch-3 sp, ch 2, [sk next ch-2 sp, sc in next sc, ch 2, (sc, ch 3, sc) in next ch-3 sp, ch 2] around, join with sl st in beg sc. Fasten off.

**Rnd 23:** Join white with sc in any ch-3 sp, sk next ch-2 sp, (3 dc, ch 2, 3 dc) in next sc, sk next ch-2 sp, [sc in next ch-3 sp, sk next ch-2 sp, (3 dc, ch 2, 3 dc) in next sc, sk next ch-2 sp] around, join with sl st in beg sc.

**Rnd 24:** Ch 1, sc in first sc, ch 3, (sc, ch 3, sc) in next ch-2 sp, ch 3, [sc in next sc, ch 3, (sc, ch 3, sc) in next ch-2 sp, ch 3] around, join with sl st in beg sc. Fasten off.

### STIFFENING & BLOCKING

**Optional:** For blocking with water, dampen finished piece, arrange and shape on a padded surface. Pin in place with rustproof straight pins, allow to dry completely, then remove pins.

If piece needs more stiffening and shaping, use fabric stiffener or starching solution. ■

# Desert Overlay

DESIGN BY MARGRET WILLSON

A multitude of scrap yarns and simple, long stitches worked throughout the design create a beautiful overlay effect and intricate look that is stunning. Unique in its reversible design, one side is as pretty as the other!

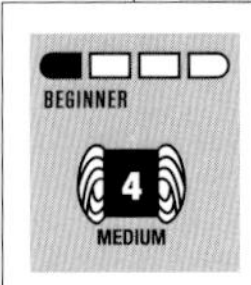


**FINISHED SIZE**
46 x 65 inches, excluding fringe

**MATERIALS**
Medium (worsted) weight yarn:
40 oz/2,000 yds/1,134g Aran
35 oz/1,750 yds/992g assorted scraps
Size H/8/5mm crochet hook or size needed to obtain gauge
Tapestry needle

**GAUGE**
14 sc = 4 inches; 5 pattern rows = 1½ inches

**PATTERN NOTES**
All rows are worked with right side facing; **do not turn rows.**

**For Fringe,** leave 6-inch length of yarn at beginning and end of each row.

**SPECIAL STITCH**
**Double crochet variation (dc):** Dc in **front lp** *(see Stitch Guide)* only of next st 2 rows below.

## INSTRUCTIONS

**AFGHAN**

**Foundation row:** With Aran, leaving 6-inch end *(see Pattern Notes)*, ch 165, sc in 2nd ch from hook and in each ch across, **do not turn** *(see Pattern Notes)*. Fasten off. *(164 sc)*

**Row 1:** Join scrap color with sc in first st, working in **back lps** *(see Stitch Guide)* only, sc in each st across to last st, sc in both lps of last st. Fasten off.

**Row 2:** Join Aran with sc in first sc, [**dc** *(see Special Stitch)* in next st, sc in each of next 3 sts] 6 times, dc in next st, sc in each of next 5 sts, *dc in next st, sc in each of next 2 sts, dc in next st, sc in each of next 11 sts, dc in each of next 2 sts, sc in each of next 11 sts, dc in next st, sc in each of next 2 sts, dc in next st*, sc in each of next 18 sts, dc in each of next 2 sts, sc in each of next 18 sts, rep between *, sc in each of next 5 sts, dc in next st, [sc in each of next 3 sts, dc in next st] 6 times, sc in next st. Fasten off.

**Row 3:** Rep row 1.

**Row 4:** Join Aran with sc in first sc, [sc in each of next 3 sts, dc in next st] 6 times, sc in each of next 7 sts, *dc in next st, sc in each of next 2 sts, dc in next st, sc in each of next 9 sts, dc in each of next 2 sts, sc in each of next 2 sts, dc in each of next 2 sts, sc in each of next 9 sts, dc in next st, sc in each of next 2 sts, dc in next st*, sc in each of next 17 sts, dc in each of next 4 sts, sc in each of next 17 sts, rep between *, sc in each of next 7 sts, [dc in next st, sc in each of next 3 sts] 6 times. Fasten off.

**Row 5:** Rep row 1.

**Row 6:** Join Aran with sc in first sc, [dc in next st, sc in each of next 3 sts] 6 times, dc in next st, sc in each of next 5 sts, *dc in next st, sc in each of next 2 sts, dc in next st, sc in each of next 7 sts, dc in each of next 2 sts, sc in each of next 6 sts, dc in each of next 2 sts, sc in each of next 7 sts, dc in next st, sc in each of next 2 sts, dc in next st*, sc in each of next 15 sts, dc in each of next 3 sts, sc in each of next 2 sts, dc in each of next 3 sts, sc in each of next 15 sts, rep between *, sc in each of next 5 sts, [dc in next st, sc in each of next 3 sc] 6 times, dc in next st, sc in last st. Fasten off.

**Row 7:** Rep row 1.

**Row 8:** Join Aran with sc in first sc, [sc in each of next 3 sts, dc in next st] 6 times, sc in each of next 7 sts, *dc in next st, sc in each of next 2 sts, dc in next st, sc in each of next 5 sts, dc in each of next 2 sts, sc in each of next 4 sts, dc in each of next 2 sts, sc in each of next 4 sts, dc in each of next 2 sts, sc in each of next 5 sts, dc in next st, sc in each of next 2 sts, dc in next st*, sc in each of next 13 sts, dc in each of next 3 sts, sc in each of next 6 sts, dc in each of

next 3 sts, sc in each of next 13 sts, rep between *, sc in each of next 7 sts, [dc in next st, sc in each of next 3 sts] 6 times. Fasten off.

**Row 9:** Rep row 1.

**Row 10:** Join Aran with sc in first st, [dc in next st, sc in each of next 3 sts] 6 times, dc in next st, sc in each of next 5 sts, *dc in next st, sc in each of next 2 sts, dc in next st, sc in each of next 7 sts, dc in each of next 2 sts, sc in each of next 6 sts, dc in each of next 2 sts, sc in each of next 7 sts, dc in next st, sc in each of next 2 sts, dc in next st*, sc in each of next 11 sts, dc in each of next 3 sts, sc in each of next 10 sts, dc in each of next 3 sts, sc in each of next 11 sts, rep between *, sc in each of next 5 sts, [dc in next st, sc in each of next 3 sts] 6 times, dc in next st, sc in last st. Fasten off.

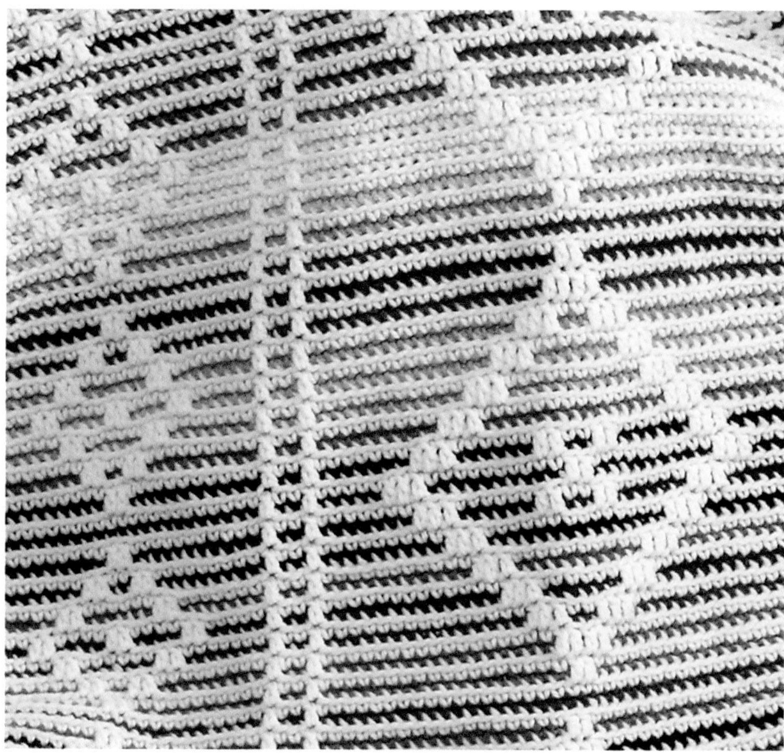

**Row 11:** Rep row 1.

**Row 12:** Join Aran with sc in first st, sc in each of next 2 sts, dc in next st, [sc in each of next 3 sts, dc in next st] 5 times, sc in each of next 7 sts, *dc in next st, sc in each of next 2 sts, dc in next st, sc in each of next 9 sts, dc in each of next 2 sts, sc in each of next 2 sts, dc in each of next 2 sts, sc in each of next 9 sts, dc in next st, sc in each of next 2 sts, dc in next st*, sc in each of next 9 sts, dc in each of next 3 sts, sc in each of next 14 sts, dc in each of next 3 sts, sc in each of next 9 sts, rep between *, sc in each of next 7 sts, [dc in next st, sc in each of next 3 sts] 6 times. Fasten off.

**Row 13:** Rep row 1.

**Row 14:** Join Aran with sc in first sc, [dc in next st, sc in each of next 3 sts] 6 times, dc in next st, sc in each of next 5 sts, *dc in next st, sc in each of next 2 sts, dc in next st, sc in each of next 11 sts, dc in each of next 2 sts, sc in each of next 11 sts, dc in next st, sc in each of next 2 sts, dc in next st*, sc in each of next 7 sts, dc in each of next 3 sts, sc in each of next 6 sts, dc in each of next 2 sts, sc in each of next 2 sts, dc in each of next 2 sts, sc in each of next 6 sts, dc in each of next 3 sts, sc in each of next 7 sts, rep between *, sc in each of next 5 sts, [dc in next st, sc in each of next 3 sts] 6 times, dc in next st, sc in next st. Fasten off.

**Row 15:** Rep row 1.

**Row 16:** Join Aran with sc in first st, sc in each of next 2 sts, dc in next st [sc in each of next 3 sts, dc in next st] 5 times, sc in each of next 7 sts, *dc in next st, sc in each of next 2 sts, dc in next st, sc in each of next 24 sts, dc in next st, sc in each of next 2 sts, dc in next st*, sc in each of next 5 sts, dc in each of next 3 sts, sc in each of next 10 sts, dc in each of next 2 sts, sc in each of next 10 sts, dc in each of next 3 sts, sc in each of next 5 sts, rep between *, sc in each of next 7 sts, [dc in next st, sc in each of next 3 sts] 6 times. Fasten off.

**Rows 17 & 18:** Rep rows 1 and 14.

**Rows 19 & 20:** Rep rows 1 and 12.

**Rows 21 & 22:** Rep rows 1 and 10.

**Rows 23 & 24:** Rep rows 1 and 8.

**Rows 25 & 26:** Rep rows 1 and 6.

**Rows 27 & 28:** Rep rows 1 and 4.

**Rows 29 & 30:** Rep rows 1 and 2.

**Row 31:** Join Aran with sc in first st, sc in each of next 2 sts, dc in next st, [sc in each of next 3 sts, dc in next st] 5 times, sc in each of next 7 sts, *dc in next st, sc in each of next 2 sts, dc in next st, sc in each of next 24 sts, dc in next st, sc in each of next 2 sts, dc in next st*, sc in each of next 38 sts, rep between *, sc in each of next 7 sts, [dc in next st, sc in each of next 3 sts] 6 times. Fasten off.

**Next rows:** Rep rows 1–31 consecutively 6 times.

Trim fringe ends even. ■

# Pastel Garden

DESIGN BY LAURA GEBHARDT

INTERMEDIATE

Decorate your home all spring and summer with freshly cut flowers from your garden. A beautiful bouquet set on this delicate centerpiece will be enhanced by the variety of subtle pastel shades.

**FINISHED SIZE**
20 inches across widest point

**MATERIALS**
Size 10 crochet cotton:
- 350 yds white *(MC)*
- 12 yds each lilac *(A)*, pink *(B)*, yellow *(C)*, light blue *(D)*, peach *(E)* and mint green *(F)*

Size 7/1.65mm steel crochet hook or size needed to obtain gauge

**GAUGE**
Center Motif = 2½ inches in diameter

**SPECIAL STITCHES**
**Cluster (Cl):** Holding back last lp of each st on hook, 3 dc in indicated sp or st, yo, pull through all lps on hook.

**Beginning cluster (beg cl):** Ch 2, holding back last lp of each st on hook, 2 dc in same sp, yo, pull through all lps on hook.

**Picot:** Ch 3, sl st in 3rd ch from hook.

## INSTRUCTIONS

**CENTER MOTIF**
**Rnd 1 (RS):** With MC, ch 6, sl st in first ch to form ring, ch 1, 12 sc in ring, join with sl st in beg sc. *(12 sc)*

**Rnd 2:** Ch 3 *(counts as first dc)*, dc in next sc, [ch 3, dc in each of next 2 sc] around, ending with ch 3, join with sl st in 3rd ch of beg ch-3. *(6 ch-3 sps)*

**Rnd 3:** Sl st in next dc and in ch-3 sp, (**beg cl**—*see Special Stitches*, ch 3, **cl**—*see Special Stitches*) in same ch sp, *ch 7, (cl, ch 3, cl) in next ch-3 sp, rep from * around, ending with ch 7, join with sl st in top of beg cl.

**Rnd 4:** Sl st in ch-3 sp, ch 1, sc in same ch sp, *(6 dc, ch 3, 6 dc) in next ch-7 sp**, sc in next ch-3 sp, rep from * around, ending last rep at **, join with sl st in beg sc. Fasten off. *(6 petals)*

**FIRST PASTEL MOTIF**
**Rnds 1–3:** With B, rep rnds 1–3 of Center Motif. At end of last rnd, fasten off.

**Rnd 4:** With RS facing, join MC with sl st in any ch-3 sp, ch 1, sc in same ch sp, (6 dc, ch 1) in next ch-7 sp, sl st in corresponding ch-3 sp on previous Motif, ch 1, 6 dc in same ch-7 sp on working Motif as last 6 dc *(1 petal joined)*, continue around as for rnd 4 of Center Motif.

**REMAINING PASTEL MOTIFS**
**Rnds 1–3:** Following Joining Diagram in numerical order for color, rep rnds 1–3 of First Pastel Motif.

**Rnd 4:** Rep rnd 4 of First Pastel Motif, joining as many petals as are indicated on Joining Diagram.

**REMAINING MC MOTIFS**
**Rnds 1–3:** Rep rnds 1–3 of Center Motif.

**Rnd 4:** With MC, rep rnd 4 of First Pastel Motif, joining as many petals as are indicated on Joining Diagram.

Follow Joining Diagram in numerical order until all Motifs have been completed.

**BORDER**
**Rnd 1:** With RS facing, join MC with sl st in ch-3 sp of unworked center petal on any corner MC Motif, ch 1, sc in same ch sp, ch 15, [sc in ch-3 sp at tip of next unworked petal, ch 15] around, join with sl st in beg sc. *(42 ch-15 sps)*

**Rnd 2:** Sl st in first ch of next ch-15 sp, ch 1, sc in same ch, sc in each ch around, join with sl st in beg sc. *(42 15-sc arches)*

**Rnd 3:** Sl st in each of next 2 sc, ch 1, *sc in each of next 4 sc, ch 3, sk next sc, sc in each of next 4 sc**, ch 7, sk next 6 sc, rep from * around, ending last rep at **, ch 4, dc in beg sc forming last ch-7 sp.

**Rnd 4:** Ch 3, 5 dc in ch sp just formed, *(3 dc, **picot**—*see Special Stitches*, 3 dc) in next ch-3 sp**, (6 dc, picot, 6 dc) in next ch-7 sp, rep from * around, ending last rep at **, (6 dc, picot) in same ch sp as beg ch-3, join with sl st in 3rd ch of beg ch-3. Fasten off. ■

**Row 11 (WS):** Join with dc in first sc, [ch 1, dc in next sc] 6 times, *[ch 1, working in front of next cl, tr in dc 1 row below cl, dc in next sc] 4 times, [ch 1, dc in next sc] 6 times, rep from * across, turn. Fasten off.

**Row 12 (RS):** Join with sc in first dc, [ch 1, sc in next dc] 6 times, *[cl, sk next 2 sts, sc in next st] 4 times, [ch 1, sc in next dc] 6 times, rep from * across, turn. Fasten off.

**Row 13 (WS):** Join with dc in first sc, [ch 1, dc in next sc] 6 times, *[ch 1, working in front of next cl, tr in next tr 1 row below cl, dc in next sc] 4 times, [ch 1, dc in next sc] 6 times, rep from * across, turn. Fasten off.

**Rows 14–17:** Rep rows 12 and 13 alternately.

**Row 18 (RS):** Join with sc in first dc, [cl, sk next 2 sts, sc in next st] 4 times, *[ch 1, sk next st, sc in next st] 6 times, [cl, sk next 2 sts, sc in next st] 4 times, rep from * across, turn. Fasten off. *(10 groups of cl)*

**Row 19 (WS):** Join with dc in first sc, [ch 1, working in front of next cl, tr in dc 1 row below cl, dc in next sc] 4 times, *[ch 1, dc in next sc] 6 times, [ch 1, working in front of next cl, tr in dc 1 row below cl, dc in next sc] 4 times, rep from * across, turn. Fasten off.

**Rows 20–35:** [Rep rows 4–19 consecutively] 6 times, then rep rows 4–9.

### EDGING

**Row 1 (RS):** Join A with sc in first dc, [ch 1, sk next st, sc in next st] across, fasten off.

**Row 2 (RS):** Join A with sl st in first st, sl st in next ch-1 sp, [ch 1, sl st in next ch-1 sp] across to last sc, sl st in last sc. Fasten off.

**Row 3 (RS):** Working on opposite side of foundation ch, join A with sc

in first ch, [ch 1, sk next ch, sc in next ch] across. Fasten off.

**Row 4 (RS):** Rep row 2.

### FRINGE

Cut 2 pieces 16 inches long. Fold strands in half, pull fold through, pull all ends through fold. Pull to tighten. Trim ends evenly.

Matching colors, attach Fringe in end of each row across. ■

# Denim Blues

DESIGN BY LORI ZELLER

Shades of blue as comfortable and familiar as your favorite pair of faded jeans make this handsome go-with-everything doily a perfect complement to your year-round decor.

INTERMEDIATE

**FINISHED SIZE**
8¼ inches in diameter

**MATERIALS**
Size 10 crochet cotton:
- 50 yds white
- 30 yds blue
- 25 yds navy

Size 5/1.90mm steel crochet hook or size needed to obtain gauge

**GAUGE**
Rnds 1–4 = 1¾ inches in diameter

**SPECIAL STITCHES**
**V-stitch (V-st):** (Dc, ch 1, dc) in indicated st.

**Double V-Stitch (double V-st):** ({Dc, ch 1} 3 times, dc) in indicated ch sp.

**Shell:** ({Dc, ch 1} 5 times, dc) in indicated ch sp.

**Cluster (cl):** Holding back last lp of each st on hook, 2 dc in indicated st, yo, pull through all lps on hook.

**INSTRUCTIONS**

**DOILY**
**Rnd 1 (RS):** With white, ch 6, sl st in first ch to form ring, ch 4 *(counts as first dc and ch-1)*, [dc in ring, ch 1] 15 times, join with sl st in 3rd ch of beg ch-4. *(16 dc, 16 ch-1 sps)*

**Rnd 2:** Ch 1, sc in first st, ch 2, **fpdc** *(see Stitch Guide)* around next dc, ch 2, [sc in next dc, ch 2, fpdc around next dc, ch 2] around, join with sl st in beg sc.

**Rnd 3:** Ch 1, **fpsc** *(see Stitch Guide)* around first sc, fpsc around next fpdc, ch 3, [fpsc around next sc, ch 3, fpsc around next fpdc, ch 3] around, join with sl st in beg sc.

**Rnd 4:** Sl st across to first ch-3 sp, ch 1, (sc, ch 3, sc) in same ch-3 sp, ch 1, [(sc, ch 3, sc) in next ch-3 sp, ch 1] around, join with sl st in beg sc. Fasten off.

**Rnd 5:** Working in ch-2 sps of rnd 2 and working behind rnds 3 and 4, join blue with sl st in any ch-2 sp of rnd 2, ch 4, dc in same ch-2 sp, ch 1, [**V-st** *(see Special Stitches)* in next ch-2 sp, ch 1] around, join with sl st in 3rd ch of beg ch-4.

**Rnd 6:** Sl st in ch-1 sp, ch 1, working through ch-3 sps of rnd 4 and ch-1 sps of V-sts of rnd 5, sc in same ch sp as joining and first ch-3 sp of rnd 4, ch 4, [sk next ch-1 sp, sc in next ch-3 sp and ch-1 sp of V-st, ch 4] around, join with sl st in beg sc. Fasten off.

**Rnd 7:** Join navy with sc in any unworked ch-1 sp between V-sts of rnd 5, holding ch-4 sps in front of work, ch 5, [sc in next unworked ch-1 sp of rnd 5, ch 5] around, join with sl st in beg sc.

**Rnd 8:** Sl st in first ch-5 sp, ch 4, V-st in same ch sp, (V-st, ch 1, dc) in each ch-5 sp around, join with sl st in 3rd ch of beg ch-4.

**Rnd 9:** Sl st in first ch sp, ch 1, sc in same ch sp, ch 3, sc in next ch-1 sp, ch 1, sc in ch-4 sp on rnd 4, ch 1, [sc in next ch-1 sp on rnd 8, ch 3, sc in next ch-1 sp, ch 1, sc in next ch-4 sp of rnd 4, ch 1] around, join with sl st in beg sc.

**Rnd 10:** Sl st in first ch-3 sp, ch 6, dc in same ch sp, ch 5, [(dc, ch 3, dc) in next ch-3 sp, ch 5] around, join with sl st in 3rd ch of beg ch-6. Fasten off.

**Rnd 11:** Join blue with sl st in first ch sp of previous rnd, (sc, ch 4, sc) in same ch sp, ch 5, [(sc, ch 4, sc) in next ch-3 sp, ch 5] around, join with sl st in beg sc. Fasten off.

**Rnd 12:** Join white with sl st in first ch-4 sp of previous rnd, ch 4, (V-st, ch 1, dc) in same ch sp, ch 2, sc ch-5 sps of rnds 10 and 11 tog, ch 2, [**double V-st** *(see Special Stitches)* in next ch-4 sp, ch 2, sc ch-5 sps of rnds 10 and 11 tog, ch 2] around, join with sl st in 3rd ch of beg ch-4.

**Rnd 13:** Sl st in first ch sp, ch 1, (sc, ch 3, sc) in same ch sp, (sc, ch 3, sc) in each of next 2 ch-1 sps, ch 7, [(sc, ch 3, sc) in each of next 3 ch-1 sps, ch 7] around, join with sl st in beg sc.

**Rnd 14:** Sl st in first ch sp, ch 2, dc in same ch sp, (**cl**—*see Special Stitches*, ch 3, cl) in next ch-3 sp, cl in next ch-3 sp, [ch 3, dc in 3rd ch from hook] twice, sk next ch-7 sp, *cl in next ch-3 sp, (cl, ch 3, cl) in next ch-3 sp, cl in next ch-3 sp, [ch 3, dc in 3rd ch from hook] twice, sk next ch-7 sp, rep from * around, join with sl st in top of first dc. Fasten off.

**Rnd 15:** Join blue with sl st in first ch-3 sp of previous rnd, ch 4, ({dc, ch 1} 4 times, dc) in same ch-3 sp, ch 3, working behind previous rnd, sc in ch-7 sp of rnd 13, ch 3, [**shell** *(see Special Stitches)* in next ch-3 sp, ch 3, working behind previous rnd, sc in ch-7 sp of rnd 13, ch 3] around, join with sl st in 3rd ch of beg ch-4. Fasten off.

**Rnd 16:** Join white with sc in first ch-1 sp of previous rnd, [ch 3, sc in next ch-1 sp] 4 times, ch 1, sc in next ch-3 sp of rnd 14, ch 4, sc in next ch-3 sp of rnd 14, ch 1, *sc in next ch-1 sp of rnd 15, [ch 3, sc in next ch-1 sp] 4 times, ch 1, sc in next ch-3 sp of rnd 14, ch 4, sc in next ch-3 sp of rnd 14, ch 1, rep from * around, join with sl st in beg sc.

**Rnd 17:** Sl st in first ch-3 sp, ch 1, sc in same ch sp, [ch 3, sc in next ch-3 sp] 3 times, ch 7, sk next ch-4 sp, *sc in next ch-3 sp, [ch 3, sc in next ch-3 sp] 3 times, ch 7, sk next ch-4 sp, rep from * around, join with sl st in beg sc.

**Rnd 18:** Sl st in first ch-3 sp, ch 2, (dc, ch 3, cl) in same ch sp, *ch 4, sk next ch-3 sp, (cl, ch 3, cl) in next ch-3 sp, ch 4, working behind ch-7 sp of previous rnd, sc in next ch-4 sp of rnd 16, ch 4**, (cl, ch 3, cl) in next ch-3 sp, rep from * around, ending last rep at **, join with sl st in first dc. Fasten off.

**Rnd 19:** Join blue with sc in first ch-3 sp of previous rnd, ch 3, sc in same ch sp, *ch 4, working behind ch-4 sp of previous rnd, sc in unworked ch-3 sp of rnd 17, ch 4, (sc, ch 3, sc) in next ch-3 sp of rnd 18, ch 2, working in front of previous rnd, (sc, ch 3, sc) in unworked ch-7 sp of rnd 17, ch 2**, (sc, ch 3, sc) in next ch-3 sp of rnd 18, rep from * around, ending last rep at **, join with sl st in beg sc. Fasten off.

**Rnd 20:** Join navy with sc in first ch-3 sp of previous rnd, ch 3, sc in same ch sp, *ch 4, working in front of previous rnd, sc in unworked ch-4 sp of rnd 18, ch 4, (sc, ch 3, sc) in next ch-3 sp of rnd 19, ch 4, sk next ch-2 sp, sc in next ch-3 sp, sk next ch-2 sp**, (sc, ch 3, sc) in next ch-3 sp, rep from * around, ending last rep at **, join with sl st in beg sc. Fasten off.

**Rnd 21:** Join white with sl st in first ch-3 sp of previous rnd, ch 4, (V-st, ch 1, dc) in same ch sp, *ch 2, working behind previous rnd, sc in next ch-4 sp of rnd 19, ch 3, sc in next ch-4 sp of rnd 19, ch 2, double V-st in next ch-3 sp of rnd 20, ch 2, sc in next ch-4 sp, ch 3, sc in next ch-4 sp, ch 2**, double V-st in next ch-3 sp, rep from * around, ending last rep at **, join with sl st in 3rd ch of beg ch-4.

**Rnd 22:** Sl st in first ch sp, ch 1, (sc, ch 3, sc) in same ch sp, (sc, ch 3, sc) in each of next 2 ch-1 sps, *ch 1, working in front of previous rnd, sc in unworked ch-4 sp of rnd 20, ch 1, (sc, ch 3, sc) in next ch-3 sp of rnd 21, ch 1, sc in next unworked ch sp of rnd 20, (sc, ch 3, sc) in each of next 3 ch-1 sps, ch 1, sk next ch-2 sp, (sc, ch 3, sc) in next ch-3 sp, ch 1, sk next ch-2 sp**, (sc, ch 3, sc) in each of next 3 ch-1 sps, rep from * around, ending last rep at **, join with sl st in beg sc. Fasten off. ■

# Country Wildflowers

DESIGN BY CAROL ALEXANDER

You can almost smell the fresh air and feel the breeze as it blows across this field of wildflowers. Larkspur and daisies bloom together with forget-me-nots and wild roses in this stunning floral throw.

**FINISHED SIZE**
46 x 65 inches

**MATERIALS**
Medium (worsted) weight yarn:
- 32 oz/1,600 yds/907g white
- 24 oz/1,200 yds/680g each soft navy and light blue
- 8 oz/400 yds/227g medium sage
- 1 oz/50 yds/28g each delft blue, lavender, bright yellow, light plum, pale yellow, gold, blue, light periwinkle, bright pink, light raspberry

Sizes E/4/3.5mm and G/6/4mm crochet hooks or sizes needed to obtain gauge
Tapestry needle
Washable fabric glue

**GAUGE**
**Size G hook:** Motif = 4 inches; completed square = 10 inches; Prickly Wild Rose = 2¾ inches in diameter; Larkspur = 2¼ inches in diameter

**Size E hook:** Forget-Me-Not = 1½ inches in diameter; Daisy = 2½ inches in diameter

**PATTERN NOTES**
Make 8 each Square A, Square B and Square C, joining as work progresses in round 3 of Edging.

Use larger hook unless otherwise stated.

To secure flowers to Motif for sewing, arrange flowers on Motif as indicated in photo, overlapping petals and leaves at various positions. Carefully lift edges of flowers and leaves and, leaving at least ¼ inch of petals and leaf tips free, place small dabs of fabric glue sparingly on under side. Smooth and gently press flowers and leaves back in place on Motif, taking care not to move out of position. Let dry thoroughly. Once glue is dry, flowers and leaves can be securely stitched in place. Sew all pieces with soft navy, working from front side of Square and underneath flowers, leave only the tips of flower petals and leaves free.

**Change color** *(see Stitch Guide)* in last stitch made.

**SPECIAL STITCHES**
**Corner scallop:** (Sc, 3 dc, ch 1, 3 dc, sc) in corner ch sp.

**Shell:** (Hdc, ch 3, hdc) in indicated st.

**Scallop:** (Sc, dc, ch 1, dc, sc) in indicated st.

**Picot:** Ch 2, sl st in top of last st made.

**Cluster (cl):** Holding back last lp of each st on hook, 3 dtr in indicated st, yo, pull through all lps on hook.

## INSTRUCTIONS

### FIRST SQUARE A

**DIAMOND MOTIF**
Make 4 Motifs for each Square.

**Row 1:** With soft navy, ch 2, sc in 2nd ch from hook, turn. *(1 sc)*

**Row 2 (RS):** Ch 1, 2 sc in first sc, sc in turning ch, turn. *(3 sc)*

**Row 3:** Ch 1, 2 sc in first sc, sc in each sc across with 2 sc in last sc, turn. *(5 sc)*

**Row 4:** Ch 1, sc in each sc across, inc 1 sc at center of row, turn. *(6 sc)*

**Rows 5 & 6:** Rep rows 3 and 4. *(9 sc at end of last row)*

**Row 7:** Rep row 3. *(11 sc)*

**Row 8:** Ch 1, sc in each sc across, turn.

**Rows 9–12:** Rep rows 3 and 4 alternately. *(17 sc at end of last row)*

**Row 13:** Ch 2, dc in first sc, hdc in next sc, 2 hdc in next sc, hdc in each of next 4 sc, sc in next sc, **sc dec** *(see Stitch Guide)* loosely in next 2 sc, hdc in each of next 4 sc, 2 hdc in next sc, hdc in next sc, dc in last sc, changing color to light blue, turn. *(19 sts)*

**Row 14:** Ch 5, sk next st, sc in next st, [ch 3, sk next st, sc in next st] across to last 2 sts, ch 2, sk next st, dc in last st to form last ch sp, turn. *(9 ch sps)*

**Row 15:** Ch 4, sc in next ch sp, [ch 3, sc in next ch sp] across to last sp, ch 1, dc in last sp, turn. *(8 ch sps)*

**Rows 16–21:** Rep row 15. *(2 ch sps)*

**Row 22:** Ch 3, sc in last ch sp. Fasten off.

Gently shape Motif into symmetrical square, defining corners.

Sew the 4 Motifs tog on WS, carefully aligning rows, with soft navy sections joined at center to form diamond.

#### RUFFLE

Join white with sl st in the sk sc on row 13 of Diamond Motif to left of any corner joining, ch 1, (sc, 2 hdc, ch 1, 2 hdc, sc) in same sc, *[(sc, hdc, ch 1, hdc sc) in next sk sc of row 13] 7 times, (sc, 2 hdc, ch 1, 2 hdc, sc) in last sk sc of row 13 just before corner joining**, (sc, 2 hdc, ch 1, 2 hdc, sc) in next sk sc of row 13 just past corner, rep from * around, ending last rep at **, join with sl st in beg sc. Fasten off.

#### PRICKLY WILD ROSE

**Rnd 1:** With pale yellow, ch 4, sl st in first ch to form ring, ch 1, 10 sc in ring, join with sl st in beg sc. Fasten off. *(10 sc)*

**Rnd 2:** Working in **back lps** *(see Stitch Guide)* only this rnd, join light raspberry with sl st in any st of rnd 1, *ch 3, (tr, dtr) in same st, ch 2, sl st in lp on center back of **post** *(see Stitch Guide)* of dtr just made, (dtr, tr, ch 3, sl st) in next st, sl st in next st, rep from * around. Fasten off. *(5 petals)*

**Rnd 3:** Working in **front lps** *(see Stitch Guide)* on rnd 1, join pale yellow with sl st in any st, ch 3, [sl st in next st, ch 3] around, join with sl st in base of beg ch-3. Fasten off.

**Row 4:** Join medium sage to back of Rose at base of and between any 2 petals, [(ch 4, dtr, trtr, ch 2, sc around top of post of trtr just made, dtr, ch 4, sl st) in same place] twice. Fasten off. *(2 leaf petals)*

Smooth flower petals and arrange evenly.

#### FORGET-ME-NOT

**Rnd 1:** With size E hook and bright yellow, ch 2, 5 sc in 2nd ch from hook, join with sl st in beg sc. Fasten off. *(5 sc)*

**Rnd 2:** With size E hook, working in back lps only this rnd, join blue with sl st in first st, *ch 1, (2 dc, ch 1, sc around top of post of last dc made, dc, ch 1, sl st) in same st, sl st in next st, rep from * 4 times. Fasten off. *(5 petals)*

Smooth and arrange petals evenly.

#### DAISY

**Rnd 1:** With size E hook and gold, ch 5, sl st in first ch to form ring, working over beg end, ch 1, 16 sc in ring, join with sl st in beg sc. Fasten off. *(16 sc)*

**Rnd 2:** With size E hook, join bright yellow with sl st in any sc, *ch 3, (tr, **picot**—*see Special Stitches*, ch 4, sl st) in same st, sl st in each of next 2 sts, rep from * around. Fasten off. *(8 petals)*

Pull beg end tightly to close center opening to approximately ¼ inch, weave in and secure on back.

**Row 3:** With size E hook, join medium sage with sl st to back of Daisy at base of and between any 2 petals, [ch 5, (trtr, ch 2, sc around top of post of trtr just made, ch 5, sl st) in same place] twice. Fasten off. *(2 leaf petals)*

Smooth flower petals and arrange evenly.

#### LARKSPUR

**Rnd 1:** With lavender, ch 2, 10 sc in 2nd ch from hook, join with sl st in beg sc. *(10 sc)*

**Rnd 2:** *Ch 3, (2 dc, picot, dc, ch 3, sl st) in same st, sl st in each of next 2 sts, rep from * around. Fasten off. *(5 petals)*

For **stamen,** with bright yellow, leaving end for sewing, ch 2, sl st in 2nd ch from hook. Fasten off.

Thread end in needle and insert through flower center from front, pull stamen firmly in place and sew securely on back side.

**Row 3:** Join medium sage with sl st to back of flower at base of and between any 2 petals, [(ch 4, **cl**—*see Special Stitches*, ch 2, sl st in top of cl, ch 4, sl st) in same place] twice. Fasten off. *(2 leaf petals)*

Smooth flower petals and arrange evenly.

Using photo as a guide, sew all flowers to square, tacking petals securely.

#### SQUARE EDGING

**Rnd 1:** Join light blue with sl st in any corner ch-3 sp, ch 1, (2 sc, ch 2, 2 sc) in same ch sp, *2 sc in each of next 7 ch sps, 2 hdc in each of next 2 ch sps *(at corner of Diamond Motif)*, 2 sc in each of next 7 ch sps**, (2 sc, ch 2, 2 sc) in corner ch sp, rep from * around, ending last rep at **, join with sl st in beg sc. Fasten off.

**Rnd 2:** Join white with sl st in any corner ch-2 sp, ch 1, *(sc, ch 3, sc) in corner sp, ch 2, sk next 2 sts, (sc, ch 1, sc) in next st, ch 2, sk next 2 sts, [(sc, ch 3, sc) in next st, sk next 2 sts] 3 times, [(sc, ch 3, sc) in next st, sk next st, (sc, ch 1, sc) in next st, sk next st] twice, [(sc, ch 3, sc) in next st, sk next 2 sts] 3 times, (sc, ch 3, sc) in next st, ch 2, sk next 2 sts, (sc, ch 1, sc) in next st, ch 2, sk next st, rep from * around, join with sl st in beg sc.

**Rnd 3:** Ch 1, *work **corner scallop** *(see Special Stitches)*, ch 1, sk next ch-2 sp, **shell** *(see Special Stitches)* in next ch-1 sp, ch 1, sk next ch-2 sp, **scallop** *(see Special Stitches)* in each of next 4 ch-3 sps, ch 1, sl st in next ch-1 sp, ch 1, scallop in next ch-3 sp, ch 1, sl st in next ch-1 sp, ch 1, scallop in each of next 4 ch-3 sps, ch 1, sk next ch-2 sp, shell in next ch-1 sp, ch 1, sk next ch-2 sp, rep from * around, join with sl st in beg sc. Fasten off.

#### 2ND SQUARE B

Rep the same rnds and rows as First Square A through rnd 2 of Square Edging, using the following flower colors:

**Prickly Wild Rose:**
Rnd 1 in pale yellow, rnd 2 in lavender and rnd 3 in pale yellow.

**Forget-me-not:**
Rnds 1 and 2 in bright yellow.

**Daisy:**
Rnd 1 in bright yellow and rnd 2 in white.

**Larkspur:**
Rnds 1 and 2 in delft blue and stamen with bright yellow.

***Note:*** *On the following joining rnd, rotate position of Square ¼ turn when joining to previous Square in order to alternate position and colors of flowers.*

**Rnd 3 (joining rnd):** Work same as rnd 3 of First Square A to first corner of joining side, on joining side, work the ch-1 of each corner scallop as sl st in the ch-1 sp of corresponding corner scallop on First Square and the ch-1 of each scallop along side as sl st in ch-1 sp of corresponding scallop on First Square, work the ch-3 of each shell as [ch 1, sl st in ch-3 sp of corresponding shell on first square, ch 1], complete remainder of rnd same as for First Square.

#### 3RD SQUARE C

Rep 2nd Square B, using following flower colors:

**Prickly Wild Rose:**
Rnd 1 in pale yellow, rnd 2 in white and rnd 3 in pale yellow.

**Forget-me-not:**
Rnd 1 in bright yellow, rnd 2 in bright pink.

**Daisy:**
Rnd 1 in gold, rnd 2 in light plum.

**Larkspur:**
Rnds 1 and 2 in light periwinkle and stamen with bright yellow.

#### ASSEMBLY

Following Placement Chart, make and join 21 more Squares in 6 rows of 4 Squares each.

#### BORDER

**Rnd 1:** Join white in corner ch-1 sp at right end of short side of throw, ch 1, *(sc, ch 3, sc) in corner ch sp, **ch 3, sc in last sc of corner scallop, ch 3, sc in ch-3 sp of next shell, [ch 3, sc in ch-1 sp of next scallop] 9 times, ch 3, sc in ch-3 sp of next shell, ch 3, sc in first dc of next corner scallop, ch 3***, sc in corner joining**, rep between ** 4 times, ending last rep at ***, (sc, ch 3, sc) in corner ch sp, ◊ch 3, sc in last sc of corner scallop, ch 3, sc in ch-3 sp of next shell, [ch 3, sc in ch-1 sp of next scallop] 9 times, ch 3, sc in ch-3 sp of next shell, ch 3, sc in first dc of next corner scallop, ch 3◊◊, sc in corner joining, rep from ◊ 6 times, ending last rep at ◊◊, rep from *, join with sl st in beg sc.

**Rnd 2:** Sl st in corner ch-3 sp, ch 3, (dc, ch 2, 2 dc) in same corner ch sp, *3 dc in each ch-3 sp across to next corner sp**, (2 dc, ch 2, 2 dc) in corner sp, rep from * around, ending last rep at **, join with sl st in 3rd ch of beg ch-3.

**Rnd 3:** Sl st to corner ch sp, ch 3, (dc, ch 2, 2 dc) in corner ch sp, *dc in each dc across to next corner ch sp**, (2 dc, ch 2, 2 dc) in corner ch sp, rep from * around, ending last rep at **, join with sl st in 3rd ch of beg ch-3. Fasten off.

***Note:*** *On rnd 4, adjust spacing of sts as needed when working between brackets to accommodate st sequence, but keeping number of sts equal between opposite sides.*

**Rnd 4:** Join soft navy in any corner ch-2 sp, ch 1, *sc in corner ch sp, ch 5, sk next 2 dc, sc in next dc, [ch 5, sk next 3 dc, sc in next dc] across, ending in 3rd dc from next corner ch sp, ch 5, sk next 2 dc, rep from * around, join with sl st in beg sc.

**Rnd 5:** Sl st in each of first 2 chs of next ch-5, ch 1, sc in same ch-5 sp, *[ch 5, sc in next ch-5 sp] across, ending in the first of the 2 ch-5 sps forming next corner, ch 7**, sc in 2nd ch-5 sp of corner, rep from * around, ending last rep at **, join with sl st in beg sc.

**Rnd 6:** (Sc, ch 1, 2 dc, ch 1, sc) in each ch-5 sp around and ({sc, ch 1, 2 dc, ch 1} 3 times, sc) in each corner ch-7 sp, join with sl st in beg sc. Fasten off. ■

| A | B | C | A |
|---|---|---|---|
| C | A | B | C |
| B | C | A | B |
| A | B | C | A |
| B | C | A | B |
| C | A | B | C |

**Country Wildflowers Placement Chart**

# Floral Harvest

DESIGN BY JOHANNA DZIKOWSKI

The quiet beauty found in the stillness of an ancient forest is reflected in the natural earth tones of this delicate doily. With this elegant accent, you can decorate your home with autumn's splendor all year long.

BEGINNER

**FINISHED SIZE**
17 inches

**MATERIALS**
Size 10 crochet cotton:
- 100 yds natural
- 50 yds spruce
- 45 yds camel
- 12 yds maize
- 10 yds orchid pink

Size B/1/2.25mm crochet hook or size needed to obtain gauge

**GAUGE**
Motif = 6½ inches in diameter
Rnds 1–6 (flower) = 2½ inches

## INSTRUCTIONS

### DOILY

**CENTER MOTIF**

**Rnd 1 (RS):** With maize, ch 6, sl st in first ch to form ring, ch 1, 12 sc in ring, join with sl st in **front lp** *(see Stitch Guide)* of beg sc. *(12 sc)*

**Rnd 2 (RS):** Working in front lps only, [ch 4, tr in same st, sl st in each of next 2 sts] 6 times. *(6 petals)*

**Rnd 3 (RS):** Sl st in **back lp** *(see Stitch Guide)* of rnd 1, working in back lps only, ch 1, sc in same st, ch 3, sk next st, [sc in next st, ch 3, sk next st] 5 times, join with sl st in beg sc, **turn.** Fasten off. *(6 ch-3 sps)*

**Rnd 4 (WS):** Join camel with sl st in ch-3 sp, ch 1, (sc, 2 dc, ch 1, 2 dc, sc) in each ch-3 sp around, join with sl st in beg sc. *(6 petals)*

**Rnd 5 (WS):** Working in same ch-3 sp of rnd 3, sl st across to ch-3 sp between 2-dc groups, ch 1, (sc, ch 4, sc) in ch-3 sp between dc of previous rnd, *(sc, ch 4, sc) in next ch-3 sp between dc of previous rnd, rep from * around, join with sl st in beg sc. *(6 ch-4 sps)*

**Rnd 6 (WS):** Ch 1, (sc, 3 dc, ch 2, 3 dc, sc) in each ch-4 sp around, join with sl st in beg sc. Fasten off. *(6 petals)*

**Rnd 7 (WS):** Join spruce with sl st in ch-2 sp, ch 6 *(counts as first dc and ch-3)*, dc in same ch-2 sp, ch 3, sc in sp between petals, ch 3, [(dc, ch 3, dc) in next ch-2 sp, ch 3, sc in sp between petals, ch 3] around, join with sl st in 3rd ch of beg ch-6.

**Rnd 8 (WS):** Sl st in ch-3 sp, ch 3, 4 dc in same ch-3 sp, *[ch 3, sc in next ch-3 sp] twice, ch 3**, 5 dc in next ch-3 sp, rep from * around, ending last rep at **, join with sl st in 3rd ch of beg ch-3. Fasten off. *(6 groups 5-dc)*

**Rnd 9 (WS):** Join natural with sl st in center dc of 5-dc group, ch 3, 4 dc in same dc, *ch 4, sk next ch-3 sp, (dc, ch 3, dc) in next ch-3 sp, ch 4, sk next ch-3 sp**, 5 dc in center dc of 5-dc group, rep from * around, ending last rep at **, join with sl st in 3rd ch of beg ch-3.

**Rnd 10 (WS):** Sl st across to center dc of 5-dc group, (ch 3, 2 dc, ch 3, 3 dc) in same dc, *ch 3, sc in next ch-4 sp, ch 3, (2 dc, ch 3, 2 dc) in next ch-3 sp, ch 3, sc in next ch-4 sp, ch 3**, (3 dc, ch 3, 3 dc) in center dc of 5-dc group, rep from * around, ending last rep at **, join with sl st in 3rd ch of beg ch-3. Fasten off.

**REMAINING MOTIFS**

Make 6 Motifs with rnds 1–3 of Flower with orchid pink.

Make 3 Motifs with rnds 1–3 of Flower with maize.

**Rnds 1–9:** Rep rnds 1–9 of Center Motif.

**Rnd 10 (WS):** Sl st across to center dc of 5-dc group, ch 3, (2 dc, ch 3, 3 dc) in same dc, ch 3, sc in next ch-4 sp, ch 3, (2 dc, ch 3, 2 dc) in next ch-3 sp, ch 3, sc in next ch-4 sp, ch 3, 3 dc in center dc of next 5-dc group, ch 1, sl st in ch-3 sp of previous Motif, ch 1, 3 dc in same dc on this Motif, ch 3, sc in next ch-4 sp on working Motif, ch 3, 2 dc in next ch-3 sp, ch 1, sl st in

ch-3 sp of previous Motif, ch 1, 2 dc in same ch-3 sp, ch 3, sc in next ch-4 sp, ch 3, 3 dc in center dc of next 5-dc group, ch 1, sl st in ch-3 sp of previous Motif, ch 1, 3 dc in same dc, *ch 3, sc in next ch-4 sp, ch 3, (2 dc, ch 3, 2 dc) in next ch-3 sp, ch 3, sc in next ch-4 sp, ch 3**, (3 dc, ch 3, 3 dc) in center dc of next 5-dc group, rep from * around, ending last rep at **, join with sl st in 3rd ch of beg ch-3. Fasten off.

Continue joining Motifs in same manner as shown in photo, joining last Motif to first, center and 2nd Motifs to close circle. ■

# Earth & Sky

DESIGN BY CHRISTINE GRAZIOSO MOODY

The powder blue sky, golden sunshine, dusty brown and leafy green of an alpine meadow are reflected in this handsome afghan, perfect for snuggling under and dreaming of a mountain retreat!

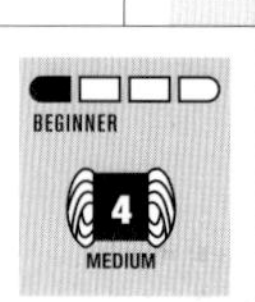


**FINISHED SIZE**
43 x 62 inches

**MATERIALS**
Medium (worsted) weight yarn:
16 oz/800 yds/454g soft white
12 oz/600 yds/340g print
1 oz/50 yds/28g scrap each of cornmeal, country blue, medium sage, light sage, buff, warm brown, light clay, brown
Size I/9/5.5mm crochet hook or size needed to obtain gauge
Tapestry needle

**GAUGE**
Rnds 1 and 2 = 1¾ inches;

Motif = 4¾ inches

**PATTERN NOTE**
Motifs are joined on 1 or 2 sides in 8 rows of 11 Motifs each.

**SPECIAL STITCHES**
**Single crochet cluster (sc cl):** [Pull up lp in indicated st, yo, pull through 1 lp on hook] 3 times in same st, yo, pull though all lps on hook.

**V-stitch (V-st):** (Dc, ch 1, dc) in indicated st.

**Picot:** Ch 4, sl st in first ch of ch-4.

## INSTRUCTIONS

**MOTIF**
Make 88.

**Rnd 1 (RS):** With soft white, ch 5, sl st in first ch to form ring, ch 1, 12 sc in ring, join with sl st in beg sc. *(12 sc)*

**Rnd 2 (RS):** Ch 1, 2 sc in each sc around, join with sl st in beg sc, turn. Fasten off. *(24 sc)*

**Rnd 3 (WS):** Join scrap color with sc in last sc, **sc cl** *(see Special Stitches)* in next sc, [sc in next sc, sc cl in next sc] around, join with sl st in beg sc, turn. Fasten off. *(12 sc, 12 sc cl)*

**Rnd 4 (RS):** Join scrap color with sl st in any sc, ch 2 *(counts as first hdc)*, *dc in next st, 3 tr in next st, dc in next st**, hdc in each of next 3 sts, rep from * around, ending last rep at **, hdc in each of last 2 sts, join with sl st in 2nd ch of beg ch-2. Fasten off.

**Rnd 5 (RS):** Attach soft white with sl st in first st, ch 3 *(counts as first dc)*, dc in each of next 2 sts, ch 1, V-st in next st, ch 1, *dc in each of next 7 sts**, ch 1, V-st in next st, ch 1, rep from * around, ending last rep at **, dc in each of last 4 sts, join with sl st in 3rd ch of beg ch-3. Fasten off.

**ASSEMBLY**

**1-SIDE JOINING**
Join print with sl st in ch-1 sp after V-st *(3rd ch-1 sp)*, ch 3, dc in each of next 7 dc, dc in next ch-1 sp, leaving 10-inch end, fasten off.

Place working Motif and next Motif with WS tog. Using rem 10-inch end and starting in ch-1 sp of adjacent Motif, whipstitch tog across next 7 dc and next ch-1 sp.

Rep, joining a total of 8 Motifs.

**2-SIDES JOINING**
Rep instructions for 1-Side Joining, working dc row on bottom of upper Motif and side of last Motif attached. Whipstitch both sides of Motif.

**FILLER MOTIF**
Make 70.

Working in sps between 4 Motifs, with print, ch 4, sl st in first ch to form ring, ch 1, sc in ring, ch 3, sl st in any corner ch-1 sp of Motif, ch 3, [sc in ring, ch 3, sl st in next corner ch-1 sp of Motif, ch 3] 11 times, join with sl st in beg sc. Fasten off.

**BORDER**
**Rnd 1 (RS):** Join print with sl st in

First Motif and Flower Center, using appropriate color for rnd 3 and same color for Flower Center.

**Rnd 4 (joining rnd):** Join white with sl st in corner ch-3 sp, ch 1, (3 sc, ch 1, sl st in corresponding corner ch-3 sp on previous Motif, ch 1, 3 sc) in same ch-3 sp on this Motif, ch 1, **joining V-st** *(see Special Stitches)* between next 2 sc, ch 1, (sc, sl st in corresponding ch-1 sp on previous Motif, sc) in ch-1 sp between next 2 dc, ch 1, joining V-st between next 2 sc, ch 1, (3 sc, ch 1, sl st in corresponding corner ch-3 sp on previous Motif, ch 1, 3 sc) in next corner ch-3 sp, complete remainder of rnd same as for First Motif.

Following Placement Chart, make and join 73 more Motifs in same manner as 2nd Motif.

When joining a corner to previously joined corners, work joining sl st into center of previous joining.

**BORDER**

**Rnd 1:** Join white with sl st in corner ch-3 sp at right end of long side of runner, ch 1, *(sc, ch 2, sc) in corner ch sp, ch 3, sc in last sc of corner group, [ch 3, sc in next V-st, ch 3, sc in ch-1 sp between next 2 sc, ch 3, sc in next V-st, ch 3, sc in first sc of next corner group, ch 3, sc in corner joining, ch 3, sc in last sc of next corner group] 15 times, ◊ch 3, sc in next V-st, ch 3, sc in ch-1 sp between next 2 sc, ch 3, sc in next V-st, ch 3, sc in first sc of next corner group, ch 3, (sc, ch 2, sc) in corner sp◊, ch 3, sc in last sc of corner group, [ch 3, sc in next V-st, ch 3, sc in ch-1 sp between next 2 sc, ch 3, sc in next V-st, ch 3, sc in first sc of next corner group, ch 3, sc in corner joining, ch 3, sc in last sc of next corner group] 5 times, rep between ◊ once, rep from * once, join with sl st in beg sc.

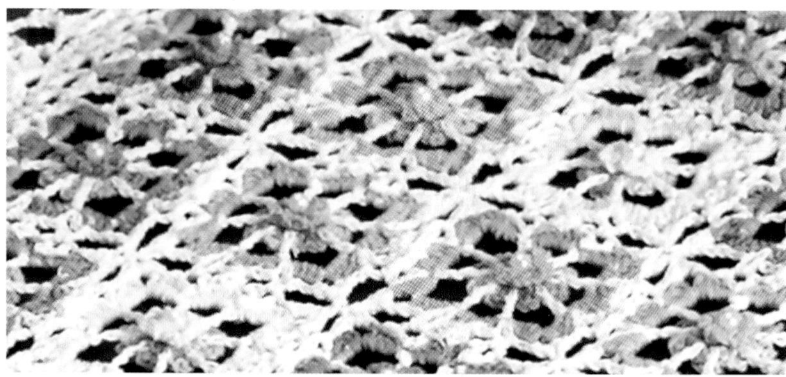

**Rnd 2:** Sl st in corner sp, ch 2, 2 hdc in same ch sp, *3 hdc in each ch-3 sp across to next corner**, 3 hdc in corner ch sp, rep from * around, ending last rep at **, join with sl st in 2nd ch of beg ch-2.

***Notes:*** *While working rnd 3, adjust spacing of sts needed between [ ], keeping sts consistent between opposite sides.*

*Total number of ch-3 sps on each side must be an odd number.*

**Rnd 3:** Sl st in next corner st, ch 1, *(sc, ch 4, sc) in corner st, sc in each of next 6 sts, [ch 3, sk next 3 sts, sc in each of next 8 sts] across, ending in 10 sts from next corner st, ch 3, sk next 3 sts, sc in each of next 6 sts, rep from * around, join with sl st in beg sc.

**Rnd 4:** Sl st in corner ch-4 sp, (**beg cl**—*see Special Stitches*, {**dc picot**—*see Special Stitches*, **cl**—*see Special Stitches*} 6 times) in same corner ch sp, *ch 2, sc in 4th sc of next 6-sc group, [ch 2, **picot shell** *(see Special Stitches)* in next ch-3 sp, ch 2, sc in 5th sc of next 8-sc group, ch 2, (cl, {dc picot, cl} 4 times) in next ch-3 sp, ch 2, sc in 5th sc of next 8-sc group] across, ending in 5th sc of last 8-sc group before corner, ch 2, picot shell in next ch-3 sp, ch 2, sc in 4th sc of next 6-sc group, ch 2**, (cl, {dc picot, cl} 6 times) in next corner ch sp, rep from * around, ending last rep at **, join with sl st in top of beg cl.

**Rnd 5:** *Sl st in next dc picot, [ch 2, **picot** *(see Special Stitches)*, ch 2, sl st in next dc picot] 5 times, **ch 4, (sc, ch 3, sc) in picot of next picot shell, ch 4, sl st in next dc picot, [ch 2, picot, ch 2, sl st in next dc picot] 3 times, rep from ** across, ending just before last picot shell before corner, ch 4, (sc, ch 3, sc) in picot of next picot shell, ch 4, rep from * 3 times, join with sl st in beg sl st. Fasten off.

Lightly starch and block runner. ■

| R | Y | B | P | V | S | R | Y | B | P | V | S | R | Y | B |
|---|---|---|---|---|---|---|---|---|---|---|---|---|---|---|
| P | V | S | R | Y | B | P | V | S | R | Y | B | P | V | S |
| Y | B | P | V | S | R | Y | B | P | V | S | R | Y | B | P |
| V | S | R | Y | B | P | V | S | R | Y | B | P | V | S | R |
| B | Y | P | P | R | S | B | Y | V | P | S | R | Y | B | V |

**Placement Chart**

**COLOR KEY**
R Medium rose
B Delft blue
Y Soft yellow
V Violet
S Spruce
P Medium peach

# Daisies

DESIGN BY DIANE STONE

Bright, happy daisies circle the center of this charming candle doily, a perfect accent for a room in need of some cheer. These flowers, with centers of gold, will warm you every time you walk by!

ERMEDIATE

**FINISHED SIZE**
12½ inches in diameter

**MATERIALS**
Size 10 crochet cotton:
- 100 yds ecru
- 50 yds light yellow
- 30 yds light green
- 20 yds dark yellow

Size 6/1.80mm steel crochet hook or size needed to obtain gauge

**GAUGE**
Rnds 1–3 = 2 inches

**SPECIAL STITCHES**

**Beginning popcorn (beg pc):** Ch 3 *(counts as first dc)*, 3 dc in same st or ch sp, drop lp from hook, insert hook in top of ch 3, pull dropped lp through.

**Popcorn (pc):** 4 dc in st or ch sp, drop lp from hook, insert hook in top of first dc of group, pull dropped lp through.

**Picot:** Ch 3, sl st in 3rd ch from hook, ch 1.

## INSTRUCTIONS

**DOILY**

**Rnd 1:** With ecru, wrap crochet cotton around finger twice to form a ring, ch 3 *(counts as first dc)*, 15 dc in ring, pull end of cotton tightly to close ring, join with sl st in top of beg ch-3. *(16 dc)*

**Rnd 2:** Ch 3, dc in same st, 2 dc in each st around, join with sl st in 3rd ch of beg ch-3. *(32 dc)*

**Rnd 3:** Ch 3, 2 dc in next st, [dc in next st, 2 dc in next st] around, join with sl st in 3rd ch of beg ch-3. *(48 dc)*

**Rnd 4:** Ch 3, dc in next st, 2 dc in next st, [dc in each of next 2 sts, 2 dc in next st] around, join with sl st in 3rd ch of beg ch-3. *(64 dc)*

**Rnd 5:** Ch 3, dc in each of next 2 sts, 2 dc in next st, [dc in each of next 3 sts, 2 dc in next st] around, join with sl st in 3rd ch of beg ch-3. *(80 dc)*

**Rnd 6:** Ch 1, sc in first st, [ch 3, sk next st, sc in next st] around, join with dc in beg sc forming last ch sp. *(40 ch sps)*

**Rnd 7:** Ch 1, sc in ch sp just made, [ch 3, sc in next ch sp] around, join with dc in beg sc.

**Rnd 8: Beg pc** *(see Special Stitches)* in ch sp just made, [ch 4, **pc** *(see Special Stitches)* in next ch sp] around, join with ch 1, dc in top of beg pc.

**Rnd 9:** Ch 1, sc in ch sp just made, [ch 5, sc in next ch sp] around, join with ch 2, dc in beg sc.

**Rnd 10:** Ch 1, sc in ch sp just made, ch 5, [sc in next ch sp, ch 5] around, join with sl st in beg sc. Fasten off.

**FIRST DAISY MOTIF**

**Rnd 1:** With dark yellow, wrap thread around finger twice to form ring, ch 1, 8 sc in ring, pull end of cotton tightly to close ring, join with sl st in beg sc. *(8 sc)*

**Rnds 2–4:** Ch 1, sc in each st around, join with sl st in 3rd ch of beg ch-3. At end of last rnd, fasten off.

**PETALS**

**Rnd 5:** Join light yellow with sl st in first st, beg pc in same st, ch 1, pc in same st, ch 1, (pc, ch 1, pc, ch 1) in each st around, join with sl st to top of beg pc. Fasten off.

**LEAVES**

**Rnd 6:** Join light green with sl st in any ch-1 sp between Petals, ch 1, sc in same ch sp, *ch 3, sc in next ch sp, ch 4, sl st in 2nd ch from hook, sc in next ch, hdc in last ch**, sc in next ch-1 sp, rep from * around, ending last rep at **, join with sl st in beg sc. Fasten off.

#### FINISHED SIZE
12 inches in diameter

#### MATERIALS
Size 10 crochet cotton:
- 200 yds each pastel variegated and white
- 40 yds light blue
- 20 yds each light yellow, light pink and light green

Size 7/1.65mm steel crochet hook or size needed to obtain gauge
Tapestry needle

#### GAUGE
Each Motif is 2 inches across.

#### SPECIAL STITCHES
**V-stitch (V-st):** (Dc, ch 2, dc) in indicated st.

**Beginning V-stitch (beg V-st):** (Ch 5, dc) in first st.

**Joining chain space (joining ch sp):** Ch 1, sl st in corresponding ch sp on other Motif, ch 1.

**Cluster (cl):** Holding back last lp of each st on hook, 2 dc in ring, yo, pull through all lps on hook.

### INSTRUCTIONS

#### FIRST ROW

#### FIRST MOTIF
**Rnd 1:** With white, ch 8, sl st in first ch to form ring, ch 2 *(counts as first hdc)*, 23 hdc in ring, join with sl st in 2nd ch of beg hdc. *(24 hdc)*

**Rnd 2:** Ch 4 *(counts as first tr)*, tr in each of next 2 sts, ch 3, [tr in each of next 3 sts, ch 3] around, join with sl st in 4th ch of beg ch-4. *(8 ch sps)*

**Rnd 3:** Sl st in each of next 2 sts, (sl st, ch 4, 2 tr, {ch 3, 3 tr} 3 times) in next ch sp, sc in next ch sp,*(3 tr, {ch 3, 3 tr} 3 times) in next ch sp, sc in next ch sp, rep from * around, join with sl st in 4th ch of beg ch-4. Fasten off.

#### 2ND MOTIF
**Rnds 1 & 2:** With variegated, rep rnd 1 and 2 of First Motif.

**Rnd 3:** Sl st in each of next 2 sts, (sl st, ch 4, 2 tr, ch 3, 3 tr) in next ch sp, joining to side of last Motif, [**joining ch sp** *(see Special Stitches)*, 3 tr in same ch sp on this Motif] twice, sc in next ch sp, 3 tr in next ch sp, joining ch sp, 3 tr in same ch sp on this Motif, joining ch sp, (3 tr, ch 3, 3 tr) in same ch sp on this Motif, sc in next ch sp, *(3 tr {ch 3, 3 tr} 3 times) in next ch sp, sc in next ch sp, rep from * around, join with sl st in 4th ch of beg ch-4.

Alternating white and variegated Motifs, rep 2nd Motif 3 times for total of 5 Motifs on this row.

#### 2ND ROW

#### FIRST MOTIF
Joining to bottom of First Motif on last row, work same as First Row, 2nd Motif.

#### 2ND MOTIF
**Rnds 1 & 2:** Rep rnds 1 and 2 of First Row, First Motif.

**Rnd 3:** Sl st in each of next 2 sts, (sl st, ch 4, 2 tr, ch 3, 3 tr) in next ch sp, joining to bottom of next Motif on last row, [joining ch sp, 3 tr in same ch sp on this Motif] twice, sc in next ch sp, 3 tr in next ch sp, joining ch sp, 3 tr in same ch sp on this Motif, joining ch sp, 3 tr in same ch sp on this Motif, joining to side of last Motif on this row, joining ch sp, 3 tr in same ch sp on this Motif, sc in next ch sp, 3 tr in next ch sp, joining ch sp, 3 tr in same ch sp on this Motif, joining ch sp, (3 tr, ch 3, 3 tr) in same ch sp on this Motif, sc in next ch sp, (3 tr {ch 3, 3 tr} 3 times) in next ch sp, sc in next ch sp, join with sl st in 4th ch of beg ch-4. Fasten off.

Alternating variegated and white Motifs, [rep 2nd Motif] 3 times for total of 5 Motifs on this row.

Always starting First Motif with the opposite color of the First Motif on row above and alternating colors across row, [rep 2nd Row] 3 times for total of 5 rows.

#### EDGING
**Rnd 1:** Join white with sl st in any corner ch sp, ch 5, *(counts as first dc and ch-2 sp)*, (dc, {ch 2, dc} twice) in same ch sp, *[ch 3, sc in next ch sp, ch 3, **V-st** *(see Special Stitches)* in next sc, ch 3, sc in next ch sp, ch 3, V-st in next sp between Motifs] 4 times, ch 3, sc in next ch sp, ch 3, V-st in next sc, ch 3, sc in next ch sp, ch 3**, (dc, {ch 3, dc} 3 times) in next corner ch sp, rep from * around, ending last rep at **, join with sl st in 3rd ch of beg ch-5.

**Rnd 2:** Sl st in next ch sp, **beg V-st** *(see Special Stitches)*, V-st in each of next 2 ch sps, *ch 3, sc in next ch sp, ch 3, [V-st in ch sp of next V-st, ch 3, sc in next sc, ch 3] rep across** to next 3 corner ch sps, V-st in each of next 3 ch sps, rep from * around ending last rep at **, join with sl st in 3rd ch of beg ch-3. Fasten off.

**Rnd 3:** Join light blue with sc in last ch sp of last rnd, ch 4, tr in last sc made, [sc in sp between next 2 V-sts, ch 4, tr in last sc made] twice, *sk ch sps of V-sts, [sc in next ch sp, ch 4, tr in last sc made] across** to next 3 corner V-sts, [sc in next sp between V-sts, ch 4, sc in last sc made] twice, rep from * around ending last rep at **, join with sl st in beg sc. Fasten off.

#### FLOWER
Make 2 light yellow.
Make 5 light pink.
Make 6 light blue.

Ch 4, sl st in first ch to form ring, (ch 2, **cl**—*see Special Stitches*, ch 3, sl st) 5 times in ring. Fasten off.

#### LEAF
Make 13.

With light green, ch 4, sl st in first ch

to form ring, [ch 10, sl st in ring] 5 times. Fasten off.

Sew 1 Leaf to back of each Flower.

Sew 1 light pink Flower to each white Motif diagonally across Doily from 1 corner to opposite corner.

Sew 1 light yellow Flower to each rem white corner Motifs.

Sew 1 light blue Flower to each rem white Flower. ■

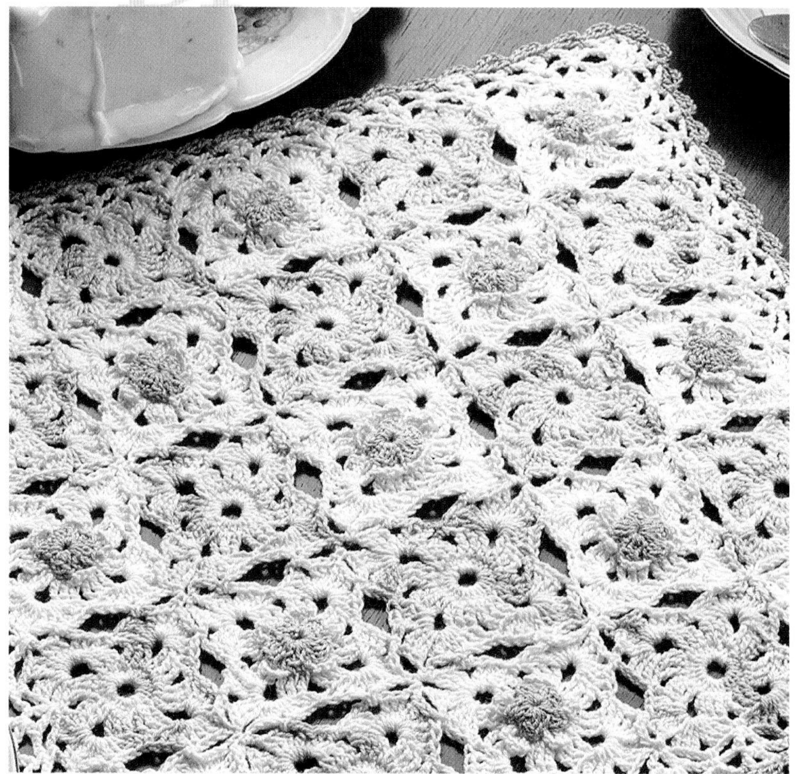

# Buttercups

DESIGN BY MAGGIE PETSCH

Rings of sunny yellow buttercups with spring green leaves adorn a lacy white background, creating flower-fresh appeal. This exquisite doily is sure to add a touch of garden beauty to any table.

ERMEDIATE

**FINISHED SIZE**
13 inches in diameter

**MATERIALS**
Size 10 crochet cotton:
225 yds white
150 yds each yellow and green
Size 7/1.65mm steel crochet hook or size needed to obtain gauge
Tapestry needle

**GAUGE**
Flower = 1½ inches; 9 sts = 1 inch

**SPECIAL STITCHES**
**Diamond:** Tr in indicated st, ch 4, 4 tr around tr.

**Beginning diamond (beg diamond):** Ch 8 *(counts as first tr and ch 4)*, tr in 5th ch from hook, 3 tr around ch-3.

**Tab:** Ch 9, dc in 6th ch from hook, dc in each of next 2 chs, ch 1.

**Double tab:** [Ch 9, dc in 6th ch from hook, dc in each of next 2 chs] twice, ch 1.

**Joined treble:** *Yo hook twice, insert hook in indicated st, yo, pull up lp, [yo, pull through 2 lps on hook] twice, rep from * once, yo, pull through all lps on hook.

## INSTRUCTIONS

**DOILY**

**Rnd 1 (RS):** With yellow, ch 6, sl st in first ch to form ring, ch 6 *(counts as first dc and ch 3)*, [dc in next ch, ch 3] 5 times, join with sl st in 3rd ch of beg ch-6. *(6 ch-3 sps)*

**Rnd 2:** Sl st in first ch-3 sp, ch 1, (sc, 5 dc, sc) in same ch sp and in each ch-3 sp around, join with sl st in beg sc. *(6 petals)*

**Rnd 3:** Ch 5, working behind petals of last rnd, [sl st between same petal and next petal, ch 5] around, join with sl st in same st as beg ch-5. *(6 ch-5 sps)*

**Rnd 4:** Sl st in first ch sp, ch 1, (sc, dc, 5 tr, dc, sc) in same ch sp and in each ch-5 sp around, join with sl st in beg sc. *(6 petals)*

**Rnd 5:** Ch 7, working behind petals of last rnd, [sl st between same and next petal, ch 7] around, join with sl st in same st as beg ch-7. Fasten off. *(6 ch-7 sps)*

**Rnd 6:** With RS facing, join white with sl st in any sl st between petals, ch 4 *(counts as first tr)*, *sk first ch of next ch-7 sp, **diamond** *(see Special Stitches)* in next ch, sk next 3 chs, dc in next ch**, tr in next sl st, rep from * around, ending last rep at **, join with sl st in 4th ch of beg ch-4. *(12 diamonds)*

**Rnd 7: Beg diamond** *(see Special Stitches)* in first st, ch 1, *[diamond in upper corner of next diamond, ch 1] twice**, diamond in next tr, ch 1, rep from * around, ending last rep at **, join with sl st in 4th ch of beg ch-8. *(18 diamonds)*

**Rnd 8:** Sl st in each of next 4 chs to upper corner of beg diamond, *ch 21, sc in 7th ch from hook *(ch-6 ring completed)*, sc in each of next 9 chs *(10-sc stem completed)*, ch 5, sl st in upper corner of next diamond, ch 11**, sl st in upper corner of next diamond, rep from * around, ending last rep at **, join with sl st in upper

corner of beg diamond of last rnd, at base of ch-21. Fasten off.

### INNER FLOWER RING

#### First Flower

**Rnd 1:** With RS facing, join yellow with sl st in first ch to the right of top of stem at base of any ch-6 ring, ch 6, working around ring, [dc in next ch, ch 3] 5 times, join with sl st in 3rd ch of beg ch-6. *(6 ch-3 sps)*

**Rnds 2–5:** Rep rnds 2–5 of Doily. At end of last rnd, leaving short end, fasten off.

Taking care that 10-sc stem at base of Flower is not twisted, tack bottom of Flower to stem with tapestry needle and short end so that sp between 2 lower petals is centered over stem.

Rep rnds 1–5 on each of 8 rem ch-6 rings. *(9 flowers)*

### LEAF PAIR

Make 9.

With RS facing, join green with sl st in center ch of first unworked ch-7 on rnd 5 of any Flower to the right of top of 10-sc stem, *ch 7, 2 sc in 2nd ch from hook, dc in each of next 4 chs, sc in next ch, ch 1, working in rem lps across opposite side of ch, sc in same ch as last sc, dc in each of next 4 chs, sc in last ch, join with sl st in beg sc*, sl st in 6th ch of ch-11 on rnd 8 of Doily directly below, rep between *, sl st in center ch of first unworked ch-7 to the left of next stem of next Flower. Fasten off.

Rep instructions for Leaf Pair between rem 8 pairs of Flowers.

### OUTER FLOWER RING

#### Stem Base

With RS facing, sk next 2 chs after leaf joining on ch-7 sp at lower left-hand side of any Flower, join white with sl st in next ch, ch 21, sc in 7th ch from hook *(ch-6 ring completed)*, sc in each of next 9 chs *(10-sc stem completed)*, sk next 2 chs after leaf joining on the ch-7 sp on next Flower to the left, sl st in next ch. Fasten off.

Rep instructions for Stem Base in 8 rem sps between Flower pairs around.

### FIRST FLOWER

**Rnds 1–5:** Rep rnds 1–5 for First Flower for Inner Flower Ring.

Rep rnds 1–5 on each of rem 8 ch-6 rings.

### LEAF TRIO

Make 9.

#### First Leaf

With RS facing, sk first unworked ch-7 sp on lower petal of Flower to the left of any Outer Flower Ring Stem Base, join green with sl st to center ch of next ch-7 sp, *ch 7, 2 sc in 2nd ch from hook, dc in each of next 4 chs, sc in next ch, ch 11, working across opposite side of ch, sc in same ch as last sc, dc in each of next 4 chs, sc in last ch, join with sl st in beg sc*, sk next unworked ch-7 sp on next Flower to the left on Inner Flower Ring, sl st in center ch of next ch-7 sp. Fasten off.

#### 2nd Leaf

With RS facing, join green with sl st in next sl st between petals to the left of leaf just joined, rep between * for First Leaf. Fasten off.

#### 3rd Leaf

With RS facing, join green with sl st in center ch of ch-7 on next petal to the left of 2nd Leaf, rep between * for First Leaf, sk first unworked ch-7 sp to the right of Stem Base on next Flower on Outer Flower Ring, join with sl st in center ch of next ch-7 sp. Fasten off.

Rep Leaf Trio in 8 rem sps around.

### DOILY BORDER

**Rnd 1:** With RS facing, join white with sl st in 2nd ch of ch-7 sp on left most of 2 unworked petals at top of any Flower of Outer Flower Ring, ch 12, dc in 6th ch from hook, dc in each of next 2 chs *(counts as first dc and tab)*, *sk next 3 chs, **joined tr** *(see Special Stitches)* over next ch and 2nd ch of next ch-7 sp on next petal, **double tab** *(see Special Stitches)*, sl st at tip of center leaf of next Leaf Trio, double tab, joined tr over next-to-last ch of ch-7 on petal of next Flower and 2nd ch of ch-7 on next petal of same Flower, **tab** *(see Special Stitches)*, sk next 3 chs, dc in next ch, tab**, dc in 2nd ch of next ch-7, tab, rep from * around, ending last rep at **, join with sl st in 3rd ch of beg ch-12. Fasten off.

**Rnd 2:** With RS facing, join green with sl st in center ch of ch-5 at top of first tab, [ch 7, sl st in center ch of ch-5 on next tab] twice, *sl st in center ch of ch-5 on next tab**, [ch 7, sl st in center ch of ch-5 on next tab] 6 times, rep from * around, ending last rep at **, [ch 7, sl st in center ch of ch-5 on next tab] 3 times, ch 7, join with sl st in sl st at base of beg ch-7.

**Rnd 3:** Ch 1, *sc in each of next 7 chs, sl st in next sl st, sc in each of next 3 chs, ch 7, remove lp from hook, sk last 2 sc of last 7-sc group, insert hook from RS to WS in next sc, pick up dropped lp, pull through lp on hook, sc in each of next 4 chs, (ch 3, sl st, ch 5, sl st, ch 3, sl st) in last sc worked, sc in each of next 3 chs, sl st in next sc below, sc in each of next 4 sc on ch-7 directly below, sl st in each sl st across to next ch-7 sp, rep from * around, join with sl st in beg sc. Fasten off. ■

# Happy Times

DESIGN BY DOT DRAKE

Coordinate your cheery colors and stitch a colorful striped throw. You'll be delighted with the new throw you create and enjoy remembering other projects you made with the same skeins of yarn.

**FINISHED SIZE**
40 x 70 inches

**MATERIALS**
Medium (worsted) weight yarn:
- 3 oz/150 yds/85g white *(MC)*
- 2 oz/100 yds/57g for each color used *(CC)*

Size H/8/5mm crochet hook or size needed to obtain gauge

**GAUGE**
13 hdc = 4 inches; 8 hdc rows = 4 inches

**SPECIAL STITCH**
**Picot:** Ch 5, sl st in 4th ch from hook.

## INSTRUCTIONS

**THROW**

**Row 1:** With MC, **picot** *(see Special Stitch)* 114 times, turn.

**Row 2:** Ch 2 *(counts as first hdc),* [hdc in next ch between picots, hdc in ch at base of next picot] across, ending with hdc in last ch after last picot, turn. Fasten off. *(228 hdc)*

**Row 3:** Join first CC with sl st in first st, ch 2, hdc in each st across, turn.

**Row 4:** Ch 2, hdc in each st across, turn. Fasten off.

**Row 5:** Join next CC with sl st in first st, ch 1, sc in first st, [tr in next st, sc in next st] across to last st, sc in last st, turn. Fasten off.

**Rows 6 & 7:** Rep rows 3 and 4.

**Rows 8–12:** Rep rows 3–7 with next 2 CCs.

**Next rows:** Rep rows 8–12 until Throw measures 40 inches from beg.

**Next row:** With MC, rep row 3, turn.

**Last row:** Sl st in first hdc, [ch 3, sl st in 3rd ch from hook, sl st in each of next 2 hdc] across to last st, sl st in last st. Fasten off. ■

# General Instructions

Please review the following information before working the projects in this book. Important details about the abbreviations and symbols used are included.

### HOOKS

Crochet hooks are sized for different weights of yarn and thread. For thread crochet, you will usually use a steel crochet hook. Steel crochet hook sizes range from size 00 to 14. The higher the number of the hook, the smaller your stitches will be. For example, a size 1 steel crochet hook will give you much larger stitches than a size 9 steel crochet hook. Keep in mind that the sizes given with the pattern instructions were obtained by working with the size thread or yarn and hook given in the materials list. If you work with a smaller hook, depending on your gauge, your project size will be smaller; if you work with a larger hook, your finished project's size will be larger.

### GAUGE

Gauge is determined by the tightness or looseness of your stitches, and affects the finished size of your project. If you are concerned about the finished size of the project matching the size given, take time to crochet a small section of the pattern and then check your gauge. For example, if the gauge called for is 10 dc = 1 inch, and your gauge is 12 dc to the inch, you should switch to a larger hook. On the other hand, if your gauge is only 8 dc to the inch, you should switch to a smaller hook.

If the gauge given in the pattern is for an entire motif, work one motif and then check your gauge.

### UNDERSTANDING SYMBOLS

As you work through a pattern, you'll quickly notice several symbols in the instructions. These symbols are used to clarify the pattern for you: brackets [ ], curlicue braces {}, parentheses () and asterisks *.

Brackets [ ] are used to set off a group of instructions worked a specific number of times. For example, "[ch 3, sc in next ch-3 sp] 7 times" means to work the instructions inside the [ ] seven times.

Occasionally, a set of instructions inside a set of brackets needs to be repeated, too. In this case, the text within the brackets to be repeated will be set off with curlicue braces {}. For example, "[dc in each of next 3 sts, ch 1, {shell in next ch-1 sp} 3 times, ch 1] 4 times." In this case, in each of the four times you work the instructions included in the brackets, you will work the section included in the curlicue braces three times.

Parentheses () are used to set off a group of stitches to be worked all in one stitch, space or loop. For example, the parentheses () in this set of instructions, "Sk 3 sc, (3 dc, ch 1, 3 dc) in next st", indicate that after skipping 3 sc, you will work 3 dc, ch 1 and 3 more dc all in the next stitch.

Single asterisks * are also used when a group of instructions is repeated. For example, "*Sc in each of the next 5 sc, 2 sc in next sc, rep from * around, join with a sl st in beg sc" simply means you will work the instructions from the first * around the entire round.

Double asterisks ** are used to indicate when a partial set of repeat instructions are to be worked. For example, "*Ch 3, (sc, ch 3, sc) in next ch-2 sp, ch 3**, shell in next dc, rep from * 3 times, ending last rep at **" means that on the third repeat of the single asterisk instructions, you stop at the double asterisks.

# Buyer's Guide

Look for the products used in this issue at your local yarn shops, department stores and mail-order sources, or contact the companies listed here.

**COATS & CLARK**
(Red Heart, Aunt Lydia, TLC, J.& P. Coats, Moda Dea)
Consumer Services
P.O. Box 12229
Greenville, SC 29612-0229
(800) 648-1479
www.coatsandclark.com

**DMC Inc.**
S. Hackensack Ave.
Port Kearny Building 10F
South Kearny, NJ 07032
(973) 589-0606
www.dmc.com

**LION BRAND YARN CO.**
135 Kero Road
Carlstadt, NJ 07072
(800) 258-9276
www.lionbrand.com

**SPINRITE**
(Bernat, Lily, Patons)
320 Livingstone Ave. S.
Listowel, ON
Canada N4W 3H3
(888) 368-8401
www.bernat.com
www.patonsyarn.com

**CARON INTERNATIONAL INC.**
Customer Service
P. O. Box 222
Washington, NC 27889
www.caron.com